FLIGHT OF GOLD

TWO PILOTS' TRUE ADVENTURE DISCOVERING ALASKA'S LEGENDARY GOLD WRECK

D1560231

FLIGHT OF GOLD

TWO PILOTS' TRUE ADVENTURE DISCOVERING
ALASKA'S LEGENDARY GOLD WRECK

To: Ed
Never give up!

KEVIN A. McGREGOR

Copyright 2013
Kevin A. McGregor

All Rights Reserved
No part of this book may be reproduced in any form or by any means, electronic
or mechanical, including photocopying, recording, or by any information storage
and retrieval system, without permission
in writing from the author.

Photographs
As credited and used with permission.
Cover image of Mount Sanford by Kevin McGregor
with aurora borealis and airplane graphic enhancements.
Airplane NC-95422 pictured on back cover and inside title page spread is the
actual plane used for Flight 4422, courtesy of Dave Edwins.
Author photograph on back cover by Randall Haslett.

Published
In the United States of America by In-Depth Editions, 2013
www.in-deptheditions.com
17 16 15 14 13   5 4 3 2 1
First Edition

Publisher Cataloging-in-Publication Data
McGregor, Kevin A.
Flight of gold: two pilots' true adventure discovering alaska's legendary gold wreck
392. : 117 ill., map
Includes bibliographical references (378-385)
ISBN 978-09889772-4-2 (pbk: alk paper)
1. Aircraft Accidents-Investigation.
2. United States-History-20th century.
3. Airplane wrecks—Alaska. 4. Mount Sanford, Alaska.
6. Alaska—History.
I. Title II. Author

2013
TL553.52.M37 2013
363.124'65 Mcg   2013939702

This book is first of all dedicated to my mother, Mae I. McGregor, and my late father, Francis A. McGregor. Their inspiration and emotional and spiritual support championed the Flight 4422 project and the writing of *Flight of Gold*.

This book is also dedicated to the thirty men whose memory is preserved on these pages and who will remain forever on Mount Sanford in Alaska.

ABOUT THE AUTHOR

A commercial airline pilot, retired Air Force major, and Desert Storm veteran, Kevin A. McGregor is an experienced mountain climber. He has climbed the high peaks of Colorado, California, and Mexico; Mount Rainier; and Kala Patar near Mount Everest. He is also an avid bush pilot who frequently flies to remote mountainous areas. He has been featured on Dateline NBC, National Geographic, CNN, King 5 TV, and many other television news programs.

IN MEMORY

THE SAILORS

Wilfred H. "Billy" Beswick, Manchester, UK

Eugene J. Adler, Fall River, MA

Morris "Max" Brooks, Bronx, NY

John R. Comshick, West Hazleton, PA

Howard A. Davidson, Bayonne, NJ

Robert William "Billy" Delaney, Keyport, NJ

Arthur L. Eilertsen, New York, NY

John V. Elkins, Richmond, NY

Eugene O. Foote, Kaplan, LA

Olav J. Jacobsen, Brooklyn, NY

John "Jackie" Joseph Jamele, Brooklyn, NY

Everett W. Jenkins, Brazil, IN

August E. Koistinen, Toivola, WI

James G. Lampman, Jersey City, NJ

Michael Marushak, Sewaren, NJ

Travis M. McCall, Tifton, GA

James G. Mooney, Paterson, NJ

Edwin Mustra, Plainfield, NJ

Robert J. Rabich, Easton, PA

John W. Rapchinski, Bayonne, NJ

Daniel C. Rice, Milwaukee, WI.

Carl F. Sigmund, Poquonock Bridge, CT

Frank J. Van Zandt, Roanoke, VA

Stanley C. Wilkowski, Bayonne, NJ

THE CREW

Captain Robert Petry, pilot, St. Paul, MN

Captain James Van Cleef, pilot, Minneapolis, MN

Jehu Stickel, copilot, Minneapolis, MN

Wayne Worsley, navigator, Minneapolis, MN

Donald Rector, flight mechanic, St. Louis Park, MN

Robert Haslett, purser, Seattle, WA

MAY THEY REST IN PEACE

CONTENTS

ROUTE OF NORTHWEST AIRLINES FLIGHT 4422

PREFACE

The story about the loss and discovery of Northwest Airlines Flight 4422 in the remote Wrangell Mountains of Alaska is true. It crashed in 1948 and remained shrouded in mystery for the next 51 years, until my fellow explorers, Marc Millican, Gerry Biasi, and I embarked on a 12-year adventure to solve many of the rumors associated with the plane's disappearance and possible treasure it carried. Although I wrote this book, the adventure was just as much Marc and Gerry's as mine, so "we" is used throughout the telling of the story.

While all of the names in this book are real, as are the main events, no one living knows exactly what happened on board Flight 4422 prior to the crash, or on the oil tanker SS *Sunset,* which was finally demolished in 1984. Nor is it known precisely what occurred during many of the expeditions to Mount Sanford, the first shortly after the crash, to the last known expedition in 1994— before our own from 1994 to 2011.

The scenario that we have constructed is based on the best information available, our experience as aviators, the factual evidence, and interviews with more than 100 individuals. Since the accident occurred in the days before flight data and voice recorders, it's not certain which captain was in the left seat, or whether the pilot or copilot was actually flying the plane when it crashed. The crash may have involved factors beyond those stated in the Civil Aeronautics Board's 1948 investigation Statement of Probable Cause. Also, the individuals we interviewed were asked to recall what they said or did up to 64 years ago. Because memory is imperfect, when necessary, we have reconstructed a likely dialogue among the characters based on what we learned. All of the letters and poems written by the sailors of the SS *Sunset* to their wives and relatives are used with the permission of their families.

Death's a fierce meadow lark: but to die having made
Something more equal to the centuries
Than muscle and bone, is mostly to shed weakness.
The mountains are dead stone, the people
Admire or hate their stature, their insolent quietness,
The mountains are neither softened nor troubled
And a few dead men's thoughts have the same temper.

- Robinson Jeffers,
    from "Wise Men in Their Bad Hours"

PROLOGUE

Towering 16,200 feet over the valley below, the icy slopes of Mount Sanford hold a secret, a secret that through the years turned into legend.

Long ago—near the top of this desolate mountain—a passenger plane crashed and disappeared. It was a Northwest Airlines prop-liner headed across the world, eastbound after a fueling stop in Anchorage. No one survived the fiery crash. That was a fact. But more intriguing were the rumors. Passed down through the years, they stirred the souls of adventurers and fortune hunters. Northwest Flight 4422, the rumors whispered, was filled with gold.

Like legs of a giant spider, long glaciers cascade down every side of the huge mountain. On the surface of one of the glaciers, a frozen human arm, entombed for 50 years, lies quietly; its upper arm, still frozen in the ice, disappears into the glacier. It is a left arm, visible to the elbow. Its long, strong fingers and thumb are well manicured and bare. The hand points accusingly north by northwest—toward what would have been the safe path of Flight 4422 around the mountain.

A few feet away, a silver ring glows with the Alaska light of a new day. On its large diamond-shaped face is engraved a picture of a building with a minaret on a black enamel background. On one side of the ring is stamped "Iran;" on the other, "1946."

One step away from the ring lies a cigarette lighter. Its mechanism is rusty, the spark wheel locked solid, and its fuel long gone. But the chrome-plated body is unmarked, glinting in the weak arctic solar rays. This glacier is not one of the beautiful, benign, snow-white expanses shown in travel brochures. It is a heaving, monstrous mass of ice, covered by a blanket of reddish and black volcanic rock. It grinds inexorably down the mountain, thawing and refreezing all the while. Plunging streams cut through its center, sub-glacial rivers run deep beneath, and crevasses open wide enough to swallow a tractor trailer. Then they freeze over, remodeling the bleak moonscape.

From an altitude of 3,000 feet, the glacier sweeps up from the valley, then curves back and forth 14 miles up the west side of the mountain. At 8,000 feet, the glacier forms two sets of crevasse-laden ice falls over another mile, then abruptly butts against a steep wall of sheer rock and ice. The face of that wall climbs almost vertically—vanishing into clouds shrouding the mountain's 16,208-foot summit. The peak is the northernmost of Alaska's Wrangell-Saint Elias National Park. A huge sanctuary, it spreads into the neighboring preserves in Canada's Yukon Territory and British Columbia. It adds up to more than 11 million acres of magnificent, remote wilderness—the largest protected area in the world.

Half a century ago, a blazing river of exploding aviation gas engulfed the steep wall of rock and ice after Flight 4422 crashed into the mountain. The fire died out two hours later, leaving only a dark, sooty stain. After a few days, all evidence of the disaster vanished beneath more snow and ice.

Fierce winds whip around the peak. They swoop up, then dive down its sides, creating microenvironments. In minutes, the weather changes from sunshine to storm. Summer rains and deep winter snows mute much of the sound on the mountain, but it is rarely entirely silent. Treacherous overhangs made of ice and drifting snow form cornices that reach out above the steep walls. When the weight or reach becomes too great, the cornices break off with the thunderous boom of cannon shots and send mighty avalanches roaring down the cliffs, where they break into smaller avalanches and spread across the glacier. Often, the excess powder sprays high into the air, forming a veil of white, hiding the cliffs, rocks, and glacier. The mountain's western face is one of the most dangerous ice and rock faces in the world.

In this serene yet hostile environment, the human arm rests unmolested...until now. Two men dressed in multicolored expedition gear kneel over the human remain. The time to give up its story has come.

JUST ANOTHER COCKPIT STORY

The captain looked up from the controls of the Boeing 747 and surveyed the cobalt-blue sky and the glacier below. "Have you heard there's an airplane wreck down there, full of gold?" he asked, glancing back at his flight engineer.

"I've heard that gold story hundreds of times. I have no idea whether it's true, but I've heard it so many times it seems like it is. It might be gold—it might be some other treasure. No one knows for certain."

He paused and gazed again at the darkening sky.

"Then again, maybe it's just another cockpit story."

The flight engineer said nothing as he stared deeply into the glacier that quickly passed out of view as the Boeing 747 cruised on at 35,000 feet and Mach .84.

Based in Anchorage for Northwest Airlines (NWA), initially as a B-747 flight engineer, Marc Millican had heard the story of the mysterious flight of gold many times; it was a favorite topic in the cockpit. Single, athletic, and just over six feet tall, the son of an Air Force pilot, he grew up around planes and lived all over the world. He graduated from the Air Force Academy in 1979 with a degree in civil engineering. After pilot training, he flew jets and worked at the White House as an aide to President Ronald Reagan. In 1983, he transferred to the Military Airlift Command at Travis AFB where he flew C-141 cargo aircraft and the massive C-5A Galaxies. On his days off, he learned to fly small planes.

Old airplane wrecks fascinated Marc. In the late 1970s, he was on a Boy Scout camping trip in Virginia when a local hunter led the troop to an old crash site in a thick forest. The metal propeller, still attached to its engine, stuck out of the ground. An illegible rusty plaque on a rotting wooden post marked the site as a reminder of the pilot who died in the crash. Marc wondered who the man was, where he had come from, and why the plane had crashed.

I met Marc in 1985 when I was also a C-141 pilot based at Travis. We became good friends over the years as we flew all over the Pacific and Asia hauling men, equipment, and anything else that would fit in the plane. Marc left active duty in 1986 to fly for NWA, but he continued to fly C-141s part-time for the Air Force Reserve. A few years later, he transferred to another squadron, where he flew the larger C-5 Galaxy. Gradually our lives took different paths and we lost contact.

Old wrecks continued to fascinate Marc. He even joined an association that attempted to solve the mystery of Amelia Earhart's disappearance, but the project moved a little too slowly for him. He liked action, not what he perceived as endless research and words.

In 1991, NWA opened a pilot base at Anchorage, and Marc was the first to sign up. "North to Alaska," he laughed, referring to the old John Wayne movie. A few weeks later, he moved into an apartment in Anchorage.

More than once, Marc has told me, "Alaska is truly God's country. It's the greatest state in the union." Its clean, crisp air, its northern lights, and the rugged serenity of its majestic peaks and glaciers captured his soul. Meanwhile, the mysterious tale of the missing flight of gold continued to fascinate him, and he decided to investigate it. He had always planned to visit the Loussac Library in Anchorage during his layovers, but never got around to it. Each time he left Alaska, he would think, *Damn, I didn't get to research that wreck again; maybe next time.*

Now, on his first day off, he visited the library and began earnestly researching Alaska's gold wreck. Staff members helped him sift through hundreds of pages of old newspapers and microfilmed records.

Years earlier, a newspaper reporter had told Marc the gold wreck was not just a rumor and that it had crashed on Mount Drum, 20 miles west of Mount Sanford's summit. But now, in an old file, Marc found a microfilmed newspaper photo taken in 1948 that showed the plane crashed on the west side of Mount Sanford, not Mount Drum.

To resolve the conflict, he drove to the University of Alaska to study a large-scale map. He found that Mount Sanford and Mount Drum were located next to each other and easily could be confused. From literature and photographs published immediately after the crash, Marc determined the gold wreck had a name: Northwest Airlines Flight 4422.

The flight was a special one, a chartered McDonnell Douglas DC-4 flying from China to New York for the sole purpose of bringing the Merchant Marines from the tanker SS *Sunset* back to New York. Other articles, published decades after the crash, mentioned that scores of people had tried to find the wreckage but failed. Marc located one article titled "Wreckage Spotted on Mount Sanford." Published in the March 13, 1948, *Anchorage Daily Times*, the story called the crash "the worst disaster in Alaska's aviation history." It indicated the aircraft had crashed on Mount Sanford and not Mount Drum, as others had told him. Later news clippings stated that a payroll, diamonds, or even gold bullion were on the plane. Yet those same articles mentioned little about the passengers who lost their lives. The article did prove once and for all that the crash of Flight 4422 was not just another cockpit story. It was real.

Marc drove to a map store and bought a three-foot aerial photo of the west side of Mount Sanford. On his kitchen table, he laid it next to the enlarged version of the microfilmed photo of the supposed wreck site. The comparison was nearly perfect. Using a magnifying glass to examine the microfilmed copy, he picked out minute geographical details of the mountain. He was astonished at how well they matched the features on the aerial photo. He thought, *I believe I know right where that airplane crashed.*

In the fall of 1992, Marc purchased a red and white Piper Super Cub floatplane. Once Alaska's lakes iced over, he swapped the floats for skis. After practicing flying his new plane throughout the winter, he removed the skis and installed huge, fat, low-pressure tundra tires. Thirty inches in diameter, they soak up punishment and spread the plane's weight, enabling landings on sand, pebbles, and mud. That spring, with the help of his friends, he learned the skills of backcountry takeoffs and landings. After landing on beaches, grass fields, riverbeds, and paved runways, he soon felt confident enough to consider an expedition to Mount Sanford, a trip that would be done in secret.

In May 1993, he cranked up the Super Cub and flew to the Gulkana airport near Glennallen, Alaska, about 50 miles from the supposed crash site. From there, he planned to fly close enough to the huge mountain to photograph the DC-4's suspected impact zone. He named his first trip to the mountain "Sanford or Bust."

After spending the night in his small tent in a green field next to the airport, Marc opened the tent flap and saw a beautiful rainbow with an arc descending into a glacier on Mount Sanford's west slope. He snapped a photo of the mountain—the first of many.

He repacked his tent, informed his friends of his plans, then started up the Super Cub, and flew easterly on a photo flight. Twenty-five minutes later, he was soaring over the northern slopes of Mount Drum, straight toward Mount Sanford at 8,000 feet. It looked much more daunting than it did from the jetliner at 35,000 feet.

A few miles away from the cliffs, on the west face, he picked out several prominent points and matched them with similar features in the newspaper article's photograph. Soon, he felt certain he had pinpointed the exact location of the wreck. He snapped several photographs while flying the plane by moving the control stick with his knees, and then flew closer for a better look.

Without warning, the Cub was caught in a wicked, turbulent updraft. The plane shuddered and rocked violently, and was tossed straight upward like a feather—up to 12,000 feet. Marc had no oxygen on board. At that altitude, he might experience a lack of oxygen to the brain and lose consciousness. His tightly cinched safety harness kept him solidly in his seat; without it, his head would have slammed against the canopy. Cameras and charts flew around the cockpit.

He managed to pull the throttle back to slow the airspeed, but the plane still soared upward. Unsure if recovery was possible, his heart pounding, he turned the plane away from the cliffs, then shoved the throttle full forward to get maximum power from the engine. Simultaneously, he pushed the control stick forward, attempting to force the Super Cub downward and perpendicular to the path of the vicious updraft.

Although the Cub's engine was putting out full power with the nose pointing nearly straight toward the ground, the little plane was still moving upward and flying backwards relative to the ground. Finally, it clawed its way free and flew out of the updraft and descended while flying away from the mountain. Thirty seconds later, Marc was safe and back in the relatively oxygen-rich air at 8,000 feet. Had the plane soared a few thousand feet higher, he might have passed out, crashed, and disappeared into the glacier.

Deciding he'd had enough excitement for one day, Marc flew back to Gulkana's airport. Although the mountain had offered him a stern warning about the dangerous wind conditions, the trip was a success; he'd taken several relatively good photos.

Half an hour later, sitting alone in the cockpit on Gulkana airport's parking ramp, the still shaken adventurer-pilot realized he would never be able to safely do anything on the huge mountain alone. Later that year, Marc flew to the mountain with a trusted friend, Boeing test pilot Dave Carbaugh. Although there was no turbulence and the weather was clear, they didn't see any wreckage. Regardless of the knowledge Marc had developed, he knew there was no way he could safely hike into the glacier without someone with climbing experience. Alaska's gold wreck would have to wait.

Marc had no idea two pilots in Colorado were also researching the lost DC-4. And they, too, had made plans to find it.

CAMPFIRE TALES

The sharp metal edges of our skis sliced into the steep slopes of snow as Gerry Biasi and I darted down one of Squaw Valley's expert ski runs. Under the bright sun, our steamy breath lingered in the clean, cold air as we hopped onto the chairlift for another ride to the top.

Safely away from the loading platform, Gerry asked me, "Did I ever tell you the story about an old airliner crash in Alaska or Canada?"

"No, I don't think so," I said. "What about it?"

"I heard about it from my hunting buddies at our Colorado camp. A long time ago, a plane crashed into a mountain in Canada or Alaska. It involved the northern lights and became a legend—rumored to be full of some kind of treasure. It's called the Gold Wreck and was supposed to have gone down in a very dangerous area."

Gerry and I were longtime friends—the kind that I trusted with my life and all of my secrets. Air Force pilot training classmates, we learned to fly supersonic jets in Del Rio, Texas. Our other interests included mountaineering, technical rock climbing, whitewater rafting, flying light airplanes, and canoeing. I was six foot one with an average build. Short, wiry, and with a shaved head, Gerry had the amazing ability to easily carry heavy backpacks over rough terrain—packs larger guys would find difficult or impossible to handle.

Over a decade, we climbed mountains in Colorado, California, and Mexico and rafted through the turbulent water of the Rio Grande's Santa Elena Canyon. We were not adrenaline junkies, but simply loved the outdoors and the freedom and beauty of the mountains. Although we were very cautious, there was one incident during which we really screwed up and learned some lessons the hard way. We almost lost our lives on Mount Popocatepetl in 1985.

Gerry, another good friend, Larry Coubrough, and I were attempting to reach Popo's nearly 18,000-foot summit, a mostly inactive Mexican volcano at the time. Metal-tarnishing sulfur fumes still puffed out of its summit caldera. Although the day was mostly clear and the climb was not technically difficult, the wind and the cold, high altitude made it very challenging.

Three hundred feet short of the summit, Larry started acting like a drunk. When I yelled to him to see how he was doing, he did not respond. He was also swaying back and forth more than I would have expected even in the strong wind. One of the reasons we missed the signs of hypoxia is that he is a nonstop, fun-loving guy and sometimes it's difficult to tell whether he's just joking around or whether something is seriously wrong. In the howling 10-degree Fahrenheit wind, we didn't notice his purple fingernails hidden by his gloves or his slurred speech and confusion—all sure signs of hypoxia. The lack of oxygen had sneaked up on him. Meanwhile, directly below us was a steep 1,500-foot-long slope of ice that ended abruptly at a 1,000-foot, nearly vertical drop.

Gerry and I were at each end of the 150-foot rope; Larry was in the middle. Each of us carried a 60-pound backpack. I stopped, took a close look at Larry, realized he was suffering from hypoxia, and immediately decided to abort the climb; he is about my height and weight, and the three of us were roped together for safety, 65 feet apart. That left 10 feet of slack rope between each of us as we started back down—not yet in the proper position to stop a fall. That was a serious error. The rope should have been taut from the beginning of our climb down.

Without warning, Larry slipped, fell, dropped his ice axe, and careened down the slope. There was no time for either Gerry or me to drop to the surface and anchor ourselves as the rope quickly tightened. Like rag dolls, we were yanked off our feet by the 250 pounds of our friend and his pack.

The three of us slid down the 45-degree slope completely out of control. Gerry and I were 50 feet apart; Larry was now 70 feet below, the three of us forming a V across the slope. Each leg of the V was a 75-foot length of nine-millimeter rope. It became a life-or-death scenario as we accelerated and headed toward the drop-off. After just a few seconds, Gerry and I rolled over onto our stomachs and tried to use our ice axes to bite into the ice. Chips of ice flew into the air as our axes scraped the surface with the screeching sound of steel against a grinding wheel. Nothing held. We slid even faster down the icy slope.

Larry's weight stretched the nylon climbing rope to its limits, but it didn't break. Our bodies slammed down on the ice again and again after being lifted slightly by the foot-deep, saucer-shaped depressions. In a final effort to stop, Gerry and I kicked hard, forcing the tips of our crampons into the hard surface.

Showers of ice again sprayed into the air as the stainless steel, inch-long spikes attached to our boots and the tips of our axes tore into the ice. Gerry's right crampon tore away from his boot and was blown across the ice like a piece of tissue paper. It was fortunate that we did not flip over and tumble. Our maneuver worked. We stopped our near-fatal slide with just 200 feet to spare.

The wind was relentless. Unable to hear each other, we communicated by using hand signals. Slowly, with one man well anchored in the ice, we painfully moved one at a time to our left, off the deadly slope and onto the ridge leading down. An hour later, we limped into the wind-battered Teopixcalco shelter hut at 16,175 feet. In Spanish, four Mexican climbers told us they saw our fall and thought we were dead men. Behind the hut, several rusted metal crosses inscribed in Spanish stood as a chilling reminder of other climbers who hadn't made it off the mountain alive. We had been very lucky.

Throughout the night, the wind continued to howl—the aluminum sides of the hut slamming against its metal frame and support cables bolted to the rock. The racket was almost enough to drive us mad. But after the nightmarish night, the morning dawned bright with a calm wind. It was a stroke of luck that none of us had broken any bones and had suffered only from sprained ankles, badly bruised legs and hips, torn muscles, and damaged pride. The left side of Gerry's face had a few red welts from impact with the ice.

We hobbled off the mountain, drove back to Mexico City, and flew to Acapulco where the evening found us counting our blessings while sipping on Mexican beers as we floated in the ocean waves lapping onto the beach. It had been a close call on the mountain.

Larry doesn't remember anything about the fall—hypoxia is like that. It can strike anyone at high altitudes. All of us had missed the all-important signs. Undaunted, the next year we climbed, without incident, to the summit of Kala Patar, an 18,000-foot peak just west of the base camp of Mount Everest.

The close call on Popocatepetl somewhat cooled my thirst for reaching the high peaks. After all, flying jets provided an equally magnificent view—without the hard physical labor. The lessons about hypoxia and carefully watching my climbing partners were something I would never forget. The accident was our fault, not the mountain's. Little did I know that those lessons would pay big dividends many years later on Mount Sanford.

On the chair lift at Squaw Valley, Gerry and I continued to discuss the strange aircraft accident in Alaska. This was a day off for both of us. He now flew for American Airlines. I was a pilot for Delta, and still flew C-141s at Travis AFB for the Air Force Reserves.

"Do you believe this legendary crash actually happened?" I asked.

He said he first heard the story from Tony Polgar, a friend of his who was a captain for Northwest Airlines. Starting just after he was hired in the 1970s, Tony heard the story from many different people.

It seems that the plane crashed at night in bad weather, fell into a glacier, and disappeared, and the northern lights may have caused it. Twenty or 30 people were on board the plane but Tony said it had never been located. It was returning from China and, although no one knew for certain, everyone believed the rumor that gold or some kind of payroll was on board. Nothing was ever recovered, including the bodies of the passengers and aircrew.

Gerry said Tony was always amazed at how the stories varied. One captain said gold bullion was on the plane; another thought it was a payroll in gold coins. Someone else said it was a load of cash or a military payroll. The only common thread among the stories was that something of great value was onboard the lost airplane, but it was never found.

Near the top of the ski lift, I asked him, "Tony's comments about the northern lights seem kind of strange, don't they? It doesn't make much sense." I've flown through and around the northern lights all over northern Canada, Alaska, and Greenland, and never noticed any magnetic disturbance or any navigation problems caused by them. "It seems to me like it is just some kind of crazy made-up story. What do you think?"

"Yup, I know it is all pretty strange," he said, "but that's the whole story— just as I heard it. It also might be one of those stories that in truth is very small and becomes bigger and bigger over the years."

Then we slid down the off ramp and skied into the winter wonderland for another great run. Gerry and I didn't see much of each other over the next few years, but he continued to ask Tony questions and whenever I talked with Gerry, I would grill him about the mystery plane. I found its story compelling.

IN 1990 I STARTED looking for information about any crash in Alaska or western Canada involving an early Douglas Corporation airplane—a DC-3, DC-4, or DC-6—with similarities to the one in Gerry's story. There were lots of them. I had just started compiling a list of 50 or so possibilities when Saddam Hussein invaded Kuwait. The Gulf War was soon in full force and my flying duties for the Air Force Reserve and Delta tied me down for more than a year. In late 1992, I continued the paper chase and seriously started investigating what Gerry and I now referred to as The Project.

Hundreds of DC-series airplanes crashed all over the world during the late 1940s and early 1950s. Back then, aviation was quite risky, and Canada and Alaska had a multitude of accidents due to the treacherous terrain and difficult flying conditions. Among the reams of old Civil Aeronautics Board (CAB) documents, I found a reference to a DC-4 accident that occurred on Mount Sanford, Alaska, on March 12, 1948. The information included the date, the place, and the fact that it was a Northwest Airlines DC-4, but not much else. I ordered a copy of the accident file.

Several months later, I was disappointed when I learned the official accident report was not available. A clerk at the civilian agency in charge of the old files said it was missing and the only complete accident reports on older crash investigations were those of the Hindenburg and Wiley Post accidents. With disbelief, I spoke with a supervisor who told me that during the 1970s the DC-4's accident report had been destroyed. In fact, due to either the U.S. government's Paper Reduction Act or a fire and water damage in an archives building, thousands of such reports had been destroyed. The report on this particular crash was one of them, gone forever. There was, however, a five-page summary available that would provide a synopsis of the 1948 investigation. I ordered a copy.

In the meantime, I located several newspaper articles that included some of the victims' photographs. I spread several 8 by 10-inch enlarged copies of those photographs across the table in my front room as a reminder of the seriousness of this project.

On a cold evening in February 1993, I returned to my Denver home from a nine-day airline trip to Europe and found a government envelope in my mailbox. I entered the house, tossed my suitcase aside, settled into my easy chair, and opened the envelope.

History flowed from each word of the Civil Aeronautic Board's summary of the tragic loss of 30 lives during the crash of NWA Flight 4422, a DC-4 on its way to New York from China. It was a chartered flight carrying 24 Merchant Mariners as passengers. Every detail matched the wild stories, except for the rumored treasure.

The five-page summary ended with this: "While the pilot was flying a course off the airway, the airplane impacted Mount Sanford which was obscured by clouds or the aurora borealis." I read the conclusion several times and wondered how the aurora borealis (northern lights) could have been the cause. Could it really be true, or had the accident board found a convenient way to close the case? It didn't seem to me to be a valid reason for the crash.

Part of the plane had been spotted the following day by a fighter pilot, First Lieutenant Willard Jenkins, flying low and fast over the glacier. He flew toward the mountain's nearly vertical wall of rock and ice. Jenkins said he saw either the wingtip or a part of the tail sticking out of the snow at the base of a long, nearly vertical wall, at the area where the top of the glacier formed a cirque (valley).

Although no CAB officials ever reached the site on foot, the accident board deemed Jenkins' sighting to be positive identification of the wreckage. Of course, none of the photos from the original report were included in the short summary. Nor was there any mention of cargo, a cargo manifest, or any treasure of any kind, including gold. That seemed odd to me. I wondered what could have spurred the moniker, "gold wreck." The accident report left several unanswered questions.

During my time in the Air Force, I learned much about aviation accident reports, eyewitness testimony, physical evidence, forensics, and how to conduct investigations. The most important thing I learned was what *not* to do: Unless absolutely required for preservation, don't remove anything, bend any of the wreckage, or even touch it. Although the accident report's conclusion puzzled me, for the first time I was convinced the bizarre story of the legendary gold wreck airplane was not just a campfire tale. What's more, it now had a name: Northwest Airlines Flight 4422.

I met Gerry a few weeks later, discussed the report, and began to make serious plans to look for the plane. Knowing the chances of actually finding such a wreck were slim to none, we agreed our primary goal was to have an aviation adventure while searching for it. Such a quest would take us into the great untamed wildernesses of Canada and Alaska. The journey itself would be worth every minute.

Throughout 1993, I scoured news articles in Denver and New York libraries and learned that many of Flight 4422's sailor-passengers had participated in World War II either as Merchant Mariners or members of the various branches of the U.S. armed forces. Most of the men were from New York and the surrounding states and had sailed on a tanker named the SS *Sunset* to Shanghai from Philadelphia. One enticing article from the New Jersey *Paterson Morning Call* on March 15, 1948, indicated the sailors were "en route home after delivering the tanker *Sunset* to purchasers in China." An article in the *Washington Post* on the same date reported that the *Sunset* had been "delivered to the Chinese government." The Chinese president at the time was Chiang Kai-shek. An *Anchorage Times* article of September 7, 1977, reported, "The tanker crew was rumored to be carrying millions of dollars in Chinese gold bullion including the money received from the sale of the tanker to the Nationalist Chinese government and their wages." That meant the crew had the gold with them on Flight 4422. But the article went on to explain that the "airline and insurance company have repeatedly denied the existence of such gold."

A March 15, 1948, article in the *Denver Post* stated that "The aurora borealis put on an unusual appearance for Denverites last night in the northern sky." On the same day, a similar article appeared in the *Seattle Post-Intelligencer* describing "One of the most spectacular displays of the aurora borealis was seen in Seattle and vicinity last night and early this morning." These stories tended to confirm the rumors and half-truths about the missing plane's association with the aurora borealis.

Gerry and I, both living in Colorado, prepared for a month-long set of flights and possible mountain climbs in search of the lost plane. With our lack of experience in Alaska and Canada, we agreed to ask around quietly and see what we could learn from others, especially from anyone already living in Alaska. The date was set for our first trip: July 1994.

I was flying the C-141 at Travis one day in March 1994 when, during a cockpit conversation, someone told me another old buddy had bought a Super Cub and kept it in Alaska. That buddy was Marc Millican. No one at the base knew Marc had been investigating the missing DC-4. What happened next is what some people would call coincidence; others would call it fate.

FATE

I landed the C-141, pulled it into its parking spot, stowed the flying charts, and placed my headset and checklist in my flight bag. As my crew of four and I stepped down from the flight deck, I watched a C-5 Galaxy cargo jet lumber in on final approach and land. Its four Pratt & Whitney TF-39 turbofan engines roared as the pilot applied the reversers and anti-skid brakes, slowing it to a stop, and taxied next to our plane. The C-5 is one of the biggest aircraft in the world, a $184-million beast, tall as a five-story building and two-thirds the size of a football field in length and width. It can carry more than 200,000 pounds of cargo over 5,000 nautical miles without refueling—a vastly different aircraft from the DC-4 missing somewhere on Mount Sanford.

By the time my crew and I finished unloading our plane, the pilot of the C-5 and his crew were climbing down the giant's two-story stairs. I recognized him immediately: Major Marc Millican. I called out to him and we met on the ground between the two planes and shook hands.

Although we had flown to the same places during Desert Storm, our paths had not crossed for more than a year. Over the constant high-pitched whining of other jets' engines being tested at idle, I yelled, "Can I meet you at the Officers Club later this evening? I have something I'd like to discuss with you—in private. Do you still live in Anchorage?"

"Sure do and sure can. See you at five," he said.

Marc's mahogany-colored 1978 Corvette roared into the parking lot of the Officers Club right on time. It was one of the special 25-year anniversary Corvette series—a thing of pride for Marc. He pulled in next to a beat-up yellow Toyota station wagon touched up with spray paint. That was mine.

The bar was dimly lit and soft music played in the background. Pilots in their olive-drab fire-retardant flight suits sat in small groups at the bar and at the well-spaced tables. Squadron patches on their sleeves identified who was with which unit. I was sipping a beer at the far end of the bar, out of earshot of the others. Marc stepped up and ordered a Black Russian just the way he liked it, with the right mix of vodka and Kahlua over ice.

"To a good life. Cheers," he grinned, as we clinked glasses.

Some folks say Marc and I could have been twins. I'm the serious one. My old laptop serves as the filing cabinet for my research, schedules, and such. Marc is more of an extrovert, fun-loving, keeping notes on numerous scraps of paper stuffed here and there. I wear what I need to wear. Marc could be a walking advertisement for an outdoor clothing catalog.

What we have in common is aviation. Marc likes nothing better than flying into his hunting cabin in the mountains with his plane on floats in the summer or on skis in the winter. Like me, he is not married. He is too busy traveling and enjoying the world to settle down, and I haven't met the right woman yet who can share my love of the outdoors and aviation. We are almost the same height, just over six feet tall. At a bit over 200 pounds, I'm a little heavier than Marc. We both have close-cropped dark hair and the weathered tan of the outdoors.

"What's happening?" asked Marc.

"Well," I said, "I heard that you're settled down in Alaska and you bought a Super Cub."

Marc grinned and nodded. "That's right; she's a beauty. The guy I bought it from and I had one hell of a tough time flying it to Anchorage from his place in Canada. Equipped with floats for water landings, our ground speed was slow. It's a long story, but I'm all checked out now."

Before joining the Air Force, I flew light planes professionally for more than two years. In contrast, Marc had learned to fly in the military's large, high-performance jets first, and then learned how to pilot small planes.

I had never been in a Super Cub, so I asked Marc how it handled.

"It handles much different than the big ones, but I've got the hang of it," he said. "I'm getting pretty good at the backcountry takeoffs and landings. A good friend of mine, Steve Karcz, has been helping me learn the ropes."

An "Alaskan pickup truck," the Piper PA-18 Super Cub is one of the bush pilot's favorites. It's a package of canvas-wrapped steel and aluminum propelled by a powerful 150-horsepower engine. Designed for very short takeoffs and landings, it can operate in places impossible for most fixed-wing aircraft. The Super Cub is the upgraded version of the original Piper Cub, with a larger engine.

The names Cub and Super Cub are interchangeable in normal conversation. The plane carries two passengers, one seated behind the other, and has been used for more than a half century in Alaska, where roads are few and small landing zones dot the landscape. These little airplanes can transport just about anything. What the pilot can't fit inside can be tied to the outside. An elk carcass, antlers, a window, and even a mattress can be lashed under the belly.

With the wing attached to the top of the Cub's fuselage, it's easy for the pilot to see the ground almost immediately below. The plane has a wheel on the tail instead of the nose to keep the propeller high off the ground during takeoffs and landings, and to clear rocks, weeds, and low brush. Most important, the plane is very lightweight and has a special high-lift wing design.

It also can take off and land at very slow speed—about 45 miles per hour, depending on its load. It requires as little as 200 feet for takeoff, and landing can use as little as 350 feet. For flying in the mountains, the Super Cub is the next best thing to a helicopter, but costs much less to operate.

With his plane and flying experience in Alaska, Marc would be a valuable addition to The Project, and that was the whole purpose of getting together with him. I was unsure how he would react, so I picked my words carefully.

"Would you consider getting involved in an Alaskan project with my buddy, Gerry, and me? It might involve the use of your Cub and could be quite an adventure."

"Maybe," he said.

Staying fairly vague, I plowed on. "Gerry and I have been researching a mystery about an airplane that crashed somewhere in Canada or Alaska. It had 30 people on board when it smashed into a glacier. We'd like to try to find it."

Marc had a strange look—half smile, half surprise. "What sort of airplane was it?"

"It's an early DC series belonging to Northwest Airlines."

Marc looked around the room, then leaned toward me. Poker-faced, he asked, "How did you hear about it?"

"Gerry told me. He heard about it from his buddies at Northwest."

"Gerry? Do you mean your American Airlines climbing buddy you've mentioned who used to refuel SR-71 Blackbirds?"

"Yup."

"Which airline crashed again?" Marc asked.

"Like I said, it was a Northwest Airlines airplane that hit Mount Sanford."

"And why did it crash?"

"It had something to do with the northern lights. It's pretty mysterious and we think it would be quite an adventure looking for it," I said. "Anything else special about it?"

"Possibly."

Marc looked down into his glass, gently swirling the ice and liquor. After a few moments, he looked at me and said, "I know all about it. It's a legend at Northwest Airlines. It's a DC-4 and I've already taken photos of the area where it supposedly crashed. I wanted to hike in on the ground and go look for it, but I couldn't find anyone I trust with enough climbing experience to go with me to check it out."

"You've got to be kidding. This was the one flying from China, right?"

"Yep," he said, "to LaGuardia, and rumored to be carrying gold. It's the only one like it and it's called 'the gold wreck.'"

I nodded. "And Gerry and I have already learned that it's a real wreck, not just some tall tale. I received the accident report summary a few months ago, but I also heard that some people thought the crash was faked. It seems…"

"It's real, all right," Marc interrupted. "There is no question about it."

"This is pretty weird, but it seems we've been separately researching the same wreck."

"One hell of a coincidence."

Marc and I had another drink and for the next hour we lost ourselves in discussing the possibilities of finding the gold wreck. He explained that it was important to him not because of any treasure but because it was a Northwest plane—his airline, and it involved his brother aviators. "It's part of Northwest's legacy," he said.

I told him what I knew: that the passengers were sailors, returning after delivering a ship named the SS *Sunset* to China. Many had WWII military or Merchant Marine backgrounds. "That makes them militarily special as well," I said. "There is a lot of honor associated with the people on Flight 4422."

And, of course, there was the rumor of a treasure on board.

"I don't know about the rumors," Marc said, "but gold or not, I would like to find that plane."

That was the commitment I had been hoping for. I raised my glass. "I think, if we combine our skills and try a fresh investigative approach, we might really have a shot at finding that wreck, or at least where it's buried. What do you say?"

He touched his glass to mine and smiled. "I'm in."

I wanted to get right to it. "The earth's current warming trend might play a role in this. I know there is one plane melting out of the ice on Mount Blanc. I think we need to move on this quickly and get to the glacier before it melts."

I made a quick phone call to Gerry to complete the pact, then told Marc, "That's it. We three are a team."

"I have some photos of where I think it crashed on Mount Sanford, but I don't want to talk about them here," Marc said. "Let's walk over to my quarters and I'll show them to you."

Marc's room at the Bachelor Officer Quarters was similar to an average-priced hotel room. This was where the part-time reservists stayed during their time at the base.

He spread a dozen color aerial photos across the bed and desk. "No one else has seen these," he said. "It was a helluva job taking them. I flew solo and held the stick between my legs to keep the plane steady."

"You're kidding me," I said. "You actually flew your Cub up there solo?"

"Sure did."

He picked up several photos of a mountain. Thick green wetlands covered the surface like a carpet spread before the giant peaks of white. The trees stopped at roughly 4,000 feet above sea level—right where the green tundra started up the gentle ridges extending from the peaks. Above that, the slopes became steep, jagged rocks, mostly covered with glaciers and thick snow. Vertical rock walls were nothing more than black masses. At the bottom lay huge jumbles of smashed blocks of ice, in glaciers pockmarked with deep crevasses.

Marc told me he had determined the airplane's location through the microfiche files in the Loussac Library. Although he had been told that the plane crashed on Mount Drum, the crash site in the microfiche photo looked more like Mount Sanford. He studied a large-scale map and figured out 4422's flight path was just north of Mount Drum, precisely on a direct path toward Mount Sanford. That's when he decided to try to find Flight 4422 on his own. "That's a lot of dangerous flying work," I said.

Ignoring my comment, he said, "Then I bought a huge blowup photo of Mount Sanford and matched that with the 1948 photo. I think I know right where 4422 hit the mountain."

I studied the photos of the mountain and looked at Marc. "This is some very serious terrain. If this is where they crashed, it's so dangerous that it makes it virtually inaccessible."

Marc pointed to one of the photos. "The news articles said the DC-4 crashed straight into the side of Mount Sanford at approximately 11,000 feet. After its impact head-on into a sheer wall, it fell down into the glacier at the 8,000-foot level. I'm sure this is the spot."

He told me about his exciting "Sanford or Bust" photo reconnaissance flight and his close call with the huge updraft on Mount Sanford's west side. On his aviation map, I noticed the caption "NO FLY ZONE DUE TO

TURBULENCE."

"What about this note?" I asked.

"That note wasn't on the chart I had last year. Anyway, I know right where to fly now to avoid the bad stuff—I learned the hard way. Trying to keep the plane under control was difficult, but I made it out okay; it was more luck than skill. I think I lost one of my nine lives."

"Did you see any wreckage?"

"Not a thing, just one hell of a lot of snow, ice, and rock."

Then he told me he thought he could climb to the crash site on the ground but he needed at least one experienced climbing companion to even have a chance of finding it. He also admitted that he knew little about glaciers.

Tossing his photos on the bed, he turned to me and said, "And then you come to me and say you and Gerry, both highly experienced climbers, are researching the same crash. Is that fate or what?"

"Maybe it was meant to be," I said. "There's a time and a place for everything and I think this is the time for us to find the DC-4. Now I have something *you* should see."

I pulled the accident report summary from a manila envelope, and laid it on the bed. "Read the last page. It seems to match what you have figured out. I think your photos are correct. It's possible we may actually be looking at the remains of 4422 right now, but can't see them. They may be hidden deep in the glacier. Certainly, somewhere in these photos, 30 men lie frozen in time and may have living relatives who care about them."

"Wow, that's pretty heavy," Marc said. "Where do we start?"

I walked back over to the table. As the more experienced climber, I studied Marc's aerial photos with a magnifying glass. I saw a jumbled mess of crevasses, obvious avalanche paths, and rock-fall hazards. Any expeditions in the area would require extreme caution. I pointed my finger to the center of the glacier—well below the rocky cliffs, cornices, crevasses, and icy slopes. I said, "Okay, Marc, you fly us there and that's where we'll begin. Maybe we'll find the wreck." Remembering the photo with the rainbow arching over Mount Sanford's west side, I added, "Who knows? Maybe we'll find a pot of gold at the end of the rainbow."

FIRST ATTEMPT

I flew commercially to Alaska in May to join Marc on a few reconnaissance missions. Our flights from Lake Hood Airport in Anchorage followed the path taken by Flight 4422 46 years earlier. Nearing Mount Sanford and Mount Drum, we flew the Super Cub at 9,000 feet—2,000 feet lower than the altitude the DC-4 had flown. The massive twin mountains loomed above us.

Although we knew it would be quicker and safer to tap the knowledge of park rangers and local bush pilots, we were determined to keep our expeditions secret. That was a decision that would add many years to our investigation, but I later realized that some things happen for a reason.

From the cockpit of the Cub, the glaciers looked as big as those on Denali (formerly known as Mount McKinley) and Mount Everest. Flying two miles away from the mountain, we photographed and videotaped the area around Mount Sanford and neighboring Mount Drum. Finding nothing of special interest, we flew a little closer to the cliffs for a better view.

We were so engrossed in the spectacle that we were caught unaware when a strong downdraft slammed us earthward. The Cub plunged 800 feet in 10 seconds. Canisters of film and other items became airborne, bouncing off the ceiling and windows of the little plane. Luckily, everything else was tied down. Marc made a quick turn away from the mountain and got us out of the downdraft. The well-built Cub handled the stress better than the two of us did.

"A bit too close to the mountain—again," Marc said into the intercom, still delicately balancing the throttle, flaps, and rudder.

"No shit," I said. "One more of those and we'll be pushing up daisies."

SIMILAR TO MOUNT EVEREST, Denali, and other huge mountains, Mount Sanford generates its own weather. It can be clear all around the massif, but huge cumulus clouds can completely cover it, creating miniature snow and rain storms accompanied by turbulent updrafts and downdrafts. We quickly learned to expect all of this at any time and any place close to the mountain, even when it seemed to be peaceful. During subsequent flights, we stayed safely away from Mount Sanford's cliffs.

After two reconnaissance flights, we'd had enough. That evening found us in the front room of Marc's home in Anchorage sorting through news articles and notes strewn across a table and the floor. The full-sized maps were covered with flight path sketches. Enlarged photos were scattered everywhere.

We spent many hours looking over the prints with magnifying glasses, searching for anything resembling a debris field or the remnant of an aircraft. It proved to be an impossible task. The muddy brown surface of the glacier was a continuous coating of multicolored volcanic rocks. Up close, it looked more like the surface of the moon than an Alaskan glacier. Even so, the pictures were of excellent quality and gave us a good idea of where we should travel on the surface. I took careful note of the crevasse patterns and the areas where the permanent landscape collided with the edges of the glacier. Obvious paths of avalanches from higher up the mountain were a major concern.

"That's a shooting gallery in there," I said. "Look at these boulders. They've broken off from the high cliffs and hurtled down several thousand feet onto the glacier at great speeds."

"It looks really dangerous in there," Marc agreed.

After reviewing the hundreds of photos and many cassettes of videotape we had taken, we saw absolutely no evidence of the crash. The photos were full of illusions. Colorful surface rocks, shadows, and reflections from the glacial ice made many things appear to be airplane parts. Ghostly images appeared to be people standing or sitting on the ice. In reality, there was nothing other than an unending expanse of ice, rock, and shadows.

Yet one week later during an airline trip in Texas, reviewing the photos in my hotel room with a magnifying glass, I was startled to see what vaguely appeared to be the nose section of an airplane. The image was high up on the rugged ridge two miles south of where the investigators of 1948 stated the airplane pieces came to rest. I sent Marc a copy of the photo. We agreed there was only one way to determine what it was—to investigate it up close, in person.

Located four miles north of the Sanford glacier, the glacier Marc studied is not named; we decided to call it the 4422 glacier. Starting at the run-out of the 4422 glacier, the Sanford River flows eight miles to the north forming a huge inverted U around Mount Drum, which is directly west of Mount Sanford. The river finally flows south, passes Gulkana, and ultimately empties into the Gulf of Alaska.

Four miles north of the bottom of the Sanford glacier, a valley mostly covered by the 4422 glacier cuts upward northeasterly 16 miles to Mount Sanford's summit. By Marc's calculations and interpretation of the news article, Flight 4422 came to rest at the top of the 4422 glacier. At the bottom, this glacier empties into the Sanford River, forming a T intersection.

On the other side, west of the T with the river, is a flat wash of sand and rocks, populated only by a few isolated bushes. At the relatively low altitude of 3,000 feet above sea level, a clear area in the bush made an acceptable spot for landing—one that would later come close to being our grave.

I flew back to Alaska in July for our first attempt at finding the crash site. Gerry Biasi was with me. We shipped four big bags of expedition gear. In Marc's garage, we unpacked everything and repacked it just as it would be once we landed in the backcountry. Then we disassembled it again for the ride in the Jeep and plane.

In addition to standard backpacking equipment such as tents, sleeping bags, and extra clothing, we carried notepads, pencils, 35mm still cameras, a Sony Super-8 video camera, and Marc's small Whisper Light stove. We wanted no one tracking where we'd been, so there would be no campfires. Three weeks of food was enough. A sterile expedition with little odor would also reduce the threat from bears—always a potential menace in Alaska.

Our plan was to do nothing but take photos and leave nothing but footprints. We would keep a low profile and enter the Wrangell-Saint Elias National Park with as little fanfare as possible. The last thing we wanted was publicity that might start a parade of treasure seekers.

By this time we had found news articles in Alaska indicating that over the years others had searched for Flight 4422. The *Anchorage Daily Times* edition of June 24, 1963, reported, "Of the 13 known expeditions, none is believed to have reached the site of the wreckage." Although some had actually told reporters they were searching for gold, no one ever admitted to finding treasure or wreckage.

Relying on my smattering of Air Force accident investigation training and police work, we mapped out a miniature accident investigation program for Flight 4422. It included documenting and photographing everything. If anyone asked, our cover story would be that we were on a climbing expedition. Gerry and I packed our usual odd assortment of bright-colored climbing gear. Marc wore the camouflage gear he normally used for hunting.

As a backup, in case of trouble in the wilderness, we always called a couple of reliable friends in Anchorage and at least one person outside Alaska. We told them exactly where we were going and sometimes gave them a detailed map of the area. Our messages included the takeoff time, route, and estimated day of return. The rule was that, if we didn't report back safely within 72 hours, something was wrong and our friends would take action. But, even with the most detailed information, any search and rescue would be difficult. That's standard operating procedure for bush pilots on every flight, no matter how short—alerting a small network of people whom they trust with their lives. Wilderness flying is risky business.

Steve Karcz and Bob Johnson were our backups on some of these flights. These highly experienced bush pilots, hunters, and fishermen knew the wilderness intimately. Although we trusted them with our lives, we only trusted ourselves with our expedition's secrets.

It was a great day for flying as we traveled toward Gulkana and the little pipeline town's airport 42 miles from Mount Sanford. I left Anchorage first, driving Marc's Jeep Cherokee at breakneck speed. Marc and Gerry took off a little later in the Super Cub. Both the Cub and the Jeep were jam-packed with gear.

The weather forecasts showed nothing but good weather in the Mount Sanford area. But Alaska is not like *outside* (as Alaskans refer to the lower 48 states). Surrounded by water on three sides, the state is pounded by huge weather systems blasting in unexpectedly from the Arctic Ocean, Bering Sea, Bristol Bay, and Gulf of Alaska. Those systems bring snow, freezing conditions, and incredibly strong, freak winds. What's more, the weather can change very quickly. The first thing a greenhorn learns is to pay close attention to weather forecasts and to listen to what local pilots with more experience say.

I once read a great book about a legendary bush pilot named Mudhole Smith. Written by Lone Jackson, the book contains a quote from Mudhole that I've taken as my mantra: "When the weather speaks, you damn well better listen or you'll pay one hell of a price."

These were the thoughts wandering through my mind during the five hours I roared toward Gulkana. I was the planner, forever weighing the odds. I again took a mental inventory of my fellow adventurers' strengths, and searched for possible weaknesses.

Marc was now a skilled and careful bush pilot who had spent six months practicing in the Super Cub. Living, hiking, and hunting in Alaska for several years, he had tremendous knowledge of the landscape and the treacherous weather conditions. He was in superb physical shape and, most important, he was a trusted friend.

Gerry was a pilot, historian, and excellent hunter with plenty of knowledge about bears. He was an experienced mountain climber, also in superb physical shape, and, another trusted friend.

It was difficult to accurately evaluate myself. Yes, I was a skilled pilot in large jets and all kinds of small planes. I also had ice climbing and glacier experience from tackling peaks in Colorado, California, the Pacific Northwest, Mexico, and Nepal. But the most important thing I brought to the team was some aircraft accident investigation experience. I'd also spent plenty of time around older aircraft and their mechanics and learned a lot about the mechanical makeup of those airplanes. In addition, I thought my research and forensic work while on the police department would help. *Would it be enough?* I wondered as we prepared to journey into the wilderness.

Marc landed the Super Cub in a light breeze, fanning the carpet of colorful flowers in the tall green grass beside the airstrip at Gulkana. I was already there and had the Jeep unloaded. The plan was that Marc would ferry us to our makeshift wilderness landing zone on the west side of the Sanford River. We had been unable to find any landing zone on the east side—where we really wanted to be.

He would make two round trips. I would go first with most of the gear. On the second flight, Marc would carry Gerry and the rest of the equipment. I could feel the excitement as we stuffed the last few pieces of equipment into every available space in the baggage compartment behind the plane's seats.

Each part of the expedition was critical, and the combination made the journey quite hazardous. Backcountry flying, strenuous glacier climbing, accident investigation, and real-time historical research had to coexist in a two-week weather window while we survived in the dangerous Alaskan wilderness—a place where anything could happen.

Besides getting injured, we could face a 60- or 70-mile walk back to civilization through dangerous bear country. Of course, the emergency radio might give us an out, but one could never be sure. We always planned for the worst-case scenario. Only fools rely just on cell phones or radios to get them out of a jam and only idiots plan on someone else taking care of them in Alaska's merciless wilderness. Precise fuel estimates and consideration of alternate scenarios were critical to Marc's planning. The penalty for incorrect calculations could be a big one—like crashing on takeoff, collapsing the landing gear, or running out of gas and making an emergency landing in a lake or forest. Thirty minutes of extra fuel is the required amount needed for any flight on a clear day.

Marc filled the plane to a level at which we could land and take off safely with plenty of fuel remaining for the return trip. I was excited as I squeezed into the back seat of the Cub, surrounded by all kinds of equipment.

"If we crash, I won't even budge an inch," I said.

"It's not exactly first class, but she'll do the job," Marc answered as he cranked up the engine.

Over the sound of the engine, he yelled to Gerry, who was waving good-bye on the tarmac, "See ya' later."

Then Marc and I lifted off from Gulkana's runway and headed east, quickly out of sight and into the Alaskan sky.

THE 1994 EXPEDITION

Dawn crawled from behind Mount Sanford in a long curve, etching its way across the clear sky. By six o'clock, the pale purple glow of sleep in the land of the midnight sun lightened to a soft blue morning haze. Fluffy white clouds hung along the western horizon, a tinge of gray clinging to their undersides. It was a great day to start an adventure.

During our eastbound flight, I flew the plane for a while, using the joystick between my knees to get a feel for the Cub, just in case I had to take over. I opened the window to enjoy the pure air and also to study the old trappers' trails threading the banks of the Sanford River. One huge bear with her two cubs wandered near the river, eating berries and fishing—slapping the water to trap fish with its claws.

At the landing zone on the west side of the river, we made several low passes to ensure that we could land safely. More important, we had to be certain we could take off again. We timed our passes to get an idea of the landing zone's length and determined it was long enough. Then we flew across the river, looking for places to land on the east side and easy places to cross the river on foot. Finding neither, we decided we had no choice but to land on the west side.

We flew around to the north, then turned south and lined up with the sand- and rock-covered landing area on the west side of the river. Descending lower and lower, the Super Cub touched down on its fat, soft tires and rolled smoothly to a stop.

Twenty minutes later we had the plane unloaded and our tent set up. Marc was ready to get airborne again. The wind from the south had increased to a steady 15 to 20 miles per hour—strong, but not critical. The Super Cub is essentially a large kite with a monster engine bolted on the front. The high-lift wings that make the Super Cub so good for takeoffs and landings also make it extremely sensitive to wind shear, crosswinds, and downdrafts.

I turned my video camera on as Marc taxied the Cub to the north end of the makeshift landing and takeoff zone. He turned the plane 180 degrees and pushed the throttle to full power, rolling southeast into the steady headwind. The Cub was airborne in about five seconds and 10 feet off the ground with the engine at full throttle when a strong gust of cold air suddenly swept down off the slopes of Mount Drum and grabbed the little plane, threatening to flip it over or slam it to the earth. Its left wing lifted high into the air and the right wing dipped down toward the earth in a 40-degree right bank just a few feet off the rough surface. I couldn't believe my eyes or ears as the Cub's right wing slammed down with the sound of an aluminum trash can being thrown hard on the pavement. The right wing hit the top of a 10-foot-high bush, but stayed in the air—barely.

Using the rudder, ailerons, and elevator, Marc fought to keep control as the plane skewed sideways, dipped earthward, and then skimmed through the tops of more bushes reaching up to drag it down. It was soon out of my sight, too low to see, but five seconds later the plane clawed its way back into the air and inched upward as the screaming propeller bit into the buffeting wind and pulled itself clear of the ground. At the same moment, standing just off the landing zone, I was slapped off balance by the same vicious downdraft.

Marc later told me he felt like he'd had a heart attack. His palms were sweating; his pulse tripped like a jackhammer. Still bouncing around like a roller coaster with a broken wheel, he managed to suck in a huge lungful of cold air and then started to breathe easier as he gained welcome height, putting clear air between himself and the treacherous, rocky surface. He'd been within inches of disaster. Another puff of wind might have sent him crashing into the ground, exploding in a fireball. On the ground, I too breathed a sigh of relief.

The 10-second drama seemed to last 10 minutes. I watched as Marc turned the plane around and headed northwest out of the valley, still rocking and rolling in the powerful tailwind. Pushing the transmit button of the handheld radio, I tried to call him, but there was no answer—only static. I understood perfectly. Marc was following the pilots' mantra: *Aviate, Navigate, then Communicate*…in that order.

Mount Sanford was already showing her anger at us—unwelcome intruders, just one more group in a long list looking for Flight 4422. We had to respect and learn to live in harmony with every aspect of nature if we could expect to survive it. *She ain't happy with us right now*, I murmured while fighting to keep standing despite the wind.

STILL SHAKEN, Marc approached Gulkana's southbound gravel strip 20 minutes later. Years of experience took over as he landed the little plane in a daze. Gerry watched with alarm as the airplane rolled almost to a full stop at the far end of the runway before Marc throttled up and taxied very slowly to the parking area, then came to a halt. He sat perfectly still in the cockpit while the engine purred at idle for about five minutes. Gerry knew something was wrong. Finally the engine sputtered to a stop and he walked to the plane and opened the right-side window.

"Rough flight?" he asked.

"Yeah," said Marc, a thousand-yard stare on his pale face.

Gerry slowly walked around the plane, inspecting it. On the underside of the right wing, two feet in from the tip, he found a long rip in the white fabric. At the tip, several green pieces of brush poked out of holes in the canvas. Gerry just stood looking at the damage for a while, then walked back to the cockpit.

"Do you know you have a rip in the right wing?" he asked.

"Um, that's what I thought," Marc mumbled. Some color had returned to his face and after five minutes or so, he released the seatbelt-shoulder harness and climbed out.

"I almost lost it," he confessed to Gerry.

It was an admission rarely offered by a pilot—especially one with more than 10,000 hours of flying time. The Super Cub was more easily repaired than its pilot's frayed nerves and ego. A mechanic at the airport checked the plane over, found no underlying frame damage, and patched the gashes and holes with special tape in just a few minutes.

Back up in the valley, there was no time to think about Marc's dangerous takeoff as I fought 50-mile-per-hour winds. Although tied down to big boulders and the bases of several bushes, my little blue tent threatened to fly away. I put another 200 pounds of rocks into the tent, scattered them in the corners, and slid my 70-pound pack along one side. Finally, I stretched out on the other side.

Sand from the river pelted the little tent. Then the rain started, slashing into the canvas in cold, horizontal gusts, testing the nylon to its limits. Luckily, it held. I curled up in my sleeping bag, safe from the rain and freezing wind.

Unable to sleep, I began to think about Marc…and the what-ifs; *What if the Cub was so badly damaged it could not be flown again? Did Marc make it back to Gulkana safely or did he crash somewhere on the way? What if I had to resort to our ultimate last-ditch backup plan—a treacherous 60- or 70-mile hike alone along the old trappers' trails lining the banks of the Sanford River?*

Hiking out had not seemed too difficult an option when the three of us discussed it over a beer back in Anchorage. But up here alone in bear country? I didn't want to consider it. I would stay put as long as possible and let our backups come into play if necessary.

Then my mind started playing tricks—trying to induce panic. I knew staying calm and cool was the only remedy—my years of military training came in handy. Then I remembered the video. Maybe I'd learn more about the damage if I could see a rerun of Marc's takeoff; maybe it would make me feel better. I switched the camera on. There was only a teeth-gritting screech—like someone dragging chalk across a blackboard. The tape was ruined.

About an hour later the driving rain slowed to a drizzle and the wind dropped to about 30 miles per hour. After piling even more rocks into the tent, I checked my emergency equipment: a backpack full of survival gear, a camera, a knife, and a gun. Opening the chamber of the Smith & Wesson .44 Magnum to check the ammunition, I couldn't believe my eyes. I closed the chamber and then opened it again: no bullets.

I quickly searched everything in the tent: my pack, the stove, the tent packing sacks, my extra pants, and each pocket in every coat. I even looked inside my boots and hat. The bullets simply were not there. *SSSHHHIIITT*!

Somehow, I must have left the ammunition in the airplane—a potentially very serious mistake. I wondered how in hell we could have blown this with all of our careful planning. Then I remembered the fresh bear scat and the deer remains of leftover bear lunches we'd spotted 200 feet away, and my heart sank even more.

I did have a can of pepper spray that was touted to be very effective against bears. But without bullets, the gun's only value was that of a rock. I thought about the old Alaskan tale about a hunter who forgot to load his rifle while hunting. With a bear in his sights, he pulled the trigger: "click, click, click" is all he heard. The bear simply strolled over to the hunter, grabbed him with his paws, and turned him over his knee. The bear then proceeded to take the hunter's rifle and shoved it right up the man's ass. The image of such an event flashed through my mind as I thought about the missing bullets. Having invaded nature's territory, I vowed if I made it out of this one alive, I'd never leave the ammo behind again. It was a stupid and dangerous mistake.

The rain dwindled to a light shower and I decided getting out of the tent would raise my spirits. Despite the gusty surface winds, the wild expanse tempted me. I decided to check out the area immediately to the south. I put on my boots and crawled out of the tent. With the sheen of new rain on the surface, the wide, pristine river valley framed by the glacier-coated mountains on three sides was nothing less than magnificent.

BACK IN GULKANA, Gerry and Marc unloaded the Cub while fighting a strong wind. Marc said he was very worried about my having to spend the night in the valley alone. Gerry tried to explain that it was almost a total nonevent for me. He knew I had done plenty of forced bivouacs in the mountains in the past and would be quite comfortable.

"What do you think about the bears?" Marc asked.

"He's got your .44 Magnum, and he'll hang up his food away from the tent. He'll be fine."

Then Marc tapped his pocket. "Yeah, but I've got the bullets," he sheepishly said.

Gerry launched into a spontaneous burst of deity-cursing expletives outlining the uselessness of an unloaded weapon and asked, "Why the hell didn't you load the gun FIRST?"

"I don't like loaded guns in the plane."

Gerry rolled his eyes. "Well, we need to do an air drop of the ammo right now, before dark."

They climbed into the Super Cub and headed east, making another hair-raising flight back to the landing zone.

I HAD HIKED a quarter mile southeast of the tent and watched the sun dip low on the northwest horizon when the faint drone of an airplane engine invaded the silence. Stumbling over the rocks, I jogged quickly back to the landing zone, arriving just as the Super Cub roared into view, passing directly overhead. Instantly, I felt relief. Marc was safe after all.

They couldn't attempt a landing due to the winds, and two-way radio communication was all but impossible in the gusts. On Marc's second pass down the center of the landing zone, I caught crackling words: "Stay clear." Then I saw Gerry in the back of the plane, waving and holding the portable radio against the window as they flew by.

The Cub came in for a third pass. This time, they flew no lower than 30 feet above the ground, swaying, jerking back and forth wildly. Halfway down the landing zone, something small flew out of the Cub's left window, hitting the ground with a solid thud. Then the plane banked steeply and peeled off to the left. Once again, it was gone quickly, flying off to the northwest.

I retrieved the package—a small brown paper bag—then laughed when I read the hastily scribbled note: "Kev, sorry about the solo bivouac but we'll see you in the morning when the winds are better. We'll try to get you some more pink snowballs. *Bueno Notte*, Gerry and Marc." The thud I'd heard was the bag containing the missing ammunition. A pair of my favorite pink snowball cakes in the bag had softened the landing.

When my buddies got back to Gulkana after the drop, the winds were so strong that two other people at the airport had to hang onto the Cub's wings to stop it from blowing away while Marc taxied in slowly, parked, and lashed the plane to the ramp. After unloading, Gerry and Marc drove the Jeep to Glennallen and checked in at the Caribou Inn. The harrowing day had given all three of us a frightening taste of Alaska's fierce and unpredictable winds. But we had managed to survive.

It was just after nine o'clock in the evening when I crawled out of the tent. Crimson rays of the low-lying sun painted the mountains a fiery red as I stood up in my expedition coat in the strong wind and light rain. Directly above me was the flight path of the ill-fated DC-4. While watching and listening to the here and now, I mentally traveled back in time—to March 12, 1948.

THE DEEP-PITCHED DRONE of the four big radial engines echoed off the steep valley walls as the silver DC-4 passed overhead, lumbering on at 11,000 feet. Thirty men sat inside the aluminum tube. Some read, some chatted, others watched the panorama of mammoth peaks pass by in the night sky bathed in the northern lights. At least two were supposed to be flying the plane.

Flight 4422 had been well past the spot where it should have turned to the left to safely clear the dangerous slopes of Mount Sanford and Mount Drum. In my mind, I watched the ship fly easterly, silhouetted by the shimmering northern lights. I saw it slam into the west side of Mount Sanford, disintegrating in a brilliant red fireball. Hairs on the back of my neck stood on end as I stared at the looming hulk of Mount Sanford—there, somewhere, were the 30 lost men.

THE NEXT MORNING dawned with a temperature just above freezing. Intermittent rain squalls hit the tent in machine-gun bursts. A few thousand feet above the landing zone, new snow coated all the mountains' slopes. Wind gusts were still too strong for any attempt at landing the Cub.

After a breakfast of hot chocolate and freeze-dried potatoes, I poked my head out of the tent.

Like a curtain opening at a stage performance, the gray bands of clouds spread apart and Mount Sanford came into full view, 18 miles away. I studied it with powerful binoculars. Its cathedral-like spires and cliffs of blinding-white snow and ice towered high into the sky. All of its cliffs, cornices, and slopes were clearly visible—and breathtaking. I whispered to the spirits of the mountains and the skies, *Tell me what really happened. Show me.*

Just as quickly as the curtain had opened, the clouds and rain returned and it closed. The wind continued to howl. It was too dangerous to venture very far from my minuscule camp.

Late in the afternoon, the temperature rose to 55 degrees, the wind slowed, and the mountains came intermittently into view. I felt safe making short two-mile hikes up and down the southwest bank of the river. Small groups of caribou on the other side watched me. They had little knowledge of the long reach of man's guns, and showed no fear of me, a strange two-legged animal. I felt myself getting in tune with nature again.

Back in the tent, I reread the five-page summary of the Civil Aeronautics Board's 1948 accident report, the only official record remaining of Flight 4422's CAB investigation: "The next morning more search aircraft arrived at Mount Sanford and positive identification was made by an Air Force pilot who was able to see the aircraft's insignia on the vertical fin. It was estimated that the falling snow and ice would cover the wreckage in a matter of days. The scene of the accident was inaccessible from either the ground or the air." The report continued, "The next day a huge weather system moved in, burying it all under many feet of snow."

I stuck my head out of the tent and looked outside, entranced by the beautiful enormity of the wilderness and its glacier winding upward to the east. At the same time, I felt sadness in the valley. There was something else I still cannot articulate. Something inside told me we had to find out what had happened—not as treasure hunters, but as human beings driven to complete something unfinished.

The three of us had to find some solid proof that Flight 4422 really existed and tell the rest of the story about the 30 spirits who wandered the remote mountain. We would have to find something that would indisputably identify the crash.

Huddled in my little tent, I knew I wasn't really alone. I could feel it.

BACK AT GULKANA, the rain poured down and the wind howled. At the Caribou Inn, the day dragged on for Marc and Gerry. Glennallen was and in many ways still is a frontier town. Not many people lived there in the 1940s, and the airstrip, three miles to the north, was known simply as "Gulkana." The radio room was a small wartime cabin made of bricks, with a tin roof. In

1948, the runway was a simple gravel strip approximately 4,000 feet in length. A few dozen private cabins dotted the woods around the airport.

When the oil pipeline connecting Alaska to the lower 48 states was constructed in the 1970s, many people and businesses arrived in Glennallen. Today there are seven sturdy hangars at the airport, warm offices, a small unmanned control tower, and a weather station. During all the growth, the town has generally kept the same layout it had in 1948.

While drinking too much coffee, Gerry and Marc traveled back and forth between the town and the airport, checking the forecasts and impatiently looking for a break in the weather. None came.

Marc was still worried about leaving me out in the bush, but Gerry reassured him. "I'm certain he's enjoying every minute of being solo in the wilderness. He's fine, don't worry."

That was true. For me, out in the bush, the time did pass quickly. I was more comfortable having the gun—and its bullets. Housekeeping chores kept me busy; I repaired the wind-damaged tent and stitched ripped pockets on my pack. Like a lazy bear, I relaxed, ate lunch, and simply hung out, soaking up the beauty of the wilderness and enjoying the solace of the mountains, a great contrast to the crazy schedule of my airline job and Air Force Reserve duties.

As the weather improved, I ventured farther up and down the sand- and rock-lined river, searching for a place to cross to save time when Marc and Gerry finally arrived. I found none. The gently flowing stream we'd seen from the air was a rushing torrent of ice-cold glacial water 10 feet wide at its narrowest, and nowhere less than five feet deep. As a tributary to the Copper River, the Sanford River is very dangerous. The locals teach their children that the Copper River has a mouth and will eat them if they fall in. It's heavily laden with silt, which fills the clothes and boots of any person who has the misfortune to fall in. Few survive.

The Sanford River is a snake pit of braided, gritty waterways that change course year to year. Other than waiting for the ice cover of winter, a person would need some type of raft to cross it in this area. We had ropes, but no raft.

I went back to camp and dined on freeze-dried beef stew and, of course, pink snowballs. Things weren't looking good. On my video camera, I recorded myself on a new tape saying, "Looks like our mission is in a little trouble right now."

At 10:30 p.m. the wind suddenly stopped and the clouds cleared. I lay back in my tent and watched a spectacular, slow sunset. Mount Sanford glistened in the rays of the setting sun—a white snowy pyramid against a background of shining stars spanning the violet evening sky. It was one of the most beautiful sights I'd ever seen, absolutely exquisite. *This is Heaven on Earth*, I thought.

I drifted off to sleep as the silence closed in, weighed down by the heavy, cold air from the mountain. I dreamed about the 30 spirits on the mountain. I now looked upon them as friends, lost somewhere in time.

Early the next morning under a perfectly blue sky, I was again scouting the river for crossings when a deafening roar surprised me. Marc and his Cub sneaked up on me. Now the 150-horsepower engine's racket echoed across the valley, interrupting the silence, with not even a puff of wind as Marc made one pass, then touched down.

Only Marc was in the plane. After the engine shut down, I asked, "Where's Gerry?"

"We gave up. He stayed in Gulkana and I'm here to take you out."

I was shocked. "You've got to be kidding. I don't think we should give up, but I don't think we can get across the river."

"We thought you would want to get out of here by now. I'm pretty sure we can get across the river. But we've lost three days and time is getting tight. It's tricky, but I'm certain we can get across. Are you okay with the time?"

"I've still got a week free. But I really don't think we can get across."

"Sure we can," answered Marc.

"Okay." I said. "Go get Gerry and let's go for it."

Two hours later, he returned with Gerry. After securing the plane by roping the wing struts and tail to large bags filled with several hundred pounds of rocks, we rechecked our equipment and headed southeast, upriver. Both Gerry and Marc refused to believe we could not cross the river somewhere. I meandered at the rear of our three-man team and watched, saying little as we skirted the river looking for a place to cross. Four hours later we were still searching. We hiked back to the Cub and untied the ropes; Marc and I took off and flew over to the east side of the river, searching for somewhere to land. It was a quick flight. Twenty minutes after takeoff, we were back where we started. Marc told Gerry, "We can't find any place to land on the other side—nada, zilch, nothing safe at all. We're done."

The three of us knew we always needed to leave plenty of slack time because the unexpected happens with regularity in Alaska. Once, after a hunting trip in the remote wilderness, our friend Steve Karcz returned to his Cub to find it sitting lopsided on a flat tire—really flat. While he was away, a bear had bitten into one of the soft rubber tundra tires and torn a two-inch chunk out of the side. Karcz spent half a day carefully fashioning a massive temporary patch that held just enough air to get the plane off the ground. He flew home praying it would not burst on landing. Luckily, the patch held. In remote Alaska, you have to leave a lot of extra time, because anything can happen.

It was six o'clock in the evening back at the landing zone when we reviewed our options. Even if we had found a way to cross the river right then, it would still take at least two more days to hike up the glacial valley. That left us with little room for delays of any kind. Now we had burned up four days and agreed it was just too tight, time-wise, to continue.

So we decided to abort our 1994 expedition. Marc and I packed up and flew out immediately. The next morning, Marc flew back to the landing zone and picked up Gerry. Noon the following day found us back at the Caribou Inn. Over lunch, we discussed our first attempt and finished with a few choice critiques:

"I feel like one of the Three Stooges," I said.

"I think we might have bitten off more than we can chew," added Gerry.

Marc was more upbeat. "It's certainly a failure, but not a total loss. We've learned a lot about the winds and the mountain. But we've got to find a landing site on the other side of the river. One thing's for certain, this ain't going to be easy."

For our team, it was back to the drawing board.

6 Colorado, 1995

COLD, HARD RESEARCH

During the winter of 1994-1995, we relied on what we knew best—our military training. The three of us completed a series of informal AARs (After Action Reports), communicating via three-way telephone calls, emails, and in-person meetings. In rehashing our mistakes, it became obvious Flight 4422 would require much time and more expeditions. Then, things changed.

In early 1995, Gerry met a wonderful woman named Martha. Sharing a love of the outdoors, they headed south to Patagonia on their own expedition. Before long, they were engaged. Understandably, Gerry's enthusiasm for the dangerous flying and expeditions to Mount Sanford waned. Marc and I wished him well and carried on with the project, while Gerry remained a trusted confidant and advisor because of his climbing experience, aviation skills, and insider's knowledge of 4422. Gerry's ringside seat provided him with a unique view of the project, and over the next several years his intuition about the associated difficulties and dangers would prove to be accurate.

With our airline jobs and Air Force duties, Marc and I traveled the world, much like the sailors and the aircrew members on board the missing DC-4. To plan our next expedition we met in Anchorage, New York, and Travis AFB. Studying thousands of photos and talking late into the night, we brainstormed many possible crash scenarios while questioning the accuracy of the 1948 accident report.

I brushed up on glaciology—the study of the geological nature, distribution, and movement of glaciers. At the Denver Federal Center archives, I spent many days locating several government aerial photos of Mount Sanford that were taken in 1957 and 1972.

Comparing United States Geological Survey (USGS)-archived images with our recent photos, I could clearly see decades-long changes on Mount Sanford's glaciers. Although there may have been times when the glacier slowed or moved down the valley in surges, its downhill progress seemed to have been more or less stable over the past 50 years. At the bottom of the 4422 glacier near the Sanford River, an enormous amount of ice had completely melted away. The photos also showed the reduction in the size of the huge cornices and the decrease in the amount of snow surrounding the valley. The glacier had receded tremendously at its lower end.

It would have been easy, but not correct, to blame the glacier's melting entirely on the world's current warming trend. Although the trend most likely contributed to the melting, Alaska's March 27, 1964, earthquake split the city of Anchorage in two and sent tsunami-type ocean waves crashing through many coastal towns, destroying everything in their paths. Deep cracks reached far into the earth. The Wrangell Mountains began to warm as those cracks allowed the discharge of a tremendous amount of heat into the mountain range. Heat was released into the peaks' volcanic calderas and glaciers. The temperature of the immediate atmosphere also rose, and the glaciers began to melt faster.

I meticulously studied all the photos, old and new. The aerial photos taken in 1972 proved to be very important. The increasingly visible blanket of rocks on the surface of Flight 4422's glacier indicated it was melting from the top down. Equally noticeable was the decrease in the amount of snow clinging to the steep cliffs that plunged down from Mount Sanford's summit. Virtually every part of the glacier was melting.

Many Alaskan glaciers have been receding for thousands of years. Stories handed down for generations among southern Alaska natives speak of glaciers that used to extend many miles into the ocean but have long since receded.

One night, while he was looking at the photos and sipping coffee, Marc said, "This sucker's been melting for at least a couple decades. It would be a wonder if any part of the plane is still there to find. That wreck's got to be scraping on the bottom by now."

I wasn't so sure. "This glacier is very complicated," I said. "Assuming the plane crashed and came to rest where the Civil Aeronautics Board said, the plane must have passed through the two sets of ice falls by now."

Then I reminded Marc that those huge crevasses may have allowed pieces of the aircraft to fall much deeper into the ice. Other parts may have stayed near the surface. It was all a matter of time, movement, and melting. Also, those streams on the glacier's surface have probably cut deep into the ice and possibly all the way to its bottom surface. There was only one way to find the truth—actually get on the glacier and study it in person.

The closest official weather station was in Gulkana. The Federal Aviation

Administration's Aviation Meteorological Observation Service there had archives of detailed climatological data back to 1948. Although the weather station was 45 miles away from Mount Sanford, the temperatures, snowfalls, and moisture content records seemed to support our observations about the glacier's changes and movement. The data indicated 1956 was a year with below-average precipitation and 1957 was an unusually warm year. That undoubtedly resulted in a lot of melting, meaning that 1957 may have been a good year to have searched for the wreckage.

The climate data indicated two notable, complicated, decade-long trends. The first was a general increase in average temperatures of two-and-one-half degrees during the 1980s and 1990s. The second was a dramatic increase of snowfall at Gulkana during the 1990s, roughly 20 inches of extra snow per year. As the temperature increased, the amount of precipitation decreased, but the actual amount of snow (as measured in inches) increased. But because it was now warmer overall, the glacier's melting trend must have increased— even though there was actually more snow on it. The bottom line was that things were changing on Mount Sanford: more snow, higher temperatures, and acceleration in glacier melting.

Two ice falls at the upper end of the glacier clearly stood out in the government's aerial photos. An ice fall is a place where a glacier breaks into huge chunks of ice as it slides over a big bump in the terrain. Within 10 years of the initial crash, the plane's debris would have had to travel through the upper set of ice falls and, later, through the lower.

If the glacier acted like many other Alaskan glaciers, we theorized that Flight 4422's debris should have neared the bottom of the second set of ice falls by 1990. We also believed that, just maybe, parts of the plane might be seen in the crevasses and among or below the huge ice blocks scattered about. But by 1995, were we already too late?

WE STUDIED THE amazing recovery of one of five WWII warplanes that had been forced to make an emergency landing on a glacier on the east side of Greenland. Those planes had been buried by more than 200 feet under tons of snow—entombed in a heaving, moving glacier. A determined group of explorers finally used a heated copper coil device to burrow down and recover one of the planes. But there was one glaring difference between the glacier in Greenland and the one we were studying: The Greenland glacier was pure snow and ice covering a huge area. In contrast, the 4422 glacier on Mount Sanford consisted of ice, snow, and a lot of volcanic rock, making it very difficult to get below its surface. Copper coil drilling would be impossible.

Marc and I agreed that the accuracy of that original report would make a tremendous difference. If the stated crash location was just off by a few tenths of a degree of latitude or longitude, we could have been looking many miles away from where it really went down—that is, if it were there at all.

During my research in the lower 48, I ran across one victim's family's story that the crash might have been faked. If that were true, it would explain why no one ever recovered anything.

All in all, it was a very strange crash.

Between airline trips, I traveled to 25 cities, most of which were in the New York area, where many of Flight 4422's victims had lived. There, I learned more about the men on board the plane and uncovered a few minor clues about the supposed treasure. I found a lot of information about the sailors in newspaper articles, but only a few short, general passages about rumored treasure. For me, the quest became personal. Through my research, the life of each man on board the plane began to unfold. Delicate pages of archived newspaper stories and faded photos provided a vivid black-and-white canvas upon which their lives played out. I soon learned that many were heroes during World War II.

I visited Bayonne, New Jersey, the home of 19-year-old John Rapchinski, and Stanley Wilkowski and Howard Davidson, both 23. The local newspapers revealed a lot about the three, including where they went to school, their addresses, relatives, and short life histories.

Photographs of each man were printed in the local newspapers in March 1948. Davidson, in particular, drew my attention. During his WWII service in the Navy, he served on the SS *Arkansas* in the battles of Normandy, Iwo Jima, and Okinawa. He was a friend of John "Raps" Rapchinski, the youngest sailor on the SS *Sunset*. Raps had also participated in WWII, but as a Merchant Mariner. A storekeeper on a cargo ship cruising the Mediterranean in 1944, Rapchinski injured his back when the ship was bombed. After a stay in a Jerusalem hospital, he returned to the sea.

The families were also mentioned in the newspaper articles, including information that could help us contact relatives. Marc and I had decided to compile a list, but we would only make contact if we found the wreck. We did not want to disturb anyone until necessary. The list we made of the brothers, sisters, wives, other relatives, and the friends of the victims became our most secret and protected data.

AN UNANSWERED QUESTION about Flight 4422 concerned the cargo. During my research about the sailors, I also found several newspaper articles that included stories about the delivery and sale of the *Sunset*. In the March 15, 1948, New Jersey *Paterson Morning Call,* Merchant Mariner James Mooney's sister, Agnes Joyce was quoted as saying, "Mooney was en route home after delivering the tanker *Sunset* to purchasers in China." The same day, the *Washington Post* reported, "The seamen were members of the crew of the tanker *Sunset*, of the Overseas Tankship Corporation, which they'd delivered to the Chinese Government."

In 1948, unlike today with computerized money transfers, it was common for large payments to be made in gold bullion. It was not much of a stretch to believe gold had been paid for the *Sunset* and that gold was on the plane. At the time, China's leader, Chang Kai-shek, was in an all-out battle to remain in power, so it was equally believable that he was smuggling gold and other treasures out of China.

The rumors of treasure on Flight 4422 were so pervasive that, on July 28, 1960, the *Anchorage Daily Times* reported, "The legend still persists—that the plane carried millions of dollars in gold bullion from Nationalist China." On June 24, 1963, a full-page article in the *Anchorage Daily Times* included this: "The four-engine cargo plane was carrying the crew of an oil tanker returning to America after delivering the vessel to the Nationalist Chinese government in Shanghai. Rumor had the plane also carrying the purchase price and the ship crew's wages in gold." And in Alaska's *Jessen's Weekly*, on June 24, 1964, reporter Tom Snapp wrote, "It has become one of the deepest mysteries of Alaska . . . According to first reports, the plane was carrying 4 million dollars in gold bullion from China."

Although we knew we would have to learn the truth about the SS *Sunset,* we decided to continue our search for the plane based on the location listed in the accident report. We would search in the jumbled mess of ice blocks and crevasses in or just below the lower set of hazardous ice falls at 7,100 feet. If we assumed that no one had ever found any wreckage, it seemed to make sense that the plane might still be somewhere above the point where the glacier leveled into a broad, relatively flat, 14-mile-long run-out.

The long winter of archival research, our monotonous study of the 4422 glacier, and discussions of crash theories left us with a thirst to get back to the mountain. We prepared to fly to Mount Sanford again, this time a little later in the summer, with longer days when the sun had warmed the frozen mountain and, we hoped, had uncovered the wreckage. Who knew? Just maybe we'd also find its rumored treasure.

The first priority was to find a safe and secure landing site on the east side of the river. It would save dangerous ferrying across the freezing torrent. We also promised each other there would be no more close calls like we had in 1994, or the one Marc had in 1993. We had to show more respect for the mountain.

This year, as an added safety factor, we decided I would fly my maroon and white Cessna 175 to Alaska from Denver. With two planes, we would fly in formation, just like we'd been trained in the Air Force. I would fly high above Marc while he looked for a landing zone on the east side of the river. If he crashed or got stuck as he reconnoitered landing strips, I would be able to drop supplies and get help fast. At least, that was the plan.

Flying around all kinds of weather and mountainous routes, it took me a week to cover the 2,394 miles from Denver to Gulkana via the Alaska-Canadian Highway. After navigating one last dangerous pass, I breathed a sigh of relief when I safely touched down in Gulkana at two o'clock on a July afternoon. I checked my answering machine and heard a message Marc had left three hours earlier. "Sorry, Kevin, I've been assigned to fly a trip to Tokyo. I can't get out of it and will be gone at least a week. Use our backups if you're going to do any flying. I'm leaving for the airport right now. See you later. Be careful."

I could only laugh. It was one of those times in life when it seems all my plans were shattered and there was nothing else to do *except* laugh. At least I'd made it to Alaska, and had a good time doing so. Looking toward Mount Drum and Mount Sanford, I decided to get something positive done for 4422. But, this year was different.

With Marc and Gerry, we had been a team of three. Gerry's departure had left two. But now, with the absence of Marc, I would venture into the treacherous wilderness of Mount Sanford alone.

SOLO

M ount Sanford stood sentry-like 50 miles away, on the eastern horizon—a craggy white fortress etched on the deep blue sky. As I stood next to my plane at Gulkana, the mountain's angry beauty took my breath away. I wondered what secrets it was protecting. *How much effort would be required to discover them?*

The volcanic massif consisting of Mount Wrangell, Mount Drum, and Mount Sanford forms the northernmost part of the Wrangell-Saint Elias National Park, often called the Mountain Kingdom of North America. The National Park Service's blunt warning to backpackers thinking of venturing there is deadly serious:

"Prospective visitors are cautioned that this is a truly vast and remote area without the usual safeguards one expects in a more developed National Park Service area. In the event of a mishap, the opportunities for rescue and evacuation are slim and response time can be slow. Adequate preparation, experience, equipment and knowledge of extreme wilderness travel and survival skills are necessities. Equipment considerations should reflect the type of trip and must include emergency rations and gear for unexpected contingencies or delays due to weather."

While parked on the ramp at Gulkana's airport, I unloaded all of the nonessential equipment from my airplane to make it as light as possible. Then I filled the fuel tanks to the top in preparation for another reconnaissance flight.

The previous winter, my mechanic, Danny Doty, and I had modified the Skylark, equipping it with a Horton short takeoff and landing kit. A special set of wing modifications, the kit allows the airplane to take off and land in shorter distances. It also allows a slower and safer speed in the event of a forced landing.

I dressed with the assumption that I could be forced down somewhere inhospitable, and I also kept a handheld emergency two-way VHF aviation radio in my pocket. Mount Drum's high ridges would block my transmissions from the glacier. In an emergency, however, I could contact a random light plane or airliner jetting high overhead. I also made the crucial backup phone calls to my friends and left the same information on Marc's answering machine.

I inspected the plane, carefully strapped in, and took off at 4 p.m. with the goal of finding a place to land on the east side of the river. I had seven hours of good daylight. Faster than in the Super Cub, I flew by Mount Drum, arriving overhead the previous year's landing strip in just 20 minutes. After flying over the strip several times, timing and measuring it, I determined I could land, but wasn't certain I could take off safely. It was too short. With five hours of fuel on board, I flew southeast over the 20-mile-long Sanford glacier just south of the 4422 glacier we were studying. Soaring farther up its long white slopes, I flew close to the summit of Mount Wrangell, enjoying the spectacular scenery. An hour later, with vast rocky ridges and crags on each side of the valley, I flew down the center of the 4422 glacier thought to be the one where the DC-4 might be hidden.

A few caribou watched as I flew down to the T intersection where the 4422 glacier's stream met the Sanford River. Searching for a place to land on the east side of the river, I flew north and south along the banks, taking my time, and increasing the search area on each pass. Two miles south of the glacier's run-out stream, I noticed a level area at least 700 feet long. It was well camouflaged among tall bushes, stubby trees, and flood zone pebbles. To see it, I had to be perfectly lined up with the landing zone. It was simple luck that I noticed it at all.

After flying several low passes down to 50 feet, I was certain I could land and, more important, take off safely. The landing zone angled northwest along the east side of the river with plenty of room for a go-around if I needed to abort the landing. After another practice landing—only down to 10 feet—I flew two more approaches and determined the landing zone would work just fine.

I zoomed back to Gulkana, landed, and notified all my backup pilots that I had returned safely. The day had been wonderfully successful and I wanted to tell Marc. But he was out of contact, somewhere in Asia. I'd had enough for one day so I hitched a ride the five miles to Glennallen and checked into our home-away-from-home, the Caribou Inn.

The Caribou's main two-story section is a modest-priced, classy designer log cabin hotel with nonsmoking rooms, a fine restaurant, and a gift shop.

During the Alaska pipeline's construction, its working men stayed in large trailer houses. Upon its completion, the Caribou Inn purchased several surplus trailers from the Tonsina Pipeline camp. In true Alaskan style, the Caribou Inn's new Pipeline Annex was a set of those trailers, which provided basic accommodations and a shared set of bathrooms and showers. Warm, inexpensive, with clean rooms, the annex was all I needed.

After a burger and fries, I climbed into bed for one more good night's rest. Just before drifting off, I remembered a glimpse of something unusual during my last pass over the new landing zone. To the west side, I'd seen something colorful flash. I wasn't sure but I thought it might have been the remnants of an airplane—a wing, maybe a tail.

Although it's never the safest thing to do, going solo in the wilderness has its rewards. The serenity of experiencing one's inner self, totally at the mercy of the unforgiving elements, is the ultimate experience. At least it is for me.

Again I weighed the risks of a solo return to the glacier. I knew very well that in the wilderness of Alaska's Wrangell-Saint Elias National Park, there was no immediate backup—no cell phones, no guarantees a radio would work. In a world totally different from cities, supermarkets, fast food, and fast cars, I would be completely on my own. In that pure and unblemished place, if I made a serious error, it was possible I might die. But I decided to give it another go.

The next morning began with filing my expedition plans with our bush pilot network. I triple-checked the pistol and its bullets, then loaded the plane. By early afternoon I was on my way to the new landing zone. I made one low pass, a second slower pass, and then, on the third pass…I aborted the landing when I recognized for certain that the colored pieces of metal were indeed those of an old wreck.

I flew back up to 5,000 feet and took time to assess everything once more. I gazed down at the meandering Sanford River. *Is it worth it?* I wondered. I recalled the words of the famous aviator and adventurer, Lt. Col. Dick Rutan: "If something's not dangerous or difficult, why do it? Who gets real pleasure out of doing something easy?"

I looked into the expanse of clear blue sky, knowing that the landing in the remote wilderness and subsequent solo climb were two of the most dangerous things I would ever do. There was still time for me to abort the trip entirely and return to Gulkana. But, I decided. *Yes, it's worth it.*

After reducing the engine's power I descended and lined up with the landing zone. It was quieter with the power down to 30 percent. A light wind from the north helped keep the speed over the ground nice and slow.

Completely focused, I edged the little plane closer and lower, and then touched down. The main wheels met the landing surface 25 feet from the south end of the makeshift runway.

The Cessna Skylark has a nose wheel, different from the tail-wheel style of the Super Cub. To keep from damaging it, I held back on the control wheel, holding the nose wheel off the rough surface as long as possible, and applied the brakes that continued to slow the plane. At 15 miles per hour, the plane's nose gently lowered to the surface and rolled to a stop.

The total landing roll distance was only 400 feet. Luckily, I brought the plane to a stop just short of a previously unseen five-foot-deep, 20-foot-wide dry wash that cut the tiny landing zone in two. If moving fast, going through that little ditch could easily have damaged the plane or caused it to flip over. Maybe that's what happened to the plane that lay nearby in pieces.

After inspecting the ditch from the inside of my plane, I taxied slowly down into, then through it and up the other side, being careful not to let the propeller hit the ground. Once on the other side, I taxied to a clear area at the north end of the landing zone and shut down the engine.

The silence was deafening. I unclipped my seat belt and shoulder harness, turned off the magneto and battery switches, got out, and walked over to check the wrecked airplane parts. Signs of corrosion indicated the crash occurred many years earlier. One piece of an aileron and two three-foot-long sections of faded white and green aluminum were all that was left.

Suddenly, mosquitoes showed up. They were as big as my thumbnail—no exaggeration—and trying to get a piece of my flesh. They bit through my clothing and swarmed over my hands and face. I quickly put on my mosquito net hood, another long-sleeve shirt, gloves, and wind pants, and that solved most of my mosquito problems. I covered my face with repellent cream, sprayed my clothes, unloaded the Cessna, and then tied the plane down with bags full of rocks. I strapped on my backpack, checked my .44 revolver, and headed toward the 10-foot-tall alders and Sitka spruce trees that covered the mountain's slopes up to the tree line. Their sweet green smell permeated the humid air as I hiked toward the glacier, finally on my way to learn what I could about the glacier and Flight 4422.

It took 45 minutes to struggle through the first mile of thick bushes covering the gentle slope from the landing zone to the river flowing from the bottom of the glacier. Branches stuck out from the bushes, snagging my 85-pound pack. Marc always said I carried too much. Maybe he was right.

It was not only arduous hiking, but treacherous, too. The thick brush often blocked my view of where I was stepping, and it would have been easy to twist an ankle or even break a leg in unseen six-inch-deep holes. In some areas I was walking on piles of rounded river rocks the size of footballs that rolled or shifted as I stumbled across them. Soon I was sweating. Thankfully, after the first mile, the mosquitoes stayed behind and I was able to shed the extra layers of clothing.

Turning to the east at the river, I tried to keep as close as possible to the roaring water on my left while skirting potential bear territory and thick bushes on my right. But round boulders on the river's banks that had been dumped by the rush of spring melt water were even bigger and more treacherous. There was no easy route to hike the two miles from the plane to the stream's source at the bottom end of the 4422 glacier. It took two hours to reach it.

At the westernmost end of the glacier, I found a 20-foot-wide river roaring out of a huge, dark ice cave at the glacier's base. Freezing water flowed down at a 20-degree angle from its underside and slammed into dumpster-size boulders, achieving the decibel level of a small jet engine. The spectacle was amazing. Thousands of gallons of water per minute gushed out from under the glacier. It did not look at all like the 1974 government photos—at least a quarter mile of the ice had melted away.

During our numerous reconnaissance flights, we had flown very close to the mountain's peak. Up there, we noticed that there had been between 350 and 500 feet of snow stacked on the summit. In time, all that snow would melt and flow out here at the bottom, some 16 miles west of the highest cliffs. This glacier had changed greatly.

How in the world are we going to find anything in this huge mess? I thought as I hiked around the rushing torrent. Then I spotted a fresh cat-like footprint in the wet sand. Maybe it was a wolverine's. Hiking near the alders, I suddenly felt as though something or someone was watching me. I began constantly looking around, but didn't see or hear anything else unusual. I also rechecked the revolver. The same fat bullets were still secure in the chamber. I hiked on, making a lot of noise so I wouldn't surprise anything.

Looking up, beyond the water rushing out from underneath the glacier, I could see that climbing out of the river valley was going to be difficult. From the plane it looked easy. But to get out of the valley, I had to climb 200 yards to the south up a 30-degree slope through an area of five-foot-tall bushes that were growing in the silt and loose rocks on top of glacial ice. An hour later, carrying my heavy pack, I made one last exhausting push to claw up 300 feet to a 20-foot-wide flat spot. Once there, I stopped and looked around. The birds were gone and the river's roar had ceased. This was the sound of true silence.

I heard my heart beat. I heard the wind rustling my hair. There, with the cold silence of the glacier, I realized the awesome task Marc and I had taken on. From high above and far away, the glacier looked placid and approachable. During our numerous overflights, it had looked more like a rocky, ice-and-mud-brown monster that was formidable yet accessible. But now, actually surrounded by it, I felt as though I were lost in the middle of a frozen, 14-mile-long landfill. It was a mix of dark purple and brown colors from the dark edge of a rainbow, dotted with an occasional orange or red boulder as big as a pickup truck, laced with strips of yellow and white rock. The cold, ice-mud sludge smelled like the bottom of a deep, wet trench. Water ran everywhere, disappearing then reappearing randomly. Searching for somewhere to camp for the night, I realized the choices were either to go back down with the potential of running into bears in the bushes or maybe a big cat beside the river, or climb even farther up on the glacier. I chose the glacier.

After scrambling up yet another hundred-foot section of bowling ball-sized rocks, I saw a small patch of reasonably smooth gravel. I dropped my pack and looked to the west, where Mount Drum loomed. To the east, the glacier rose gently. Just beyond it, I could see Mount Sanford's snowy summit—the closest view yet. It was incredible.

I was used to high altitudes, but at just 4,000 feet, I was exhausted. Pitching my dome tent on a small flat area, I weighed it down with large rocks. Then I heard a munching sound nearby. Quickly, I pulled out the gun and cocked it. I also removed the safety clip from the pepper spray on my belt, so it was ready to use. Carefully peering around a rock, I saw a big porcupine, 60 feet away, lazily dining on the skull and horns of a freshly killed Dall sheep—just another link in the natural food chain. I think Mr. Porcupine was just as surprised to see me as I was to see him that high up on the glacier. I was relieved and my blood pressure returned to normal.

After dining on rehydrated freeze-dried spaghetti Bolognese, I crawled into my sleeping bag.

From the rocky perch, I watched the great golden ball of the sun drift down the silhouetted northern slopes of Mount Drum, then melt into the horizon. In the valley far below, the Sanford River's meandering braids of silver glacier runoff merged and disappeared into the setting sun. Darkness finally descended somewhere around midnight.

I kept a log of that trip and wrote, "Tired but excited because I'm finally in a position to climb and make a good survey of the suspected wreckage area. I'm still 10 miles or more away, but I think I can make it in the morning, providing I can find a safe route up. This glacier is treacherous, got to get off quickly. Marker wands—critical. I plan to get a good night's sleep, and then hike up the glacier in the morning. I think I can make it up and back to base camp in a day with no problem. That is my plan."

I was wrong. Eight a.m. found me awakening to another perfect day as the sun beat down on the tent, turning it into a sauna. Mr. Porcupine was back, breakfasting on the remains of the sheep, paying little attention to me. Not to be outdone, I cooked up some instant cinnamon oatmeal and hot chocolate, packed for a one-day hike, and soon was ready to go. Carrying my day pack with emergency equipment, I planned to return by 10 p.m. at the latest.

The glacier turned out to be a 14-mile obstacle course of volcanic rock, the last three miles bordered by 3,000-foot-high, steep cliffs from which rocks plummet like mortars into the glacier.

I stayed on the glacier for two miles—until I was higher than the natural bear habitat of bushes and trees. Having marked my route with wands, two-foot-long bamboo poles with bright survey tape attached to the tops, I transitioned off the glacier and hiked up the dirt and grass game trails on the south side of the glacier. To my left was the glacier with its volcanic debris, caves of ice, crevasses, and turquoise pools of silty water.

I passed the first valley we'd seen from the air. It was too rough and full of bushes to use as a landing zone. An hour later, I passed the second. I thought this area had potential and would check it out on my way back down. Two miles later, the game trails stopped and I had to hike either on the glacier or in the ditch between it and slopes of loose rock to my right. This was the last area with green grass and a point easily seen from the glacier. So I named this spot Green Point. From there, I had a commanding view of the entire glacier and Mount Sanford. Through my binoculars, I watched plumes of white powder spray into the air as a large slab of snow broke away from the snow pack near the summit. A few seconds later, I heard the crack of its breakaway.

It was 1 p.m. when I left Green Point. It was too dangerous to hike on this glacier by myself. So, I hiked in the trench between the ice and the rock slopes. I had traveled one mile when the slope to my right began to move. The rock slide sounded like a dump truck unloading boulders, gritting and scraping against each other. I jumped out of the way and, with several long strides, got onto the glacier just clear of the tumbling boulders' path. After placing two wands as a warning, I continued up the trench for half a mile. Then, I had no choice other than to stay on the glacier at its edge where it was mostly stable, yet out of reach of rocks shooting down from the cliffs on my right. It took five hours to cover the last five miles.

AT 6 P.M. I FINALLY stood on stable ice at 6,800 feet—the bottom of the lower set of ice falls. I had made it. The half-mile-wide glacier immediately in front of me was a cascade of jumbled snow and ice pinned between the mile-high vertical cliffs on each side, forming a magnificent amphitheater.

The ice falls sloped upward easterly for one-and-a-half miles at about a 30-degree angle to 8,500 feet. From there the glacier shot straight up the cliff to 13,000 feet. Then it gently sloped back again to the east toward the 16,200-foot peak. Behind me, the glacier spanned just over one mile in width between the ice ridges and flowed gently downward roughly 14 miles to the southwest.

It was an incredible sight. The glacier was riddled with all kinds of volcanic material embedded in the flowing ice. Here at the top there was much less rock, less than one foot deep. At the bottom, like a 14-mile-long huge conveyor belt, the glacier had a five-foot blanket of rocks on its surface. High above me, Mount Sanford's summit was pure white against the deep blue sky; every wrinkle on her ancient face stood out, enhanced by the low angle of the sun.

Somewhere near here in their icy tomb, 30 spirits were frozen in time. I stood there for a long time, overwhelmed by the sight and my feelings. I had learned much about those men. Now their ghostly names churned in my mind—so much so that I thought I was actually hearing them. *Davidson, Rapchinski, Wilkowski, and Delaney.* Others crept in. *Comshick, Eilertsen, Adler, Foote.* What did all of this mean? Why was it so vivid? It was a magical place and a surreal experience—the kind I'd read about in fairy tales.

I looked down the glacier, then up the huge slope to the mountain's summit, and whispered into the air, "Talk to me, tell me what happened."

The only answer was the sound of a gentle breeze, drifting across the rock and ice.

Mentally drifting back to March 12, 1948, I envisioned the crash as if I were watching a movie. The northern lights shimmered red, green, and blue. Yellow streaks shot through the sky as the roar of the four engines shook the canyon, echoing off the steep walls. Then came the explosion, with its vertical river of fire. The red-hot wreckage fell slowly, almost reverently, down the cliff for 3,000 feet before coming to rest in a steaming, charred mess, burning holes in the ice and snow just up the glacier from where I stood. The fire roared for nearly an hour, then dimmed to a faint glow. It flickered one last time as its light and the lives of 30 men faded into the frigid darkness. Alone in the silence of the wilderness, I fought hard to hold back tears.

I recalled the heroic efforts of a brave young pilot named Layton Bennett and his student, Jerry Luebke. The accident report stated the two pilots had fearlessly flown to Mount Sanford immediately after the crash. Flying along the Sanford River just before midnight and nearly blinded by the northern lights, the two men searched, hoping against hope they might find someone alive. The next day, a military pilot thought he had spotted part of the plane's tail sticking out of the snow. Within two days, it was all buried by more snow; nothing was ever recovered.

I snapped several photos and made marks on the map. Staying only on non-crevassed, stable ice, I combed the immediate area, looking for wreckage or a sign of the missing plane—anything that might indicate I was in the right place. I found nothing. But I knew this was the right place—I could feel their presence. Flight 4422 and its men were very close. And so too, perhaps, its legendary treasure.

Then I began to notice a whiff of a slightly pungent odor. It was definitely out of place on a wilderness glacier that usually smells like clean mud. It was akin to a greasy smell, like old rags in a garage or auto repair shop abandoned long ago. But I saw nothing unusual on the lonely glacier 50 miles from nowhere. And there was no way in hell I was going any farther down or up the glacier to find out. The strange smell dissipated as quickly as it had come.

Just to the north of the glacier's center, I spotted about 20 unusual three- to five-foot-tall, perfectly formed cones dotting the ice. I recognized them as dirt cones, each was made of ice and was covered with reddish or brownish volcanic ash three to five inches deep on all sides, formed due to the constant growing and shrinking of the underlying snow. They were shaped so perfectly, they looked as though they might have been man-made. I made careful note of their location.

Then I took a moment to survey my surroundings, and that's when I felt an inner peace come over me, a peace I'd been searching for my entire life. In a place where the line between life and death was blurred, I was completely content and perfectly calm. At the same time, I reflected on the way the 30 men on board Flight 4422 had met death. Certainly they did not leave the world with the calm I was feeling now. Their deaths were startling and violent. I considered how I would react to such a sudden end of life, and I felt a deep connection to the 30 souls that rested somewhere nearby. As I surveyed my glacial surroundings, with not a single piece of wreckage in sight, I knew for certain that sometime, somehow, we would discover Flight 4422. My solo journey had been well worth it.

Rousing myself from this reverie, I shivered and looked at my watch. It was then I realized I had made a mistake. It was 8:30 p.m. Time seemed to have stood still in this hauntingly beautiful place. Where had the last two hours gone? I wanted to stay, but could not because my overnight gear was many miles away near the bottom of the glacier. That had been another mistake.

Before leaving the amphitheater, I placed a four-foot-long aluminum memorial marker stake in one of the piles of scree adjacent to the glacier. On the stake, weeks earlier, I had stamped "In Memory of Flight 4422, crashed March 12, 1948." This spot was well clear of any avalanche paths, and off the immediate flow of ice. The stake had two purposes: to serve as a memorial, and to measure the movement of the huge piles of scree just off the ice. I named the area below the lower ice falls the Amphitheater of the Souls. By the time I'd completed the task, the warm sun had already dropped noticeably lower on the horizon. Reluctantly I grabbed my pack and headed down—back toward my base camp.

It wasn't long before I realized just how big an error I'd made. I had lingered too long. The yellow ball of the sun was now split in half by Alaska's western horizon. Soon it would be dark. Traveling downhill on a good trail with good light, I could have covered the 14 miles back to the camp by midnight. But now, high on the glacier, fingers of frozen air descended into the valley, mixing with the chill coming up from the ice. The temperature dropped rapidly to 20 degrees.

The ground lost all definition. Distinct spokes of light pierced the cold air in the land of the midnight sun. Exquisite copper-colored sunrays reflected horizontally off the bottom of a high, thin layer of clouds and onto the glacier. I can still see it now—burned into my mind forever, like a fine painting brushed by the creator himself, the surface of the glacier changed from dirty white to shimmering gold. It was breathtaking.

My downhill pace in the darkness was much slower than when I hiked up. Rocks shifted beneath each step. This was a great way to break an ankle.

By 10:30, I had covered only a mile and had to call it quits. It was simply too dangerous to continue. I wished I had my full pack so I could pitch the tent, boil some water, have a hot dinner, and stay another day. Now I faced a forced bivouac with minimal equipment. Thin, high clouds moved in overhead and blotted out any light from the stars. It was getting dark and cold, and I was tired—a potentially dangerous combination.

I unpacked the tiny orange emergency tent and other contingency gear that I always carried on such trips. Setting up my bivouac off the ice but well clear of the fields of boulders seemed reasonable. I found a spot in a low pocket, mostly out of the wind.

To fight off the cold, I wore my brownish orange expedition parka, a thick down jacket that would keep me toasty warm as long as it didn't get too wet.

A pair of waterproof overpants added an extra layer of insulation for my legs, and a red woolen balaclava stocking hat pulled down over my neck and ears left only my eyes, nose, and mouth exposed. I had a huge pair of mittens for my hands. I reminded myself to save every bit of strength as I munched on energy bars and sucked on some candy.

In the darkness, I pulled out my emergency candle and lit it. There is something primordial and comforting about fire. Whether it's a huge bonfire or a small, single flame, to man, fire is special. It can provide a feeling of warmth without providing much heat, and a feeling of cheer in a time of absolute dread.

The light from the little flame flickered brightly inside the tent. From a mile away, it would have been barely visible—a tiny glimmer of light at the edge of a huge glacier. From the bottom of the valley or from an airliner overhead, the fire would not have been visible—as though neither the fire nor I existed.

I had been cavalier in my planning, but my emergency contingencies were working. It was not a survival situation, but I needed to be extremely careful. Any deterioration in conditions, like an injury or early snowstorm, could put me in real danger.

To relax my feet, I removed my heavy climbing boots. It felt great, but soon my feet became cold. So I slipped the huge expedition mittens onto my feet like giant slippers. That worked great; my feet were toasty warm in just a few minutes. I was feeling quite content until the candle started to burn through the side of the plastic wall of the tent. I blew it out—darkness.

I clicked my flashlight on. It provided just enough light so I could double-check where each item was in the small tent. To save the batteries, I turned it off; darkness again. I tossed and turned in the black of the night until I found a position where the bumps and curves of my body more or less fit the rocky ground. Though I was exhausted, sleep wasn't easy; occasional avalanches roared high up on the mountain. The glacier next door groaned and squeaked. As the temperature dropped even lower, the noises from the ice and avalanches ceased; when the glacier went to sleep so, finally, did I.

I woke to what my blurry vision interpreted as a blaze. The tent was glowing, orange and then red. It was on fire! The candle must have… but no, it hadn't. As the fog of dreams cleared, I realized I was witnessing a spectacular light show courtesy of the aurora borealis. I poked my head out. The sky had cleared and was so bright I could see all the way across the valley a mile and a half away. Yet I could not see up onto the high slopes of Mount Sanford.

It was 2 a.m. A cold sky full of warm celestial curtains waved silently in the breeze. Mostly blood red, some waves were shimmering orange while others were tinged with emerald green. *This must be what Heaven looks like,* I thought. The curtains moved gently back and forth with a peaceful rhythm. Although some have said they could hear the northern lights, I heard no sound at all.

Was Mount Sanford showing me the same lights that might have lured Flight 4422 to its doom? The rainbow night sky continuously changed. It was odd; a warm, heavenly display soared above, while the glacier retained its wet-cement smell and its bitter cold.

At one point, pure white laser-like beams of light shot down like a conical celestial headlight. The surface of the glacier reflected the glow for a few minutes. Then the shimmering curtains of the aurora borealis returned. Twenty minutes later, the northern lights evaporated into the thin, icy air. I was left in total darkness with the cold biting into my bones. Alone, but not lonely, and unafraid, I toughed it out at my bivouac spot just off the glacier. Tossing and turning, I was unable to sleep. Never in my life had I wanted the dark and cold of the night to pass so quickly. I wanted to get warm, get going, and check out the potential landing zone.

AT 4:30 A.M., a pale, dirty-white smudge of dawn appeared over the mountains. It was the first hint of light and I warmed up by moving quickly as I packed. Within 10 minutes I was on the trail again with just enough light to see my way. Spurred on by the thought of a hot breakfast and a nice nap, I hustled along, although good sleep was still 12 long miles and many hours away.

I skirted the dangerous rockslide area, being careful when I came upon the two wands I'd placed, then scrambled out of the trench and rejoined the ridge at Green Point, well clear of the scree fields. Continuing downhill, I moved quickly over the game trails, and reached the valley containing the second potential landing zone at 6:30 a.m.

Now with plenty of time, I took a moment to survey the valley. I was certain it was an acceptable landing zone, but would have never tried to land there without actually being there, walking on the ground, first. The valley had well over 2,000 feet of a rough but usable landing and takeoff surface, leaving just enough room for a Super Cub. One drawback was that it was a dead-end landing area with little chance of a go-around. It also looked as though it would flood rapidly if there were a lot of rain.

Flying in and out would require steep turns just after takeoff and just before landing. Any wind from the south, east, or north could create serious problems. Landing at this 4,800-foot altitude would be no picnic and taking off in a fully loaded airplane would be even more dangerous. But I was certain Marc and his Super Cub could do it safely.

This takeoff and landing zone would save at least eight miles of difficult hiking each way and eliminate having to cross the most difficult terrain. It would also give us more time onsite to search for the wreck. Moreover, it would keep us farther away from bear country, which was something I was anxious to avoid. I said out loud, "Perfect." It's one of my favorite words.

Hiking out of the northwest end of the little valley, I was perplexed when I spotted debris from an old campsite. Covering a 50-foot by 50-foot area, it appeared to have been a heavy-duty base camp for several people. Rusty tin cans, a white enamel basin, broken glass jars and bottles, and strange pieces of broken, dull metal were strewn about. Someone had dug a large pit into the side of the hill, perhaps to form the foundation for a cabin or to construct a storage cache.

Off to one side was a five-gallon gasoline can. Upon closer inspection I saw it was date-stamped 1951. I looked carefully for anything resembling airplane parts, but found none.

From the amount of debris lying around, I figured whoever camped here either came in by plane or had some sort of ground transportation, pack animals, or both. It may have been a hunter's camp, but it seemed too far away from the valley. Of course, it may have been the camp of someone looking for Flight 4422's gold.

After photographing the area, I headed down the grassy ridges toward base camp, the thought of a nice nap spurring me on.

The sun finally rose over the summit of Mount Sanford and the warm rays gave me a breath of new life. It was a great day. The night had been nearly coffin-like cold, and it gave me a sense of what it might feel like to be *in* the glacier. Now, as I scurried down the game trails, I felt totally in tune with nature. All around me was a display of striking ice peaks, deep chasms, caves, and inaccessible aqua blue tunnels of ice and snow.

After several hours of retracing the route down the brown and green slopes, I spotted the first wand on top of one of the rock and ice pinnacles. I climbed up to it and then scrambled along the two-mile path marked by more wands, which led directly to the tent. Without the wands, it would have been extremely difficult if not impossible to find the tent hidden in the jumbled glacial mess.

With my light pack, I'd made it all the way back to my camp quickly, arriving at nine in the morning. Minus the overnight stop, it had taken only six hours and 15 minutes to return. The trip up had taken nearly 10 hours.

The sun was now well above the high summits and warmed the campsite. Mr. Porcupine and the sheep's horns were gone. I spread out on my sleeping bag inside the tent and appreciated the sun's warm glow. Two birds chased each other among rocks and chirped in the glowing day as I rested. A few giant bugs zipped around—more welcome evidence of life. They were bugs, yes, but beautifully alive—a stark contrast to the lifeless tomb of the cold night I had spent 14 miles up on the glacier.

Short, disrupted naps are part of my life as a commercial pilot, so after two hours, I woke up warm, refreshed and happy. I looked out of the tent and saw on the skyline a mother caribou and her calf grazing. For a moment, I thought about what a great place this would be to camp for a few days, explore a little, and observe the wildlife. But then I reminded myself that this was only a small part of a bigger mission—much bigger—and I had to move on.

My solo expedition had been a resounding success. I'd found a place to land on the east side of the river, located and inspected the new landing zone halfway up the mountain, and had made it all the way to the ice falls. *I'll be back next year,* I thought. I knew Marc would want to go.

I packed up the tent, stowed everything in my backpack, and started down the steep last half mile of the glacier. As I took one final glance to the east, Mount Sanford disappeared behind the piles of ice and rock.

After two hours of retracing my route, crashing through bushes, trees, and small streams, I was back at the Cessna. It was still in one piece, undamaged. I untied the ropes holding the plane to the bags of rocks, emptied them, and stowed the bags on board along with my pack. After checking the plane, I hopped in and switched on the ignition. One spin of the starter and the engine roared into life. I warmed it up for five minutes and taxied down the makeshift runway toward the south end. *Don't mess it up now,* I thought, as I passed the pieces of the old wreck.

I made a 180-degree turn at the end of the takeoff zone so that I faced northwest—into the wind and toward the wide, slightly descending end of the valley. Then I shut down the engine, climbed out, and pulled the airplane backwards about a hundred feet into the weeds and bush, obtaining every inch of takeoff distance possible. Then I strapped in.

Eighteen years of flying had made me one with the plane. I fired up the engine again, then pushed the throttle full forward. As soon as it started rolling, I pulled the nose wheel into the air to eliminate any possible damage to the nose gear or propeller. The plane picked up more speed as its main wheels bumped along the gravel strip. At 45 miles per hour, it lifted into the air 50 feet before the ditch that cut the takeoff zone in two.

I flew just north of Mount Sanford's neighbor, Mount Drum, and headed for Gulkana. The men lost in the glacier would have to wait for another day. But they now had a friend, a friend who would not give up until their story was told.

Half an hour later, the Cessna Skylark rolled onto the runway at Gulkana. What a relief. The first thing I did was make calls to my emergency backup friends, informing them I had returned safely.

ON THE AIRPORT'S south ramp stood a huge metal hangar; its open doors revealed a highly polished turbine helicopter inside. Still grimy from my hike, but curious about a local helicopter service that might know something about Flight 4422, I walked over and spoke with its pilot, Al Sebaka. As he showed me around the helicopter, we talked about Mount Sanford and the local area. We had a circuitous discussion in which we both understood the topic was Flight 4422 and its rumored treasure, but never directly mention it. "I flew a guy around up there last year," Al said. "He was a captain for NWA."

Although Sebaka didn't mention the captain's name, I already knew it was Ed Becker. In 1994, Becker hired a helicopter to search for Flight 4422. He then wrote an article about his search in the December 1994 issue of Northwest Airline's *Contrails* magazine. Although the article did not mention the pilot's name, Sebaka acknowledged that he was indeed the pilot of that helicopter.

Eventually, Sebaka would reveal to me that he had flown Becker all around Mount Sanford's 4422 glacier, the ice falls, and its steep walls, all the way up to the supposed impact point. They flew close to the glacier's surface, searching for wreckage in the area below the ice falls, but found nothing. He told me Becker had spent many thousands of dollars for the charter flight. Sebaka and Becker conducted the most detailed aerial, modern-day search undertaken before 1995. I didn't mention that I had just been up on the 4422 glacier looking for Flight 4422, but was certain Sebaka had figured that out. After thanking him for the tour, I walked over to Ellis Air Taxi, where I gave myself a badly needed shave and wash-up in the restroom.

Marc was still flying in Asia and there was no way I was going to go back to Mount Sanford that trip, so I packed up for my flight back to Colorado. I fueled up, filed an FAA flight plan, checked the weather, and took off. A little later I landed at the town of Tok, Alaska, where I stayed the night.

Misty low clouds and overcast skies socked in the field for one day, then cleared just enough to allow me to fly out. I retraced my route over the Alaska Canadian highway to Whitehorse. Due to bad weather to the east, I changed my route, southerly, toward Dease Lake, Canada, where I refueled. While flying to Smithers, my next fuel stop, unforecast heavy rain, thunderstorms ,and lightning blocked my route. To make matters worse, fog and low stratus clouds began to form as the sun set. Soon, the entire area would be covered with impenetrable ground fog—a recipe for disaster. I had to land immediately or be stuck on top of a solid layer of low clouds with no way of safely getting to the ground.

I remembered seeing what looked like a very rough landing strip a few miles back to the north, so I whipped the little plane around. I had a choice of landing on the strip or the highway next to it. I chose the strip. After two quick, low approaches down to 20 feet, I brought the Skylark in just as thick fog began to creep across the field. The plane touched down with a loud thump and stopped in less than 300 feet. I was lucky—20 feet farther down the runway lay a three-foot-wide boulder. Several children and a group of adults came running out. I learned that I had just landed on the brand-new, not yet complete, backyard airstrip of Jack and Larz Hagen. They had cleared the trees and bulldozed the runway through a forest of hundred-foot-high spruce trees a few weeks earlier.

JUST AFTER NOON the next day, the sun melted away the fog and I took off for Denver, arriving the next evening. While flying to Colorado, I had plenty of time to think about the wreck on Mount Sanford. I felt a strange new force from the mountain and it now drove me as never before. It wasn't the gold or rumors of treasure. It was something else that I still couldn't identify. During my bivouac alone next to the cold, remote glacier, I had felt something. Maybe it was the spirits of the men of Flight 4422, maybe it wasn't. But something had reached deep inside me and would not let go. A few weeks later, another fall season crept over the desolate slopes of Mount Sanford, followed by the winter's blinding blizzards. Avalanches ripped across the cliffs, and down sides of the mountain, probably burying our newly discovered landing zone under 10 feet of drifting snow, making it inaccessible for another year. The temperature dropped below minus 50 degrees. Inside the glacier, little changed as the mass of ice and rock inched away from the mountain carrying everything inside it toward the river and on toward its ultimate destination, the sea.

MYSTERY OF THE MISSING FILES

Winter and spring of 1996 found us working on more research, Marc in Alaska, me in the lower 48 states. By July, we had two large briefcases bulging with information: the official 1948 accident report, a stack of news clippings about the crash, treasure stories, details on DC-4s and their military counterpart, C-54s. We had charts and photos going back five decades, and a battered laptop full of notes. Near the entrance to Travis Air Force Base in California, a DC-4 sister ship to Flight 4422, was on permanent display. The plane had been a key part of airlifts during WWII and subsequent years. Technically a C-54, it was now part of the base museum.

Every time Marc or I worked as Air Force reservists at Travis, we photographed and studied this plane. Coordinating with the museum's curators, we spent hours inside and outside the plane, crawling all over its huge frame. We learned the important facets of its construction, making it possible for us to identify DC-4/C-54 parts in the glacier if we found them. Relative to the C-141 and C-5 jets we now flew, this C-54 was a grandfather. Sadly, it would never fly again.

The C-54 at Travis had web-fishnet-type seats that ran lengthwise from the front to the aft of the passenger compartment. According to Dave Edwins, Shanghai's station manager in 1948, Flight 4422 had large passenger-airliner type seats known as MacArthur seats. Other than that, the C-54 at Travis was nearly identical to 4422. One day, I sat in the copilot's seat and ran my fingers over the throttles, across the instrument panel, and held the control wheel just as the copilot would have. Sliding into the captain's seat, Marc buckled in with the seatbelts to get a feel of the plane. Then we swapped seats and repeated the process. I noticed that the windshield was small, with far less visibility than newer jets.

Hundreds of photographs of the C-54's details filled our files. The construction of the walls, the floor of the passenger compartment, and the layout of the radio operator and navigator's stations were the types of things that might be important if we located airplane parts strewn on or in the glacier. Outside the plane, we carefully studied the engines, wings, tail, the plane's huge tires and struts, the complicated retractable gear assembly, and the maze of hydraulic, fuel, and electrical lines.

Most of the legends associated with Flight 4422 seemed far-fetched and baseless. We needed to pin down the true history not only of the airplane but of the ship, the SS *Sunset*. We felt we had to trace their histories all the way back to their construction. FAA records indicated Flight 4422's plane had originally been a military C-54 and was then leased to Northwest Airlines after modifications to make it a DC-4. To find more information, I visited the Air Force Historical Research Agency (AFHRA) at Maxwell Air Force Base in Alabama. AFHRA retains the official historical files of the Air Force. All the original records of ex-Air Force and Army Air Force aircraft are kept there. If the records exist, they would have them.

It wasn't the first time I had visited Maxwell. I'd attended the USAF's Squadron Officer School there in 1985. It had been a tough course. Now I enjoyed walking around the showcase air base, with its well-manicured lawns, trees, and shrubbery. I watched as the newest officer training school recruits marched by in formations—just as I had done 16 years earlier in San Antonio. They all looked like high school kids. For the first time, I felt the twinge of age.

The target of my search was serial number 35966, the military's official number for NC-95422. But the master records locater list of all aircraft indicated that the plane had yet another number—the C-54, military registration number 45-513. Only when it entered civilian capacity with Northwest Airlines in 1946, had it become NC-95422.

An hour of careful searching left me disappointed. The plane's history file, known as the aircraft record card, wasn't there. Literally thousands of airplane files were in perfect order before and after 35966, aka 45-513, but the one file I was looking for was missing. Maybe someone misfiled the record or had checked it out. I inquired at the research desk. "It has to be here," said the young woman at the desk. "Those files don't walk away from here. We have very strict controls, and no one has signed it out."

Perplexed by the missing file, two other specialist staff members soon joined the search. An hour later, they had failed to find it, and no one had any idea how long it had been missing.

But another half hour later the chief returned from an archival area restricted to AFHRA employees pushing a two-foot-tall stack of files in a big crate. "I have some good news," she said. "This is the backup file for this group of planes. No one touches these but us."

After a few minutes of shuffling through many numbered folders, she located what should have been the appropriate set of files.

"Here we go. What was that number again?"

"Three-five-nine-six-six," I said.

After a few moments she said, "I have no idea what is going on here. That file isn't in here, either. There has to be a mistake. Primary files have been misplaced before, but I've never seen an aircraft record missing from the backup files as well as the primary. Let me go and check the master file list again."

She again disappeared into the archives not open to researchers. After 30 minutes she returned with another specialist who held a single, two-inch-wide microfiche roll that obviously had not been used in some time. The dry rubber band around it had lost its elasticity and broke into several pieces when she pulled on it.

"Let's take a look at this…carefully," she said. "It's another old backup made sometime in the 1950s or '60s. If it's not in here, it might not be anywhere. Are you certain this is the correct aircraft number?"

"Your own records show it's 35966/45-513."

The specialist delicately opened the box, carefully attached the reel to a nearby microfiche reader, and slowly ran the film onto the rollers. Thousands of aircraft card copies whizzed across the screen. Finally, the magic numbers appeared—35966.

"Here it is," said the chief. "We've got it."

A little cheer came from the others behind the front desk. Who says research can't be fun and exciting? Backlit on the screen was the answer to my expensive two-day journey to Alabama. I made printed copies, videotaped the files, and even photographed them in case this one official record disappeared or disintegrated.

Several pages of the microfiche information had been marked "Classified" or "Secret," but were now declassified. Using other previously classified encoding and decoding lists, I translated the information and determined the general history of the plane.

As a brand new C-54, the plane used for Flight 4422 was manufactured by the Douglas Corporation and released to the U.S. Army Air Force in June 1945. It flew missions in Europe and Africa near the end of WWII, then was transferred to bases on the west coast of the U. S. in late 1945. From there, it flew many more missions in the Pacific and Indo-China until June 1946.

It was common for U.S. airlines to lease or purchase WWII military surplus C-54s. Most of these planes were modified slightly and redesignated as DC-4s, bolstering the fledgling airline industry. The military records confirmed that after its military service, the plane was leased to Northwest Airlines in 1946. The last entry in the record indicated the military had written it off its books to "REC" [reclamation] in late 1948, well after its crash on Mount Sanford. Legally, the U.S. government still owned the plane when it crashed and disappeared into the glacier.

Knowing the plane's history was important. But the fact that the primary and first backup files were missing or possibly stolen seemed strange. The records chief remained baffled. It certainly seemed as if someone had intentionally removed both files. Without the second backup file on microfiche, no official record of 35966/45-513 would have existed. I wondered, *Why would anyone want to make 4422's military history disappear? What was so special about this particular plane?* Those were just two more questions added to the long list associated with Flight 4422.

That evening, back in the Bachelor Officer Quarters, I reviewed my copies of the files. Working late into the night, I deciphered the details of the plane's 1940's destinations and maintenance. I was amazed to discover that 45-513/NC-95422/35966 had been based at Travis AFB for a short time in 1945. Marc and I had probably walked the same paths as the pilots who flew the plane during WWII.

The next morning I grabbed some breakfast, then walked back to AFHRA where I studied the previously secret history of the 10th Rescue Squadron assigned to fly 4422's search-and-rescue mission. Declassified files showed that the squadron had flown a total of 14 hours and 30 minutes, a distance of 2,175 miles, during the search. The summary stated:

"Missing aircraft found on Mount Sanford at the 9,000 foot level. Only fin of plane was visible. There was no sign of life and it was determined that it would be too hazardous to attempt to reach the wreckage because of the danger of avalanches."

Although there was no mention of cargo, the records seemed to be consistent with the CAB report. But despite all of our research, there were still missing pieces. I couldn't find any cargo manifest for the plane—nothing about it in Alaska or the lower 48 states. That was unusual. Additionally, because the plane was in civilian status at the time of the crash, there was no military accident investigation. Nor was there any copy of the CAB's investigation in the military files.

The only reference to any cargo was the CAB's statement in the five-page summary report: "The weight and balance was within limits." I wondered how the CAB could have determined that fact without a cargo manifest—a manifest that must have been well protected, hidden, destroyed, or never existed. Without the CAB's entire official report, there was no way of knowing.

OUR RESEARCH INTO the DC-4 had been extensive and laborious. But as difficult as that research had been, it was easy compared to finding answers about the T-2 tanker ship, the SS *Sunset*. It took many years to accumulate bits and pieces of information about the *Sunset* from insurance company records, government agency archives, books, and individuals. In probate (death) records, I found copies of last letters and postcards sent home by some of the ship's sailors. These helped retrace its route to China. Various library chronicles regarding WWII ships also provided clues.

Was the *Sunset* the key to the rumors of treasure that may have gone down with the plane lost in Alaska's wilderness? Marc and I were determined to find out. It took years of research, but the fog of time and space began to clear and the complete and true story of Flight 4422, the SS *Sunset,* and the lives of its men slowly emerged. It went something like this… .

Rainbow over Mount Sanford from Gulkana Airstrip in 1993. This is the first photograph Marc took of Mount Sanford. *Photograph by Marc Millican.*

Marc Millican and his 1957 Super Cubat Gulkana, Alaska in 1994. *Photograph by author.*

Gerry Biasi (L), the author, and Marc Millican (R) in Anchorage getting ready for the first expedition to Mount Sanford in 1994.

Aerial view looking east at the west end (bottom run-out) of the 4422 glacier. *Photograph by author.*

Raging run-out stream at the bottom of the 4422 glacier. The water is deep, and dangerous. *Photograph by author.*

First close-up view of lower ice falls taken in 1995. The plane wreckage must have passed through here in the 1970s or 1980s. *Photograph by author.*

Author's Cessna 175 at the Sanford east landing zone in 1995. This would be the primary backup landing zone for the remainder of the project. *Photograph by author.*

First view of the glacier looking northwest from the ground; taken in 1995 during the solo trip from what we called Green Point. *Photograph by author.*

Looking west from top of the west end of glacier toward Gulkana and north slope of Mount Drum. Note the tent and how small it is in the massive landscape. *Photograph by author.*

First view (1995) of Cub Valley from the ground. 1951 campsite is on the immediate left just out of view. *Photograph by author.*

1994 landing zone/camp site west side of Sanford River. Mount Sanford is 18 miles away in the background. Marc and Gerry left the author there for two nights due to weather. *Photograph by author.*

A dirt cone just below the lower ice falls. It is solid ice approximately five feet tall covered with volcanic debris. Near the top, on the right side is author's hand print in the ice showing the approximate scale. *Photograph by author.*

THE VOYAGE OF THE SS SUNSET

The voyage of the SS *Sunset* had begun on December 19, 1947, at the port of Chester, Pennsylvania, in the damp glow of a cold winter morning. Yellow lights glowed through the *Sunset*'s portholes high up toward the center of the oil tanker, and a few dim lamps lit the deck. The low drone of the ship's huge engines permeated the air. A bell clanged on a marker buoy somewhere out in the channel. The ship was part of the U.S. Merchant Marine fleet, and the members of its crew were called Merchant Mariners.

A T-2 oil tanker ship built for WWII, the SS *Sunset* was never used as such during the war. As a surplus WWII ship, she was acquired from the U.S. government by the Texas Company (CALTEX) in 1947 and took her place in the fleet of the Texas Company's carrying company, the Overseas Tankship Corporation (OTC). This entity was jointly owned by the Texas Company and the Standard Oil Company of California. She was flagged by OTC in Panama and carried throughout the world.

One of the Merchant Mariners, Billy Beswick, roomed in a house in Staten Island, New York. While signing up for the cruise two weeks earlier, the 23-year-old had befriended two other sailors: 24-year-old Howard "Howie" Davidson and 19-year-old John "Raps" Rapchinski—both from Bayonne, New Jersey. The three of them had met at the union hall in Bayonne. During the week before departure, they met a few other members of the *Sunset*'s crew on the streets of Bayonne. They all had something to celebrate: WWII was over, they'd won, and they were excited about embarking on a lucrative and adventurous three-month journey that would take them halfway around the globe.

Billy Beswick's real home was England, but most of the *Sunset*'s sailors for that voyage lived in New York and New Jersey; some came from other states. They were a mix of young and not-quite-young, with a taste for travel and adventure. All had been toughened, in one way or another, by WWII.

Howard Davidson was a big, good-looking guy. The war had already matured him beyond his years. He had spent four years in the Navy as a rangefinder, manning the mighty guns of the USS *Arkansas*, a 27,000-ton, 16-gun battleship that served in both world wars. While firing those huge guns, he was wounded by flash burns during the D-Day invasion of Normandy and blinded for several days. After recovering, he again sailed on the *Arkansas* in the battles for Iwo Jima and Okinawa. Working on the *Sunset* was easy by comparison.

Just before going off to war, Davidson had met Audrey Catt from Jersey City. It was a chance encounter on a crisp and clear Easter Sunday morning—April 5, 1942—a beautiful day in Bayonne for the wedding of his sister, Flory. Davidson and a friend had decided to kill some time before the wedding by walking through the Hudson County Park at the north end of Bayonne. Miss Catt also was out for a walk, with a girlfriend—two good-looking boys, two beautiful girls. Their paths crossed and they struck up a four-way conversation. After a token show of reluctance, she gave Davidson her telephone number. It was love at first sight for both of them.

The next day, he called her, and they soon began dating. Davidson was tall and lean, with hazel eyes and blond hair. Audrey Catt was bubbly and full of fun, a beautiful brunette. Their romance blossomed throughout the war, despite their separation and countless unknowns. Then one day the war was over and Davidson returned home. She flew into his arms and they were soon married. Like so many couples right after the war, they had little money so they moved in with his parents. Meanwhile, Davidson became a Merchant Mariner with the Overseas Tankship Corporation, one of the best jobs around. In addition to excellent pay, the position offered a tax break: Because OTC tankers were registered in Panama, the crews paid little or no tax.

It wasn't long before the young wife was pregnant. The couple was ecstatic, and their daughter, Denise, became the apple of her daddy's eye. Davidson's parents were delighted with their first grandchild, and loved her even before she could call them Nana and Pop-Pop. Home life was good, but Davidson's long time away from home began to take its toll. Each trip made it harder for the tough WWII veteran to leave his family. Finally, the couple made a decision: Although sailing in the OTC ships provided a very good income, this cruise to China would be his last.

Howard Davidson and his four brothers, Robert (Robbie), Warren, Norman, and Leroy, were all buddies. Howard and Robbie were especially close, and were saving money to buy a gas station together. Robbie attended the Merchant Marine Academy before WWII, and then spent the war on the high seas just like his brother. Now he wanted to sail with Howard on one more trip—on the *Sunset*. They figured their combined wages would provide more than enough money to buy the gas station they had their eyes on. Howard signed up right away, but when Robbie went to sign on a few days later, the *Sunset*'s complement was full. As the best alternative, he signed on to one of the *Sunset*'s sister ships, the *Wagon Mound*, which was scheduled to leave Chester three days later than the *Sunset*, but would arrive in Shanghai on the same day as its sister ship. The plan wasn't perfect, but it seemed reasonable. The two brothers would at least fly home together.

All seemed well until one afternoon about two weeks before the *Sunset* was to sail for Shanghai. Nana and Pop-Pop were visiting Robbie, Howard, and their families at Robbie's house, just a few blocks from Howard and Audrey's. As was common at the time, an elderly lady rented a room upstairs. All the Davidsons were together talking and having a good time in the front room on the main floor when the old woman called down to Nana, "Would you please come up here? I must talk with you."

Nana went upstairs. Although the boarder knew nothing about Nana's sons' planned voyage, she told her, "I have some terrible news for you, and you must believe me. It is true. Very shortly, two of your boys will go away together and only one will come home."

With disbelief, Nana asked the old woman to repeat it, then asked how she knew. The woman said nothing more—she just stared out the window. Nana went back downstairs and relayed the strange message to the rest of the family, but no one paid any attention. It was soon forgotten.

The war had made the sea even more dangerous than usual. Live mines were still scattered throughout the oceans, and sunken vessels posed unseen navigational hazards that could rip the bottoms out of ships. But no one was worried about a simple cruise in an oil tanker during peacetime. All the Davidsons figured the two brothers could handle anything, and their chances of getting hurt were very slim.

When departure day came, December 19, 1947, Howard had a difficult time leaving. Just before he sailed, he turned to his wife. Looking intently into her sweet face, he said, "I don't think I can face leaving home like this ever again. This will certainly be my last voyage."

She lit up like a flower in full bloom.

Then he boarded the ship, the ropes were cast off, and the *Sunset* slowly pulled away from the dock. Somewhere out in the channel, the bell of a marker buoy probably rang. It would have been a mournful sound as the ship disappeared into the cold morning mist.

THERE WERE 29 working sailors and 15 officers on the *Sunset.* Their actual numbers varied during the two-and-a-half month cruise as crewmembers joined the ship at some ports; at other stops, some men left the ship. In general, the officers worked in three, five-man shifts. The working sailors usually numbered eight men per shift.

Many of the men were engaged to be married, or newly married with young families. The *Sunset* was also young. Only three years old, it was one of OTC's fleet of 53. From Chester, Pennsylvania, she sailed due south through the Caribbean, carrying fresh water to the oil docks at Curacao, Dutch West Indies. Under clear skies, she offloaded the fresh water from Bayonne and filled her tanks with oil.

Her route was not set in stone; she went where the oil market took her. Although there was an initial plan, the sailors never knew exactly when or where they might end up. At the *Sunset's* cruising speed of 13 1/2 knots, the length of time the sailors would be away from home was at best an educated guess. But the sailors and their families were used to this kind of uncertainty.

Curacao offered an additional attraction for the crew. It was a place where gems of all types, including uncut diamonds, could be purchased at highly discounted prices. Several of the *Sunset's* men undoubtedly shopped for the precious stones.

Most of the men had served in the Army or Navy during WWII. The rest were among those unsung heroes who worked on the unarmed Merchant Marine ships. While carrying desperately needed supplies from America to Europe and Russia, these ships braved German U-boat wolf packs. The men of the *Sunset* had seen their share of ships blown in two, destroyed, and sunk.

Among them was August Koistenen, who had served in the Army during the war. His six brothers served in the armed forces during WWII and his sister, Hilma, had joined the Women's Air Corps (WACS). Koistenen saw action in New Guinea and Guam, and had suffered an injury during a freak accident when he was struck by a heavy sack dropped from an airplane engaged in target practice.

After his discharge in 1946, he spent a summer in a freighter on the Great Lakes, then joined the Merchant Marines. A kind and gentle man, during one period of vacation he taught his niece, Dorothy, to drive a Model T.

One of the younger members of the crew was 21-year-old Bobby Delaney, a native of Keyport, New Jersey. This was his first voyage on the *Sunset* and his first assignment with OTC, but he was no novice. During five years as a Merchant Mariner for the Standard Oil Company, two tankers had been torpedoed out from under him. He'd also survived a case of malaria.

Back in Keyport, his father, two sisters, and his fiancée waited for Delaney. He'd become engaged just a few days before the *Sunset* sailed. Delaney had told his family that the other sailors informed him OTC was going to sell the *Sunset* to Chiang Kai-shek.

It was common knowledge that in 1948 in China many things were paid for in gold, the only stable money in Asia. Throughout the world, gold bullion was often transported back and forth between countries to pay off debts or make loans. It seemed to make sense that the *Sunset* was going to be sold and paid for in gold. True or not, Delaney's word would give birth to one of Flight 4422's legends.

Delaney loved the sea and was excited about the cruise, but he was sad about leaving. He kissed his fiancée goodbye and told her he'd write her as often as he could and that they would get married as soon as he returned.

Frank Van Zandt worked in the engine room as an oiler—applying oil and grease to the engines' bearings to keep them running smoothly. His lanky, 170-pound, six-foot frame made it easy to get to the hard-to-reach places. He had honed his skills over several years on the sea. He had a rough side, though—he had his jaw broken during a shipboard fight a few years earlier. As is common with some people who are gone much of the time, his life at his Roanoke, Virginia, home was somewhat unsettled. He and his wife had separated after just three years of marriage and had no children. Van Zandt spent much of his time at sea.

In contrast, Robert "Robbie" Rabich was a perpetually cheerful guy who kept everyone around him laughing. His father, George Rabich, had been a Merchant Mariner years earlier but now owned and operated a pretzel factory on Line Street in Easton, Pennsylvania. Growing up around the business, the young man had learned well and was a natural businessman. He said he had fallen in love with Alaska and its pioneering spirit, and had decided that right after the cruise he was going to move north—to the land of the midnight sun.

Two hundred miles north of Bayonne, in Fall River, Massachusetts, another well-seasoned sailor left home for the sea. Twenty-four-year-old Eugene Adler bid a similar sad farewell to his young wife, Phyllis, who was one month pregnant. However, Adler didn't know it yet.

One of the most devoted family men on the ship was Lieutenant Carl Sigmund. Thirty-four-years-old, Sigmund was a big, muscular man who had graduated from the U.S. Maritime School in New London, Connecticut. During the first few years of the war, he worked for the Electric Boat Company in Groton, Connecticut, as a radio operator on submarines. In 1944, he joined the Coast Guard. After the war, he received a letter and a medal from

President Harry Truman for his bravery escorting Atlantic convoys. A boxer and a writer, Sigmund wrote for a sports magazine and had published a book, *Salty Tales*. He wrote continually and carried the unfinished manuscript of a second book with him.

Between seagoing trips, he spent as much time at home as possible. A loving father, he brought home big bags of money from his world travels. Due to the extremely strong dollar at the time, the money was not worth much. But he and the children had a lot of fun playing with the foreign currencies.

While at sea, when he wasn't writing books and magazine articles, he penned long letters home to his wife, Harriet. Like all the other sailors, he hated being away from his family for long periods. But with a glut of men back from the war, good jobs were in short supply, and he needed the work.

The Sigmunds had six children, but fate had been cruel to them. In 1946, a Model T Ford backfired in the street outside their home and sparks from the backfire set the house ablaze, burning it to the ground and killing two of their children, Winkie and Dotty. Their five-year-old son, Carl Junior, was badly burned and nearly died of his injuries.

The tragedy brought the couple even closer, but it also caused Harriet Sigmund to worry constantly about her family. She believed she had developed a sixth sense, and now it spoke to her. Just before her husband set sail on the *Sunset*, she told other family members that she had a strong premonition she would never see him again.

FROM CURACAO, the *Sunset* headed to England. Somewhere in the North Atlantic, the crew celebrated Christmas Day with a turkey dinner. Twenty-one-year-old Edwin Mustra assisted the chef. His three years as a ship's cook, second class, in the U. S. Navy during WWII made him a valuable cook's assistant. It was an easy trip for Mustra because his cousin from Sewaren, New Jersey, 22-year-old Michael Marushak, was there to show him the ropes. It was Marushak's third OTC cruise and he already knew all the ports and all the little tricks that made the cruise more enjoyable. He had talked his cousin into going on the cruise as an adventure as much as a job.

But Christmas is a difficult time for families separated by the sea. The married men felt homesick. Howard Davidson slipped away from the party and sprawled out on his bunk to write a letter, pouring out his heart to the family he missed badly:

Christmas, December 25, 1947
    My darling wife and baby, I'll start by saying I'm sorry for not

writing sooner but we left early in the morning we got back to the ship and yet have not got to port. We are now on our way to Venezuela to load up and from there to Europe. It's to take us 15 days to cross so we think it may be either Sweden, Norway, or up that way.

Well, how are both my babies coming along, fine I hope. I sure miss you both and you already know how I love you both. I hope you and [the baby] had a nice Xmas. What did she think of the Xmas tree and did she get a lot of presents? We had a swell Xmas dinner with turkey and all the trimmings. The crew and officers all seem okay so far.

It sure is lonesome for me when I am away from my darling wife and I'm always thinking of you. As I've said a million times, I love you so very much sweetheart. Give the baby a kiss for me and tell her that daddy sure loves her. Take care of yourselves and don't worry about anything.

Love-as ever and always,
Your loving husband

He tucked the letter away, planning to mail it the first chance he got.

The fully loaded *Sunset* continued that leg of the cruise, northeasterly toward England, a country still rebuilding after the devastation of WWII. The monumental reconstruction effort required a continuous supply of oil.

With no more Nazi subs to worry about, Stanley Wilkowski would have enjoyed the peaceful sunrises. He had been on a ship that had been blown up by a sub during the war. Two months later he woke up in Africa with no recollection of how he got there. One minute he was in the ocean; the next, he woke up in the desert. John "Raps" Rapchinski may have joined him on the ship's deck. Other than the sounds of the Atlantic's eternal waves and the low drone of the engines, it would have been quiet. Rapchinski was also on a ship in the Mediterranean that was torpedoed and destroyed. He was in the ship's storeroom when it blew up, and he escaped before it sank. He seriously injured his back in the explosion and spent several months in a Jerusalem hospital.

However safe the young men felt, the oceans were still dangerous. Leftover mines from the war still dotted many parts of the seas. In fact, Merchant Mariners received bonus pay when sailing through waters known to be mined.

Back in Bayonne, Wilkowski's mother and siblings had a tough time making ends meet. His father had died in 1934 and now the family relied on the younger man's wages. Things were hard at Rapchinski's home as well. His mother, sisters, and brothers relied on him, too. His mother couldn't write in English and still signed her name with an X. She and her husband had emigrated from Poland in the 1920s, but he died in 1940.

The ship's bow plowed on through the deep blue of the Atlantic and the bell on the *Sunset* clanged. Shift change—time to go to work.

New Year's Eve, December 31, 1947, found the *Sunset* two-thirds of the way across the Atlantic Ocean. The chef and Edwin Mustra would have worked their magic again with another fine feast. Captain P. J. Barbe may have led the crew in a toast. Then they may have sung "Auld Lang Syne."

A Norwegian, Barbe had survived U-boat torpedo attacks and half-ton shells dropped by dive bombers while he ran the Atlantic convoys during WWII.

TEN DAYS LATER, the *Sunset* passed the half-sunken piers and bombed-out buildings still marking the docks and wharves of Liverpool. It docked two miles upstream, at the Dingle Oil terminal in the Mersey River. Some of the men stayed on the ship to operate the oil pumps, delivering the badly needed supply of oil. Others, like Bobby Delaney, were given shore leave. He headed straight to a big red pillar-mail box, pulled the letter to his fiancée from his coat, slipped it into the mail slot, and went directly back to the ship. The bars and clubs didn't interest him. He had plenty of company with his thoughts of home and the future.

Billy Beswick headed for the train station, as he always did when he was in this part of the world. This time, though, he was accompanied by two shipmates, Rapchinski and Davidson. Full of youthful energy, they hopped on the train and went to see Beswick's family in Old Trafford, about an hour's ride away from Liverpool. Twenty-three-years-old, tall and slim, Beswick had a quick grin, a twinkle in his eye, and an air of mystery that girls found irresistible. An adventurer, he was born in the United States when his father was posted there with the British Foreign Service. That gave him dual nationality.

He had made headlines in Britain during the war when he became the first Brit to enlist in the U.S. Navy. He loved it, and he loved that the U.S. sailors were better paid and wore better-cut uniforms than their British counterparts, which meant more girls. Grumpy English lads had a saying about American servicemen during the war: "Oversexed, over-paid, and over here."

With his looks and charm, Beswick truly had the proverbial girl in every port. He had two families as well: one where he grew up, in Seymour

Grove, Old Trafford—a suburb of Manchester that is now famous for its soccer stadium—and the other family, the McKews, on Rice Avenue, Staten Island, New York, where he based himself after joining the Navy. He even had different names. In America he was Billy; in England he was Wilf, short for his given name of Wilfred.

With the McKews of New York, he lived in an upstairs apartment with a wonderful view to the west. Their daughter, Elizabeth "Betsy" McKew, had adopted him as her uncle. She was like another little sister to Beswick and on this particular voyage he had a special mission. He had promised he would bring her a doll from China.

That evening in England, Beswick, Rapchinski, and Davidson walked down the wide driveway of the brick house on Seymour Grove—a pleasant, three-bedroom, single-family home with a small front porch. Beswick had three brothers and two sisters. His youngest sister, Pearl, knew he was a true hero and an explorer. She idolized him and always wished he could spend more time with her. He spun wonderful stories of his travels, and Pearl could listen for hours. Her brother was her window to the world and his stories let her drift away from war-ravaged England. The nylon stockings and exotic presents he brought were treasures in a country still struggling with post-war rationing. Beswick explained to Pearl how he had recently transferred out of the military into the U.S. Merchant Marine. On this cruise, he was going farther than ever—to Hong Kong or Shanghai, China.

The evening passed quickly and soon it was time to say goodbye. As Beswick walked through the gate with Rapchinski and Davidson on either side, his kid sister ran down the driveway to wave him out of sight. Holding back tears, she yelled, "Come back soon."

He glanced back and waved to Pearl, smiling as he turned the corner. Then he was gone.

THE SOUTH RIDGE

M arc Millican was jet-lagged. After a week and a half of flying a Northwest Airlines 747 between New York and Tokyo, the only thing he wanted to do was sleep. He arrived at his home in Anchorage after midnight and slept until well past noon. Lying in bed in a half-asleep state, he tried to remember exactly where he was. Tokyo? New York? Travis AFB? Gradually, the familiar furnishings of his bedroom took shape. He groggily rolled out of bed and made his way to the shower.

Marc's bachelor pad is a comfortable two-story house on Campbell Lake with a dock for his plane. His house is always neat, but the garage was packed with his Jeep Cherokee, tents and camping equipment, a snowmobile, and a canoe.

Having flown in from New York the night before, I was already downstairs in Marc's kitchen reviewing charts and documents after an early morning trip to the sporting goods store, where I'd purchased a few last-minute items. I had extracted the Jeep from the garage and placed the expedition essentials in neat little piles, ready to load into Marc's Cub. Because I'd discovered the new landing zone at the elevation of 4,800 feet, we didn't need two light airplanes; we would be able to get by with just the Super Cub. Marc finally meandered down the stairs and poured a stiff cup of coffee. I asked him if he was ready to go.

"No way," he said. "I have to check my mail, go the bank, and have a ton of other things to get caught up on before I can leave. It'll be awhile. By the way, what day is it?"

Such is the life of international airline people with dizzying schedules and generally unstable lives. Two hours later Marc was his usual jovial self, dressed and ready for another adventure. We reviewed every detail of our research and spent several hours rechecking the equipment and loading the Super Cub. This year we would carry some special climbing equipment, including ropes, ice hammers, ice axes, ice screws, snow anchors, and climbing harnesses. If we climbed the entire the south ridge, we would need all of it.

Our series of expeditions to find Flight 4422 followed a building-block approach. Each year, we learned more about the mountain and glacier by being there and experiencing it firsthand. Meanwhile, at our homes, we had a complete database of information in case we found the wreck or its victims. And as we learned more about the victims and their families, we became more passionate about the project. In fact, it began to approach an obsession. We had already spent thousands of dollars and hundreds of hours and we were just getting started.

I'd made it all the way to the base of the icefalls in 1995 and found nothing. Despite numerous high- and low-altitude photographic flights over the glacier and all around Mount Sanford and Mount Drum, we had seen no evidence of the lost plane. Now we would check out the one place we hadn't looked—the south ridge.

Using the new landing zone, we planned to climb from there south to the high ridge at 8,000 feet, paralleling the glacier. Climbing farther east, up the crest of the ridge, we would be able to view the entire glacier with binoculars. If anything important were visible, we thought we would be able to see it from that vantage point. More important, we would be high enough on the ridge to view some unusual features we'd seen in our aerial photos. One feature looked like it might be the airplane's nose.

Our latest theory was that the Civil Aeronautics Board's 1948 report might have been mistaken. We thought it was possible the airplane tail or wing tip seen lying in the glacier by the rescuers in 1948 did not include the entire plane, but only part of it. Maybe the DC-4 hit the ridge and only the part of the plane that included the tail section had fallen down into the glacier, and the rest of it was scattered elsewhere on the mountain. There were many possibilities, so we would keep our minds open.

Weeks earlier, Marc's mechanic, Voight Clum, had removed the skis from the Super Cub and installed wheels with huge balloon tires—necessities for the backcountry trip. Clum was always curious about our activities. He never pried, but always warned us, "I hope you boys have backups for whatever you're doing and wherever you're going."

The answer was always in the affirmative. Pilots' lives are in the hands of their skilled mechanics, and Marc and I trusted Clum completely. With the two huge tires bulging from the landing gear and our goals as big as Mount Sanford herself, we departed Lake Hood Airport at 7 p.m. Two hours later, we touched down in Gulkana.

After a comfortable night at the Caribou Inn, we woke to bright, clear skies. The weather forecast, however, wasn't good. Three stationary low-pressure systems lined up like soldiers south of Valdez, a hundred miles south of Mount Sanford. If the systems edged northward, the entire Copper River basin could easily be socked in as the low pressure sucked in moisture-laden air, creating low clouds, rain, or even snow. If the low-pressure systems moved south, east, or stayed where they were, nice weather would prevail over Mount Sanford. The lows were not good news. We needed clear weather.

Before leaving for the bush, wise and experienced pilots stuff themselves with food in case they need extra energy for some unforeseen event. One of Marc's buddies, Jeff, always said, "Eat well. You can't snowshoe five miles on a salad." After a big breakfast and a careful recheck of the airplane, its fuel, and its contents, we took off once again for the wilderness of Mount Sanford.

We flew directly to the clear area near the Sanford River where I had landed in 1995. After flying a few low passes to get familiar with the area, Marc pushed the power up and flew toward the new landing zone with an altitude of 4,800 feet.

Looking down at it from 6,500 feet, he said, "Are you sure about this?"

"Yup," I said, "I know we can get in and out of here. The surface is certainly as good as the place we landed in 1994, but the approach is going to be pretty hairy."

ON OUR FIRST PASS at 6,500 feet, the roar of the Cub's engine spooked a grizzly bear. With long, quick strides, he clawed his way up the hill to the south, his brown fur rippling and glistening in the sun. We made a circular pass over the top of the ridge and saw a flock of about 50 Dall sheep. The bear apparently had been hunting the sheep when our plane startled him.

Our second pass was at 6,000 feet. Marc scrutinized the landing zone and the dogleg flight path. We learned that, from just 250 feet directly above the center of the glacier, he would have to maneuver the plane down into the little notch separating the glacier from the valley, make a hard left turn, and then touch down without hitting the 8,000-foot mountain directly ahead of us.

After completing the second pass Marc added full power, but the plane didn't climb into the air like it should have—an unseen downdraft swept in from the ridge to our right. The little plane moved perilously closer to the mountainous slope on the east end as Marc gingerly turned it to the left, back toward the glacier and away from the rock-covered slopes. There wasn't enough room to turn right. "That's all the power we can get," he yelled into the intercom. "I think we're in a downdraft. Hold on!"

I was as silent and still as a rock. There was nothing I could do other than hold on tight as the little plane cleared the east end of the notch-hill by about 25 feet. Marc gently and skillfully brought the plane farther left toward the glacier. By holding the nose up and keeping the wings at their maximum angle of climb, he conserved every inch of space between us and the surface. The engine roared and the propeller clawed away at the thin cool air, but the Super Cub sank even more. We were so low that some of the glacier's seracs actually rose higher than the plane.

Time seemed to slow down as small greenish blue tairns (glacial lakes) passed 20 feet underneath us. Arches of ice reached into the sky, framing some of the little ponds. The rock scree on top of the ice looked like a nut coating on a white ice cake. The scenery was a magnificent frozen brown, blue, and white fantasyland—beautiful but deadly. If we crashed into any of those icy pits, we would never be seen or heard from again. I braced for the inevitable impact, thinking *what a beautiful place to die.*

After what seemed like an eternity (in reality no longer than 30 seconds), we began to gain height above the cold and wet glacier. We were not climbing at all—the glacier dropped away as it descended toward its run-out into the Sanford River. One mile down the glacier, the Super Cub started gaining altitude, well out of the downdraft. I breathed a sigh of relief. We had just learned one more critical lesson unique to this terrain: In the evening, air generally rushed down the glacier into the valley far below. From my hike in 1995, I already knew that in the mornings, the air generally rushed in the opposite direction up the valley, providing a slight headwind and better conditions for taking off. This was critical information for the future.

Safely back high in the air, I called over the plane's intercom, "Wasn't that a little tight?"

"Yeah," Marc replied, "There went another one of my nine lives. We have a new rule. Once below 1,000 feet above this landing area, we will be committed to landing."

"You mean committed to the nuthouse, don't you?"

"No comment. The surface looked acceptable to me—rough, but good enough. What do you say? Let's give it another try. You'll have to talk me down."

"Okay. But cross off two of your nine lives. This close call counted as two."

WE PREPARED FOR another attempt at landing. There would be no go-around this time. One way or another we would end up on the ground. I piloted the plane while Marc relaxed for about five minutes and surveyed the landing zone one more time. Then he took back the stick. "I've got the plane now," he said. "Let's go for it. This time's for real."

The approach and landing was a two-man operation requiring Marc's flying skill and my year-old memory of the little valley. We made one pass at 6,000 feet and swung far out to the north side of the glacier. Turning back, he set up a nice long, stable approach. After we turned at the notch, I said, "See that grassy knoll on the left, 250 feet ahead? Do not touch down before it or we might flip over. There is a little ditch there and it's probably full of water. Touch down just beyond it."

Marc added just enough power to clear the ditch. The plane hit with a thud, 10 feet past the grassy knoll. Its left main wheel touched down hard, causing a little water to spray up from a small stream, then lurched five feet back into the air and slammed down on the right wheel. Marc fought to keep it straight, added a little power, and stabilized the plane while it traveled over mounds of grass, wet rivulets, and softball-size rocks. He brought it to a stop with 25 feet to spare. "That was pretty tough but we made it."

"Wow, that was one hell of an approach. Nice job," I said.

"That's real teamwork," he replied, and shook my hand over the back of his seat.

IT WASN'T BAD for the first landing in a remote and unfamiliar area. The Cub's altimeter read 4,800 feet. At that high altitude, we knew that later on the takeoff would be difficult due not only to the altitude, but also because of the rough surface. The winds and other weather conditions would have to be just right. At least for now, we were nicely positioned to continue our search for Flight 4422. After two minutes of letting the engine run at idle so that it would cool off, Marc shut it down and we climbed out.

Silence enveloped us as we stood in the remote valley. The sudden change from the brain-rattling approach and constant intercom chatter caught us off guard. It took us a full 30 minutes to calm down and adjust to the solitude of wilderness. For me, it was great to be back in the valley. I felt right at home. Marc drank three pint bags of juice after the difficult approach and landing. Finally, he settled down and became comfortable with the solace of the new surroundings. The beauty and serenity of the wilderness calmed our souls.

"Let's call this Cub Valley," he said, "for the Super Cub."

And that's how the remote valley halfway up the side of the 4422 glacier, on the southwest side of Mount Sanford, got its name.

"Okay, I got us in here," Marc said. "Now it's your turn. Let's find 4422."

After putting the airplane to bed with ropes and rocks-in-a-bag, and repacking our heavy backpacks, off we went, this time to the south. Trickling waterfalls led the way up the grass-covered banks of a small stream lined with boulders. We followed the stream to its source in a meadow on top of the ridge, close to where Mr. Bear's sheep had been grazing.

Another grueling five-hour hike to the northeast along the top of the ridge took us to 8,500 feet. Occasional five-minute breaks allowed us to shoot some photographs and catch our breath.

With high-powered binoculars and a telescope, we scanned every inch of the huge glacier far below and the ridge to the east, but saw nothing out of the ordinary—only rocks, water, snow, and ice. Behind us, ominous dark clouds formed and began moving in from the southwest. One or more of the low-pressure systems must have started moving toward us—not a good sign.

Looking far down into the glacier, we picked out my 1995 bivouac spot several miles west of the ice falls, but were unable to see the strange red and brown cones I'd studied at the foot of the falls. Perhaps they had melted, but the glacier certainly should not have moved enough in one year to obliterate them. If they had melted, that would be a small yet important indication of the glacier's warming. Perhaps the mercury had risen enough so that the lost plane and its occupants would be revealed by the thawing glacier.

As we climbed even higher and farther east on the ridge, clouds filled the sky and the wind started howling. We could feel the increase in humidity as the cold, wet air moved in. Just before the visibility dropped to zero, we got one chance to carefully scan the ridge. We could see the feature that looked like the plane's nose section and now we were able to see that it was just another illusion caused by shadows, snow, rock, and ice. Clearly, it was not a part of a plane.

Gusts of cold wind from the south slapped us hard. Within minutes, the gusts changed to a steady 55-mile-per-hour gale. Mount Sanford's temperament had changed; she now hid her face behind a white and gray veil of clouds. Snow flew off the highest peaks, trailing several hundred yards into the sky.

At first, the huge avalanche was out of view, but we could hear loud snapping sounds similar to cracks of lightning, followed by a roar like a freight train, as tons of snow and ice ripped down the nearly vertical slopes below Mount Sanford's summit. Through a break in the clouds, we saw the powdered snow billow into the sky as chunks of snow and ice careened past the DC-4's 1948 impact area and down into the glacial cirque above the ice falls. Huge cornices 50 feet thick broke away and fell down the overhanging cliffs—apparently overloaded by the pressure from the gales of wind and weight of new snow. It was not just one avalanche, but a set of many roaring downward at more than a hundred miles per hour past the 8,000-foot level. The white plumes rose thousands of feet into the air, engulfing the entire upper glacier far below. But the white fury didn't stop there; it hurtled down past the ice falls and onto the stable portion of the glacier where I had stood the previous year. The avalanches' plumes billowed even higher, obscuring the top quarter of the 16-mile-long glacier for just over 10 minutes.

I swallowed hard as I realized we would have been directly in the avalanches' paths if we'd hiked to the top of the glacier, as I had done the previous year. We might have been buried alive.

DEEP IN THE WILDERNESS of Alaska, we had just dodged another bullet. Having viewed the powerful spectacle firsthand, we were convinced there was no way anything other than natural rocks and ice could have remained on the cliffs at the plane's supposed point of impact. We also knew there was no way we were ever going to enter the area above the ice falls; to do so would be suicidal. "If anyone ever went up there, they were crazy," I said.

Marc agreed. With snow blowing all around us, the sudden change in the weather meant only one thing. At least one of those wicked low-pressure systems must have started moving north. The moisture sucked in by the low system could result in a huge snowstorm, easily stranding us for days or even weeks. Three or four inches of snow would make it tough, but a foot of the white stuff would be catastrophic. The landing zone also could be flooded, rendering it unusable. With moderate snow already whipping around us and the wind howling like a banshee, our next decision was easy.

"It's time to get out of here," I yelled into the wind.

Marc yelled back, "Let's go."

We moved quickly—straight into the one-inch flakes of driving snow. The extra weight of our backpacks was actually an advantage because it prevented us from getting blown off the ridge. We didn't need a compass; all we had to do was stay on the highest point of the ridge as we descended.

We could have toughed it out, thrown up the tent, and stayed to see if the weather would get better. But after nearly crashing the Super Cub in 1994 and the close call during our first landing in Cub Valley, we had agreed we were not going to take any more unnecessary risks. Enough people had already died on this mountain. We hustled back down the snow-covered, windblown ridge. After we descended just 1,000 feet, the weather changed dramatically. The snow became light rain as we moved through several layers of clouds down to the 6,000-foot level. Once we were off the ridge and only 500 feet above Cub Valley, a few orphaned rays of the setting sun broke through the lowest clouds and mist for a few minutes. We breathed a sigh of relief.

Cub Valley was cold that evening. The beams from our flashlights formed long tunnels in the mist—the only light as we neared our campsite, totally exhausted. The reflection of the Super Cub's white fabric raised our spirits, but visibility was only a few hundred yards in the mist. That could be a real problem for flying out. Aviation-wise, our little one-way landing/takeoff zone was a challenging combination of high altitude, rough surface, clouds, and unpredictable winds. It was no place for amateurs.

But it was a safe harbor—well protected from the raging south wind. After quickly setting up the tent and boiling hot water for a freeze-dried dinner, we slid into our sleeping bags and wolfed down high-energy food. Despite the winds howling through the night high up on the ridge, I slept well. Marc stretched out and tried to relax, but still jet-lagged from his recent flight, he only got an hour of sleep.

The ridge visit of 1996 was finished. Even though we had seen no aircraft debris, we were not disappointed. We'd viewed most of the glacier from the ridge and determined that the possible nose section was nothing more than an odd formation of rock. This was a big puzzle with many pieces that could only be solved one at a time. We also knew, despite our exhilaration and caution, that we were living dangerously.

MORNING FOUND EVERYTHING in the valley lightly coated in snow and frost under gray skies, and a mix of rain and snow continued to pelt us. It would have been a good day to stay in our sleeping bags, but we were awake by 5 a.m. I crawled out of the tent and hiked up the little hill on the north. The mist and light rain seemed to stay up the glacier. I was amazed to be able to see five miles down the glacier to the west toward the Sanford River. Directly above, ominous clouds hung very low, giving us a ceiling of 400 or 500 feet; the blanket of solid clouds provided just enough room above the ground to escape from the valley.

Fortunately the temperature rose slightly and the groundcover of snow began to melt. There was no time to lose. Skipping breakfast, we packed the Cub as fast as we could. After pushing its tail back into the sparse weeds, Marc cranked the engine and warmed it up. I ran 300 yards to the top of the little hill to the northwest to make another check on the weather. I could still see down into the glacier and out to the valley floor—but just barely. I sprinted back to the plane, huffing and puffing.

Above the noise of the engine, I yelled, "The clouds are coming down fast."

Marc commanded, "Strap in. Let's go—now!"

Taking off from Cub Valley was challenging. The mountain loomed ahead slightly to our left, disappearing into the clouds. From our starting point, it was impossible to see over the small ridge on our right, down into the glacier. Marc had to trust my judgment and fly straight down the small stream that started in the valley's east side, then make a hard right turn and fly around the west end of that hill above the 1951 campsite. After he made it around the corner, he'd have to fly blind for a couple of moments until he could see northward in the direction of the glacier. Once over the ice, he would have to turn back to the left down the glacier.

One big concern was that if the engine quit on takeoff, or just before or over the glacier, a crash would probably be fatal. There was nowhere smooth for us to land among the icy crevasses during the first intense 60 seconds of flight. We had to do it right the first time. There was no room for error in Cub Valley.

The engine purred smoothly in the moderate rain and mist. I had barely finished strapping in when Marc pushed the throttle all the way forward, demanding full power from the Cub's engine. He concentrated on the takeoff like a jeweler cutting a million-dollar diamond. Off we went, bumping and rolling over the rough surface. I sat perfectly still and silent in the back.

Marc raised the tail after just a few seconds. The big tundra tires lifted off the gravel-and-rock-covered surface at 40 miles per hour. Ten feet in the air, he turned the plane to the right 40 degrees, flew over the 1951 campsite, and headed through the low spot between the hill and the mountain as planned, squeezing past the rocks on the right and left.

Five seconds later, we were flying just above the glacier and its spectacular array of cathedral-like ice spires, rock peaks, valleys, and glacial tarns. To our right, less than a half mile up the glacier, gray clouds formed a solid wall. To our left, down the glacier, we could still see into the valley. Our red and white plane startled two caribou grazing on the ridge as we flew over. They galloped into a brush-filled wash.

Menacing clouds hovered only 200 feet above the plane as Marc turned it back to the left, soaring straight down the glacier, whose icy surface dropped away as it continued its gentle downward slope into the valley, toward the Sanford River. Within minutes, we were soaring smoothly 400 feet above the ice—and relatively safe. The weather had made it a close call.

Rain pelted the windshield as we headed west. Behind us, several inches of new snow covered the glacier and blanketed the mountains on each side of Cub Valley. The snow must have been much deeper higher up on the ridges and the previous day's climbing route was most certainly covered by new snow. The glacier with its secrets receded into the mist and clouds. But we knew we would be back; Flight 4422 had captured our souls.

In the span of only four minutes, we flew over what had taken me four-and-a-half hours to hike down the year before. Unfortunately, that snowstorm would prevent us from searching again in 1996. The area high above Cub Valley was most likely already buried underneath at least a foot of snow, making it impossible to survey anything from the ground or the air.

At 6:30 a.m., Marc glided the Super Cub to a nice touchdown at Gulkana. Light rain fell. No one else was at the airport; its fuel pumps were turned off and locked. Scores of other small planes were parked in neat rows, soldier-like, awaiting their next assignments.

CLIMBING OUT OF the Cub, I looked across the parking ramp and imagined the flurry of activity at the little airstrip back on March 12, 1948. Marc and I were walking in the footsteps of Layton Bennett, Jerry Luebke, and the others who had tried so desperately to find Flight 4422. I envisioned the two pilots taking off into a night sky filled with the northern lights to search for the plane. I imagined the investigators' endless questions that still lingered after so many years.

Although it was early, Marc telephoned Steve Karcz and our other pilot buddies to let them know we were safely out of the remote mountains. An hour later, Lynn Ellis showed up and turned on the fuel pumps. We refueled the Cub, filed a flight plan, and flew through moderate rain back to Anchorage.

Over the next week, the weather continued to deteriorate in the Copper River basin. Up on Mount Sanford, if we had delayed our exit even by half a day, we would have been stranded—no question about that.

Our 1996 expedition had not gone as planned, but we had become more comfortable with and informed about conditions on Mount Sanford. Because we had not noticed any major movement of the large rocks near the glacier's south edge, we realized that most of the glacier's movement must have been confined to the narrow center section. This was a clue to the plane's whereabouts and it demanded a more detailed study of the glacier.

Back in Anchorage, over a couple beers and a good dinner at Marc's house, we once again reviewed our photos and evaluated all our theories about the crash. Nothing indicated the CAB report was wrong, but we had found nothing that supported it, either. We recapped our latest set of expeditions: By 1993 Marc had obtained basic historical research and flew over the crash area. Gerry and I had completed some research. In 1994, we'd conducted aerial surveys and photo flights. But, we'd aborted our first expedition. In 1995, I'd gone solo and hiked visit to the Amphitheater of the Souls and Cub Valley. I surveyed the upper glacier and had viewed the ice falls. Although we'd lost Gerry as a climbing partner, he would remain a good part of the team with whom we could discuss our most secret plans. Our 1996 south ridge survey had given us a bird's-eye view of the glacier and eliminated an odd-looking feature as being the nose section on the ridge. Most importantly, we learned that Cub Valley worked well as a landing area and that the lower backup landing zone on the east side of the Sanford River was acceptable.

As we discussed the 1996 expedition late into the night, we didn't feel demoralized by the fact that bad weather had curtailed our search. We were just as fired up as ever, and we tried to understand why we were so driven to solve this mystery, one that had eluded so many people for so many years.

By now we had spent at least $40,000, including airplane time, fuel, maintenance, expedition equipment, and lots of research costs. The tab was really starting to add up and we were beginning to feel the financial burden. We had not found any of the wreckage, and we agreed that the chances of finding it were pretty slim. Yet we still felt we had a chance—better than finding planes that have crashed into the sea—which was all we asked for. Everything still seemed to point to the glacier.

We agreed it was worth one more try. If nothing else, Marc would have visited the base of the ice falls enabling him to describe the suspected crash site in an article he wanted to write for the Northwest Pilots Association magazine. Another look at the position of the aluminum memory marker I'd left in 1995 might reveal something about the glacier's movement. I also wanted to find out what happened to those peculiar cones I'd seen in 1995.

Just after midnight, Marc dropped me off at Anchorage International Airport with four duffel bags of equipment. We said *so long* and I boarded my flight. Exhausted from the expedition, I fell asleep as soon as I took my seat in the Boeing 767. Once the plane reached cruising altitude of 35,000 feet, the pilots reduced the engines' power and I woke up. Raising the cover on the window, I saw Mount Sanford's summit in the distance, jutting above the thick low-level clouds laden with rain and snow. A thin veil of northern lights waved above its summit as if to say, "We are waiting."

I drifted back to sleep and dreamed of my cold night bivouacking on the glacier one year before. It seemed like a very long time ago.

DURING THE REMAINDER of 1996 and early 1997, we continued to locate more pieces of information. From reams of court records and data in libraries across the U.S., we learned more about each victim of the crash and about the SS *Sunset*. The sailors' and aircrew members' personal stories intrigued us, spurring us on.

I was astounded when I found records of many of the lawsuits filed by victims' relatives. They provided a wealth of information and opened new avenues of research. Yet each bit of data created more questions. One special aspect of our research was locating living relatives. If our search for the plane was successful, we soon would want to contact them, and these records contained clues to help us find them.

The files revealed that many questions lingered—painfully unanswered for half a century among the friends and families of those lost. Answering those questions became the primary goal of our Flight 4422 project. Of course we would still have to identify the plane if we found it. Maybe the tail with the plane's registration number was still near the surface of the ice. A logbook would do, or maybe an engine, or something personal from one of the passengers or aircrew. So far, we'd drawn a blank.

Marc and I agreed that 1997 would be our last attempt. We were aware of how lucky we had been in 1996. We hadn't been caught in the huge set of avalanches, we had narrowly escaped being stuck in deep snow on the mountain, and we had not crashed into the glacier during our first low fly-by of Cub Valley. But we had pressed our luck to the limit. How many more chances did we have before disaster struck? Meanwhile, whetting our appetites was our research, which continued to fill the voids in our knowledge of the lives of the 30 men who had gone down with the plane.

England to China in the SS *Sunset*, January 1948

LETTERS

The SS *Sunset* rode high in the cold brown water of the River Mersey as she left Liverpool, England. Seawater ballast was all she had in her tanks. She rounded the headland of Wallasey, cleared the Isle of Anglesey off northwest Wales, then charted a course southeast around the tip of Spain and through the Strait of Gibraltar into the Mediterranean. She was heading to the oil-rich states of the Persian Gulf. The first stop—Port Said at the northern end of the Suez Canal.

On deck, a few of the sailors enjoyed the hot Mediterranean sun. Others, most of them homesick, may have sat in the shade of a tarp tied between the rigging, writing letters home. Among them were Bobby Delaney, Billy Beswick, Carl Sigmund, Eugene Adler, Howie Davidson, and Everett Jenkins. In addition to personal notes, their letters recorded important details of the ship's movements, their pay, and life at sea. Three years had passed since the end of WWII, and information about the ship's movements was no longer censored. On January 22, Davidson wrote:

> "Dearest Audrey and Denise,
> How are both my sweethearts coming along? Fine I hope in all ways. I want both you babies to take good care of yourselves for me as I'm sure anxious to see you and I want you both in the best of health and all.
> Darling, the days and nights are sure lonesome without you and I love you and miss you more and more each day. It will be awfully good to be home again and by the time you get this letter, it will be soon for me to be along.
> We are now two days out of Port Said and that's where I hope to mail this or at Suez. We are now about off the coast of Turkey or near Abyssinia. From Suez to Aden it will be about 6 days and from

Aden to Bahrein (Arabia) is another 9 or 10 days and another 20 to Shanghai. Half of the load goes to Hong Kong which no one is sure if we'll take it or the Chinese. But, we know Shanghai for sure. That is if the revolution there is over. I guess you heard about it on the radio – we did anyway. According to the officers, we will be in China about the 25th of Feb. – so you can see it won't be long now.

Well darling how's the weather back there? I know it must be cold but I hope not too bad. This is when you should miss my cuddling up to you and vice versa (I hope you do anyway – don't be mad remember I love you anyway). No fooling darling I miss you something terrible and in all ways. I'm going to hug you to pieces when I get hold of you – I think as soon as I get home – be it morning noon or night, off to bed I'm taking you. I'm sure you'll love that won't you – at any rate you can bet your girdle I will.

And now but of course never least a few questions about our precious baby. How is she darling. I can't wait to see her and I'm sure she's walking all over the house. Oh how I miss her – both you and she will never know. I can't explain how awfully I want to see her, hug, kiss and love her. She's so cute and we really have a fine baby daughter there. Kiss her and hug her for me and tell her that daddy misses her.

Give my love and regards to all and tell mom and pop all the news I've told you. Keep your chin up darling and I'll not be far behind this letter – I'm sure it will be sooner than expected. God bless you and the baby and think of me as I think of you both and miss you so much.

Your loving husband,
'I love you so.'
For you and baby!
XXXXXXXXXXXXXXXXXXXXXXXXXX [Kisses]"

The ship sailed on through the Suez Canal into the Red Sea, where the air was even hotter. On February 1, Davidson wrote again:

"My precious wife and baby,
Here's hoping this letter finds you both doing well and all O.K. I'm not so sure this letter will get off at Bahrain, Arabia, which is our next port but its possible I hear. We are due there Feb 3 or this Tues. From there we are going to go back to the Red Sea (which we went through a week ago). And unload at Aden. From Aden back to Bahrain and on to China. That

is the orders to now but of course they may change again. If this does happen (which I and many others doubt) it will make the trip another 10 days to 2 week longer. I hope that news is not to disappointing to you – if its so I won't be home till about the middle of March.

By the time you get this letter, you should have gotten one check by then. I hope so as I know you can use the money. Please don't go without anything for you or the baby when the check comes. Get all you need or please to get, don't worry about having any left. Just get things you need and don't do without anything for yourself and baby.

Darling you'll never know how I love you and [the baby] and the terrible way I miss you both. It's like hell worrying about if you both are alright and happy. I hope you manage to get to the show once in a while to enjoy yourself. When I come home you and I will go to NYC for a night or two if it can be arranged to see a show of some kind. Darling I think of you and dream of you so very much.

Darling you mean the world to me and I could never live without you. This is probably the last time I'll be away from you as I long for you too much when we are apart. I am counting every day and minute till I am home again with you and my darling baby. I can't wait to see [the baby]. I suppose she's walking all over and talking more than ever. I'm going to hug her (you too) so tight when I get home. She's such a cute and good baby. Hon and we're pretty lucky to have such a daughter.

I hope you are missing me as its unfair the terrible way I long for you. Your loving is something I could never go without. To hold you in my arms and love you is all I live for. Your kisses and caressing is what keeps me living and happy. The nites are endless and empty and the days are weary and long when I am not near my darling wife. You are not replaceable darling so please take care of yourself for me. I would die broken hearted without you dearest. I love you I love you and I love you.

It is getting time for me to go to the galley and have my evening toast and tea before I go to sleep. And dream of the sweetest, cutest, prettiest and loveable wife of mine. So darling keep that pretty little chin up and kiss the baby for her daddy and tell her I love her. Till I write again or till I can take you in my arms I'll say goodnite, my angel. Oh how I miss you dearest.

Your faithful husband,
XXXXXXXXXXXXXXXX [Kisses]
It won't be long darling (chin up)"

Sailors throughout the world knew about long months of separation, but that didn't make it any easier for them. As a single man during WWII, Everett Jenkins had two Merchant Marine ships blown out from under him, one by a torpedo and the other by a mine. A realistic man, Jenkins accepted whatever fate might befall him. But once married (on December 2, 1947), he decided he'd had enough of the high seas and planned to settle down after this cruise on the *Sunset*.

The ship crossed the Gulf of Aden into the Arabian Sea and rounded the eastern shore of Saudi Arabia, turning northwest into the Persian Gulf. At Port Said, instructions were received to head for Bahrain, a tiny, oil-rich island halfway up the western shore of the Persian Gulf. There, she would refill her tanks with oil. On February 12, 1948, Davidson wrote another letter to his wife:

"My Darling wife and daughter,

To begin I must tell you I love you and my baby ever ever so much. I miss you both something terrible and the days can't go fast enough till I am again with you.

As I said we may go to Aden – well, we are. We are due in about midnight tonight and it is now 7 PM. We will be here a few days and then back to Bahrain – they are both in Arabia. From Bahrain, we will positively go on to Shanghai.

As far as I know we are due in China on March 11 or 12th and in New York on the 14th or 15th. That is about when to expect me darling – no sooner. The heat is terrific here and I guess you are probably having freezing weather home. You should see the swell sun tan I have darling. I hope it stays on till I get home. They say its mighty cold around China now. I'll probably freeze there.

So how is my two little angels coming along – great I hope. Boy hon it sure will be great to be home with you two again. I can just picture Denise walking all over the place. I look at both your pictures often and then is when I really get homesick for you. It is impossible for me to tell you how awful I miss you and your loving. I'm going to crush you to pieces when I get my arms around you. Naturally you can imagine the terrific physical urge I have for you. I dream of you quite often darling and when I wake and find you gone, I feel of low.

For some reason the engines are making a hell of a pounding that I can't concentrate. These officers don't know a damn about our ship. By the way darling, I received three of your wonderful letters at one time in Bahrain. They sure were good to get. Only a few letters came to the whole crew and I got three of them. Lucky me. It's good to know you are both okay and I hope I get more soon. Those letters had the east 44th St. address but I still got them OK. If I were you, I wouldn't write after March 1st as I'll probably not get them.

I'll close now darling but will always continue to love you and miss you and long for you. Give the baby a kiss for her daddy.

Love as ever,

XXXXXXXXXXXXXXXX" [Kisses]

Five days later, on Tuesday February 17, 1948, Davidson wrote another letter home:

"Dearest Darling,

Happy birthday to you my dear wife and I hope many more only with me by your side. No dearest I didn't forget your birth day or the baby's (on the 5th) either. I'll bring you both something when I come home which won't be long now. You can expect me on about the 14th or 15th of March.

Now how is the two sweetest girls in the world doing these days. Fine I hope and all being well. Just imagine hon, our precious darling is a year old already. Oh how I can't wait to see her and of course you too dearest. I sure love you both something awful. I am constantly thinking about and dreaming of you both. It seems like years since I've seen you and the time can never go fast enough till I am with you. Every evening I sit on deck and look at the stars and day dream of you. I am not going to leave you or Denise ever again as I get too lonesome and homesick for you. Since we were married I can't seem to get used to sleeping alone and I don't like it. You know what I mean so its not necessary to say – "don't get me wrong." I have but one darling and it's you sweet. I love you so and I always will love only you. I love Denise too but it's a different way of course. Ever since I left, I live day to day only waiting to get home to you.

We have just left Aden on Sunday and are going back to Rasintura or Bahrien to load and our orders say straight to Shanghai. Everyone doubts any change in them and most hope not. At Bahrien we will get mail and I am sure there will be some for me. There just got to be but if not, I know it couldn't be your fault. Nothing could be wrong and be my sweet wife's fault. Oh how I love you.

*During the first week of March you should receive another allotment
check. Use it as you need it and don't go without anything you or the
baby need. The money is there for you so don't be afraid to use it.*

*The heat here is awful and I sweat night and day. The engine room
and fire room are as hot as hell. I sure hope it cools off near China. So
my angel, I come to close another letter hoping you are getting all I
write. Take care of yourself and our darling daughter and remember I
am longing to be with you. I love you darling and kiss [the baby] for her
daddy.*

Love-to the sweetest wife on earth.
Your husband,
XXXX"

The mail system was very efficient. At Bahrain, when the crew pumped
the *Sunset's* tanks full of crude oil again, they had a chance to mail their
letters, most of which would arrive in the States within 10 days. The ship left
Bahrain and sailed through the Indian Ocean, South China Sea, and East
China Sea. The crew couldn't wait to get ashore and head for home, courtesy
of Northwest Airlines.

JUST LIKE THE Merchant Mariners of the *Sunset*, aircrews did not
necessarily stay together for an entire trip. While sailors signed on and off the
ship in different places in the world, Northwest Airlines formed its aircrews
in various ways. Over a two-week trip, a captain and copilot would usually fly
with several different pursers, flight mechanics, and navigators.

During the first week of March, 1948, 27-year-old Northwest Airlines
Captain James Van Cleef packed his bags in Minneapolis, Minnesota, in
preparation for a week-long flight to and from Alaska. He roared down the
highway to the airport in his brand-new green 1948 Studebaker. A quick
study and a genuinely nice man, Van Cleef didn't waste money. Like many
pilots, he was aware of the ups and downs of the industry and was fairly
conservative. With a reputation of quality and reliability, the Studebaker
reflected his conservative lifestyle. After parking the car in the employee lot,
he walked to the pilot office and signed in for his trip to Anchorage where he
would be part of the crew taking over NWA Flight 4422, a chartered flight
transporting the *Sunset's* crew back to New York via Alaska and Canada. At
Northwest Airlines, these chartered flights were known as "Caltex charters."

On the other side of town, DC-4 Flight Mechanic Donald Rector kissed
his wife, Mary, goodbye and hugged his two children. He too was assigned to

fly the Caltex charter, joining it in Anchorage.

In Seattle, Robert Haslett followed a similar routine. He kissed his wife, patted his one-year-old son, Randall, on the head, and drove to the airport. A flight purser for Northwest, Haslett would take care of the 24 passengers scheduled to be on his fight from Anchorage to Minneapolis.

HOMEWARD BOUND

On the *Sunset*'s bridge, Captain P. J. Barbe decided it looked safe and pulled the lanyard, sending an angry cigarettes-and-whiskey blast from the foghorns signaling the SS *Sunset*'s arrival in Shanghai, China, on March 11, 1948. With a load of oil from the Middle East, she powered her way through the cool waters of the Huangpu River as the 16,000-ton T-2 oil tanker completed her three-month voyage. Like magic, walla wallas and junks appeared out of the mist and floated all around the ship as it dropped anchor. Having been surrounded by ocean water for the best part of three months, the sailors couldn't wait to get off the ship as she moored in the deep water in the middle of the Huangpu.

As soon as the captain ordered the engines idled, a crew of about 30 Chinese seamen swarmed aboard to pump oil out of the *Sunset*'s tanks. The 24 American working sailors were replaced by sailors of Chinese nationality who were paid about one-fourth the wages the Americans received. Captain Barbe and his 12 Scandinavian officers stayed with the ship. Three of the American sailors, all firemen, also stayed on board for a few hours to train the Chinese and ensure the ship's safety until the newcomers learned the ropes. Two other American sailors also stayed on the ship. They were "observing engineers"—trainees previously unfamiliar with the ship's big diesel engines.

The American sailors grabbed their bags and clambered into ferry boats called walla wallas. Soon they felt the firm, dry land of Shanghai beneath their feet. Their long trip was over and now they could relax and look forward to flying home the next day.

The *Sunset* arrived to a scene of controlled chaos in Shanghai's harbor. It was chaos born of WWII. Perhaps 12 million people jockeyed for a piece of the action after eight years of Japanese occupation. There was no city plan, haphazard policing, innumerable small uncontrolled businesses, and rampant inflation. One U.S. dollar traded for 500,000 CNC—Chinese

Nationalist Currency. You literally needed a wheelbarrow of Chinese cash to buy a loaf of bread.

China's revolutionary war was well underway, with President Chiang Kai-shek's Nationalists and the Communist Red Army fighting for control of the nation. Although Chiang Kai-shek's rule was in serious jeopardy, for the moment Shanghai and its world-class seaport were still relatively safe; the heavy fighting was still well outside the city limits.

Shanghai means "on the sea." The city spreads across a huge expanse of flat river delta 10 to 16 feet above sea level, and the river flows directly into the sea. As one of the biggest natural deep-water harbors in the world, Shanghai was one of the centers of East Asian trade.

It has always been a wild town. Decades earlier, its name became a verb—shanghaied. Desperate 19th-century ship captains sent out snatch squads to kidnap drunks in bars around the seaports of San Francisco, New York, London, and Liverpool. The stupefied souls awoke to find themselves on the high seas and were forced to work their way to China or wherever the vessel was headed. If they refused, they paid dearly.

The SS *Grand River,* a sister ship of the *Sunset,* had arrived in Shanghai five days ahead of the *Sunset.* The radio officer, Bernie Hopkins, received a radiogram from New York: "MONEY REQUIRED—U.S. EQUIVALENT—CNC ONE BILLION FIVE HUNDRED MILLION. PLEASE CABLE SEPARATE AMOUNTS FOR PERSONNEL REMAINING ON BOARD AND ONES SIGNING OFF."

Hopkins immediately sent the message up to the *Grand River*'s captain to alert him of the galloping inflation and to warn him not to pay off any of his crew in China. The *Grand River* offloaded its oil and exchanged its U. S. working crew of sailors for Chinese nationals. Then, as scheduled, the *Grand River*'s American sailors flew safely to New York on a Northwest Airlines chartered Caltex flight similar to that on which the *Sunset*'s men would travel.

Farther inland, the civil war raged on between Chiang's forces and the Red Army, whose leader would later become famous as Chairman Mao. Chiang was losing and would flee to Taiwan the next year. Later, many people would hint that Chiang had already planned to operate a government in exile and was shipping out items of great value—art treasures, cash in many foreign currencies, and gold.

Across the sea to the south, Japan was still paying war compensation to the Pacific islands it had occupied, and those countries demanded payment in gold. In fact, everyone wanted gold. Cargo planes, usually loaded at the last minute, were considered to be safer than ship transportation. Sometimes only the captain knew gold was on board, and it often was not documented. While many officials attempted to keep things legal, smuggling was big business in the rough-and-tumble, postwar world. Gold was king and Shanghai was the ultimate frontier town.

OTC and its ships were all registered in Panama, a flag of convenience. This was a common practice of shipping lines, enabling them to avoid paying higher union wages and the high taxes in less obliging countries. The registration under a foreign flag also allowed them to skirt some expensive maintenance inspections.

After leaving the ship, John E. Brown, of the Texas Company (China) Limited, provided the U.S. crew with accommodations in Shanghai. He also ensured they made it to their flight back to the States.

Brown watched as the sailors' duffel bags were taken off the ship and put in the bonded storehouse of Chinese Customs, meaning that technically the baggage never landed in China, This way, the sailors did not have to declare any of their souvenirs, gifts, and whatever else they had collected on the voyage. The Panamanian consul was also there overseeing the paperwork as 24 crew members signed certificates of discharge and verified their pay records, known as a square accounts. Their work contracts stated they would still get per diem until they arrived in New York.

Travis Moses McCall, one of the *Sunset*'s sailors, was the Merchant Mariners' union steward. He would have watched as the paperwork was signed by the sailors, insuring accuracy. After the sailors quickly scribbled their signatures, they walked away from the Texas Company's offices, joking and laughing. Still wobbly from months on the sea, it would have taken the men several days to lose their sea legs and walk without swaying. Most of them probably headed to the nearest bar, just a few blocks away.

McCall didn't go with the others. Instead, he went to Shanghai's millinery district. In one of the shops, he picked up the large roll of red Chinese silk he'd ordered for his cousin's wedding dress. With his purchase under his arm, McCall probably headed back to the Seamen's Club and joined the celebration of another successful cruise. An avid cigar smoker, he would have puffed on his cigar and told the others about the silk.

A 37-year-old veteran of the sea, McCall had a long, handsome, and slightly weathered face. His dark hair was well trimmed and his dark eyes gleamed with patience and understanding. Far away, at his home in Tifton, Georgia, his two young sons frolicked under the watchful eye of their mother, Collene. She was used to doing things on her own, but always looked forward to a time when her husband could stay home.

Tifton was a typical small town, where it seemed everyone knew everyone else and much of their personal business. When home, McCall enjoyed his tobacco and worked part-time at Joe Pappa's cigar shop. Smoking was extremely popular during WWII, and was one of the sailor's few pleasures at sea. He always had a spare cigarette for another sailor.

Each sailor had a choice: He could fly to New York, remain overseas, or return home by any means available. Travel by air would be the fastest, but commercial aviation was still in its infancy and considered to be risky. Not all the seafarers were happy with this novel form of transportation. Nearly every week, the newspapers printed stories of the latest plane crashes. Back in the U. S., many major league baseball players refused to fly. An article in the *Cincinnati Times* on March 12, 1948, reported "officials realize that sooner or later a whole ball club will be wiped out." That was aviation in 1948.

Near the wharf, Eugene Adler mailed a letter to his wife, Elizabeth. He had just learned she was pregnant and wrote, "I would happily forgo transportation by air if boat transportation was available."

But no ship was available. The letter would arrive a few weeks later. Another sailor, Olav Jacobsen, had a girlfriend back in New York. He may have written a letter but didn't have time to mail it.

In the cool predawn hours, the sailors arrived at the airport's ramp and their sea bags were weighed and loaded. Later, there would be much speculation about what, if any, additional cargo was loaded. However, there was no paperwork associated with anything other than the sailors' belongings. Many would wonder if Chiang Kai-shek, losing ground to the Communists, had smuggled gold or other treasures onto Flight 4422. The sailors knew nothing about this, nor did they care. They just wanted to go home.

ON FRIDAY, MARCH 12, 1948, the Northwest Airlines DC-4 sat on the tarmac at Shanghai's Lungwha Airport, fueled and ready to go. The four-engine plane's polished aluminum finish gleamed, showing off the company colors: dark blue trim with red stripes, the circular NWA insignia painted on each side of the tail.

Just before leaving, passenger-sailor Arthur Eilertsen made a phone call to his best friend and brother–in–law, Frank Oravetz, back in Ohio. Eilertsen and Oravetz had a small business making and selling men's rings. Eilertsen told Oravetz he had been successful in purchasing the items they needed to make some more rings. Wearing one of the rings, Eilertsen assured Oravetz his purchases were safe and sound.

Dave Edwins, NWA's Shanghai station manager, was in charge of making the plane ready for departure. Edwins had instructed his ground crew to reconfigure the DC-4 by replacing the 36 standard seats with 24 comfortable MacArthur seats, its name attributed to the famous WWII general, Douglas MacArthur. One of his duties was to reduce the plane's weight every way he could to make it legal and safe. The aft section of the DC-4 contained a 180-gallon oil tank from which oil could be pumped into the engines in flight. One way to save weight without compromising safety was to remove some of the oil.

Edwins walked across the ramp, climbed into the cockpit, and asked the captain if it was okay to take half of the oil out of the reserve tank because it would save about 500 pounds. The captain knew less weight would make the takeoff safer and approved Edwin's request. However, the DC-4 would still be near its maximum allowable gross weight for takeoff to Tokyo, the first of six long legs to New York.

Many people watched as the ground crew readied the plane. On its aft, left side, the plane's huge double cargo doors allowed oversize cargo to be placed on board. But that morning, only the forward half of the huge special double door was open, for its passengers.

Just before departure, Edwins completed the cargo manifest, a sheet of paper detailing the cargo on the flight. On the lines used to list the cargo and its weight, he simply wrote "N/A." Then he turned in the document to the Chinese customs office.

THE EARLY MORNING rays of the rising sun pierced the mist and fog as 24 sailors from the *Sunset* arrived at the Seamen's Club in various states of alertness. The night on the town in Shanghai was fun, but they were ready to go home. They awaited transportation to Shanghai's Lungwha Airport, where a chartered airplane was ready to take them to New York's LaGuardia Airport.

Flight 4422 was not a normal airline flight. Northwest Airlines had contracted with the Overseas Tankship Corporation (OTC) to safely and expeditiously transport OTC's sailors back to New York after their delivery of oil tankers to China, the Philippines, or elsewhere in Asia. One of many such flights, it would return the sailors to New York in only two days—extremely fast in 1948. As part of that contract, NWA had provided a $25,000 life insurance policy for each sailor-passenger. One by one, the 24 *Sunset* sailors climbed up the stairs and entered the plane.

The *Sunset's* crew would fly home in a DC-4, small by modern jetliner standards. In 1948, it was aviation's workhorse—the 747 of its day. It was the civilian version of the military's C-54. Each of its four radial engines could produce 1,450 horsepower.

TAKEOFF FROM SHANGHAI commenced at 9:10 a.m. In New York, it was 9:10 p.m. the previous evening, Thursday, March 11. With a synchronized roar from its four Pratt & Whitney radial engines, Flight 4422 picked up speed and lumbered down the runway. The plane lifted off, struggled into the air, continued higher, and disappeared into the steel-gray morning sky. Three-bladed Hamilton Standard propellers, 13 feet in diameter, pulled the plane through the air while it climbed. An unpressurized plane, it did not normally fly higher than 10,000 feet because above that altitude the crew would have to wear uncomfortable rubber oxygen masks. The plane most likely climbed to its cruise altitude of 9,000 feet. After two-and-a-half months at sea, the sailors were on their way home.

Most of them sat back and relaxed while reading or chatting. Some smoked. Eugene Adler, however, probably couldn't relax. He didn't like flying very much. To take his mind off the flight, he thought about being a father.

For James Mooney the flight was both nostalgic and special—it would be his last. He'd flown many times during his 20 years as a Merchant Mariner and had returned from the Orient once before by plane. Soon, he would be back home in Paterson, New Jersey. He was 40 and single, but there was still plenty of time for a family.

Arthur Eilertsen was ecstatic to be making his first flight. Another tough ex-Navy man from Brooklyn, Eilertsen had obtained a job on the *Sunset* as an ordinary seaman with the help of his brother-in-law, Frank Oravetz. Just like the Davidson brothers, they had planned on working the *Sunset*'s cruise together. They had told Eilertsen's sister, Anna, "It would be just like old times,.

Eilertsen and Oravetz had served together in the Navy for two years during the war. In their jaunts to countries throughout the Middle East, they had gone on many liberties together. They were the best of friends—the kind who trusted each other with their lives. Just before their departure on the *Sunset*, Anna, Eilersten's sister, became very worried—so worried that at the last minute, she didn't want either man to go on the cruise. "Frank, you aren't going," she said. "I know something bad is going to happen."

Both men grumbled about her fears, but Anna's husband, Frank Oravetz, respected her wishes and canceled his plans. Eilertsen decided to work the cruise without his brother-in-law.

Now sitting comfortably in the DC-4 on his way home, Eilertsen had nothing to worry about. The cruise had gone well, and he would be home in a couple days. But, Eilertsen had many problems with his teeth. As the unpressurized plane continued to climb, trapped air in new cavities in his teeth would have expanded and probably began to hurt.

Eilertsen's teeth had always given him trouble and after the long ocean cruise, with no opportunity for real dental treatment, he knew he could be back in the dentist's office soon, something he didn't look forward to. He had had a lot of dental work, even before he enlisted in the Navy. In fact, despite his young age, he already had a partial denture.

Eilertsen may have massaged his jaw and smoked a cigarette as he peered down at the waves that were getting smaller as the airplane climbed. As he sat in the well-padded seat, he may have gazed at the reflection coming from the silver and gold colored ring on the ring finger of his left hand. Then he may have double-checked his carry-on bag. When he'd telephoned Oravetz, he'd told him that, in the ship, he'd had to hide the small pouches he carried. Now, they were safe in his bag and within reach at all times.

By the 1940s, Northwest Airlines had realized the cost-saving efficiencies of Great Circle travel and flew the northerly "inland" route to and from Asia over Alaska and Canada. Not having the globe-hopping range of modern jets, the propeller-driven aircraft of that era flew the Great Circle route with a few strategic refueling locations. The DC-4's flight from Shanghai to New York was planned to take 49 hours.

The first stop was Tokyo, roughly 1,100 miles or four-and-a-half hours after takeoff from Shanghai. After landing, the 24 passengers would have exited the plane. Some probably smoked as they stretched while the aircraft was refueled. Thirty minutes later, the sailors climbed back up the stairs and strapped in for the long over-ocean leg to their next refueling stop.

Eleven hours later, they touched down at the small island of Shemya. One of the westernmost points of Alaska, Shemya is a small, frigid, wet, incredibly bleak outcrop above the crashing waves of the Bering Sea just south of the Arctic Circle. At the extreme western end of the Aleutian Islands, it's the final link in a chain of 70 atolls that sweep 1,100 miles into the ocean in a southerly arc. The ragged tops are the signs of a mostly submerged mountain range that once joined America and Russia.

The relatively warm air above a near-freezing sea gives Shemya some unique atmospheric conditions. Like something in a horror movie, the island can become invisible, shrouded in a solid cloud layer stretching from the ground to 2,000 to 3,000 feet above the ocean. Within this cloud there is bizarre weather: drizzle, rain, snow, and howling winds that sometimes exceed 60 miles per hour.

Man's propensity for war made Shemya a strategically important aviation outpost. Due to the limited range of aircraft during WWII, U. S. aircrews taking the fight into Asia breathed a sigh of relief when they spotted the foggy sanctuary rising up from the gray sea.

At this desolate place, Wesley Brum, an off-duty NWA flight mechanic, waited for Flight 4422. He planned to hitch a ride on the plane to his next assignment, a common practice for off-duty crew members.

Brum boarded Flight 4422 while it refueled before departing for Elmendorf Field in Anchorage. He may have sat in an extra aircrew seat in the cockpit known as a jump-seat. After takeoff, he talked with the flight crew on duty, and noted that everything seemed normal with the plane. One by one, the Aleutian Islands passed underneath as the plane flew on to Anchorage. Each mile took the sailors closer to home. Three more stops and they would be back in New York. At least, that was the plan.

LAST CHANCE

We planned one final attempt to find the lost plane. It was a two-pronged approach. First, we would conduct a detailed air search of the entire mountain from my 1972 Turbocharged Cessna 210 Centurion. Turbochargers compress the engine's intake air, allowing the engine to continue to develop sea level power at much higher altitudes than a plane without a turbocharger. We could fly my Cessna all the way up to 25,000 feet, which would allow us to make a quicker and safer airborne search than from Marc's Cub. On a second trip, we would take the Cub and land near the mountain, and follow my 1995 route to the bottom of the ice falls. During the climb, we would again search every bit of the glacier with binoculars and a small scope. If we didn't find anything on this final effort, we thought it might not be possible to find Flight 4422— at least not in this lifetime.

Unknown to either Marc or me, in eastern Canada Randall Haslett, the son of 4422's purser, also had decided to try to find Flight 4422. Over many years, Haslett had discovered only bits of information about the legendary plane's demise, and it frustrated him greatly. Now that he had learned more, he planned an expedition to Mount Sanford in search of answers. At the very least, he wanted to see exactly where the plane crashed. His timing was uncanny—the last several days of July 1997—exactly the same time we planned to be on the glacier.

My research had taken me all over the world—to the homes of the men on Flight 4422, and to the ocean world in which they had lived and worked. The huge expanse of the seas fascinated me. While learning about Wilfred Beswick, I stood on the banks of the Mersey River in Liverpool, England, watching the ships sail in and out of the oil jetties just as the *Sunset* had in January 1948. In Istanbul, on an afternoon marked by thunderstorms, I watched cargo and tanker ships enter and exit the Black Sea via the Bosporus. On foggy days in Amsterdam, I listened to ships blasting their foghorns as they made their way across the waterways. Finally, I began to understand the lives of the Merchant Mariners on Flight 4422. I also began to love the sea, a place foreign to land-locked Colorado where I had grown up. But, I had not found Randall Haslett then.

One of the wild rumors about 4422 was that the FBI had been involved in the investigation of the crash. Marc sent a Freedom of Information Act letter to the FBI in search of information relating to the crash. Several months later, the FBI replied, saying it had no information.

IT WAS A MILE-HIGH, blue-sky morning in early July 1997 when I took off from Aurora Air Park, Colorado; my parents were with me. Despite a few areas of light rain and low clouds, we had a wonderful time. Just as I'd done in 1995, we flew over Wyoming and Montana and then followed the Alaskan Canadian Highway all the way to Alaska. Before I got to the serious business of the 1997 expedition, we spent a few days touring Anchorage and Alaska's deep seaport, Seward. Babbling brooks and streams packed with fish, a variety of wildlife, and the Cook Inlet's 22-foot tidal flows provided plenty to see.

One morning, I woke up at 3:45 and discovered a clear blue sky and almost no wind. We took advantage of the weather and flew about 45 minutes north of Anchorage to Denali. At 200 miles per hour, our small plane seemed to barely move relative to the gigantic mountain as we flew by its eastern buttress.

We passed the prominent points: the Kahiltna glacier, the West Buttress, the Moose's Tooth, and South Summit—all spectacular in the pure white of the early morning. Still in view were trailheads and tracks of those who had attempted climbs to the summit earlier in the season. A few colorful ski planes looked like bugs sitting far below on the glaciers, transporting climbers to and from the mountain's ice—on landing zones.

We arrived back in Anchorage at 7 a.m. It had been one of the rare crystal-clear mornings with spectacular views of the entire massif of Denali and its cascading white glaciers. But now it was time to get back to the business of Flight 4422.

My parents flew back to Colorado commercially; I remained in Alaska. Marc returned from another international flight late the next afternoon. After a day of jet lag recovery, we repacked for one last trip to Mount Sanford. By now, packing had become somewhat routine.

Marc took off in the always-dependable Cub from Lake Hood airport at 3 p.m. I departed in my Cessna 210 an hour later so we would arrive in

Gulkana at about the same time. As ex-military pilots, we had earlier briefed and planned flying in formation just in case I caught up with Marc. Indeed, I joined him about 40 miles west of Gulkana. We flew in formation the last 15 minutes and landed at Gulkana.

We hadn't been to the landing surface at Cub Valley in 1997. So Marc parked the Super Cub and strapped into the Centurion while I kept it running. We took off and headed to Mount Sanford. Fifteen minutes later, we were over Cub Valley's landing zone and could see that the sand and rock area appeared to be dry and in good condition.

For an hour, we scrutinized Mount Sanford high and low, snapped numerous photos, and ran the video camera until the batteries died. At one point, we flew a few hundred feet from the impact point on the cliffs at 11,000 feet. Looking down into the chutes that descended onto the glacial surface, we viewed the area where Flight 4422 had come to rest. From our viewpoint off the mountain, we saw only rock and ice, but gained a valuable perspective only attainable from a planc. The immensity of the cliffs and grandeur of the mountain never ceased to amaze us; 4422 really was a needle in a haystack.

Flying close to the mountain's upper slopes, we gained a new appreciation for the thick snow and ice. Monstrous cornices varying from 300 to 500 feet in thickness clung to the ice fields sloping down from the summit and hung over the edges into space. It was no wonder there were such large and continual avalanches into the glacial cirque one mile below.

After flying over several more ridges and glacial valleys reaching down from the mountain, we flew down the center of the glacier believed to encase Flight 4422. Marc took over the controls of the Centurion while I studied the glacier, noting minor changes in the crevasse fields' patterns and undulating surfaces.

"That is one rough and rocky glacier," I said, "except for where I accessed the valley by climbing through the bottom end of the glacier. It's a damned good thing I didn't try to go over the whole thing by myself back in 1995."

"It looks more like the surface of the moon," Marc said.

AT 200 MILES PER HOUR, the Centurion covered the area quickly. But its small wheels and retractable landing gear made it impractical for landing in the rough backcountry, so we headed back to the Super Cub at Gulkana.

Completing monotonous preflight and pre-expedition checks one last time, we swapped out camera batteries, took off in the Super Cub, and headed back to Cub Valley, where we repeated the arrival procedures we developed in 1996. After two high passes, we readied for an approach and landing. Unfortunately, just as we started our approach, threatening cumulus clouds began to rush over the ridge a thousand feet above.

Big raindrops pelted the windshield and dark streaks of airborne dirt flew off the ridges—certain signs of strong, gusting winds. We could expect downdrafts or wind shears at any time. It was too dangerous to attempt a landing, so Marc made a right turn and flew away from Cub Valley.

But just after we started our turn, violent gusts hit the Cub, jerking the little plane back and forth, up and down, in moderate turbulence. Below and a little way behind us, we could see dirt and other debris blowing and swirling all around Cub Valley. Once again, we had narrowly missed being smashed against the ground by the unpredictable and violent winds of Mount Sanford. We flew down the glacier to our backup landing zone eight miles away—the landing zone I had located in 1995. We had been lucky again…or was it that someone or something was looking out for us?

Before leaving Gulkana we had carefully calculated our fuel supply, as always. To be as lightweight as possible, Marc had allowed 15 minutes of extra fuel for one divert in addition to the required 30 minutes of fuel on top of the amount needed to fly back to Gulkana. Now, if it worked out just right, we would be able to land at the lower landing zone and still have enough gas to fly back up and make another approach and landing in Cub Valley.

Six minutes after leaving Cub Valley, caribou watched our strange little red and white Cub land southbound and roll to a stop on my backup landing zone on the east side of the Sanford River. Just as the wheels came to a stop, buckets of heavy rain began to fall. We were exasperated by the continued bouts with the weather and other problems.

I looked out the window. "I guess we have a little shower, eh, Marc?"

"A Colorado little shower," he said. "I sure hope nothing electrical shorts out on the plane and we get stuck out here. It's just one thing after another going wrong, one after another."

IT WOULD HAVE been easy to give up and fly back to Anchorage. From wind and rain to snow, low clouds, avalanches, bad information, and misinformation, difficulties seemed to plague our expeditions. But that's just the way it is in the wilderness of Alaska. Mother Nature is unforgiving and relentless. We had to play by her rules, or not play at all.

An hour later, the rain stopped and the sky began to clear enough for one more chance to land at Cub Valley.

"What do you think about the fuel level?" I asked.

Marc peered at the manual sight gauge. "I can see exactly where the level is and it looks like we have enough fuel to get to Cub Valley, make one approach and landing, and still have our 30-minute reserve. But if we have to abort our approach for any reason at all, we'll have no choice except to fly straight back to Gulkana."

I looked at the gauges and didn't see any fuel in them at all. "Marc, I don't see a thing."

"Of course you don't, put on your glasses."

Indeed, 19 years of flying had taken its toll. With my spectacles, I could just barely see fuel in the bottom of the little viewing tubes. That meant we had exactly one hour of gas, no more and no less.

"Trust me," Marc said. "I know exactly what the gauge levels mean in this particular plane."

His Super Cub has one gasoline level indicator tube on each side, near the cockpit's ceiling. The tubes actually have gas in them directly from the fuel tanks and show the precise level of the gas in the tanks. It's an extremely reliable system, used in many bush planes.

"Okay," I said, "I guess you're right. Let's go."

At 8:30 p.m., Marc cranked up the engine, taxied the zone's north end, pushed up the power, and took off. Ten minutes later, after one quick circle above the landing zone, he brought the little plane down uneventfully in Cub Valley. It was too late to start hiking, so we put the Cub to bed, set up camp, and slid into our sleeping bags.

The next morning dawned cold and clear. High on the western slope of the buttress immediately east of Cub Valley four Dall sheep peered down at our tent. They were always there, so we named it Sheep Mountain.

After a light breakfast of oatmeal and power bars, we picked up our 85-pound backpacks and started up the mountain, following my 1995 route. Initially, we walked along the game trails meandering up the soft grass hills on the south side of the glacier. The sheep and caribou cared little about us, and kept their distance.

Climbing with our heavy packs was difficult and slower than when I hiked with only my day pack. But with the two of us on the trail the climb was much more enjoyable and safer than when I was solo. We stopped often to snap photos and look through binoculars at the entire glacier and the slopes of the valley on each side. We were determined nothing would escape our scrutiny on this final trip.

Occasionally, we climbed a little higher on the slopes. We could actually look down into the glacier, but we saw only rock and ice. No wing tips stuck up and no tail section was visible. There was no evidence whatsoever that Flight 4422 or its occupants had crashed here.

IT WOULD TAKE us 10 hours to ascend my 1995 route. Finally, we climbed away from the grassy knolls ending at Green Point. Now, we had to get down and dirty on the actual glacier's edge where the rocks of the valley butted against the ice. We slipped all over the ice and wet rocks, setting off many small rock slides. Above, the blue sky gave way to thick clouds, and the temperature plummeted.

The glacier's edge was melting away. Water dripped from the ice, plopping into small ponds with the ticking sound of nature's infinite clock. Rock and grit loosened and plunged from the ice into the water. Surface rivers of glacier water wandered here and there, on top, then underneath and through the middle of the rock and ice, appearing and disappearing virtually anywhere. This was the business end of the unending cycle of glacial creation and destruction that began at the dawn of the last ice age.

Marc didn't like the rough going. "Hiking over these big marbles on this ice rink is one certain way to break our necks," he said.

Meanwhile, I kept up a steady patter of what I hoped were encouraging words: "It's just around the corner," and "It's just over that rock, can't you see it yet?" "It's just a few hundred feet more to the ice falls."

Basically, it was complete balderdash to pass the time, but I hoped it would help keep us going over the roughest parts. Marc soldiered on, trusting my judgment about getting to the ice falls. One step followed another as we made our way up the side of the icy monolith. I cautioned Marc as we passed the area of the rock slide I had encountered in 1995. Above us to the right, an occasional boulder shifted on the slopes with an unnerving scraping sound. My wands marking this dangerous spot, placed two years earlier, were nowhere to be seen—probably buried. Then, nearly exhausted, we passed my bivouac spot. The low area, just a few feet off the ice, didn't look as accommodating as I remembered it. In fact, it was not a very good spot at all, but at least it was out of the wind, a safe place to hunker down for a few hours. I pointed it out to Marc.

"You slept in that depression?" asked Marc incredulously.

"Yup. This is the spot. I'll take any port in a storm…I guess."

AT 6 P.M. WE DRAGGED our tired bodies into the Amphitheater of the Souls, just below the ice falls. Marc was astonished by the glacier, which sloped down from the 2,000-foot run-out. He just stared at the 3,000-foot, nearly vertical face down which the wreckage had supposedly fallen. The glacial cirque with the huge cliffs above it was basically one huge avalanche-making machine—an extremely dangerous place indeed. Up close, it was even more impressive.

Sometimes, to experience such a place and embrace its danger is to really live life. Then and there, life takes on a new meaning. In this case, the feeling was intensified by our knowledge that somewhere nearby 30 human beings had met a violent, tragic death. The immensity of the amphitheater was overwhelming for both of us. The feeling cannot be captured by photos or video—one simply has to be there. We stood for 20 minutes looking up at the massive mountain. At any second, ice and snow could have cracked off and created an avalanche that could have covered us. But we were transfixed by the huge rock outcroppings, the sheer walls of ice, and the incredible amount of snow clinging to the steep cliffs. Despite having flown over the area numerous times, we now saw it from a whole new perspective.

Then the clouds thickened and light rain began to fall. Several small ice cornices broke away and created small avalanches that cascaded down Mount Sanford's face. Marc just stood there, mesmerized. The rain didn't seem to matter to him.

Standing next to him, I thought about the events of 1948. I thought about Travis McCall, whose wife and children suffered tremendously from both his loss and subsequent years of unsuccessful lawsuits. I thought of Howard Davidson, whose brave brother, Norman, volunteered to jump into this magnificent frozen chasm in the cold of winter to search for his brother and any other survivors. The image of a young boy flashed through my mind: Carl Sigmund, Jr. He had nearly burned to death in a tragic house fire the year before his father was lost on this mountain. I thought about all the victims—both the crew and passengers—of this disaster.

The enormity of the amphitheater with its soaring slopes reminded me of my glacier climb on Mount Rainier back in the 1970s. The day before the climb, as I flew into Seattle, Mount Rainier appeared to be no problem. But that was the 30,000-foot view. The next day, at Paradise base camp, incredible excitement gripped me and my two climbing partners, Richard Hoyt and Joan Winsor. They were experienced climbers; I was the novice. My legs felt like jelly as I looked up into the dramatic Nisqually glacier, then on up to the Rainier's 14,000-foot summit. Two days later, we nearly made it to the summit but turned around just 300 feet short of the top because of a heavy blizzard and zero visibility. It would have been nice to make it to the summit but the ultimate goal was getting down safely. We did that despite a harrowing night bivouacking on the side of Nisqually.

Now, at the base of the ice falls of Mount Sanford, that same feeling captured me: the pure excitement of climbing—exhilarating, scary, and challenging, and every time I wonder if I'm equal to the task.

We set up our tent in a relatively safe area on the side of the Amphitheater next to the memory stake I had placed there in 1995. The three-foot piece of aluminum did not appear to have changed or moved in two years. Then, in the cold rain, Marc and I hiked over the relatively flat area of the glacier, just below the ice falls.

Horizontal rays of the setting sun pierced the sky just below the clouds, illuminating the surface of the glacier with an eerie gold hue, accentuated by sparkling rain and snow that coated the rocks and ice.

The glacier we were standing on was alive, and we had to be sure we never forgot that little detail. Crevasses—even the hardest ice—change all the time and can open up quickly. Climbing history is littered with fatal crevasse and ice accidents—even among expert climbers. Some people have walked only a few feet from their tent and disappeared forever into the abyss.

We carried a climbing rope and traveled for three hours, investigating the area up to the edge of the ice blocks known as seracs that had tumbled down through the ice falls. As we walked across the Amphitheater, we heard the glacial ice groan and crackle beneath our feet. Above, long waterfall-like sounds echoed through the valley from avalanches high up on the slopes. Some lasted several minutes and could be heard but, disconcertingly, not seen.

Slipping and sliding on the wet conglomerate, we saw nothing out of the ordinary except the remains of the strange dirt cones, nearly perfect conical formations of ice, three- to five-feet-tall, I'd investigated two years earlier. Now they were gone. In their place were flat circles of red and brown soil eight feet in diameter. By 1997, I'd studied information about similar cones in other northern countries and learned the cones were common on some glaciers. The red and brown volcanic material adhering to the outside surface had protected the ice inside for some time.

All of this indicated that the glacier had melted significantly in two years. Exactly how much we didn't know, but our educated guess was a foot or so. Regardless of the specifics, it was an important clue about the glacier and its continuous downsizing.

By the time we completed our evening survey, the light rain had increased to moderate, with intermittent snow. At 10 o'clock, we returned to the tent. Snow replaced the rain while the few remaining rays of the setting sun disappeared.

"Just what we need, more snow," I said.

Snow could devastate our expedition because we had to be able to actually see the surface to find any parts of Flight 4422. New snow also would make hiking over the ice and rocks even more treacherous.

Nice and dry in our sleeping bags in the tent, we fired up hot water and ate another dinner of freeze-dried spaghetti and discussed the entire saga of 4422 again. Basically, we simply refused to believe that an airplane as large as a DC-4 could have vanished without a trace.

Because I'd been there before, I was comfortable in the Amphitheater. More important, living at 8,200 feet in Colorado, I was well acclimated to the high altitude. Marc, who lived at sea level, understandably didn't feel very well. He had developed a headache, was slightly dehydrated and a little dizzy, and suffered some hypoxia at our camp's relatively high altitude of 6,800 feet. He also was still experiencing jet lag and was increasingly concerned about his Super Cub waiting far down the valley. The snow was becoming a major issue.

After a thorough in-tent discussion of the pros and cons of the situation, we decided that even though we still had a week of slack time, we would wait only one day for the weather to clear at our high camp. If it didn't improve, we would start hiking out, which would give us four days of padding for bad weather. We both felt that our luck was running thin and we were not willing to test it further. Things were not looking good. Marc drank lots of water and swallowed some aspirin.

Drifting into a half-sleep, we listened to the roar of avalanches cascading down the cliffs high above and the groaning of the glacier's ice below. At the top of the 14-mile-long run-out of the glacier, our small blue nylon tent swayed back and forth in the snow. The pitch black of the night was broken only by a few faint stars occasionally peeking between the clouds. We knew tomorrow was our last chance.

MARC WAS AWAKE first, well before the sun approached the top of the mountain. The snow had stopped and the inch or so from the night before already was melting. I awoke to find him peering high up on the cliffs through the spotting scope. He thought he saw something that could be an engine. Then he thought he saw a propeller high up on the cliff at the 11,000-foot level of the impact site, nearly two miles from our location, but he couldn't be certain. Maybe it was an oxygen bottle, or it might be just an optical illusion. There was really no way to tell for sure what the items sticking out of the snow might be.

I just gazed out over the immense glacier; I had already experienced the illusions on the ice and was certain it was a futile effort to look for anything higher up. Even so, I tried to take a few photos through the telescope. They came out marginal at best. Although something might still be hanging onto the cliffs, after 50 years it was extremely unlikely.

Finally, with reluctance, I said, "We'll never know for sure what's up there because we aren't ever going. That would be suicidal." We took turns peering through the scope, hoping for a glimpse of just a single piece of the DC-4—anything that would provide positive identification of the wreckage.

For two more hours, standing at the bottom of the ice falls, we used binoculars and a small spotting scope to carefully look at everything above us in the ice falls and cliffs. But there was nothing resembling an aircraft part or anything else unusual. Even if something was there, the mountain's multicolored conglomerate rocks made it very difficult, if not impossible, to discern wreckage from rock and ice. Maybe Flight 4422 really had disappeared without a trace.

At 9 a.m. we reluctantly began to stuff our gear into our packs for the long descent. It was over. Just like so many before us, we too had failed, finding exactly nothing to confirm the existence of the DC-4 or its occupants. I reached down and removed the memory stake I had placed in the moraine in 1995 and put it in my pack. We would leave the area absolutely clean.

We paused to look up at the glacier for a last few moments, then lifted our packs and prepared to start the descent back to the Cub. Then both of us, at almost the exact same moment, stopped and laid our packs down on the ice. I turned and peered down into the serpentine length of the glacial expanse meandering into the west. Marc gazed up in the opposite direction—to the cliffs. We both felt a warm breeze drift down the frigid glacier. Goosebumps formed on my back, and Marc turned around to face me. Then we both looked into the bowels of the glacier stretching 14 miles down to the Sanford River.

With its tumbled mass of undulating ice hills, crevasses, and an indescribable mess of rocks and ice, it seemed impenetrable. It was a dangerous place to go—especially with backpacks. No one in his right mind would hike into that.

Just above a whisper, I said, "Hey, Marc, what do you think about giving this one last good try by going right down the middle of the glacier—right into its guts? We can't wear crampons—it's too rocky. It could take two days, maybe three. And then we might actually have to climb all the way back up here to get out. But, that might be our last hope."

Marc was silent for a moment as he looked up onto the high cliffs. Finally he said, "That sounds okay to me. I think the Cub is safe and the weather still might be OK. Anyway, going down the glacier can't be any worse than that junkyard of marbles and ice we came up through, can it?"

With a just-dare-me look, I shifted my eyes toward him and said, "Oh, yes, it can be much, much, more difficult and extremely dangerous. How lucky do you feel?"

"I think I've used up five or six of my nine lives on this project so far."

"So you still have a few left. Let's do it."

REINVIGORATED WITH A plan of action, we discussed the details and dangers of glacial backpacking and how we would travel while conducting one final search on the way down. During our four-year saga, the very center of the glacier was the only place we hadn't examined up close and in person. We thought it was possible, but unlikely, that we had missed something in the middle, out of view from the glacier's edges, or from the air. We wondered *Could Flight 4422 have passed through the lower ice falls by now?*

We hoisted our packs once again and started down. The sky yielded to a darkening translucent layer of clouds at 8,000 feet. As we descended, that layer thickened as the clouds moved and bumped against the side of the mountain. On the surface, there was no more breeze, just dead calm. We considered each step carefully as we made our way over the treacherous rocks covering the slippery ice. Small, volcanic rocks, some as sharp as glass, tried to penetrate the soles of our boots at each step. Even with thick-soled boots, it was very uncomfortable; our heavy loads made it even worse. Occasionally, we jumped over four-foot-wide open crevasses—one small leap of faith after another. Fog began to form and a spooky mist covered the glacier as we ventured lower and deeper into the valley of ice. With the memory stake sticking out of my pack, we continued downward into the very soul of the glacier, traveling back in time and into the pages of history.

THE ABYSS

Flight 4422 touched down at Elmendorf Field in Anchorage, Alaska, in the early evening of March 12, 1948. It had been a long flight in the DC-4 from Shanghai with stops at Tokyo and Shemya. Once again, the *Sunset's* 24 sailors got off the plane to stretch. Scheduled to work a later flight, mechanic Wesley Brum also departed the plane.

The working flight crew packed up their personal gear, donned their warmest coats, and left the plane. Another aircrew would take over. The men responsible for refueling the plane pushed ladders across the icy ramp and filled the wings' fuel tanks all the way to the top. The mechanic checked in with the aircrew and confirmed the plane was in good shape.

After everyone else was off the plane, sailors Jackie Jamele and John Comshick eased down the steps to the tarmac. Having broken both legs in WWII, and never fully recovered, Jamele was probably sore and stiff from the long flight. He and Comshick likely walked to the edge of the airfield's parking ramp where the snow was piled high, far from the plane and its fuel. Jamele may have lit one of his favorite cigarettes, Luckies. The warm smoke would have felt good. Comshick also would have felt aches and pain from injuries sustained when his Jeep hit a mine in Italy during the war. The cold, damp evening air of Alaska would not have made it any easier for either of the WWII veterans.

Eugene Foote might have shivered as he stood on the tarmac and thought back to his days in the war in the Mediterranean. Now he probably looked forward to some time off in the warm and green forests of Louisiana and may have dreamed about dropping a line into the water, catching some catfish, and frying them up.

Back on the ramp, Tiny Eglund worked hard getting the DC-4 ready for departure. As one of NWA's ramp agents, he worked with several others whose tasks included restocking the galley, cleaning the plane, refueling, and loading the cargo. With no wagons of passenger baggage or crates of cargo to load, it was a relatively easy flight to work. But Eglund did notice some kind of box in one of the plane's cargo areas. Oddly, it was covered with several tarps. He asked another ramp agent about the unusual piece of cargo, but the other man said, "It's one of those things you are not supposed see."

In other words, mind your own business. It wasn't uncommon to run across such items. As the primary air transport for the U. S. military, NWA flew all kinds of military freight and protected cargo. Sometimes it was stamped "Classified" or "Secret." Occasionally only the captain knew what was placed on board, and there was no documentation at all—especially with small items.

Eglund initially ignored the piece of cargo and went on with his work. A little later, he visited the cockpit to deliver some paperwork. There, he was surprised to see a document with PAYROLL stamped on it. He was not a man who got excited easily, but the payroll item, along with the strange piece of covered cargo, got his attention and became something he would remember and talk about. He never would find anyone who knew at which station the unusual piece of cargo had been loaded, where it came from, or what it was.

Most of the Merchant Mariners on board Flight 4422 were oblivious to the cargo and cared only that there were only a couple more scheduled stops before reaching LaGuardia: Edmonton, Canada, and Minneapolis, then to New York.

Just before the plane was ready to depart, sailor Dan Rice mailed a letter to his father. It said, "I'll be home in a few days," just as he had done on the completion of his previous cruise. Dan was single and had joined the Merchant Marine in 1946 after years of sailing the Great Lakes. With more than 60 nieces and nephews back home in Wisconsin, he had no shortage of family.

All the sailors must have been telling each other, "Another day in the air and we'll be home. This sure beats several weeks in a ship."

A NEW FLIGHT CREW of six, three of them pilots, boarded the plane in Anchorage. Captain Robert G. Petry was one of the two captain-qualified pilots on board. A 30-year-old bachelor, he had flown this route many times for the Army and amassed 8,324 flying hours, 728 in DC-4s. This flight was his 24th for Northwest. Petry was fun-loving and well-liked by many of the Northwest aircrew members. Now he was finally going to settle down and marry his fiancée, Rose, back in Minneapolis. But he had no plans of giving up flying. Petry was a man of the world and he loved the wide-open skies.

The copilot was also experienced. First Officer Jehu (pronounced Jay-hugh) J. Stickel, 34, had flown 4,772 hours, 779 of them in DC-4s. Originally from Zanesville, Ohio, Stickel's first marriage was to Dorothy Helriggle. They had a son, but he died at six weeks of age and the couple divorced. In December 1947, he married ex-stewardess Pat Scott. She had been in the first class of Northwest Airlines stewardesses who weren't required to be nurses. Stewardesses had to be single, so she quit her job to marry Stickel. They had been married for only three months when he left for his trip on Flight 4422. He and his new bride planned to start a family as soon as possible. Some people thought Stickel was going to quit flying and go back to being a plumber. However, according to his wife, he had decided he would continue to fly despite the risks.

Northwest's System Chief Pilot in 1948, Captain Joe Kimm, considered Stickel to be "one of the most professional and conscientious co-pilots we had at Northwest." Still, in 1948, an aviation career was considered adventurous and risky for a new husband.

Back home in Ohio a few months earlier, Stickel had told stories to family and friends about the exciting trips he'd been on, enthralling them with the close calls he'd had in the mountains of Alaska. Just before leaving Anchorage, during a telephone call to his friends in Zanesville, he said he would be flying the leg from Anchorage to Edmonton.

Captain James G. Van Cleef was the second captain on board Flight 4422 and, at 27, was one of Northwest's youngest captains. He grew up in Nampa, Idaho, and had flown Northwest cargo and transport aircraft between Anchorage and Edmonton on contracted flights for the Army during WWII. He was an old hand at flying this route.

Officially and legally, it was Captain James Van Cleef who was listed on the official crew manifest as the pilot in command of Flight 4422. He had logged 4,453 flying hours, 733 of them in DC-4s. Earlier, he had traded some trips with a few other pilots so he could get back home quicker. Stickel and Van Cleef had just returned together from another airline trip to Asia.

And, although no one at Northwest knew it, Van Cleef's relatives understood that he was tired of long-haul flights in heavy aircraft. He had already completed the required paperwork for joining the Navy and was looking forward to the excitement of flying fighter aircraft. Thus, Flight 4422 was scheduled to be one of his last flights for Northwest.

Flight 4422 had a purser, the title for a male flight attendant, Robert J. Haslett, 27, from Seattle. He looked a little like a young Frank Sinatra. A graduate of Seattle's Lincoln High School, he served three years in the Army during the war as a teletype operator for a bomber wing in North Africa and Italy. His long, slender fingers were perfect for his military duties as well as his personal interest as an artist.

As the war had drawn to a close, Haslett married his Canadian girlfriend, Margery Lindgren. During a traditional wedding, she wore a long, white bridal gown with a veil and he wore his Army uniform. They made a handsome couple as they cut their three-tier wedding cake. Since then, he wore his large gold and silver wedding ring—on his left hand. Aircraft had fascinated Haslett during the war, and he decided he wanted to work in the new world of passenger airlines.

Wayne W. Worsley served as the navigator. From Racine, Wisconsin, 31 years old and single, Worsley was a serious young man constantly searching for a deeper meaning to his life and the world. After earning a degree in English at a college in Sturgeon Bay, Wisconsin, he'd become a schoolteacher and coached some of the athletic teams in Sturgeon Bay.

In 1939, he discovered flying when he joined the Marine Air Corps as a navigator/bombardier crewing Mitchell B-25 bombers. He performed well in the Pacific and became a navigation instructor at Quantico Marine Station. Leaving the Air Corps as a captain at the end of the war, he applied to Northwest Airlines and was hired as a navigator. During his time off, he studied law at Marquette University and doubled as a flight ground instructor at Mitchell Field, Milwaukee. By March 1948, he had logged 2,556 hours of flying time. According to his brother, Gail, he loved everything about aviation.

Worsley sometimes expressed his thoughts about life and death through poetry, and he shared some of those with his close friend, Helen Lang, including one he titled, "Heaven":

"I do not think of heaven as a place
Where streets are paved with gold or precious jewels,
Where bright, winged souls strum golden harps through space,
For such would seem a paradise for fools.
I only hope it is a place where one may dance
While gently healing winds blow fresh and free.
Where every face will wear that radiance
That shone from yours
When last you looked at me."

No one knows if Worsley was actually working as a navigator during the flight. Although he was on the flight crew list, he had told relatives that he would not be on duty and was only deadheading home on Flight 4422. The route flown east of Anchorage was equipped with radio navigation aids. Navigators were not considered necessary on overland routes, like this one. To complicate matters, at that time Northwest's navigators were involved in a dispute with the company over the long hours they had to work. Worsley may have been going on strike at the completion of Flight 4422.

Long hours in the air provided Worsey with time to ponder and try to put meaning to and understanding of his life and the world. A few months before the crash, he had written a poem that turned out to be prophetic:

> "Why does he love such things
> As stars and sun and stranger lands,
> And northern lights upon steel wings
> And routes few men have spanned?
> Why can he not love simple things
> The things a woman's heart demands?
> Why did he make me cut the strings
> That bound the dreams we planned?
> Someday the angry elements
> He now so foolishly defies,
> Will seek him out upon the raft
> And dark his green-brown eyes.
> I wonder if he'll love me then
> And curse those hateful, foreign skies?"

Donald L. Rector was the sixth member of the new crew. Twenty-eight, good-looking, and a real gentleman, Don had recently married Mary McDowell, a ticket agent for Northwest Airlines in Chicago. At home, he always had a pleasant smile and kind words as he tinkered with mechanical things, fashioning new and interesting machines. He may have even built one of the first go-carts.

His stocky build was perfect for mechanical work. He was always bringing home odds and ends, many from Asia.

Altogether, the crew of Flight 4422 had amassed more than 20,000 hours of flying time, a vast amount by any standard; they knew their airplane and their route extremely well…perhaps too well.

AT 8.12 P.M. ALASKA time on Friday, March 12, 1948, the DC-4 left Anchorage for Edmonton, Canada. In New York the clock read 12 minutes past midnight on Saturday, March 13. Captain Robert Petry was in the left seat of the DC-4 as it taxied for takeoff. Jehu Stickel was probably in the co-pilot's seat and flying the leg from Anchorage to Edmonton. James Van Cleef would have probably sat in the cockpit's jump-seat for takeoff. Wayne Worsley may have been sitting in a spare rest seat and not in the cockpit. No one knows whether the pilots changed seats before takeoff or in flight.

Snow banks were piled around Elmendorf Field's ramp, but the runway was plowed and clear. Although exhausted from the numerous time zone changes and the long hours in the air, the sailors on board had only one thought: They'd be home soon. After more than 24 hours of flying from China, even the most nervous mariners had become confident—maybe even blasé about air travel.

Alaska's winter sun had set 6:54 p.m. and the sky was black when Flight 4422 roared down Elmendorf Field's runway and lifted gently into the cold night sky. Its fuel tanks were once again full for the 1,432-mile flight to Edmonton. To the northwest, the moon appeared as a tiny sliver. Two days earlier, the lunar phase had been that of a new moon. Now, the almost unnoticeable slice of moon officially would set at 9:32 p.m. The sky was dark…very dark. As the plane climbed, the moon was so low on the horizon that it was soon hidden behind the peaks of the Alaska Range, 10 days before the spring equinox.

In 1948, in the rural and wilderness areas of Alaska, nighttime surface lighting visible from the air was rare. The night of March 12 was particularly dark. NWA Captain Warren Avenson said, "In Alaska, on a moonless night, it was so dark we couldn't tell if our eyes were open or closed."

Once airborne, one of the aircrew raised the landing gear handle, the DC-4's chrome-plated hydraulic landing gear struts and wheels retracted into the underside of the nose and wings, and the landing gear doors closed. The nose gear strut rested gently in its retracted, horizontal, nose-to-tail position. Freed of the drag, Flight 4422 accelerated to its cruising speed. The pilot set the autopilot on a north heading, to follow the air route over Wasilla, north of Anchorage.

James Van Cleef may have headed back to a rest seat aft of the navigator's station, out of the cockpit. He might have thought about his new Studebaker, waiting for him in the Minneapolis parking lot.

On some routes pilots stayed on course with the aid of radio range stations dotted along their routes. Those range stations sent out audio Morse code signals in four directional radio beams pointing roughly north, south, east, and west, depending on what was necessary. The centerline courses of the range stations transmitted a steady tone. If the left was the dot-dash of the letter A and the right was the dash-dot of the letter N, and the pilot wanted to fly out on the centerline of a radio beacon's signal, he tuned in to the correct frequency and listened for the steady tone on his earphones. If he started to hear an A, he was drifting to the left. Hearing an N meant he was drifting right.

If on duty, the navigator carried out the task of listening to the range stations. Once on course, staying there was relatively easy. But, if the plane was off course, it was difficult to determine exactly how far off. Most pilots became proficient at range station navigation and could safely navigate by the system without the aid of a navigator, as was the case when flying east of Anchorage. A few of the stations were manned. The operators provided the aircrew with someone on the ground to talk to, and transmitted updated weather information. But there were long segments when the flights were out of range of any radio communication. Aircraft radio, radar, and navigation were relatively primitive in 1948—the horse-and-buggy days of aviation.

On 4422's flight deck, most likely, two pilots actively flew and navigated the plane. East of Anchorage, on an overland route, not having a navigator on duty normally presented no problem. But something changed that made this flight different.

At 8.28 p.m. the gleaming DC-4 passed over Wasilla Intersection, 35 miles north of Anchorage. At that point, the north course of the Anchorage radio range intercepted the east course of Skwentna radio range. The steady tone would have indicated the flight was on course.

At 8:28 p.m., Flight 4422 checked in on the radio. Someone on the crew reported, "Flight 4422 over Wasilla at 2028."

Three minutes later, at 2031, the flight reported that it was at its cruising altitude of 11,000 feet.

One of the pilots would have turned the autopilot to a heading farther right, on a course northeast, toward the Wrangell Mountains. The autopilot held the airplane on the heading selected by the pilot; it could not automatically follow the course. Don Rector, the flight mechanic, would have been monitoring the engines by watching rows of dials above his desk.

Rector's station was just aft of the cockpit, more or less in a dark hole on the side of the corridor between the cockpit and the passenger compartment. The lights on the pilots' panels and the engineer's panel would have been turned low to allow their eyes to adjust to the darkness. That way, the pilots might have been able to see at least a few of the sparse lights on the ground. Dim, uncertain silhouettes of the mountains on each side of their route may have been in view.

At 8.42 p.m., someone on the crew made a radio call indicating they were on course over a navigation point named Sheep Mountain, 35 miles east of Wasilla. On the top of the mountain was Sheep Mountain non-directional beacon (NDB), 031 degrees magnetic, and 85 air miles from Anchorage. These NDB radio transmitters were marked on aviation maps and sent out a specific signal in all directions. By flying directly over them, the aircrews knew exactly where they were. A lost pilot could navigate to beacon by flying a box pattern and judging the strength of the signal. Flight 4422's next navigation checkpoint was Gulkana.

At 9.03 p.m., Flight 4422 passed over the general area of the Gulkana radio range station and was generally on course, 159 miles from Anchorage, on a bearing of 034 degrees magnetic, at 11,000 feet. No one knows if the aircrew or passengers were wearing masks delivering brain function-sustaining oxygen.

THE BENNETTS WERE aircraft communicators for the Civil Aeronautics Administration and worked at Gulkana's aircraft communication station. Layton had gotten off work at 4 p. m. His wife, Lou, was due to start work at midnight. Maurice Benningfield, the Bennetts' good friend and the third aircraft communicator at Gulkana, was on duty until midnight.

Layton Bennett and his wife were home chatting quietly in their living room when they heard the distant roar of a big plane at 9:03 p.m. But, looking outside, they couldn't see the plane. Other citizens of Gulkana did see the plane but wondered why it flew south of Gulkana, about four miles south of the planned course. To the east, the aurora borealis flickered in the night sky, a common and beautiful occurrence.

THE AURORA BOREALIS—the northern lights, the greatest light show on Earth—erupted all around Flight 4422 in a giant, silent fireworks-like display that no man-made creation could match. Mother Nature, in all her glory, was spectacular.

Created by superheated atoms in the thin upper atmosphere above the earth's poles, the northern lights are visible when those atoms are bombarded by high-speed electrons and protons streaming earthward from the sun. The earth's magnetic field and gravity play a part in the apparent movement. That night, they were brighter than anyone in Gulkana had seen in a long time. On the flight deck, the passengers and crew probably had the same borealis experience—spectacular and distracting.

In the passenger compartment, the sailors must have watched in awe.

Even the oldest sailors, John Elkins and Brooklynites Max Brooks and James Lampman, must have been impressed, having seen the northern lights and other spectacular sights many times during their travels, but nothing like this.

Arthur Eilertsen also would have loved it, enamored with aviation. British sailor Wilfred Beswick, also hooked on aviation, probably felt the same way. Years earlier, he had signed up for naval aviation but just missed qualifying for the program.

The lights hung in spooky silence from the sky in great curtains of orange, red, green, and gold. They danced and waved seductively. An unusual amount of humidity in the air created an illusion that made the lights seem to extend farther down than normal—all the way to the earth's surface. That created deceptive shapes, blending the white slopes of the mountains with the sky, a phenomenon that easily could have disoriented the pilots.

On the ground 20 miles to the northeast of Gulkana, at 35 degrees below zero, young hunter Sy Neely was camping in a tent. He, too, was looking in awe at the spectacular display of celestial colors. In the cold silence, Neely heard the barely audible crackling sound made by the northern lights on the earth's surface. But, he knew nothing about the airplane flying south of him.

THERE WAS A shortcut from Gulkana to the Snag intersection just across the border in Canada. Many pilots knew about the route, which passed just north of 16,208-foot Mount Sanford and its 12,002-foot neighbor, Mount Drum. Normally, planes would fly the approved, legal, but slightly longer route to the town of Northway, then southeast, over Snag intersection and on to Whitehorse, Canada. However, radio operator Ken Crewdson told me that on clear days, pilots sometimes took the shorter route and did not fly over Northway.

A plane flying the shortcut would fly east from Gulkana and pass about two miles north of Mount Drum. Three minutes later, the shortcut would barely miss the summit of Mount Sanford, passing close to its northernmost ridge. But a pilot had to see the mountain to keep from hitting it.

In order to safely clear that ridge, a plane would have to climb a little higher than 12,500 feet. Once safely past Mount Sanford, it could descend quickly and fly on to the east, directly to Snag intersection and then to Whitehorse.

The approved route provided a large safety margin by staying well clear of Mount Sanford's summit. However, the shortcut saved as much as 18 minutes. To the pilots of 4422, the night may have seemed clear enough—perhaps they may have chosen the short cut to save time.

AFTER PASSING GULKANA, a change of direction (left) to 023 degrees magnetic was critical for Flight 4422. The change in course from 046 degrees to 023 degrees would have turned the plane safely north toward Northway, well clear of the mountains. But no one changed the plane's heading. The pilots may have been flying the plane manually and were distracted by the northern lights. Or, maybe the autopilot was still engaged but not selected to turn onto the route toward Northway—maybe they simply forgot to turn. Or, it is possible the pilots intentionally risked their lives and that of the passengers by directing the plane to continue straight ahead toward Mount Sanford, hoping they would be able to fly around it, visually. The only thing that is certain is that the plane never made the turn. Flight 4422 roared straight toward Mount Sanford.

Two minutes after passing Gulkana, someone on the flight deck made the required position report via radio. "Flight 4422 over Gulkana at 2103 (9:03 p.m.), estimating Northway at 2136 (9:36 p.m.)."

The plane would have been traveling approximately 220 miles per hour at 11,000 feet. This radio call indicated they were planning on flying over Northway. But, that is not where they were heading.

In the passenger cabin, the sailors may have may have pressed their noses against the windows in silent wonder of the beauty of the aurora borealis. On the flight deck the pilots' eyes would no longer have been adjusted to the darkness. More than likely, no one could have seen where they were heading because the terrain was basically indiscernible. No one may have been listening to the navigational radio aids that would have indicated they were flying even farther off course.

The aurora borealis shimmered and danced in front of the plane and all around it. Like the mythical sirens to the ancient sailors on the high seas, the lights beckoned Flight 4422 to the deadly mountains.

Someone on the flight deck made a second radio call at approximately 9:12 p.m. and repeated the Gulkana position report. At the small Northway radio station, operator Ken Crewdson heard the report, repeated it, and acknowledged it to Flight 4422 on a backup radio voice circuit.

Just off the right wing, the pilots may have vaguely seen the outline of a huge mountain and thought it was Mount Sanford. But they were flying in a sea of disorienting colors slanting in various directions. It would have been difficult, if not impossible, to make out anything for certain. And then suddenly, Flight 4422 slammed into the western side of Mount Sanford.

THE ALUMINUM AIRCRAFT, flying at 293 feet per second, smashed into a nearly vertical wall of rock covered by thick ice and snow. The powerful engines, weighing 1605 pounds each, were operating at cruise power. Spinning propellers drilled into the ice and scraped against the underlying rock at 11,000 feet. The blades screamed in an agony of twisting, snapping steel. Pieces of the radial engines' cylinders, sticking out like spokes of a wheel, were torn off; others were deformed as easily as if they were putty.

The airplane shattered into thousands of pieces. Large sheets of aluminum ripped from the plane's wings, walls, and floor and crumpled as though made of paper. Seen as a fireball from fifty miles to the west, the brimming fuel tanks split and exploded. Instantaneously, the west side of the mountain lit up—the flames from the ignition of thousands of gallons of aviation gasoline.

During the impact, seats, cargo, and personal items flew forward and shot into the air and against the mountain. The aircrew and passengers were slammed against metal, ice, and rock. Human remains were flung into the cold night air, flying well clear of the huge fireball. Hurtling through the frigid darkness, the human flesh immediately started to freeze. The tremendous force of the impact destroyed the plane and everyone on board.

Blazing fuel descended and melted a narrow, long black gash down the face of the ice-covered rock, flowing toward the glacier far below. In a classic battle of fire and ice, the gasoline burned furiously, dripping steam and flames farther down the mountain. A small ring tumbled through the chaos and down the mountain. It was diamond-shaped with a thin silver band around the rim and a picture of a minaret on the face. On one side of the face was stamped Iran; on the other, 1946.

No one on board the plane felt a thing—nothing. Thirty lives ended in an instant, lost forever to their friends and loved ones. A shower of airplane fragments, human remains, ice, and snow tumbled and slid slowly, almost reverently, into the remote eternity of the glacial chasm far below.

Kevin McGregor (L) and Marc Millican (R) with Marc's 1957 Super Cub in Cub Valley on Mount Sanford, Alaska, in 1996 at 4, 800-foot elevation. *Photograph by author.*

Sanford River winding its way toward Gulkana, Alaska. Layton Bennett and Jerry Luebke followed this river while trying to find Flight 4422 the night of March 12, 1948. *Photograph by author.*

Flight Mechanic Donald Rector (center looking at camera) in Shanghai, China, with members of his aircrew. Circa 1948. This may be the last photograph ever taken of Rector. *Courtesy Polly Rector Logan.*

T-2 tankship SS *Sunset* in Cape Town, South Africa, in 1947. This is the only known photograph of the vessel taken as the SS *Sunset.* Its name was later changed to *Caltex Lisbon, Toyosu Maru,* and *Toyosu.* Note Table Rock in the background. *Courtesy of V. H. Young and L. A. Sawyer, ship photographers, Seatoun, Wellington, New Zealand.*

Eugene J. Adler   Wilfred Henry Beswick   Morris "Max" Brooks

John R. Comshick   Howard A. Davidson   William Delaney

Arthur L. Eilertsen   John V. Elkins   Eugene O. Foote

Olav J. Jacobsen   John Joseph Jamele   Everett W. Jenkins

August E. Koistinen

James G. Lampman

Michael Marushak

Travis M. McCall

James G. Mooney

Edwin Mustra

Robert J. Rabich

John W. Rapchinski

Daniel C. Rice

Carl F. Sigmund

Frank J. Van Zandt

Stanley C. Wilkowski

Robert Haslett, purser

Robert Petry, pilot

Donald Rector, flight mechanic

Jehu Stickel, copilot

James Van Cleef, pilot

Wayne Worsly, navigator

Northwest Airlines DC-4 NC-95422 circa 1947, Alaska. Note number 422 painted on fuselage just below the captain's window. Paint scheme is that used before becoming the "Red tail fleet." *Courtesy Northwest Airlines history department.*

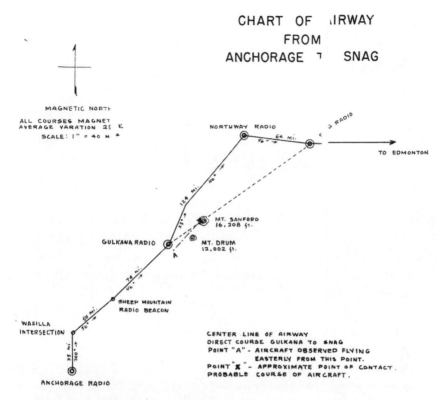

The aircraft route chart from the Civil Aeronautics Board accident report summary shows how after passing the Gulkana radio range station, Flight 4422 continued straight forward (dashed line) toward Mount Sanford for reasons unknown, rather than making the turn to the left toward Northway. The radio range stations broadcast audio tones to assist pilots in staying on course.

 March 12, 1948, 9:14 p.m.

AFTERMATH

In the small town of Glennallen, 45 miles west of Mount Sanford, 15-year-old Helen Cameron crossed the street and walked up to her parents' front porch at exactly 9:14 p.m. after watching a movie at the town's makeshift theater operated by her father, William P. Cameron, directly across the street. Her father was still locking up the theater while she stood on the dark front porch, shivering in the 35 degrees-below-zero air. To the east, the aurora borealis fanned across the sky, creating a spectacular show over the Wrangell Mountains.

Suddenly, Helen saw an even brighter light—a fiery blast on the mountain. The flash lasted only a few seconds and then diminished to flames. *It's the sun*, she thought. *No, it's a volcano; Mount Sanford has erupted.*

Her father, having completed locking up, also saw the flames. He ran up to the porch and told her, "A plane's gone down." He squinted toward the flickering flames. To pinpoint the location of what he thought was a crash, he grabbed a ski pole and placed it on top of a waist-high rectangular flower pot and pointed it directly toward the flames.

Meanwhile, many other of the town's children also saw the explosion. Twelve-year-old Carole Neely saw a momentary flash in the eastern sky and noticed a flaming streak running down the west side of Mount Sanford.

In the inky black of the long winter night, interrupted only by the northern lights, Cameron figured anything that he could do to help rescuers zero in on the wreckage might prove to be a lifesaver. He called the CAA radio station near the Gulkana airstrip. Pan Am Radio Operator Layton Bennett already knew about the situation because his phone at home had been ringing off the hook with calls about the crash. Someone else ran and banged on the Bennetts' door, but they were already on the phone to Maurice Benningfield at the CAA station.

Benningfield also had seen the fire. He used a pair of scissors to etch permanent lines on the door jamb of the radio station lined up with the runway lights, to pinpoint the location of the flames. Layton and Lou Bennett already had a good idea what might have happened. She headed for the station while her husband sped over to Gulkana's airstrip to ready his plane for a search. There might be survivors, they figured.

Layton Bennett was a good-natured, boisterous, sturdy frontiersman type of guy who loved adventure. If adventure wouldn't come to him, he went looking for it. Born in Woodland, Washington, he'd moved to Alaska in 1939 and hired on as a 19-year-old radio operator for Pan Am, the operating company of the Civil Aeronautics Administration's aviation radio stations. In 1942, he signed up with the Army Air Corps at Randolph Air Force Base, Texas, where he met Lou, a young, dark-haired beauty from Rockdale, Texas. The cheerful, handsome pilot and the gentle woman from Texas fell in love, becoming husband and wife in 1944.

It was the beginning of a wonderful and exciting life for both of them. To his frustration, the Air Corps kept Bennett as an instructor. "You're too damned good. I need you here," his commander had said.

Figuring another way out, he repeatedly asked to be assigned to helicopters because he saw their potential in war. Instead, the Air Corps had assigned him as an instructor in B-29 bombers. The war ended before he had gotten a chance to see any action. In 1946, he left the Air Force and, with his wife and new son, Eric, moved to Gulkana to work as aircraft communicators. On his off time, Bennett flew hunters and fisherman to and from the remote bush of Alaska.

As the flames flickered on the distant mountain, Bennett shoved a fire pot under the engine of his Luscombe, a light bush pilot's plane made of aluminum and fabric that was popular with mountain flyers. "At 30 degrees below zero, engine oil turns to molasses," he said. "Try to run any engine at that temperature, without heating it, and you'll soon burn out the bearings, seize up the pistons, and generally speaking make one hell of a mess."

Bennett prepared the plane by warming the engine's oil before spinning the propeller and then dusted the snow off the skis and wings. He cleared the windshield and yelled to student pilot Jerry Luebke, "Load up the emergency equipment."

To the east, the aurora borealis still hung like curtains and flashed on and off, brighter than anyone could remember.

"We're all set to go," Luebke said. "Do you think we can find someone who made it through alive?"

"I don't know, but we'll give it our best shot."

It took more than an hour to get the Luscombe's engine warm enough to start. Finally, Bennett cranked her up and he and Luebke took off into the clear starlit night. They followed the frozen Sanford River, snaking their way between the valleys descending from Mount Drum and Mount Sanford. It took a bold, experienced pilot to fly it on a night like this. It was nothing less than heroic. They were halfway to Mount Sanford when the aurora borealis flared up again, covering the entire sky.

"Did you ever see anything like it?" Luebke asked.

A hanging, shimmering curtain of light suddenly blocked out the world.

Bennett peered through the windshield. "I'm not seeing what I'm doing. I know exactly where the mountain is. I just can't see it. I'm flying blind."

He thought for a moment then said, "I know this country. I'm going to stay right over the river. That way we won't hit anything."

They looked down, keeping the river in sight, occasionally looking over the landscape for any sign of the plane.

The Luscombe flew back and forth across the frozen river as the two men scoured the mountain between bursts of the aurora, straining their eyes, looking up into the glacial valleys, but they saw nothing. Even the fire from the crash had burned out. It was pitch black again, but suddenly the aurora borealis flared up with renewed intensity. Reluctantly, Bennett turned the airplane around. If he crashed, he would be of no use to any survivors.

Well after midnight, the two men landed back at Gulkana's ice- and snow-covered runway. They met Lou Bennett, Maurice Benningfield, and many others who had gathered in the radio station, grabbed hot cups of coffee, and waited to offer help.

"Couldn't find a thing," Bennett told the waiting crowd. Then the talk started.

One person asked, "Where was that plane coming from? China?"

Someone else yelled, "What's it carrying?"

Removing his extra cold-weather gear, Bennett answered offhandedly, "I don't know. It's probably full of gold from Chiang Kai-shek or something like that."

Outside the little radio building, through hushed conversations, the story quickly passed from one person to another that the airplane that had crashed on Mount Sanford was full of Chiang Kai-shek's gold.

AT NORTHWAY, ALASKA, just after Flight 4422 made its last radio call repeating its Gulkana position, Northway's radio operator, Ken Crewdson, used his teletype to forward the position report to Northwest Airlines' headquarters in Minneapolis.

Fifteen minutes later, Crewdson received a phone call from Benningfield, who said, "I can't contact NWA Flight 4422. Can you try to contact them?"

Agents from Northwest Airlines Flight Control section also called Crewdson and excitedly asked if he was talking to the flight. Crewdson told them he had just taken the report and passed it on. The man on the phone gruffly said, "That is not what I mean. Are you talking to them NOW?"

In the lonely one-man radio outpost, Crewdson immediately fired up the radios and again tried to contact 4422. There was no answer, just static. Over the next hour, Crewdson tried to raise the plane on several frequencies, but there still was no answer. Fifty years later, tears would run down Crewdson's cheeks when he realized he was the last person to talk to anyone alive on Flight 4422. It was a heavy burden, one he would carry to his grave.

Alaska's Tenth Rescue Squadron got the report of the missing DC-4 and immediately launched its B-17 into the dark night. The huge bomber, turned search-and-rescue plane, arrived over the scene 30 minutes after Bennett and Luebke aborted their search, but the B-17 crewmembers saw nothing—no fire, no survivors. On the way, the pilot carefully watched his navigation instruments and reported that radio reception was normal and that his magnetic compass worked fine. A second search plane, a C-47 from Ladd Field near Fairbanks, Alaska, took off just before midnight, searched, and reported the same sad news.

The human response to the crash was as great as it could have been in 1948. But attempting a rescue 50 miles deep in the wilderness of Alaska, in the dead of a subfreezing night, was an almost impossible task.

There was a third search plane. Just before midnight, a Pan American DC-4 took off from Seattle on a red-eye cargo flight to Fairbanks. Three pilots were on board: the two line pilots assigned to fly the trip, and Chief Pilot Ralph Savory, who was administering a flight evaluation. Two hours after takeoff, they were flying over Juneau when they were told a plane had gone down on the west side of Mount Sanford. A few hours later, they flew over its summit, searched, but saw nothing unusual. By then, the northern lights had disappeared. Only darkness remained.

In Anchorage, NWA Flight Mechanic Wesley Brum heard the terrible news of the crash and quickly realized he had been the luckiest man around—having gotten off the ill-fated plane. NWA Mechanic George Holm had been on the airport ramp in Minneapolis on Saturday, March 13, 1948, assigned to Flight 4422. Expecting an evening arrival, Holm was notified the plane would not be coming; it had disappeared in the mountainous wilderness of Alaska.

THE CRASH OF FLIGHT 4422 was the worst airline disaster in Alaska's history and demanded a maximum effort. Overnight, it transformed the tiny, quiet crossroads village. As the closest town to Mount Sanford, Glennallen became the center of activity for the search, possible rescue, and subsequent investigation. It was a bunkhouse town of bush pilots and laborers working for the Alaska Road Commission. There were three streets of log cabins sitting at the junction of Route 4 from Valdez and Route 1, the main road to Anchorage. Route 1 would eventually link with the Alaska Highway, which stretches 1,523 miles from British Columbia to Fairbanks then connects to another highway that runs a thousand miles north to the Prudhoe Bay oil fields.

Glennallen had a bar, a gas station, and the Camerons' makeshift movie theater doubling as a bunkhouse. Electrical power was intermittent and most inhabitants heated their homes with oil-barrel stoves—a steel oil barrel turned on its side with a chimney welded into what then became the top. Piled full of blazing logs, and with a good draft running through it, a barrel would glow red hot, making homes cozy. Some enterprising residents wrapped coiled copper piping around the chimney and ran water through it to make a rudimentary central heating system and hot water for washing.

Beginning at 6 a.m. the morning following the crash, many people began descending on Glennallen. They would total more than 200 over the next few days, including investigators from the Civil Aviation Administration (CAA), the Civil Aviation Board (CAB), and Northwest Airline's own investigation team. Alaska State Troopers arrived, and, of course, reporters and photographers. The U. S. Army arrived and then, quietly, FBI agents, in their obvious, nondescript cars, showed up and started asking questions—lots of questions.

Young trapper Sy Neely returned from his hunting trip and watched the G-men travel about town interviewing nearly everyone. Neely, as well as many of the other residents, wondered why the FBI was there. "What was so important about Flight 4422?" they asked each other.

Maybe it was from the FBI men, maybe the military or CAB officials, but somehow information filtered down to the local population indicating there was some kind of payroll or gold bullion on board the wrecked DC-4. The search for the plane continued.

THE TENTH RESCUE Squadron, with five planes and a helicopter, conducted what was up to that time the largest search-and-rescue operation in Alaska's history. Fourteen airplanes from U. S. Army bases were involved in the official search. Additionally, eight P-51s and a C-47 from the 57th Fighter Group helped scour the remote mountains. Another C-47 came from Base Operations to help.

Then-classified archives recorded that the Tenth Rescue Group spent 14 1/2 hours flying around the mountain looking for survivors, logging 2,275 miles. Previously classified records of the Canadian North West Air Command marked, Secret, indicated its unit at Whitehorse, Yukon Territory, was standing by to assist with the search-and-rescue mission.

Among the Tenth Rescue Squadron's 25 officers and 150 enlisted men were two eight-man squads specially trained for land rescue missions. They also had one paratroop team, two dogsled teams, and three M29C all-terrain vehicles known as Weasles—perfect for traveling through Alaska's wilderness. The ground crews prepared to travel to the crash site, but they needed to know exactly where to go, if it were possible to get there.

Local pilot Jim Hurst, flying a CAA DC-3 from Merrill Field, Anchorage, was the first official search pilot to spot what he thought was debris from the DC-4. He was a veteran mountain flier who knew exactly what to look for. His plane was full of officials from the CAB, CAA, and Northwest Airlines.

It was 9 a.m. on the morning after the crash when Hurst spotted the wreckage from a distance. One hour later, Army First Lieutenant Willard Jenkins, from Monticello, Arkansas, got an extreme close-up view from his C-47. During two descending right turns, just above the glacier, he spotted the NWA logo on the airplane's tail fin sticking out of the snow. Another pilot who flew his fighter very low, just above the glacier, spotted the wreckage and pulled up just before hitting the wall of rock and ice. He pulled farther back on the stick and intentionally continued looping over backwards, then he abruptly rolled upright and flew away from the mountain.

What appeared to be the shattered wreck of the DC-4 lay in an extremely dangerous and wide half-round glacial cirque. The remnants of the plane had been melted down into the glacier by blazing aviation gas. Jenkins reported that he could clearly see the point where Flight 4422 had apparently impacted the ice-covered cliff 2,500 feet above the wreckage.

Later that morning, Layton Bennett flew to the crash site again. While flying parallel to the face of the ice cliff at 10,000 feet, he saw a long dark scar that started above his plane, at 11,000 feet. Four horizontal dark spots indicated precisely where the four engines impacted the mountain, destroying the oil reservoirs, splattering the black liquid onto the cliffs of ice, snow, and rock.

The dark streaks came together and formed one long black trail of death down onto the glacier far below. Bennett followed the path down as far as he could but soon realized it would be impossible to land on the glacier or anywhere near the crash. On the surface of the glacial circular area at the base of the cliffs, he saw what looked like thousands of tiny pieces of the plane scattered about. *There's no way anyone lived through that,* he thought.

Another Glennallen bush pilot, Cleo McMahan, flew over the crash site just a few hours after Bennett's flight. Perhaps because it was later in the day, McMahan was able to fly very close to the crash site and was certain that he saw what he thought was a large portion of the tail section. He could even see smoke still curling up from it and was also convinced there were no survivors.

Less than 12 hours after the crash, the wreck was already disappearing. Avalanches tumbled on top filling in the low spots, then covered the debris. The chances of the military's ground crews making it to the site became even dimmer as snow began to fall. Two days later, the military officials agreed it was beyond their capabilities to reach the remote site. They cancelled the ground searches.

Meanwhile, far away from Mount Sanford on March 13, 1948, at the homes of the relatives of all the *Sunset's* crew, the first of many sad telegrams arrived:

> "WE ARE ADVISED BY NORTHWEST AIRLINES THAT THE PLANE ON WHICH [SAILOR'S NAME] WAS ENROUTE TO NEW YORK FROM SHANGHAI HAS BEEN UNREPORTED SINCE EARLY THIS MORNING. SEARCH IS NOW UNDERWAY BY AIRLINE ARMY AND CIVIL AERONAUTICS AUTHORITY AND AS SOON AS WE HAVE ANY FURTHER INFORMATION WE WILL INFORM YOU. W P GAYNOR JR VICE PRESIDENT OVERSEAS TANKSHIP CORPORATION."

Only one other chance of reaching the wreckage remained. Fred Ewan and Jake "Jack" Butler were two of Alaska's most famous dog mushers. The two strong young Athabasca Native Americans (known as Eskimos by most) were comfortable traveling in the middle of the wilderness during the dark, freezing winter. Ten miles north of Gulkana, at the native town of Gakona, they prepared their dogs and began to pack their sleds for a hazardous trek 40 miles across the deep snow from Gakona to the crash site.

They wanted to try to find survivors, but they had also heard the stories about gold being shipped on the plane. Ewan and Butler talked about their intentions publicly, keeping nothing secret.

Interestingly, despite government officials' knowledge of their proposed expedition, and despite talks between the mushers and a few government officials, neither Ewan nor Butler was told exactly what they would be looking for. It was all done by whispers and innuendo. Ewan and Butler thought that if they could make it to the site and recover the gold or whatever valuable treasure there was, they would get a big reward. Ewan said, "Whatever was onboard that plane, the government people wanted it badly...very badly! They told us, 'You'll know what it is when you find it!'"

Apparently, no official wanted to take responsibility for having leaked information about what was on board the plane. There was nothing in writing and the cargo manifest—if there had been one—never surfaced.

The snow-covered slopes and fields of the green wilderness around Mount Sanford were Ewan and Butler's backyard. Having hunted there since childhood, they knew it better than anyone. Ewan's parents and grandparents lived on that land their entire lives. Considering two routes, the two mushers felt it might be possible to cover the 40 miles with their dogs and sleds despite the difficulties of breaking a new trail. Unique problems on the glacier itself would have to be tackled once they got there. But they never got the chance to try.

It seemed that Mother Nature was throwing everything she had at Flight 4422. Three days after the crash, just before Ewan and Butler were scheduled to depart, a new storm blew in and dumped well over a foot of snow at the lower altitudes. The two highly experienced Athabascans knew the storm must have dropped several feet of snow higher up on the mountain.

Thunder from unseen avalanches echoed throughout the Copper River basin as tons of snow and ice crashed down into the glacial valleys. It was obvious the crash site was being covered by more tons of snow and ice, making it far too dangerous for anyone to attempt accessing the DC-4. Ewan and Butler called off their expedition. There was simply no way they could safely reach the site, no matter what was offered, or by whom.

In Glennallen, it remained an accepted fact that Flight 4422 carried a payroll—possibly gold, or some other kind or treasure. But, there was no way to get to it—at least not in March 1948.

Late winter and early spring snows continued to blanket the mountains and more avalanches buried most of the crash site even deeper. With the experienced dog mushers having given up, the last card had been dealt. There were no more official plans to reach the site. The mystery of the plane and the men on board would have to wait for history to take its course.

IN BAYONNE, NEW JERSEY, the Davidson family refused to give up.

Howard's brothers—Robert, Warren, and Norman—and their friend, Ronnie Kramer, a paratrooper in WWII, contacted the rescue center in Alaska. Athletic, fit, and well trained by the Navy, Norman led the group's efforts. During WWII, he had served on the USS *Montauk IV* (AN-2/AP-161/LSV-6) throughout the Pacific. The ship was involved in several invasions, and he reasoned that a search and rescue would be much less difficult than surviving the battles he had seen. These tough, young men were ready and willing to go into the wilds of Alaska to search for Davidson.

Several other men from New York and adjacent states, all relatives and friends of those on board Flight 4422, traveled to Alaska. They volunteered to go to Mount Sanford in search of survivors. But government officials refused to allow any such efforts. They made it clear they weren't going to permit anyone to search for 4422. They reasoned that having to rescue the rescuers was the last thing anyone needed. Experienced Alaskan mountain climbers agreed that it would be suicide to parachute into the site or land a plane on the heaving, treacherous glacier.

Of course, the government's quashing of all rescue attempts only raised more questions about what, if anything, of value was on the plane. The question lingered: Was someone hiding something about 4422? By March 14, only two days after the crash, most of Flight 4422 had disappeared under the snow and ice. The families of the passengers and crew received another telegram:

"WE HAD HOPED BY THIS TIME TO HAVE SOME ENCOURAGING INFORMATION FOR YOU BUT REGRET TO REPORT NONE IS AT HAND. REST ASSURED IF ANY ENCOURAGING NEWS IS RECEVED YOU WILL BE ADVISED IMMEDIATELY. W P GAYNOR JR VICE PRESIDENT OVERSEAS TANKSHIP CORPORATION."

But the plane had been found. On March 17 the families received one last devastating telegram:

"WE ARE EXTREMELY SORRY TO REPORT CORONERS INQUEST MT SANFORD ACCIDENT REPORTED VERDICT OF DEATH. CORONERS JURY VERDICT CONCLUSIVELY ESTABLISHED INSTANT DEATH OF ALL PERSONS ABOARD WITH FURTHER FINDINGS THAT IMPOSSIBLE TO REACH SCENE OF ACCIDENT AND ANY ATTEMPT WOULD

ENDANGER LIVES OF SEARCHERS WITH NO POSSIBLE
GAIN DUE TO TERRAIN AND GLACIAL ACTION. RELIGIOUS
SERVICES ALL FAITHS TO BE CONDUCTED FROM
NORTHWEST AIRLINES PLANE OVER SCENE OF ACCIDENT
WEDNESDAY MARCH 17." W. P. GAYNOR VICE PRESIDENT
OVERSEAS TANKSHIP CORPORATION.

There was no hope for survivors, but the last letters mailed home by the
sailors were still in the mail.

JUST EAST OF CHINA, another OTC T-2 tanker, the *Grand River*, headed out
to sea. Its radio officer, Bernie Hopkins, heard the news of the crash of Flight
4422. He looked out at the Chinese sailors on the deck and wondered if there
could have been a mistake and that it was actually his previous American mates
on the *Grand River* who were the ones lost. They had also been swapped out
with Chinese sailors and scheduled to fly back to New York. After rechecking
the flight schedules and making a few radio calls to other ships, he was relieved
to learn his ex-shipmates had departed on a flight three days ahead of Flight
4422's sailors. They were already safely in New York.

Even so, something didn't feel right. Something compelled Hopkins to
make an extra copy of the *Grand River*'s original official personnel work and
pay records. Then he quietly slipped them into his briefcase. Months later,
after the completion of his cruise, he filed them away in his personal mariner's
archives at home in New Zealand, where they would remain untouched for
half a century.

In the Territory of Alaska, the newspapers reported that "the passengers
on board the lost plane were sailors coming back from China," and that "they
had just been paid, in Shanghai, after the long voyage." It wasn't a stretch of
the imagination to believe their pay was in gold because they were paid in
China, where gold was king.

MEANWHILE, THE RAMP AGENT, Tiny Eglund, told other Northwest
Airlines employees about what he had seen: a box in the cargo compartment
covered with tarps as well as some kind of paper in 4422's cockpit stamped
"PAYROLL." And the rumors continued to proliferate.

In Shanghai, another OTC tanker, the *Wagon Mound*, dropped anchor
on March 14, 1948. On it, Howard Davidson's brother, Robert, worked. It was
two days behind schedule because while the *Wagon Mound* was being loaded
in Bahrain, a labor dispute had erupted and fighting broke out among the

men. To make matters worse, the Norwegian sailors on board had gone on strike. "Better wages, less time on duty, and more respect," the Norwegians had demanded.

The *Wagon Mound*'s American sailors supported the Norwegians through a work stoppage. The underlying problem was that lingering hate and suspicions from WWII infected the work environment. For one thing, the Norwegians didn't like the German chief engineer.

To settle the dispute, the captain threw the rowdiest strikers into the brig, but it only held four men. So he ordered the chief engineer off the ship, stranding him in Bahrain. Then he threatened to have the other sailors thrown into the Bahrain prison. That finally got the men's attention. Begrudgingly, they went back to work after a two-day delay—a delay that saved Robert Davidson's life.

After anchoring in Shanghai, the *Wagon Mound*'s sailors went ashore to board another DC-4, a charter flight identical to the *Sunset*'s, also bound for New York. Upon arriving at the plane, NWA's Shanghai station manager told the sailors that the DC-4 with the *Sunset* crew on board had crashed on a mountain in Alaska and all aboard were feared to be dead.

Robert Davidson had missed flying home with his brother Howie by two days. Devastated by the news of the plane's crash, he telephoned home to Bayonne and confirmed the horrible news. They already knew about the crash. Then he and his shipmates boarded their DC-4 and headed for home via Alaska.

It was a long, cold flight for all on board. Davidson tossed and turned, unable to sleep. He couldn't help but wonder about Howie. *Did he suffer? Was he lost? Did he freeze? Did he starve? Or, maybe he's still alive.* The loss of his brother was unthinkable. During that cold flight, Robert decided he had to do something. He would try to find his brother, or at least find some answers.

The DC-4 carrying the *Wagon Mound*'s sailors followed virtually the same route as Flight 4422, and touched down at Elmendorf Field in Anchorage. Davidson told the ramp agent, "I'm getting off here. I'm going to find my brother."

On the ramp, a huge argument ensued among Robert Davidson, NWA officials, and the military police. It went on for 30 minutes. In the end, Davidson was given an ultimatum by the officer in charge, a major: "Either get back on the plane or go to jail. You are not getting off here."

Distraught, with no options, he got back on the plane.

Large flakes of snow drifted through the air as the plane took off from Elmendorf. Inside the DC-4, it was cold, dark, and noisy. Davidson covered himself with several blankets and tried to sleep. But instead he sat there, staring into space with the four engines droning in the background. He couldn't eat any of the fresh sandwiches on board; he was lost without his closest friend and brother. It was hard to hide his tears.

An hour later, the plane passed Mount Sanford, on course, well to the north of the mountain. Looking out the window, Davidson saw nothing. Mount Sanford was hidden by another fierce snowstorm. There were no beautiful northern lights, just the cold, relentless darkness of the north. Turning toward Northway, the plane followed the correct course. It roared directly over Gakona, the home of Fred Ewan, who intended to get to the wreckage.

Davidson began to wonder: *Why were they so stubborn about not letting me look for the plane and my brother?* The truth was that it was far too dangerous. In Bayonne, the brothers' dreams of the gas station vanished. There were no good answers and no closure. Howie's young wife, Audrey, was devastated. She realized that the old woman's warning had come true: Only one of the brothers had returned from their voyages. She sobbed as her year-old daughter, Denise, crawled around the house, giggling. As the girl got older, the heartbreaking loss of her father would leave a gaping hole in her life.

In Pelican Lake, Wisconsin, Daniel Rice's last letter arrived at his father's house. The hopeful words, "I'll be home in a few days," would never come true. One week later, Robert "Billy" Delaney's sister, Florence Sherff, received a similar note in her mailbox. Two weeks later, Collene McCall received a letter from her husband, Travis. He wrote, "I'm flying home. See you soon, honey." The roll of silk he purchased for his cousin's wedding dress never arrived.

Three full weeks passed before Phyllis Adler received her husband's last letter, with the haunting sentence, "I would happily forgo air transportation if a ship was available."

Harriet Sigmund's sixth sense had been correct, and Anna Eilertsen Oravetz was glad she had kept her husband, Frank, from going on the cruise. But now, she was lost without her brother, Arthur Eilertsen.

Back on Staten Island, little Betsy McKew couldn't understand why her adopted uncle, Billy Beswick, didn't show up with her Indian doll. The loss left the family in a kind of dream state. Nothing seemed real anymore.

Even later still, Jackie Jamele's grandmother, Maria, fished a letter from the mailbox at her home in Waterbury, Connecticut. She recognized her own handwriting on the envelope. It was a letter she had sent to 21-year-old Jackie, hoping it would catch up with him in Shanghai. Across the front of the envelope was a postal worker's unintentionally cruel scrawl: "Undeliverable."

And for more than half a century, the photograph of Robert Rabich, with his wide grin, holding his service pistol, would be displayed by his nieces and nephews. He would never join the many extended family members who later moved to Alaska. Over time, their uncle grew into a family legend, just as would Flight 4422. To the Rabichs, Robert became bigger than life.

At the Minneapolis airport, Captain James Van Cleef's fiancée waited for his return from the two-week trip. She had heard nothing about the accident. It was late Saturday afternoon when a Northwest Airlines employee told her the tragic news. In the company parking lot, snow and ice piled up on top of Van Cleef's new green Studebaker. As time passed, the frozen mantle disappeared. Dust formed on the car's surface and its luster began to fade. The beautiful car he loved so much waited in vain for its owner for several weeks before his brother removed it. Its odometer read 150 miles.

THE COPILOT, Jehu Stickel, had often visited his hometown—Zanesville, Ohio. There, he thrilled his young niece, Jan, with stories of his flying and the places he had been, including Alaska. Her uncle was Jan's window to the world. She was 16 when the plane disappeared. Her very first flight took her to Minneapolis for the memorial service for the aircrew members.

Northwest Airlines Captain Chet Eklund was a check pilot who had often flown with Jehu Stickel. Eklund said he could not believe Stickel would ever have let any airplane wander off that course from Gulkana to Northway. Eklund said, "When flying northeastward from Gulkana, he was the one first officer who never let a captain make any error toward Mount Sanford. He always corrected well to the west of Gulkana. Stickel was one of our most conservative, conscientious copilots."

ON MARCH 17, 1948, NWA Captain Charles Wesley "Charlie" Ryan, with pilots Ralph Nelson and Dudley Cox, flew another Northwest Airlines DC-4 over the crash site where airborne funeral rites were conducted by Protestant, Catholic, and Jewish clergymen. They said prayers and through the open passenger door dropped several colorful wreaths onto the mountain in a tribute to the 30 victims. Then the DC-4 made a reverent, wide-climbing, 180-degree turn and flew off to the west, leaving the remains of Flight 4422 in a cold, permanent silence. Those on board saw no evidence of the plane, now covered by snow and ice.

THE CAB'S EIGHT-MAN board of inquiry convened at the Radisson Hotel in Minneapolis on April 16, 1948. CAB investigators interviewed as many witnesses as possible while looking into the possibility of sabotage or hijacking, but found nothing suspicious. Stories circulated that the sailors had been rowdy, but nothing like that was ever proven.

Among many witnesses, Layton Bennett discussed his search flight and testified about the extremely bright northern lights he and Jerry Luebke witnessed the night of the crash. Bennett said, "The aurora borealis was extremely bright that night. It was like looking straight into a car's headlights."

Bennett also told the board members that he and Luebke did not see any of the wreckage that night. Ken Crewdson, the radio operator who last communicated with Flight 4422, explained the radio calls he'd received.

The board concluded the cause of the accident. Its official statement read: "The board determines that the probable cause of this accident was the pilot's failure to see Mount Sanford, which was probably obscured by clouds or the aurora borealis or both while flying a course off the airway."

THE WORLD'S ATTENTION soon moved on to other things. In Eastern Europe, the Cold War continued to develop. The United States was terrified of an invasion from the Reds. Communists were already in Canada. Newspapers ran stories about the potential annihilation of the United States. Maps of international Armageddon covered entire pages, with Canada clearly being the shortest route to the U. S. It was also a time when the Central Intelligence Agency (CIA) gained power and expanded quickly from its formation in 1946 as the U. S. Army's Signal Corps. In California's Mohave Desert, secret aviation tests continued as pilots and engineers made major advances in aerospace technology.

Then the Berlin Airlift grabbed the headlines during the first big crisis of the cold war. The Soviet Union blockaded the railway and canal access to the Allied-controlled sector of Berlin. The Soviets did this in an attempt to force the British sector to accept food and fuel from the Soviet Union, therefore, in practical terms, giving control of the sector to the Soviets. The blockade failed in May 1949 due to the incredible airlift which delivered more food and fuel than the railway and canals had done previously. In one year, the U.S. and its allies flew more than 200,000 flights full of food and fuel into the British sector. This was a huge embarrassment for the Soviet Union.

WITH NO RECOVERED bodies or wreckage, the fate of the lost DC-4, the men on board, and its rumored mysterious cargo of treasure passed into folklore. Except for the friends and relatives of those lost, nearly everyone forgot about it.

Despite the CAB's report and several pilots' reported identification of the plane in the glacier and the signs of fire on the ice and rock, information about what caused the crash was not as clear, nor as readily available, as it would have been in an accident where a plane was recovered. Several theories arose and the families of those on board received conflicting information from various sources.

Some people went so far as to speculate that Flight 4422 had not crashed. One victim's family was told that the plane and its load of gold had been hijacked by the sailors. Another family was told the crash was faked and the plane was flown to Russia. Still another story theorized that the aircrew had been asphyxiated by exhaust smoke entering the cabin, a legitimate problem in aircraft in the 1940s.

Flight 4422 became a ghost plane of sorts, lost in Alaska. With no conclusive information and no closure, the friends and relatives of the dead men were left with only grief and unanswered questions.

16

RUMORS

The rumors were already rampant. There was gold on Flight 4422. No, it was a military payroll in cash. Wrong again; it was a military payroll all right, but it was in gold coins or bullion. No, it was Chinese gold being smuggled out by Chiang Kai-shek, away from the Reds. Whatever was or was not on board the plane, the U. S. government expressed a great interest in the flight's disappearance.

While in Minneapolis to testify at the accident's hearings, but away from the official meetings, Ken Crewdson heard many people whisper about "a stack of gold bars" having been on Flight 4422, but he never heard or saw anything official about such cargo. There were many airplane crashes in 1948, but none of them received as much attention as 4422.

NWA mechanic George Holm was also in Minneapolis during the hearings. Over the next several days and weeks, he heard many experienced Northwest pilots talking on the ramp. He heard one say, "Flight 4422 cut the corner up there. Instead of going up to the northeast and around the mountains, they took the shortcut."

Other aircrew members weren't so sure. Holm also heard people around the ramp say, "The sailors on board had just been paid in China and had lots of money with them."

One of the more bizarre rumors he heard was, "Since the sailors had so much pay, maybe some of the aircrew members were playing poker with them in the passenger compartment."

Holm admits things were more relaxed on the charter flights than the mainline passenger flights, but he knew many of the aircrew members personally, and he believed such an idea was far-fetched. Regardless of what was going on inside the hearings, outside the meeting rooms, people were already referring to Flight 4422 as "the Gold Wreck."

William P. Cameron recalled that, in Gulkana, local folks were told the sailors "had been paid off in gold by the Chinese. At the time [1948] we were told the gold amounted to around $25,000. Since that time, I have heard tales of the gold amounting to $250,000 and $500,000...Kind of like the tales of lost gold mines."

Speculation was rampant, but the fact was that no one knew what had happened. And few if any knew for certain what cargo was on board the missing plane. But the truth didn't matter; human beings like to believe in legends, the unknown, things out of reach—untouchable. It makes ordinary living more exciting, adding a little spice to life. Far from the hearing in Minneapolis, people in Alaska were also calling Flight 4422 "the Gold Wreck."

Other than rumors of treasure on board the plane, there was a legitimate reason people wanted to find Flight 4422: insurance. That was the reason behind the first known ground attempt to locate the plane.

Explorer/hunter/trapper/fisherman George Hayden, originally a Nebraska rancher, first traveled to Alaska in 1940 on the Alaska Steamship Line. His goal was to find a quick $20,000 in gold to restock the family's cattle ranch. Unlike most gold hunters, he was successful. He found gold in the Little Brennan River near the Copper River. After just one year in Alaska, Hayden returned to Nebraska, restocked the family's cattle, got married, and returned to Alaska in 1942.

A remarkably industrious and ingenious man, he quickly became a licensed fishing and hunting guide in the Gakona and Glennallen area. Then he started a commercial fishing business at Nakiski on the Cook Inlet which he operated for almost 40 years. He spent eight or nine months each year in the territory, returning to his Nebraska home during the coldest months. Hayden was on the beach of the Cook Inlet cleaning fish in March 1948 when he heard about Flight 4422's accident. News of the crash was being broadcast virtually nonstop on the radio. All over Alaska, he knew, whether factual or not, it was widely understood that Flight 4422 was the "Orient Express Flight" from China to the U.S.A. and that everyone on board was loaded with money, bringing their life savings and everything they owned from Asia. Some people talked about pearls having been on the flight, and others talked about gold and cash. Everybody was talking about it because it was the biggest news in a long time.

He didn't pay much attention to the wild stories until a brother of one of those on board the flight put an advertisement on the radio and offered a $10,000 cash reward. The ad was broadcast on the Tundra Times, a daily AM radio program where, as an established practice, anyone could send messages for free.

It was a great service. Friends and relatives in the bush could receive messages simply by listening to the radio station. A typical message went something like this: "This one's for John Smith. Sally is delayed one week in Seattle; tell Roberta to go ahead and smoke the salmon by herself."

Another might have said, "John Smith sends his love to his wife and says he bought enough dog food to last the entire winter and will return home next week."

In late summer of 1948 George Hayden heard a radio message, "The surviving brother of one of the men lost on the recent crash on Mount Sanford is offering a $10,000 reward to anyone who can bring back proof that his brother died in the crash of Flight 4422. Contact him at the Westward Hotel in Anchorage."

The brothers apparently had been business partners and the survivor had to provide more proof of his brother's death to make a valid claim on the insurance policy.

Within days of hearing the reward offer, Hayden contacted three friends: William Moore, who worked at or owned the Anchorage U Drive Car Rental agency; a young man named Bill James, and a Native American from Chickaloon, a small Alaska town west of Gulkana. They decided it was worth trying to get to the wreck and collect the $10,000 reward.

Viewing the upper portion of the glacier from Gakona, just north of Gulkana, with strong field glasses, Hayden and the others saw what they thought was the plane's tail section high up on the glacier. There was no time to lose, so the team of four departed Gakona in the fall of 1948. At least two small snowstorms had already blanketed the ground with six to eight inches of new snow. Their plan was to have just enough snow to be able to travel by dogsled, but not too much to make trail blazing difficult. They were strong and in good shape and thought it would be relatively easy to make it to the crash site.

Using one small boat as a ferry, they floated their nine dogs, the sled, and the rest of their equipment across the partially frozen Copper River just east of Glennallen. Then, with only a compass and no maps, they headed east and broke trail in deep snow. They reached a small cabin on the trail late the first evening. Unfortunately, the snow was much deeper than they had anticipated.

After breaking trail for two more days, they were totally exhausted when they reached a second cabin beside a lake. After a good night's rest, they headed out again. Five hours later, they finally made it to the extreme northeastern slopes of Mount Drum. But they were wallowing through two feet of snow. With 15 miles remaining to reach the bottom of 4422's glacier, they gave up. Breaking the new trail demanded too much from both men and dogs. Retracing their trail, they took two days to return to Glennallen.

Hayden's "Insurance Expedition" journey was the first known non-aviation attempt to reach Flight 4422. It lasted less than a week. Although it was a determined and courageous effort, the four adventurers made it only about halfway to the crash site. They never tried again.

The next attempt came in the summer of 1949, when a group of four climbers from Anchorage tried to make it up to the crash site. They ascended the northeast side of Mount Sanford and set up camp at 9,500 feet, near the edge of a nearly vertical cliff of ice. With 1,000 feet of rope, their plan was to lower one of their team into the glacier. Three men winched the lone climber down the ice face. Unfortunately, their 1,000-foot rope was about 500 feet short, and the climber never reached the glacier. It took two days to winch him back up the cliff. Two days and one night, freezing while dangling on a rope above the deadly glacier with rocks shooting down each side, must have been terrifying. They aborted their attempt.

Back in Anchorage, rumors continued to flourish. One newspaper article repeated the claim that the *Sunset* had been sold to Chiang Kai-shek in Shanghai, that the payment was in gold bullion, and the payment was reported to have been on Flight 4422 when it crashed. Even wilder stories appeared in other publications, most of them claiming there was some kind of treasure on Flight 4422—far too many stories to ignore.

GOLD AND THE GLACIER

The merest whiff of gold has driven men to the most inhospitable corners of the world. It was one of the reasons early pioneers headed west. Although Mount Sanford's frozen glacier was at least as hostile and inhospitable as the Klondike, it didn't cool the gold fever. Men ventured to Mount Sanford in twos, threes, and fours during the summer over the years—groups of men with the desire for untold wealth in their eyes.

Glaciers move; they slide across the underlying surface at varying speeds. There are two sets of ice falls in Flight 4422's glacier on Mount Sanford's west side. The higher of the two is slightly less than a half mile from where the DC-4 was believed to have come to rest in 1948.

As the glacier moves downhill through ice falls, it breaks up, splits apart, and opens. Large crevasses expose the dark and ominous interior of the glacier. Some pieces of debris may stay frozen on or near the surface. Others may fall into the crevasses. Once past an ice fall, the glacier closes up again, hiding whatever is inside.

In 1957, there had been relatively little snowfall on Mount Sanford. With low snowfall and the glacier's movement, and despite the fact that the wreckage of the DC-4 had been entombed for nine years, 1957 seemed to open a window of accessibility to individuals hell-bent on finding the Gold Wreck.

The expeditions started early that year. The March 11 edition of the *Anchorage News* reported that three men—Harland Lewis, Ken Kunkel, and Bernie Levitt of Fairbanks, all 24 years old, departed in early March to find the wreckage. They flew from Phillips Field near Fairbanks with pilot Walter Lyons, who dropped them off at a landing strip at the mouth of the Sanford glacier.

The three told the newspaper reporter they had proof that the "U.S. Commissioner at Gulkana signed a certification shortly after the crash stating that the plane carried a shipment of gold the Chinese Nationalists had paid for the tanker. The gold was supposed to include the wages of the 24 men." The newspaper article also reported: "According to another rumor, the ship is supposed to have on board a tape recording of a conversation between President Franklin D. Roosevelt and Chiang Kai-shek."

Whether or not they reached the site or found any of the wreckage is unclear. What is known is that they spent one week trying to reach the site and that during one of Lyons' takeoffs or landings, a ski broke off the airplane, an Aeronca Chief. A second pilot, Claude Rogers of Glennallen, flew them out safely several days later.

That summer, two soldiers from Fort Richardson near Anchorage tried to find the DC-4. Not much is known about them other than that they failed and were injured in the process. One is believed to have broken his leg. There is no information about how they got to and from the glacier.

Then there was one very serious group of men—four, maybe five. They were hard-bitten men, shaped by a lifetime in the hostile terrain of Alaska. All four worked for Alaska Freight Lines (AFL) in Anchorage. In June, after work one day, they began plotting their moves during a secret meeting behind the locked doors of an old wooden aircraft hangar. AFL was the biggest trucking company in the territory, transporting anything and everything throughout Alaska. AFL trucks traveled north across ice roads to the DEW Line (Defense Early Warning Line), and south via the Alcan Highway to and from the lower 48 states carrying fuel, heaters, generators, electrical supplies, tools, building materials, portable buildings, winter clothing, dried food, and tons of survival equipment. They transported cargo for anyone, including the U.S. government.

AFL's truck shop was a converted WWII hangar at Merrill Field where the men worked. One of the foursome was a refrigerator engineer who maintained the trucks' Thermo King coolers. Another was a driver, and the other two were mechanics. All were in their 30s and 40s. They saw Flight 4422's treasure as their chance to hit the jackpot.

Late at night with no one else was around, their big, gnarled hands, permanently etched with grease and grime, moved across maps, tracing routes and weather and the movement of the glacier. When they were ready, they loaded their gear in an old pickup truck, telling others they were going on a hunting trip. One of the men, John Henniger, owned a government surplus Weasel, an all-terrain vehicle capable of driving through the bush.

The first time up on the mountain that summer, they saw something that took their breath away. It was one of those moments when the fickle weather and the heaving glacier grudgingly cooperated to reveal some of the mountain's secrets. Forty feet above the men, part of the DC-4's fuselage stuck out from the ice. Dark blue and red patches of paint were still on the aluminum. It appeared to be part of the plane's aft section, tantalizingly close, but just out of reach. These men were used to using monkey wrenches, not ice axes. The overhang put it beyond their limited climbing talents. They needed ladders.

They returned to Anchorage where they toiled for weeks, late at night after everyone else had gone home. They told no one where they had been, although two friends heard the drills and saws and wondered.

The men built several sturdy aluminum ladders. With specially made slots enabling the ends to join, the ladders would take them across crevasses and around the icy overhang. It was a race against time; they wanted to get back on the mountain before winter set in and buried the wreckage again. They disappeared again, telling almost no one where they were going. A week later they slipped quietly back into Anchorage.

While constructing a canopy over the back of one of their pickup trucks late at night, they confided in two good trucking friends, Al Renk and Dean Hart, telling them about their expeditions to Mount Sanford. Then they left town. It would be a long time before anyone heard anything more about them.

THERE WAS ONE other known trip to the mountain during the summer of '57—a solo venture by a young man who worked at Gulkana's Flight Service Station, which provided aviation weather and flight planning. For many years prior, the young man flew his J-3 Cub up to Mount Sanford in search of the gold wreck. He didn't tell anyone the details of his trips. But airplane charter operator Lynn Ellis's father watched the flight service man come and go many times each summer. On at least three occasions, the young man had an aluminum ladder tied to the bottom of his plane. His route of flight headed straight toward Mount Sanford and the glacier thought to harbor the plane wreck full of treasure.

Some people noticed that the young man kept skis on his plane all the way into the early summer. Apparently, he landed on a grass area adjacent to the glacier, or found an acceptable place to land on the ice and snow. Then in the autumn of 1957 without any warning, he quit his job and left Glennallen. No one ever heard from him again.

It had been a very busy year indeed for Flight 4422's glacier.

SEVEN YEARS LATER, all hell broke loose in Alaska. Tectonic plates shifted, the earth's surface shook violently, and the city of Anchorage was nearly destroyed in the epic earthquake of March 27, 1964. Streets were ripped apart, buildings demolished, and 115 people killed by the disaster. Tidal waves smashed hundreds of miles of Alaska's shoreline, destroying everything in their paths and re-forming some of the coastline.

Most certainly, in Mount Sanford's ice falls, many of the precariously poised ice blocks (seracs) and crevasses collapsed. The earthquake would have buried anything resembling the remains of an airplane clinging to the open cliffs of ice.

From deep down in the earth and almost without notice, small semi-permanent cracks broke through the protective shell on the surface. This allowed heat to rise from the superheated magma trapped far below. In what would become the Wrangell-Saint Elias National Park, the heat started a gentle warming of Mount Wrangell, Mount Sanford ,and the adjacent peaks. The glaciers on each started to feel the heat.

Centuries-old ice began to give way and slowly melt. It was the beginning of yet another cycle of nature humans are only now starting to understand and appreciate.

Another 33 years passed while gold hunters mounted many expeditions to the fabled crash site, but found nothing. Thousands of tons of snow fell, huge cornices formed on the high ridges, and ferocious avalanches swept down the mountain thousands of times—just as they had for centuries and will for many more.

Rain fell, froze, and partially thawed in Alaska's summer sun. But Mother Nature was not constant. Some seasons saw huge amounts of snow, others less. Some winters were relatively warm, and others were extremely cold, leaving the glacier's surface frozen late into the summer.

The glacier traveled at a distance that varied with the seasons, sometimes moving little if any. At other times, it surged in its crawl down to the Sanford River. During the half century following the crash of Flight 4422, the glacier's movement down the mountain averaged 265 feet annually, an agonizingly slow pace for man but light speed for nature.

The glacier is a living, dynamic entity. While moving over large rises or steep areas, the glacier acts like the slices of an open loaf of bread gently moving forward as it is bent over the edge of a table. The slices separate and create crevasses. When back on a relatively flat area, they close back together. The internal pressure that is created is enormous. When released, the result is a sound like rifle shots or exploding mortar shells, commonplace in the mess of huge blocks of ice and snow. These broken pieces, seracs, can be as large as buildings and often weigh several tons. They lie precariously in odd positions, some waiting to fall over at any moment to crush whatever lies beneath.

Few things survive in the glacier's slow but certain path. Anything beneath the glacier is ground into microscopic bits by the tremendous weight of snow and ice. Inside the glacier it's possible that something might survive, although squeezed like the layers of a cake. On top of the glacier, sporadic avalanches roar across its undulating surface without warning. From a distance, the glacier is beautiful and forms long, elegant white ribbons that meander gently down the slopes of the mountain. The glacier is unpredictable; sometimes the new snow and ice blows over the crevasses, freezes, or builds upon the top of the crevasses, forming bridges of thin snow or ice. Rivers of water barely above freezing cut across the surface, through the center, and sometimes completely underneath the ice, entirely hidden. One false move on a glacier can result in death.

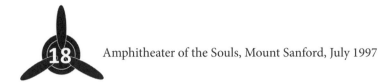

DESTINY

Following the warm gust of wind coming down from the glacier, Marc and I hiked down into the glacier. Over the jumbled mass of ice and rubble, we traced a wide, double-zigzag pattern to cover as much territory as possible. Less than a mile from the base of the lowest ice fall, water melting off the glacier's surface formed a small glacial stream that flowed into a larger one. The wider stream formed a jagged dividing line between the north and south halves of the glacier. We were looking for just one piece of Flight 4422—anything that would confirm its existence.

Marc was about 40 feet in front of me, negotiating his way down the loose rocks and wet ice close to the small stream. I was looking beyond him, trying to spot a place on the other side where we could safely climb out of the stream, when I saw something out of place—a partially coiled rope on the other side of the water.

As we got closer, we saw that it was a small length of dark hemp rope, lying just above and southwest of the stream. Most of it was coiled in a pile and appeared to be very old—not like today's ultra-strong nylon climbing ropes. It had five or six braids and looked like a common twisted hemp rope. The uncoiled end was partially covered by a boot-sized rock.

We uncoiled the rope, which measured 26 feet, and photographed it. Its ends were frayed and ripped, not cut. In the air near the rope was a slight odor like rotten fish. We knew the rope, having already deteriorated significantly, would soon crumble into dust and blow away or disappear in the glacial water runoff.

We wondered if it was a piece of evidence. There was no way to be certain. Maybe it belonged to a climber. Taking note of its location, we continued deeper into the glacier.

Two minutes later, Marc shouted, "Hey, Kevin, come look at this, and bring the camera."

He pointed to a small piece of twisted aluminum glinting in the dim sunlight. Three inches long and an inch wide, with several deformed rivets, it obviously had been violently separated from whatever it had been connected to. Even though there were no manufacturer's markings, it seemed to be a piece of an aircraft. Even if it came from an airplane, it wasn't necessarily a piece of a DC-4. In Alaska, airplane wreckage is scattered all over the state, easily misleading those searching for a specific plane's remnants. Another possibility was that this small part might have fallen off something flying high overhead. Or it could have been dropped by a hiker, although unlikely. Regardless, we were quite excited at the prospect it could be part of the DC-4.

We started hiking and had only traveled 50 feet when Marc spotted a small fragment of hard plastic, one-and-a-half-inches long and three-eighths-inch thick. It looked like it might be part of a window. A few feet away, another piece of plastic protruded from the gravel beneath a large rock. It showed evidence of burn damage that would have been consistent with Flight 4422's explosive fireball. That created some more excitement. I thought, *hmmm, we may be on to something here.*

After photographing the items, we started down-glacier again, and found nothing else in the immediate area. Even though the aluminum and plastic parts were small, the discovery was exciting and indicated we might be on the right path.

The sky darkened a little more and occasional showers fell in a calm wind as we searched back and forth over the ice hills covered with ancient volcanic rock debris, a scene that resembled the surface of the moon.

Thirty minutes later found us a half mile farther down the glacier. We crossed over a small rise and stopped in our tracks. There before us, in an area the size of a football field, were hundreds of aluminum aircraft pieces. We moved quickly from piece to piece. Most were battered or bent. Some were the size of a fingernail, barely visible and wedged between surface rocks. Most ranged from two inches square to a foot long; a few were larger. There were also ragged pieces of wet blue canvas about three inches in length, short pieces of wiring, and three-eighths-inch-diameter black and gray rubber hoses up to a foot long. The time capsule of an ice-enshrouded airplane's debris field was opening.

Marc and I had opposite reactions to our find. Marc excitedly hurried around, looking over a wide area. I buried my excitement and took my time carefully studying each piece, trying desperately to find any shred of evidence of its identity. But I found none.

After an hour, we left this mother lode of parts and cautiously proceeded down the glacier in search of anything that could identify this wreckage. We tried not to be distracted by the fact that we had actually located a crash site.

Two hundred feet farther into our descent, we came across a green piece of corrugated aluminum measuring roughly three feet by two feet. It certainly came from the floor of an aircraft. Its edges were extremely rough, as if it had been ripped from its supporting structure with tremendous force. Clear black-penned engineering marks, letters, and numbers scrawled by the aircraft factory's mechanics were visible—as though they had been written yesterday. Dark green, zinc chromate corrosion-resistant paint still coated most of the flooring and was as good as new. There was no question this was part of a large aircraft—not a small airplane like my Centurion or Marc's Super Cub. We had located the debris field of a major crash. But the question remained, was it that of Flight 4422?

"This is some pretty heavy stuff," Marc said.

"Do you smell anything?" I asked. "I smell a faint whiff of the same odor I noticed in 1995—like oil or grease."

"I really can't tell. My nose is kind of stuffed up."

"Let's be super careful now and try not to get too excited."

Staying close together, we continued down the glacier. Low clouds now lingered just above the glacier's surface. The hills of ice became more pronounced; dangerous crevasses were close by. Step by step, my good buddy and I journeyed through the glacier and remnants of a crash of a yet unknown plane.

AHEAD, A FAINT OUTLINE began to take shape—a hundred-foot mountain of rock and ice rose above the glacier. And near the top of the huge ice hill loomed two huge propeller blades. We both stared as though it were an apparition that might disappear at any moment. But it didn't. The blades were real.

The two of us walked up to the blades which stood on end angling away from each other 10 feet below the top of the 100-foot-high hill of ice. It was no wonder we hadn't seen them from either the air or the glacier's sides. The silver blades were perfectly camouflaged among the multi-colored rocks, and they were just far enough below the ice and rock peak to be invisible from the air or the sides of the glacier. One had to be right on top of them to see them.

Marc said, "These are incredible and one still has stenciled numbers on it."

"Holy cow, this really is something! This might identify this at 4422," I said.

The blades were attached to a round hub that measured roughly one-

and-a-half feet in diameter. The hub had begun to rust and was partially embedded in the ice. The third blade was missing and most likely broke off during impact. The hub exuded a strong smell of grease.

I pulled out my video camera and Marc read the stenciled information on the blades. "Model Number 6507-A-0 and Serial Number RRL6377."

I wrote the blade numbers in my notebook. Each blade measured six feet in length. With the hub in the center, that made the total arc of the blades 13 feet in diameter, consistent with the size of those on DC-4 and C-54 aircraft.

Marc said, "What about this serial number and model number? Can we track them?"

I opened our aircraft files and shielded them from the rain with my poncho.

"I don't know about the serial numbers, but the model is the same."

Indeed, the propeller blade model 6507-A-0 matched the one listed in the accident report, but that didn't prove a thing. Those propeller models were used on all kinds of planes back in the '40s and '50s. But it sure looked promising. I took out my still camera and photographed the blades.

"What we really need," I said, "is some part of the plane with identification numbers—like a piece of the fuselage or tail with the registration numbers painted on it."

Of course in this scattered field of debris, we both knew that finding something like that was remote at best.

The damp, rusty smell of rain-coated metal was in the air as I slowly ran my fingers across the leading edge of one of the blades. Half-century-old scrapes and quarter-inch deep pits covered its surface. I also found a large gouge, halfway down the front side of one blade.

"This had to have been the initial impact spot of this blade," I said.

After the nose section, these leading edges of the propeller blades were next to hit the rock and ice. The blades were curled slightly, indicating that at least this propeller's engine had power at the time of impact.

As we looked around at the jumbled mess of airplane parts, ice, and rock, our mood changed from the excitement of adventure to the sobering realization that we were in the midst of a long-hidden grave. Real people, each with a personal story, had lost their lives here, and these inanimate metal parts strewn over the cold and desolate expanse served as their tombstone.

A long silence ensued. We blinked with watery eyes, looking in opposite directions from the hill of ice. Whether or not this was Flight 4422, it was certain that people perished in this violent crash. If it was 4422, this was the grave of 30 men.

It was one of those moments that stir one's soul—a moment remembered for a lifetime, impossible to describe, and filled with opposing emotions. Conrad Anker and his team, the climbers who found George Mallory's body (lost in 1924) on the north side of Mount Everest in 1999, must have felt the same way: torn between the euphoria and excitement of discovery and bitter sadness at the loss of life.

The mere thought of the existence of any treasure like gold bullion, diamonds, gold coins, or cash in the pockets of those lost would have been cruelly out of place. We stood there quietly for a long time.

Finally, I said, "No human remains so far."

"Not yet," Marc said. After a pause, he said, "Let's call this Propeller Point."

"Okay. And let's get on with it before we freeze."

Marc left me and the blades and hiked up to the top of the hill of ice. I yelled, "Be very careful; we don't know what's on the other side. This water on ice is slicker than shit."

He yelled back, "You're right. The other side of this hill drops way off down into the river—at least 50 feet nearly straight down."

I finished photographing and videotaping the propellers while Marc made a controlled descent from the top of the ice hill back toward my left, away from the ice cliff, slipping and sliding a hundred feet down into a miniature ice valley. At the bottom, a two-foot-deep, six-foot-wide stream flowed. Halfway down, Marc looked to his left and saw another partially buried propeller blade about 75 feet to the west of Propeller Point. It was the same size as the others, but had no markings. The single blade was still attached to its own hub; its two sister blades were gone—snapped off.

Slowly, a picture of the impact scenario took shape. All three of the propeller blades had massive leading edge impact damage and twisted ends, signs that the engines to which they had been attached had been operating with a significant amount of power at the time of impact. In other words, at least two of the plane's four engines appeared to have been running at a high power setting when the crash occurred.

Marc made it down to the stream's edge. Immediately upstream he spotted several foot-high cascades; 50 feet downstream, a small waterfall made of ice. Several hundred feet farther downstream, the water plunged into a dark hole underneath the glacier. The bottom and sides of the stream were pure ice. With no way to stop, to fall in was certain death.

A few moments later above the roar of the icy water, Marc called out, "There are all kinds of little things embedded in the ice down here. Come on down."

I told him I would be there in a few minutes, after taking more pictures. I also warned him to be careful of a crevasse or cavern. "I know," he said. "There's one just downstream. I can hear it. The water disappears into darkness. I'll wait for you."

Ten minutes later, Marc was still standing at the glacial river's edge. I started down the slope of volcanic, grit-covered ice to join him. Halfway down, I stopped to investigate a 10-inch-long piece of twisted hydraulic line; then I continued down the slope. When I was about 10 feet from Marc, I tossed it to him.

At first, it seemed Marc had made a good catch. But the hydraulic line popped out of his hand, bounced off his left boot, and landed on the gritty sand-covered ice next to the icy stream. When he reached down to pick it up, something caught his eye: Six inches in front of his left boot was a razor-blade-like sliver of metal protruding from a small pile of sand on the ice. Slowly, he pulled it out.

THE GLACIER THOUGHT to harbor Flight 4422 is 16 miles long from the very top of the ice falls to its run-out at the bottom. It varies from three-fourths of a mile to one mile in width. A needle in a haystack would be easy to find in comparison to locating something smaller than a man's wallet in any one of Mount Sanford's numerous glaciers. Marc had found that needle.

He examined the four-by-three-inch piece of rectangular aluminum, then said, "I think this is an engine identification plate!"

"You've got to be kidding me," I said. "No way."

"Yes. There is an engine serial number and model number here."

I quickly joined him and gazed at the slightly crumpled, scratched, gouged, but shiny surface. It read,

ENG. NO. 107507

ATC. 230

MODEL 2SD13G.

"Kevin," Marc said. "Look at this: It's got all the right type of numbers and the little holes for attachment rivets."

He was right. In fact, the piece of aluminum looked exactly like the data plates we'd studied on the C-54's engines at the museum at Travis AFB.

This was the Holy Grail—an engine identification plate. The question lingered: *Was it the right one?*

"Marc, we were meant to find this."

"I know I caught that line and I don't know how I dropped it. It just kind of popped out of my hand and fell right by that data plate," he said. "I never would have seen it otherwise."

Rain fell again from the darkening clouds—appropriate weather for looking into an open grave. I pulled out a few dampened pages from the stack of files in my backpack. Sheltered by my poncho, I shuffled through them, found what I was looking for, and stared at Marc, in shock.

"The engine type doesn't match what's listed here for Flight 4422."

The official FAA records indicated the engines attached to the wings of NC-95422/35966/45-513 were model R-2000s, not 2SD13Gs. I didn't know what a 2SD13G was.

"This could be the correct wreck," I said, "but we'll have to do some more research. I don't think this'll be easy."

Disbelievingly, Marc said, "Everything else seems right so far. Could it really be a different plane?"

"It could be. Everything else adds up. It's the right place, correct blade model, and generally seems to be the right type of plane. We'll figure it out somehow."

Disappointed, we continued our search toward the west. We located hundreds of other parts, photographed some, and admired the workmanship of yesteryear's engineers and mechanics.

Down at the glacial stream, open sinkholes surrounded us. Frigid streams appeared out of nowhere and disappeared into the ice. Caverns of ice, plus huge, curved, undercut ice ledges and smooth-surfaced caves, created a sort of endless ice palace. We became hoarse yelling back and forth over the roar of the near-freezing water rushing in the streams in the glacier and on top of the volcanic grit-dotted ice.

On this glacier, the meandering streams on and beneath its surface acted like knives cutting slowly through butter. A complicated natural action, the undercuts are formed when the streams turn a corner and slice back under the ice. Sometimes the rock-laden ice ceiling above can no longer support the weight of ice and rock and simply breaks off and collapses, burying everything underneath. Then, as the broken ice melts away, the volcanic material that was inside or on the top of the ice either washes away or forms a surface of sand and rock, covering whatever else was buried. It's a natural action that releases parts of the plane from the ice then reburies some of them. The scenario is water on ice, with the only variable being temperature.

We continued on and 250 feet upstream from where we found the data plate we came upon another stunning discovery: a WWII radial engine with twin rows of seven cylinders. That was consistent with a Twin Wasp radial type engine, the same style as Flight 4422's engines. Specification of Pratt and

Whitney, the engine's manufacturer, indicated this type of engine weighed 1,605 pounds when new. Of course, this one had sustained major damage.

As I snapped photos, I saw that the seven cylinders on the front were smashed as though they were made of putty; a few were partially sheared off. Piston rods dangled from the cast-iron block, but the blue paint on the P & W engine gleamed like new. The data plate was missing, and the engine had only recently melted halfway out of its glacial encasement. It was possible that the data plate found downstream by Marc might have come from that engine. So far, it was the only piece of the wreckage we'd found that might identify or eliminate this plane as Flight 4422. It was a crucial linchpin to the entire project.

WE WERE CERTAIN we were the first persons to see the engine since the plane crashed. More than likely, the engine was frozen in the glacier well before either of us was born. We were viewing and touching history.

Aircraft parts were strewn all about. It was sad to see such beautifully fashioned creations of aeronautical engineering haphazardly tossed about in this cold, lonely place. Like teardrops, water dripped off fuel pumps, pieces of plastic, wire, and aluminum. A few threadbare shreds of clothing lay about with no way to identify what kind of clothes they were or whom they had belonged to. With 30 people having perished, it would have been reasonable to expect to find human remains. But we'd found none: not an arm, leg, or bone; absolutely nothing human.

Next we came upon a nose gear strut 100 feet northeast of Propeller Point. The strut's beautifully chromed surface was as good as the day it was made and only a little of the bare steel at one end showed signs of rust. Moving it slightly, I guessed it weighed at least 75 pounds.

The strut was a six-inch-diameter piece of pipe, about 20 inches long, with walls at least a half-inch thick. With the landing gear retracted, the strut lies in the under-nose area of the plane. One end of the strut was crushed longitudinally toward its center, like a soda can stood on its end and partially crushed by stepping on it, clear evidence the DC-4 to which it was attached had endured an incredible front-to-back impact.

The excellent condition of the strut was amazing. Pure steel normally should have been completely rusted over after 50 years. But this was a glacial time capsule. Like the engine, the strut had been recently released from the glacier's icy grip. Circular compression damage around the strut indicated that the plane had impacted straight into whatever it hit, consistent with Flight 4422's supposed direct impact with the cliffs.

"Looks like there were no last-minute heroic turns, no last-minute pull-ups, no warning," I said.

Marc nodded. "At least no one suffered."

Then the skies suddenly opened up and the rain grew heavier. The already near-freezing temperature dropped dramatically. Although there was a tremendous amount of information just waiting to be studied, Marc and I were exhausted. We had to stop our search and concentrate on just a few special parts that might tell much of the story and possibly identify the wreck.

We set up our tent just off the debris field. After a 10-minute rest break, we bundled up in all of our waterproof cold-weather gear, marked the tent's location with a large fluorescent poncho, and headed back into the middle of the glacier. We placed wands along our way in case the weather turned worse and visibility decreased.

At the stream-bed crossing, we marked both sides with several bright orange wands, and then jumped across the six-foot-wide stream. Climbing up the other side was difficult, requiring the use of our ice axes. Once on top, we found a dinner knife with the handle missing. "INSICO" was stamped at the base of the blade. That was the type of butter or dinner knife used on airliners of the 1940s. A four-foot section of aluminum airframe and several electrical pumps and rusted electrical relays lay on the stream's north side.

The ice and near-freezing wet rocks made for slippery footing as we examined numerous pieces of aluminum aircraft skin and all kinds of metal scraps, steel pipes, wires, and black rubber hoses. One large piece of aluminum aircraft skin had dark blue and red paint on it, consistent with Northwest's 1948 paint scheme.

Fifteen minutes later I stopped in my tracks, dumbfounded. An undamaged, 16-foot, single-piece aluminum ladder lay adjacent to a pair of 1950s or 1960s European-style collapsible crampons, the kind that attached to leather climbing boots. Just east of the ladder was a 30-foot-long rope. It was not state of the art equipment and the rope was neither nylon nor polypropylene. It might have been manila rope. Someone had been here before. But had that someone been on the wreckage site for the purpose of finding the wreck? Or was it just coincidence?

I examined the ladder and saw that the rungs had scrapes consistent with someone wearing crampons. Climbers use ladders to cross glaciers. Maybe it was just some climbers who had these implements here. But it certainly seemed suspicious that this ladder, rope, and crampons were within 400 feet of Propeller Point, and they happened to be right in the middle of the north half of the debris field. Marc said, "More than likely it was a gold chaser."

From the north side of the stream, we could see the entire debris field. It was more than a mile long and a half-mile wide. In terms of research capability, maybe it was bigger than the two of us could handle.

Clouds billowed above, the rain fell harder, and fog formed over the glacier. Totally immersed in our search, we hadn't noticed that three hours had passed while we combed the northern area, investigating and recording parts of the wreckage. The excitement left us somewhat dehydrated, wet, and very tired—the perfect recipe for hypothermia. We had to stop.

It was a good thing we'd marked our route with wands. Without them, it would have been easy to become disoriented in the low visibility. From the glacier's north side, Propeller Point was nowhere in sight. We hiked back following the wands. We climbed back up the south side of the icy valley. Finally, in the general area of the tent, the orange poncho emerged as a beacon in the fog and rain. It seemed farther away than we had remembered, but it was home.

It was only 4 p.m. but dark enough to be 9. Marc fired up the camp stove, heated water for hot chocolate, and we munched on energy bars and slid into our nice and dry sleeping bags. Marc went right to sleep, but I worked on the data associated with the search for another 15 minutes, then tried to sleep. I could only catch a few occasional winks; my thoughts were a whirlwind of the day's events. I tried to analyze the whole picture and determine the next appropriate steps. That engine identification plate baffled me. Everything else in the debris field was consistent with 4422, but the data plate's engine model number didn't match. My records indicated 4422's engines were R-2000s not 2SD13-Gs. Had we missed something in the airplane's archives? As raindrops pelted the tent, I flipped back through the 20 pages of aircraft records we'd brought with us, but found no answers.

The plane's location was perplexing. If this was Flight 4422, it was farther down the glacier than we had thought and had been moving about 30 percent faster than we'd figured. The glacier must have surged greatly in the past. Maybe the earthquake of 1964 had something to do with it. There were no records about this glacier on Mount Sanford to tell for certain. Scientists throughout the world had been recently discussing climate change. Maybe that was at the root of the fast glacial movement. At 6 p.m., the rain still showed no signs of letting up and I finally dozed off.

IT MAY HAVE BEEN the sound of the wind or just a gnawing, uncomfortable feeling that Marc had, but at 7:45 p.m., he sat up straight, woke me and said, "We have to leave." I suggested we wait until the rain stopped. Totally exhausted, I went back to sleep, reasoning that we still had several days to use in the valley. Marc tried to go back to sleep but was too concerned about the changing weather. It wasn't long before I too sat up in my bag. Something was wrong—things outside the tent had changed. I listened intently. The cold wind was shrieking across the high ridges. In the valley, the rain continued to pour. Now, I felt it, too: an unshakable feeling that said, "Leave, NOW."

"Marc," I said, "what was that you felt a while ago?"

"That we have to leave. NOW. I still feel it!"

"In this heavy rain?"

"I just know we have to go. And I'm very worried about the Super Cub."

"Okay," I said, "let's roll."

Marc is always meticulous while packing and unpacking; everything in its place and accounted for. Not this time. I couldn't believe it. For the next 10 minutes, his actions were like someone in an old high-speed movie reel. He was out of his bag, boots put on, sleeping bag stuffed, backpack packed, and already taking down the tent before I was even out of my sleeping bag. I was still putting on my rain-soaked boots when he said, "I'm ready to go. What's taking you so long?"

He was standing there like a camouflaged statue in the pouring rain. Quickly, I joined him.

We left Propeller Point at 8 p.m. in a miserable mix of cold, soaking rain and intermittent snow. The mythical site vanished into the darkness as we descended over a treacherous glaze of slush on the misty, moisture-laden glacier, the dim beams of our flashlights cutting through the dark and fog. Behind us, the debris field returned to total darkness. The 30 men would have to wait just a little longer.

Using my crevasse probe, we poked around and avoided questionable places on the glacier. We negotiated a descent over an unknown route, attempting to find an exit point. This is where the mentally mapped image I had of the crevasse fields and the glacial hills paid big dividends. As Marc had flown the Cub during our many over flights, I noted rough headings to avoid some of the largest glacial ponds, crevasse fields, and the most dangerous, steep cliffs of ice. Most important, I had spotted several potential exit points.

During my solo trip in 1995, I had taken note of exactly where an ice bridge spanned the gap between the glacier and a point just below the place we'd named Green Point. We had seen the bridge on the climb up as well. Hopefully, it would still provide a link to the grassy slopes off of the glacier. But we had to find it first.

We were two miles down the glacier from our tent site when things changed. A loud shotgun-like blast, followed by a roar, shook the valley and broke the monotonous sounds of hiking in the dark. We had heard that sound before—in 1996. It was unmistakably an avalanche careening down from the highest parts of the cliffs. We couldn't tell how far down the glacier it traveled. All we could do was listen to the invisible freight train, and keep moving— fast. Our destinies were now out of our hands. The ice would determine our fate. Five minutes later, the roar subsided and the valley returned to its peace, interrupted only by the sound of raindrops mixed with wet snowflakes and our boots on the trail.

Based on the volume and length of time we had heard the avalanche, it may have gone far enough to cover the newly discovered debris field. It may have reached the area just below the ice falls, where we had set up our tent and hiked one day earlier. We didn't know and we certainly weren't going back up to find out. It was just one more of the mammoth avalanches that had fallen for centuries and would continue to fall in the future. For the fourth time, we had narrowly avoided a disaster on the mountain. Were we just lucky—or was it something else protecting us?

We were on high alert now, our senses sharpened by the life-and-death situation. We were attuned to everything: the sounds and smells of the glacier, the clouds, the changes in the wind, and to things we felt but did not necessarily understand. We also listened to each other. We still weren't sure what had made us leave the glacier in a pouring rain at seemingly the worst time possible. Was it luck or was it fate? An hour after leaving the debris field, I yelled, "It's right here; we nailed it."

Like a bridge over a moat, a thin, hundred-foot-long ice and rock bridge spanning the chasm below came into view. It crossed over treacherous moraine and frigid running water. If the bridge broke while we crossed it, we would slam onto piles of sharp volcanic rock and into the freezing water 30 feet below. We decided to cross one at a time.

I went first, approaching the bridge cautiously as though walking on glass. As I stepped onto it, the ice groaned under my weight. I barely breathed, taking one step at a time. After five minutes, I reached the grass. Marc, who weighed a little less than me, moved across quickly. With sighs of relief, we were free of the icy clutches of the glacier.

THE CHANGE WAS IMMEDIATE. The solid ground covered with wet grass felt like luxurious carpet compared to the uneven, jagged, boot-piercing surface of the glacier. Taking no break, we hiked quickly for almost two hours, scurrying down the green slopes and muddy game trails toward the entrance of Cub Valley. The rain didn't bother us. Soon, we smelled the lush vegetation—a welcome change from the dusty, concrete smell of wet rocks on ice.

A few lingering rays of the setting sun broke through the clouds as we stumbled the final steps into camp. The Super Cub was still there with inflated tires and no fabric torn by bears. Relieved, we dropped our backpacks onto the grassy surface. A misty glow of evening's twilight provided the only light to help us erect the tent.

My watch showed 10:45 p.m. when we finally had the camp set up. Although wet and tired and still 50 miles or so from the closest civilization, we felt right at home. It was far too late to fly out; taking off in the dark from the mountainous back country is one sure way to die.

Inside the tent, warm and dry in our sleeping bags, we had time to contemplate the day's events. Marc asked, "Was it real or was it just a dream up on the glacier? Did we really find a debris field?"

"I don't know for certain," I said with a snicker. "Let me check."

I turned on my video camera. It squealed from the high moisture content, but sure enough there were images of propellers, an engine, and the data plate. The battery died after a minute. "It was real, all right. It's right there."

But Marc was already asleep. I lay back, exhausted. That night we slept well, hoping for an easy departure the next day.

AT 5:30 THE NEXT MORNING, we woke to find that the blue and yellow tent had held up well under the downpour that had continued through the night. Some of its seams were finally starting to succumb to the rain running down its sides. Water had snuck in through places in the nylon where one of us had accidentally leaned against it. We used dirty socks to soak up some of the drips and small pools of water forming on the floor and in the tent's corners. We also strung a laundry line across the inside of the tent in a mostly futile attempt at drying a few things. Everything was soaked except our sleeping bags.

I slipped out of my bag, put on my parka, and went outside for a peek. The visibility in Cub Valley was less than a fourth of a mile in the rain and mist—a death sentence for flying a light plane in the wilderness. We couldn't even see the hill at the west end. Long, opaque bus-sized lumps of clouds drifted just above the surface. Some people would call it fog. Rather, these were the tops of the layer of clouds in the valley.

When I was a child in Colorado, I watched clouds like these while lying on the grass and wondered how it would feel to be inside them. Now I knew. I could reach out and touch them. Although the temperature was near freezing, the clouds felt warm—kind of like a celestial, somewhat smothering, blanket. And they were pure white.

Occasionally, I caught a glimpse of ice spires jutting up from the glacier. New, pristine snow sparkled on top of them. *Maybe that's how heaven looks*, I thought. In the distance, I could hear avalanches roaring down from the high cornices and snow chutes seven miles up the glacier.

Unfortunately, unlike our 1996 departure from Cub Valley, I couldn't see down the glacier at all. The valley below and the flight route back to Gulkana were totally socked in.

Because we had already used our extra fuel during the diversion flight to and from the lower landing zone three days earlier, we had only enough fuel to make it straight back to Gulkana, with exactly 30 minutes of reserve. We had one shot at taking off safely. If we screwed up, we would be landing in the soft surface of the taiga, forest of small trees, and right in the middle of dangerous bear country. We went back to sleep in our sleeping bags and waited for a chance to escape.

Each hour, dressed in an orange-brown parka and boots, I crawled out of the tent, sprinted 200 feet up the eastern slope of the valley, peered down into the glacial valley below, then returned to the tent. I had found a position from which I could check the weather in the valley to determine when and if we could safely depart. Marc stayed in the tent as the pilot resting on alert so he would be ready to go when and if the weather cleared enough to take off. Piloting the Cub was his job; I did the support functions during this part of the expedition. This is how we had set it up years earlier, and it worked well.

We had made a wind sock of a thin, pink plastic bag taped to bamboo poles. It showed that the wind was coming from the southeast—the wrong direction. We needed wind from the west, or no wind at all. That southeasterly wind created a good tail wind for cruise, but was bad for takeoff and landing. Unfortunately, with winds from the east, we also could experience dangerous downdrafts after takeoff. There was nothing to do but wait, sleep, and wait some more. By noon, the rain let up somewhat and the clouds had lifted up from the valley. For the eighth time, I ran outside, returned, and reported back to Marc.

"I can see about six miles down the glacier toward the Sanford River valley. The wind sock shows nearly calm wind. What do you think?"

Marc scrambled out of the tent and joined me.

Fingerlike strands of clouds still hung in the air and slowly moved across the glacier's surface. A few minutes later, the wind sock shifted a little more. Now a warm breeze flowed up into Cub Valley from the west, actually creating a little headwind that would help the takeoff performance. More important, it indicated that no dangerous downdrafts would come off the ridges to the south or east.

Marc agreed it was time to depart. "This is marginal, but I'm afraid to wait any longer because it's so late in the day. The cumulus clouds might build up at any time and really mess us up."

I agreed. "Let's go."

Leaving Cub Valley was always risky, just a matter of degree. After quickly repacking the plane, we saved gas by grabbing the leading edge of the plane's tail, then pushing it several hundred feet backwards into the weeds to achieve the longest possible takeoff distance. Then we strapped into our seats and Marc started the engine. He allowed it to warm up and gently pushed the power up to the limit, repeating the takeoff of 1996. The airspeed increased and the Super Cub bumped along the makeshift takeoff zone.

Just after liftoff, we reached the edge of the hill on the right, made the hard right turn at the end, then climbed gracefully away from Cub Valley and out of the wash. Within seconds, we were once again skimming 40 feet above the wicked ice spires reaching up from the frozen glacier. A minute later, with several hundred feet of altitude between us and the ice, we were back in the relatively comfortable zone of safety, descending back down the glacier.

Looking back to the east, I could see nothing. Mount Sanford was totally socked in again. Directly in front of us, only the lowest slopes of Mount Drum were in view. Rain spattered against the windshield. Mount Drum's ridges and valleys rose silently into the clouds and out of sight.

As the Super Cub flew directly under the path the DC-4 had taken in 1948, I thought of Captain Bob Petry, Captain James Van Cleef, and First Officer Jehu Stickel, the pilots of Flight 4422. Had Marc and I been with the lost pilots and their plane in the glacier? If so, what did it mean? If the debris field was that of Flight 4422, why had we been able to locate it and, apparently, not the others before us? I watched as Mount Sanford and its glacier disappeared behind the curtain of clouds.

The lower valley had good visibility—Marc could see at least 10 miles and everything seemed to be good. We flew just below the clouds at 2,000 feet over the northernmost slopes of Mount Drum and the flat taiga to the west. Then we noticed we were not making good time. Headwinds! While we were on the mountain, a weather system had moved in and created 20-to-

30-mile-per-hour winds from the west. That ate seven minutes more of our precious fuel, and made us both uncomfortable.

Marc babied the engine and did some quick calculations, figuring the best power setting for the headwind situation at the low altitude. Thankfully, Gulkana came into view just as both fuel level indicators bounced against "E." Marc flew directly to the end of the runway, made a tight left turn to the runway, and touched down. All the practice with Steve Karcz had paid off.

Safely on the ground, we taxied onto the quiet ramp. Marc pulled out the mixture lever, bringing the engine to a stop. We sat there for a few minutes in total silence, relieved at having made it back safely from an incredible few days.

My Cessna Centurion was still there. After calling our friends and closing our personal flight plans we refueled the Super Cub. The aviation fuel kept pumping for several minutes. We had landed with 20 minutes of fuel remaining. Thanks to the required fuel reserves, it had worked out well. I refueled my Centurion, and we took off in both planes and followed our route back to Anchorage.

What a week and what an accomplishment. We were proud and satisfied with our find, but knew we had to ascertain if the debris we found was really from Flight 4422. We had no idea of the immense amount of research that lay ahead, nor did we know what surprises Flight 4422 had in store for us.

Mt. SANFORD   16, 208'

● 1948 Impact site 11,000'

● 1948 Resting Place 8,000'

1997/1998 Debris Field 6,800'   1997/1998 ROUTE

1996 ROUTE

1995 SOLO/1999 ROUTE

○ Cub Valley Landing Zone 4,800'

Flight Path

188

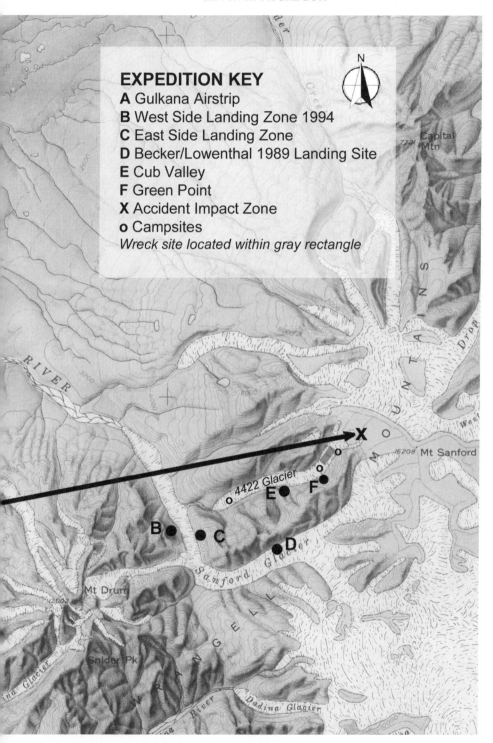

EXPEDITION KEY
A Gulkana Airstrip
B West Side Landing Zone 1994
C East Side Landing Zone
D Becker/Lowenthal 1989 Landing Site
E Cub Valley
F Green Point
X Accident Impact Zone
o Campsites
Wreck site located within gray rectangle

Author with rope found on glacier approximately a half-mile west of the lower ice fall. The rope could have been on Flight 4422 or used by other explorers. *Photograph by Marc Millican.*

The first piece of wreckage found was a small piece of twisted aluminum with pulled rivets, consistent with a large aircraft. However, it did not offer conclusive proof of the discovery of Flight 4422. *Photograph by author.*

This small piece of plexiglass with burn damage on its exterior was most likely part of one of Flight 4422's passenger side windows. *Photograph by author.*

Engine cowling from an R-2000 series engine, approximately two feet long. *Photograph by author.*

This propeller with two blades and hub measures 13 feet from tip to tip and is consistent with a DC-4's propellers. *Photograph by author.*

Original stenciled model and serial numbers remain on the propeller blade after more than 50 years in the glacier. *Photograph by author.*

This propeller hub is from the second propeller found on the glacier. Note the thickness of the broken blade at the arrow. Tremendous shear force would be required to break it in this fashion. *Photograph by author.*

This photograph was captured just as the author and Marc Millican spotted an engine (arrow points to it) in the valley below Propeller Point. A close-up view of the engine is seen on the facing page. *Photograph by author.*

A close-up view of the engine data plate after recovery from the glacier. *Photograph by author.*

A Pratt and Whitney R-2000 engine (modified as a 2SD-13G) as it rests in July 1997 having just melted out of the glacier. This engine's data plate is most likely the one found downstream. *Photograph by author.*

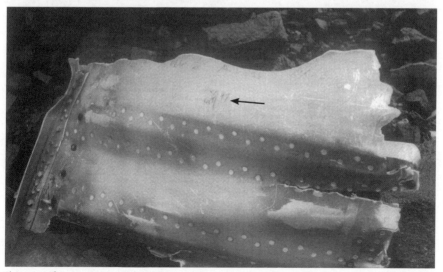

This significant structural piece is about three by five feet, and was a portion of a floor panel coated with zinc chromate paint. Note original aircraft engineer's written notations at arrow. *Photograph by author.*

Author (L) and Marc Millican (R) studying a DC-4 nose landing gear strut. *Photograph by author.*

Marc Millican crosses a glacier stream on an ice overhang. If he had fallen into this stream, with nothing to hold on to, he could have been swept downstream where approximately 300 feet west the stream completely disappeared underneath the glacier. *Photograph by author.*

The serial and model numbers on this piece of a Stromberg engine component provided another way to identify the plane. *Photograph by author.*

The collapsed area on this chromed nose landing strut seen in July 1997 indicates that the aircraft impacted Mount Sanford nearly straight on. *Photograph by author.*

Marc Millican on South Ridge. *Photograph by author.*

Glacier stream valley below Propeller Point where the engine data plate was found in the sand. The engine is upstream a few hundred feet. *Photograph by author.*

Author on South Ridge just before white-out in snow. *Photograph by Marc Millican.*

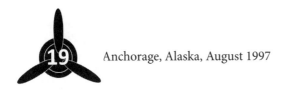

BUDDIES

Safely back in Anchorage, Marc and I reviewed what had happened. We thought, okay, we've located what we believe might be the wreckage of Flight 4422 which, after 50 years, has begun to melt out of the glacier. We always knew there was a chance of finding at least a piece of the wreckage, but were stunned when we found so much. We also knew that the engine ID plate would be one of the keys to a positive identification. There was also a chance the model and serial numbers stenciled on the propeller blade might lead to a positive ID. But we weren't sure where to find such data.

I contacted Northwest Airlines and traveled to Minneapolis in an attempt to get more information about the flight. The employees I talked to said they had absolutely no records of Flight 4422. It seemed odd that such a huge company would not keep files of an accident in which 30 people had died.

Once again, I queried the NTSB and the FAA, but hit another dead end. The engine and propeller serial numbers simply were not on any of the plane's FAA files and the original accident report had been destroyed. The Air Line Pilots Association (ALPA) also tried for more than a year to find records, to no avail.

Another immediate problem was deciding how we should handle the discovery we had made. The most logical thing to do was to contact the National Park Service's headquarters in Anchorage. Despite later media reports to the contrary, that is exactly what we did.

Bruce Collins was the aviation director of the National Park Service in Alaska. Two days after getting back to Anchorage, we met with him at his office in downtown Anchorage and told him we had found a large, unidentified aircraft debris field in one of the national park's glaciers. We mentioned it might be NWA Flight 4422, but didn't mention the fact that we thought the wreck might be the one known as the Gold Wreck. Collins quizzed us about the wreck's age, type of aircraft, and specifically whether there were any human remains. We answered the best we could and told him about the eight years of research that led to the discovery. We also said we would not be able to get back to the site until the next year due to weather and glacial conditions. The access window was limited to one month—July—each year.

Collins said he would like to know about it as soon as we were certain of the wreck's identity, and at that time we should also contact the local park headquarters, in this case, at Wrangell-Saint Elias. If we ever discovered any human remains, we were to contact him immediately. He cautioned us that it probably wouldn't be any big deal and not to expect much. "There are old wrecks scattered all over Alaska and many buried in the national parks," he said.

Our discovery just didn't seem very important to the Park Service. We left the Anchorage headquarters disappointed, having expected an immediate and significant reaction to what we considered an incredible find. Nevertheless, we decided to persevere, but with extreme caution—physically and legally.

THE PROJECT HAD BEEN mentally taxing for Marc and me. To get away from it for a while, we flew Marc's Cessna 185 float plane to a secret fishing location (as they all are) one hour from Anchorage. A clear blue sky reflected on the mirror-surfaced lake as Marc landed on the water. We unloaded our fishing gear and hiked 30 minutes to a fast-running stream where the lake flowed into the sea. Thousands of pink salmon swam upstream to the lake—rush hour for the fish, heading home to spawn. I had never seen anything like it.

The stream was cold, but alive—a stark difference from the cold glacier. You could walk across the stream and come down on a live salmon with each step. After less than an hour of fishing and battling the giant Alaskan mosquitoes and gnats, Marc had three fish. I hooked at least a dozen, but landed a big fat zero, breaking the fishing line every time. A great fisherman I am not. But this was wonderful and one of the experiences that makes Alaska famous.

During the second hour of our stay, a local approached from 200 yards downstream. The big black bear looked as if it might be coming right over to eat our 20-inch fish lying in the grass, or us. After all, it was lunchtime.

"Here comes a great big bear," I yelled.

"Just keep fishing," Marc said.

Unholstering his .44 Magnum pistol, with bullets loaded, he was ready for whatever might happen. It was an odd sight: Marc cast his line with one hand, holding the pistol high in the air with the other. We kept one eye on the bear, one on the fish. I continued to break my fishing line, setting the fish free.

Thankfully, Mr. Bear kept his distance. Splashing in the water, he swatted at fish and grabbed enough for himself. Then he sat back on his rear, looking like a giant teddy bear, and ate his fish for 30 minutes. Finally, he wandered off into the deep grass, never bothering us or our fish. It was a wonderful time; a vivid contrast to the cold glacier some 200 miles away.

Wispy cirrus clouds called mare's tails floated high up in the atmosphere; lower clouds began to form a few thousand feet above the sea, indicating a change in the weather. It was time to leave. We hiked back, loaded the plane, and under a sky of pink and red clouds, flew back to Campbell Lake in the midst of a beautiful Alaskan sunset. On Marc's porch, the aroma of grilled fish soon filled the air. With just the right touch of lemon and some other spices, the fresh salmon provided a wonderful dinner.

From Wrangell-Saint Elias National Park to Denali, to the fishing stream, I had experienced much of Alaska at its finest. Life was good. But it was the lost airliner and its occupants that had lured me to Alaska's wilderness. Far away, in the frigid depths of the glacier, the mystery patiently waited.

Time had run out. Our 1997 journey came to an end. Early the next morning, I drove Marc to the NWA crew entrance. Fifteen minutes later, he climbed the three-story stairway to the Boeing 747 cockpit. The crew started the engines, the giant plane lumbered down the runway, then roared off to Tokyo—over more of the route Flight 4422 had flown 49 years earlier.

A few hours later, I reluctantly loaded my Cessna 210, cranked up the engine, and headed northeast. I planned to follow much of 4422's route by flying via Gulkana, Snag intersection, and Whitehorse. After that, I planned to follow part of the Alcan Highway through Canada and fly south directly to Denver with only two fuel stops: Quesnel, British Columbia, and Great Falls, Montana.

Forty miles northeast of Anchorage, at 10,500 feet, I heard the eerie sound of an ELT (Emergency Locator Transmitter). It's an ear-piercing tone that starts high and descends quickly in about one-second intervals. The sound is heard on the civilian VHF emergency frequency of 121.5 and used only for emergency communications and locating downed aircraft. This ELT signal lasted for only three seconds. I turned the plane around to see if I could locate the ELT signal by figuring out which valley it had come from. I began to hear it again, faintly. The signal works by line of sight; if a mountain is in the way, you won't hear it. I called Anchorage air traffic control on my

VHF aircraft radio and notified them I was receiving an ELT signal. I also told them I would fly southeast toward the Knik glacier—where the signal seemed to be coming from—to investigate further.

Part of the brotherhood of aviation is that pilots watch out for each other. This was one of those times. After flying up a valley to the east, I followed the ELT radio sound, which became stronger and stronger. While flying toward what might be an accident, my mind flashed backed to 1985 when I had been involved in a similar kind of search.

Assigned to Laughlin Air Force Base, just east of Del Rio, Texas, as a T-37 instructor, I was administering a student evaluation ride with Second Lt. Vincent Kramer when the military air traffic controllers, in coordination with the Air Force's operations office and the FAA, directed us to search for a downed aircraft. Thunderstorms and rain had shut down the base for three hours. My student and I were the first to take off after the massive line of thunderstorms finally passed by.

Upon receiving the directive to search, I terminated the check ride. Now we were an official two-man search team in our jet. We followed the heading assigned by air traffic control toward the missing aircraft's last known location. Within minutes, we heard half of the ELT signal on the military UHF emergency frequency, 243.0. After two five-minute "S pattern" searches, we sighted the airplane.

A medium-size twin-engine aircraft had smashed into the hard, West Texas surface. The plane appeared to have crashed upside down and there was no sign of survivors. We notified air traffic control of the location, and within 20 minutes a U. S. Border Patrol helicopter and other authorities arrived on the scene. For Lt. Kramer and me, it was a somber flight back to Laughlin AFB.

Later we learned that, having just dropped off his passengers at Del Rio International Airport, the pilot was the only occupant of the plane and he had died on impact. The NTSB investigation into the accident determined that the airplane's tail had come off in flight, apparently due to inappropriate repairs made years earlier after a gear-up landing. The unfortunate pilot was not at fault. Once the tail was ripped from the plane, the fuselage was out of control. But its pilot may have been fully conscious until the incredible impact.

Now, over Alaska's Knik glacier, I hoped the ELT signal was false. I hated the sound of the ELT. It always brought news that was either good or bad, rarely anything in between. The hair on the back of my neck stood on end as the signal grew stronger. After just a few minutes, I saw a tail draggertype aircraft on a sandy, rock-washed area between two crevassed areas of glaciers. The plane had flipped over on its nose, then onto to its back. There was no smoke or fire.

My heart pounded as I flew low enough to see the entire situation. There was no way I could land the Centurion on the glacier. During my second pass I saw another pilot—he'd landed his own airplane a quarter mile to the east and had just reached the wrecked plane. I flew by the flipped airplane three times, very low, just to the north. I felt much better with the second pilot on the ground. He saw me, backed away from the plane, and, with his arms both straight up in the air, signaled "all was well." Just then, the pilot of the wrecked plane crawled out from the wreckage.

I waved my wings and zoomed at full power back up to 10,500 feet. Once in radio contact again, I notified the air traffic controller of what I had seen and that apparently the pilot of the wrecked plane was safe. The controller said he also had just been notified from another source by radio that the second aircraft was on the scene and things were under control.

My heart rate slowed down and I got that somewhat elated feeling that occurs when something turns out well despite dire possibilities. The sight of that crash and my flight to help out was a bit disconcerting, considering the 4422 project. But this small airplane crash was the way it was supposed to work—a good ending to a potentially bad situation.

I had spent 45 minutes in the downed airplane's area and still had plenty of gas and the required reserve to make it to Whitehorse, Canada. I rejoined my original course and cruised on toward Mount Sanford and Snag intersection.

For the next hour, I held to the exact course and altitude Flight 4422 had followed to Gulkana. Then, rather than flying to Northway first, I took the shortcut directly to Snag—the same path many other pilots had taken in the 1940s. I couldn't help but wonder if the pilots of Flight 4422 had intentionally taken this same shortcut, as implied in the CAB's 1948 report and by many other pilots' conjectures.

The northernmost shoulder of Mount Sanford passed under my right wing as I turned a little more to the northeast, just enough to miss the looming mountain. Maybe that was what the pilots of Flight 4422 had intended on doing, but no one would ever know for certain. This trip revealed just how easy it is to misidentify Mount Drum for Mount Sanford. At cruise speed, only three minutes separate Drum's cascading glaciers and white slopes from Sanford's deadly cliffs. I could see that on this course, in any low visibility or darkness, it would be easy to mistake one mountain for the other.

Originally, I had planned to take more still photos while passing by Mount Sanford, but I had to concentrate completely on flying. The valleys were still socked in with rain and snow—all the way down to 4,000 feet above sea level. The weather in Flight 4422's glacial valley where we had been searching remained just as it had been when Marc and I flew out of Cub Valley three days earlier. If we hadn't left the site when we did, there was a good chance we would have been stuck there.

I thought about the word "home" and how the concept changed for me depending on what was at hand. When we were searching on the glacier, the tent had felt like home when we hiked back to it in the cold rain. Cub Valley felt even more like home after we hiked off the dangerous glacier. After that, nearly 50 miles west, Gulkana became home, then Anchorage and Colorado. Now, the familiar flight controls of the Cessna Centurion fit like a glove. It was another home—one in the sky that I was used to.

That sky took us all over the world. As military and airline pilots, we traveled the globe and more or less made our homes wherever our travels took us. In truth, Marc and I were not much different from the sailors traveling the world or the globe-trotting aircrew of Flight 4422; we were made of the same fabric. Maybe that was the unseen bond among all of us.

Safely past Mount Sanford I turned farther north and, with two fuel stops, flew back to Colorado where a familiar bed waited. This time, I flew quickly, with no weather delays. One day later I landed at Aurora Airpark, Colorado, in the wee hours of the morning. After pushing the airplane back into its hangar and unloading the expedition equipment, I drove to my Colorado home and slept for 12 solid hours.

DURING THE NEXT YEAR, we continued our research, spending thousands of hours poring through archives all over the United States. I reviewed dusty books in several U. S. courthouses and in England. Lawsuit records, probate files, custody reports, and many other documents provided a wealth of information about the plane, the men, their relatives, and their lives.

Growing up in landlocked Colorado, I wasn't familiar with the oceans and sea life. Learning about the SS *Sunset* and the Merchant Mariners, who traveled the world in ships, fascinated me. I learned to love and respect the oceans and men of the sea. I also studied the history of China and Chiang Kai-shek, which I found to be full of omissions and contradictions. The questions lingered: Was there gold or a payroll on 4422? Or maybe something else of treasure-like value?

Marc and I interviewed many people with firsthand knowledge of the events preceding and following the crash. They provided additional important tidbits. I took special note of all the information relating to the passengers, aircrew members, and their relatives. At some point, we knew we would be contacting the relatives. Twice I flew to Haines, Alaska, and interviewed Layton and Lou Bennett. He told me about the amazing bright and blinding aurora borealis he had encountered that fateful night. His 1948 student pilot, Jerry Luebke, confirmed every detail of the incredible story. The Bennetts also said they were sure someone had actually made it to at least part of the wreckage in the 1950s and brought out a propeller hub, but they had no photos or proof.

"I know they brought out something big because they broke the pack board I lent them," Layton Bennett recalled.

Lou said she remembered seeing someone bring back pieces of uniforms and perhaps a pilot's hat.

But those were only sketchy memories from long ago and most of the names associated with those events had been lost to time. It became clear that many people had been to the glacier in search of the missing plane and its rumored treasure.

Marc continued to dig through various archives in Alaska and found information about the growing list of known expeditions. Many people recalled that part of the tail section was visible for years after the crash. But again, there were no photos or other proof.

Then, one day, an interesting piece of photographic archival data appeared.

In December 1997 I again flew to NWA's headquarters in Minneapolis seeking more data regarding Flight 4422. It was five degrees below zero, snow was falling, and the ground was frozen rock hard. I rented a car and made it to the NWA main office, a red brick building with few windows. I met with a clerk in the historian's office. He told me they had no information whatsoever about Flight 4422. I asked if he had any old photos of DC-4s. Thirty minutes later he returned with a box of photos of old aircraft, including DC-3s, Martin 404s, Boeing 747s—but no DC-4s. My visit was a total waste of time. It turned out that the clerk was just filling in for the vacationing historian. He probably didn't even know where everything was kept. I left the office and spent the afternoon researching records in the city's courthouses, but discovered little of importance. I headed back to the archives on the East Coast.

Two months later Marc attended his annual pilot training in Minneapolis and agreed to try his hand at obtaining a DC-4 photo. Between training classes he visited the same office I had gone to. Luckily, the historian was there, and he brought out a large box of old aircraft publicity photos, different from the ones I had seen. Marc reached into the box and randomly pulled out two photos. "These look like DC-4s to me," he said. With a quick glance, the historian confirmed Marc's observation and told him he could use the photos.

That evening, Marc left a message for me saying he acquired two photos of NWA DC-4s and that he had already mailed them to my house in Colorado. A week later, I returned home from an international trip and found a large envelope waiting for me. After lighting a fire and whipping up some hot chocolate, I sat in front of a blazing fireplace and opened the package.

Sure enough, Marc had succeeded. I gazed at two beautiful photos of NWA DC-4s. One shot showed the front and left side of the plane. The other was taken from the left side and aft of the plane, apparently on the tarmac at Shemya, Alaska.

The photos of some of the sailors were a constant reminder that the project was about real people, with real names and families. For the purposes of the project, I didn't see them as dead men, but as friends—aircrew members and Merchant Mariners missing somewhere in the unexplained folds of time. In the center of the photographs of these sailors spread across my front room table, I placed the airplane photos. Light from the fire reflected off the sailors' faces as I examined the photos of the plane. In the first shot, I noticed a number on the side of the plane, just below the captain's window. I went to my office, retrieved a six-inch magnifying glass, and examined the number; "422" was as vivid and clear as it could be. Incredibly, the ghostly photo was actually that of NC-95422, the missing plane.

Stunned, I sat back for a few minutes, and then looked again. There was no question about it. It was real—422 was NWA's abbreviation for NC-95422.

Then I studied the other photo. On the top surface on the right wing, as was common in the earlier days of aviation, were the aircraft's registration numbers in bold print. Though the numbers were barely legible due to the angle of the wing in the photo, I slowly picked out N…. 9….5….4….2….2.

I broke out in a cold sweat. Not one, but two photos of Flight 4422 were in our possession. *What are the chances of that?* I wondered.

One of the other photographs on my table was that of Flight 4422's aircrew. The two captains, the copilot, navigator, flight mechanic, and purser were all there—looking at me. The copilot, Jehu Stickel, seemed to have a special kind of all-knowing grin. I grabbed the phone and dialed Marc's cell number.

I heard his groggy "Hello."

"Sorry, Marc, but I had to call. You know those photos you sent me?"

"Yeah. Do you realize it's midnight here? I have a training flight in the simulator beginning in six hours."

"Sorry about that. Marc, both of the photos are of the plane we're looking for."

"You're kidding." Now he was fully awake. "Are you certain?"

"Yep. Both photos have the plane's numbers on them."

After a long silence, he said, "All I did was reach into the box and pull out two photographs. I only made sure they were DC-4s. The historian didn't even look at them closely, other than to see they were DC-4s."

"These are photos of NC-95422," I said.

"This is getting pretty spooky. Make some copies and send them to me in Anchorage. I'll have a look at them later. Right now, I've got to get back to sleep for the simulator. But thanks for letting me know. Anything else you need me to try to get here in Minni?"

"Nope, you really did a bang-up job getting these. Good luck on your simulator check ride."

"Okay, thanks. See ya' later."

OVER THE NEXT FEW DAYS, I made several phone calls from my house in Colorado. Identifying the engine data plate got top billing. Nothing in the plane's official FAA files contained the serial number. Perhaps a positive identification could be made through peripheral research. I thought we might be able to identify Flight 4422's engine serial numbers by comparing those of sister aircraft built and modified the same time as NC-95422. P & W issued engine serial numbers sequentially when manufactured. Perhaps, numerically, we could bracket the right serial/production numbers for the engines.

I called some experts on radial engines and the FAA. I was chagrined to learn that in 1948 the serial numbers of the engines were not included in the FAA's official airplane files. That year and earlier, the individual engine serial numbers were only required to be documented in the airline's own company files. In the case of NC-95422, NWA said they had no files. But, the rules changed in 1951. It was a long shot that would take more time, but I sent out requests for the FAA's records of NC-95422's sister airplanes' files—all 14 DC-4s assigned to NWA in 1951, including their 56 radial engines.

Several months later, I reviewed all of NC-95422's registration documents in search of any scrap of information we may have missed. Sure enough, I was astonished when I found something in small print on the bottom of one page. I found the notation: "R-2000s REPLACED WITH 2SD13Gs." I read it again. It was true. NC-95422 had been equipped with the same type of engine model listed on the data plate we'd found. Somehow, we'd missed the notation.

I spent all night looking through hundreds of other pages, trying to find any reference to engine numbers; there was none. I excitedly left a message for Marc with the news. Although it did not prove a positive match yet, it was very good news and one more step toward the truth. With the matching propeller model and now a matching engine model, I knew we were on the right track. Regardless, we still had to obtain a confirmation of the serial number 107507.

Pratt & Whitney (P & W) manufactured many thousands of R-2000 engines during and after WWII. We learned many of them were modified later to become 2SD13Gs, with efficiencies suited to airline operations. It was still possible that two DC-4s or some other large plane crashed on Mount Sanford. We had to learn the truth and learn it soon, because we intended to hike to the site again in late summer 1998 and we needed to know if we were visiting the site of Flight 4422's demise.

IT ONLY TOOK a few weeks to receive the files of NWA's sister DC-4 aircraft dated later than 1951. Those files included each engine's individual serial number. We were making progress.

The engines' serial numbers were consistent in numerical sequence with serial number 107507. They were within plus or minus 100 numbers of the data plate found on the glacier. If correct, serial number 107507 had been delivered about the same time and had most likely been delivered to NWA in the same block of engines from P & W. If NWA still had Fight 4422's original logbooks, the engines' serial numbers should have been in them. I checked with NWA one more time, but the airline again said it had no such records. I felt as though we were closing in quickly on the data plate's identity.

To search for propeller models and serial numbers, I went directly to the source and to its senior propeller expert, Kirk Chamberlain, Hamilton Standard Propellers. He told us that, other than documentation in each airplane's logbooks, there was no way to verify the serial number of any of the propeller blades. Since Northwest Airlines had none of the NC-95422 aircraft records, there was no way to track the propeller serial number.

Chamberlain said, "We've been down this road before. During WWII and subsequent years, tens of thousands of those propellers were manufactured at each of at least eight manufacturing plants all over the United States.

Hamilton Standard's records of those props were destroyed long ago."

That ended our research on the propeller blades. Then, another amazing coincidence happened.

A FEW MONTHS AFTER giving up on the propeller blade research, I was on my rest break while flying a Boeing 767 from Europe back to New York's John F. Kennedy airport. We were somewhere over the North Atlantic Ocean when I began a conversation with a pleasant, unassuming gentleman sitting next to me named Frank McAbee. We talked a little, and then McAbee asked me about the Pratt & Whitney (P & W) aircraft engines on the plane. After a little more pilot talk, it became clear that he was much more interested in jet engines than an average passenger. He finally revealed that he was a P&W representative; in fact, he was one of P&W's top management people in Europe. I had a hard time hiding my excitement. *What are the chances of this?* I thought.

I explained to McAbee that I was working on a history project and asked if there was any way P & W could help identify an engine serial number from an engine manufactured during or just after WWII. He told me he would check into it, but warned me that, unfortunately, P & W's history department was closed during the company's recent cutbacks, so the request would be difficult. I wrapped up our conversation and napped for two hours.

When I woke up, McAbee surprised me and said he had been thinking about my request. Then he handed me a piece of paper with a name and phone number on it. "Try this number, and tell him it was me who told you to call."

Wow! I thought. If this contact resulted in identifying the plane, it could be as good as gold for Marc and me in our attempt to identify the wreckage in the glacier. Of course, there was still another kind of gold that had gotten many people's attention ever since the plane crashed in 1948.

Golden, Colorado, November 1997　**20**

GOING FOR THE GOLD

The legendary flight of gold created a siren call heard far beyond the borders of Alaska that was answered by many. Expeditionary teams that went to the mountain and the 4422 glacier varied widely in degrees of experience and success in their attempts to find the wreckage. In addition to those expeditions in 1957, there were scores of others. It's amazing that no lives are known to have been lost during those adventures.

Some expeditions were "solo" trips; others were large, well-coordinated, quasi-military groups of five or more people. Then there were a few unofficial ventures made up of military personnel. Some expedition members were expert climbers. Others had never set foot on a glacier. Several groups flew to the glacier via light airplanes and landed in several locations, then hiked to the supposed crash area. Some even traveled by horseback.

There were also those men who simply walked the entire 65 to 75 miles through dangerous bear country on trappers' trails adjacent to the Sanford River—all the way from Gulkana and Gakona. Some groups drove special vehicles to cover the hostile terrain. Boats were used by several expeditions to cross the river and streams. Others tied 50-gallon barrels together, forming makeshift barges. The toughest men simply used rubber rafts or waded and swam across the dangerous river, moving skillfully with and around the strong, cold currents.

In surprising acts of boldness, a few of the men actually went to the newspapers before they departed, divulging many details of their treasure-hunting plans. Most of the expeditions, however, were conducted in secrecy and involved as few people as possible. In many cases, decades passed before anyone knew they had even made it to the 4422 glacier.

In 1960, the largest known group attempted to locate the plane. The July 27, 1960, edition of the *Fairbanks Daily Miner* told the story of a team of seven men who carefully hid their objectives, or so they thought. They arrived at Mount Sanford via several trips in a light plane, then hiked up the glacier.

One week into their expedition, their pilot, 18-year-old James Cassady, Jr., and team member Frank Whaley, Jr., 27, flew out to Fairbanks to get supplies. At the supply store, Whaley casually picked up the local newspaper and was stunned to read about himself and his group on the front page. "We'd hoped to do this quietly," Whaley said later in a subsequent response to a reporter's inquiry.

The word about their expedition leaked when team member Ralph Lucas's wife became concerned after not hearing from her husband for several weeks. From Hawaii, she called the newspaper office in Fairbanks and innocently asked if there was any news about the men trying to find the Gold Wreck on Mount Sanford. "The cat was let out of the bag," Whaley said.

A bit miffed at his wife, Ralph Lucas said, "I hardly think she would expect me to mail her a letter from atop the mountain."

That team included Oskar Webber, Roger Bridenburg, Peter Emerson, and Rennie Carson, and later claimed to have made it all the way to Flight 4422's impact zone, but found no wreckage. Meanwhile, the story slowly made its way around the world—all the way to New Zealand.

ONE OF OUR BIGGEST breaks in understanding what really happened on the *Sunset* came from a response to an article titled "Mountain Treasure Hunt to Begin Again." The article appeared in the April 8, 1963, edition of the *New Zealand Herald* and described the endless hunt for treasure at the site of Flight 4422 in search of a lost payroll or cargo of gold. Merchant Mariner Bernie Hopkins, living near Auckland, New Zealand, read the article and wrote to "his worship the mayor," George Sharrock in Anchorage. The *Anchorage Daily Times* printed Hopkins' letter on June 24, 1963.

Hopkins had been the radio operator on the *Sunset*'s sister ship, the SS *Grand River*. He also was the officer in charge of the payroll on the *Grand River*, so he knew how the payrolls worked on the OTC ships. After reading the article in the *New Zealand Herald*, Hopkins wrote to the mayor in an attempt to dispel at least the rumors of a payroll for the Merchant Mariners on the plane. He said, "It was most unlikely that the crew of the *Sunset* was paid in gold in Shanghai as this was certainly not the case with others of its sister ships."

I telephoned Hopkins' home of record in Waiuku, New Zealand. Sure enough, he answered the telephone. Once he was certain who was calling and what the call was about, he told me, "I've been waiting for this call for a very long time."

A man in his 70s, Bernie Hopkins held the keys to understanding the operation of the ship and its crew's financial affairs, ultimately paving the way to laying to rest several of the rumors associated with Flight 4422. Here's how he explained it to me: The *Grand River* left Shanghai five days before the *Sunset* arrived. He was the one who filled out the payroll records for his ship's crew in a procedure identical to that used on the *Sunset*. After carefully reviewing their "squared accounts," the Merchant Mariners signed them, indicating that they would be paid in full when they arrived in New York. There was no sailors' payroll accompanying them on the plane. Hopkins told me "that rumor was bunk". Thus, I was convinced one of Flight 4422's treasure rumors was untrue. However, that didn't eliminate the possibility of some other kind of payroll being on board the plane.

AN INTERESTING PAIR of expedition situations on Mount Sanford occurred in 1989 when six people, not including their bush pilots, made it to the 4422 glacier. The original plan called for one expedition team, but ended up being two, one led by NWA Captain Ed Becker, and the other by NWA Captain Robert Lowenthal. In short, it became a race for the gold.

The original expedition was planned during a layover at NWA's hotel near Tokyo, Japan. Becker carefully outlined his plans to seek the treasure said to be on the lost DC-4 and invited Lowenthal to go with him. After discussing his plan to find the fabled airliner, Becker gave Lowenthal the phone number of the place where they would rendezvous at Glennallen, Alaska.

Over the next several weeks, Becker contacted Hartmut Pluntke, the NWA ramp agent who had heard, firsthand, Tiny Eglund's rendition about the secret box he had seen on 4422 in 1948 and the papers marked "payroll." Pluntke, an experienced glacial mountain climber from Germany, understood he had been invited to be part of Becker's search for Flight 4422.

Upon Lowenthal's return to his home in Florida, he spoke with his wife and decided to go on the expedition. Lowenthal's 15-year-old daughter, Kristi, decided she would like to go, too. Kristi was in great shape. Lowenthal phoned Becker and let him know that they would be going, but also that they would be there one day late. Originally, Becker had proposed to go on a Monday. But, Lowenthal could not arrive in Anchorage until Monday night and wouldn't be in Glennallen until Tuesday. After arriving in Anchorage, Lowenthal phoned Becker who was in Glennallen. Becker sounded surprised when Lowenthal called him to confirm their plans.

Becker asked, "How did you get this number?"

"You gave it to me, you turkey," said Lowenthal.

Becker told Lowenthal he was going to go ahead as planned. Lowenthal told him that he and Kristi would fly in and catch up to him on the mountain.

Lowenthal and Kristi rented a car and drove straight to Glennallen. There, they happened to meet Becker's wife at the bush pilot's office. That pilot was the same bush pilot Becker had used. That pilot flew the three of them, Bob, Kristi, and Becker's wife, on a reconnaissance flight up to the glacier to see how Becker was doing. Becker had a radio with him and Lowenthal spoke to him from the plane.

Becker said they were making fair progress in the difficult terrain. They?—Yes. Unknown to Lowenthal, Pluntke had helped Becker hire two expert mountaineers, Vern Tejas and Rick Ford. Becker's team of three had landed adjacent to the Sanford glacier about 12 miles or so from the ice falls on the glacier he thought was 4422's. However, Becker had left Pluntke behind at Gulkana's airport. Pluntke was disappointed.

From the small plane flying overhead, Lowenthal and the others saw Ed and his two climbing partners high up in the glacier, actually in the lower set of ice falls. They had made good progress. Lowenthal snapped a few photos of Becker and the others in the ice falls. Then, over the radio, Lowenthal told Becker they would fly in the next day and look for them.

Captain Becker was a person who really thought there was gold on Flight 4422. Lowenthal heard another pilot say that Becker had said he was going to use the money to buy Continental Airlines.

Upon returning to Gulkana, Lowenthal anticipated a short time of repacking followed by flying in to land near Mount Sanford. However, the pilot told them he would not fly them in because he didn't think they had the proper equipment for the trip despite Lowenthal's showing him all of their equipment. The pilot wouldn't budge. Lowenthal got the impression Becker had asked the pilot NOT to fly them to the landing zone.

Then, Lowenthal noticed Pluntke lingering at the airport. Pluntke told Lowenthal Becker was being careful about his money and probably decided that he did not need Pluntke. Now, Lowenthal saw Pluntke as the perfect man to join him and Kristi on their own expedition. All they needed was someone to fly them in. That afternoon they located bush pilot Ken Lewis, who, Lowenthal said, "was a pearl."

Early the next morning they flew, one at a time, to the same landing area near the Sanford glacier Becker had been taken to. It was on the south side of the high ridge separating them from the unnamed glacier where Flight 4422 supposedly disappeared. There were now two expeditions, six people in all, in the same area, at the same time, in search of the same airplane, its treasure, and answers to the same burning, mystery-laden questions. This was the largest human population in the valley since the 28-day 1960 Lucas/Weber seven-man expedition. Kristi was the only woman to ever visit the glacier.

After Lowenthal and his team landed, they packed up and started up the steep ridge to the north. Pluntke carried most of the water and food. Since they had heard Becker's team had taken a 30-06 rifle with them, they also carried a 12-gauge shotgun, just for bears. Pluntke's pack was huge but he chugged up the mountain like a locomotive. Kristi and Lowenthal carried the sleeping bags, tent, and shotgun.

They had climbed to about 6,000 feet elevation when the lack of oxygen became noticeable. Kristi was a high school track star so it was Lowenthal who was the one huffing and puffing. Halfway up the ridge, Lowenthal's sleeping bag slipped out of the tie cords and bounced all the way back down the hill. He was already so exhausted that the prospect of repeating that climb was more than he could bear. Kristi took pity on her father and took off down the slope and retrieved it. When she returned about 20 minutes later, Lowenthal noticed that her lips were blue from the exertion. After a 10-minute rest, she recovered just fine. Lowenthal vowed to be much more careful. It had become clear that any mishap could turn into a dangerous situation.

After climbing to the top of the ridge, they had to head east along the top for a few miles. From that point, they had a commanding view. They took a break on the ridge, then started down the other side into the glacial valley.

The slope down from the ridge consisted of talus, more-or-less flat rocks. Some of them were three feet in diameter and slipped easily. Roped together with Kristi at the bottom and Pluntke at the top, the three started down. Suddenly, Lowenthal heard a deep roar—about an acre of loose boulders moved all at once, then stopped. Lowenthal's knees instantly turned to jelly. That roar had scared the hell out of the trio.

Rather than take a chance on the loose talus, they decided to hike down the rock surface immediately adjacent to a notch in the slope. Halfway down the notch, a frozen creek formed a thousand-foot-long ice chute. A short time after starting down, Lowenthal tripped over a rock and flipped over directly onto the ice. Without the rope, he would have accelerated and been seriously injured, if not killed. Pluntke immediately sat back with the rope around his hands and caught Lowenthal before he fell even 10 feet. Stopped, Lowenthal carefully removed his pack, placed it on the rocks next to him, and recovered. Reaching the bottom of the notch, they found themselves on a narrow, flat, grassy path below the talus slopes.

From there, they hiked up the grassy game trails to the spot where the path came to an end and where they actually had to get onto the glacier. That is where they quit. Trembling from the exertion of the climb, with rocks whistling down from above, they realized it was too difficult for them to continue. Every five minutes or so, they heard the roar of an avalanche or rock slide and realized there was no way anyone was going to recover any gold from this glacier.

Although they found no evidence of Flight 4422, they did find a perfectly blue sky and mountains that were a creamy, dazzling white. "It was wild, beautiful, and exciting," Lowenthal said. "That is why I came to this place. The adventure, the sheer enjoyment of being in such an unspoiled spot, and the special joy of sharing this with Kristi was the treasure I was seeking."

On Thursday, August 10, 1989, Lowenthal's group returned to the landing area at 11:30 a.m., just in time to catch up to Rick Ford, the last member of Becker's team to fly out. Becker and Vern Tejas had already departed in their pilot's plane. Pluntke, Lowenthal, and Kristi were all flown out by Ken Lewis and back at Gulkana by 2:30 p.m. The two climbing parties had, unknowingly, passed each other while Lowenthal's team was traveling to the glacier. Regarding the search for gold, apparently there was no further communication between the two climbing parties...ever.

HISTORY WILL RECORD that NWA Captain Ed Becker did in fact make at least two unsuccessful, yet admirable expeditions, in 1989 and 1994, to the site in an attempt to uncover the wreck's secrets. In a 1989 *Anchorage Daily News* article, Becker is quoted, "We took a lot of pictures, but we couldn't see any evidence of the aircraft or the bodies."

The "Raiders of the Lost Aircraft" in Northwest Airlines flyer *On Course* magazine in early 1994 quotes Becker as saying "We were about a half-mile away from the wreckage and I could see parts of a propeller and oxygen bottle. But we couldn't get to the plane. It was just too dangerous because of the threat of avalanches in the area."

A December 1994 article about Becker in the same NWA magazine stated, "His second trip in August 1994 proved futile," and that "Unfortunately between 1990 and 1994, there was a huge rock slide and the wreckage is now covered with at least 100 feet of rock, snow and ice."

Becker also stated there was rumored to be a sealed container with secret war or historical documents, but Marc and I never found any proof of this.

Captain Becker spent a lot of time and money attempting to find Flight 4422. He and pilot Al Sebaka spent many hours flying high and low over the glacier and up and down the high sidewalls, and avalanche chutes. They were so close to the walls of the upper valley near the impact site, Sebaka was afraid they might get hit by one of the huge rocks flying off the rock and ice side-walls. One story circulated that Becker had been hanging out of the helicopter on a rope, but that was not true at all. He did take lots of photos and video.

Although both teams returned safely from their attempts on August 10, 1989, neither was successful in locating the wreck or any of the rumored treasure.

BY 1993, THERE HAD been more than 25 expeditions to find Flight 4422, involving more than 100 people and numerous aircraft.

There were many accidents during these attempts. In 1957, Walter Lyons broke one of his plane's skis. During the trip by two Fort Richardson soldiers, one was injured. At least one plane bent its propeller during the trips. Adjacent to the landing zone on the east side of the Sanford River, just below the bottom of the glacier, there were parts of a wing, a tail, and a bent airplane frame, evidence that one plane was destroyed.

In the early 1950s, one explorer became separated from his teammates. After spending a week searching for him on the glacier, his friends presumed him to be dead, probably having fallen into a crevasse, and then left the glacier and reported him missing. A month later, during a flyover of the glacier, pioneer bush pilot Jack Wilson spotted the man.

Wilson thought he saw a bear eating wild berries at first. Then he noticed the clothes, more like rags tied together, moving in some bushes. That's when he realized it was a man. After landing nearby to check on the man, he saw him running toward his plane. Although the man was starved and half crazy, Wilson picked him up and flew him back to Gulkana. After nothing more than a quick thank you, the man took off walking down the highway. Wilson never heard from him again, but was sure he was the missing explorer. Bush pilot Cleo McMahan had a similar experience regarding a man from a treasure-hunting group McMahan had flown in. Unable to cross a wide creek, the man had gotten separated from his group and was thought to have been washed away. McMahan flew back several times in search of him. Some time later, McMahan found him. He'd grown a long white beard, was wearing gunnysacks for shoes, and had been living on blueberries.

Over the years, the legend of the mysterious treasure continued to grow. In a March 11, 1957, United Press International article titled "Fairbanks Trio to Seek Gold on Wrecked Plane," treasure hunter Harland Lewis was quoted as saying, "The U.S. commissioner at Gulkana signed a certification shortly after the crash stating that the plane carried a shipment of gold the Chinese Nationalists had paid for the tanker. The gold was supposed to include the wages of the thirty crewmen."

This added fuel to the already red-hot rumor fire.

Most of the men and women involved with the expeditions were seeking only the rumored loot. But others had different motives, such as trying to solve the mystery of the lost plane—for personal reasons or for evidence related to insurance claims. Although there were no official reports of the early expeditions actually finding the wreckage, each group of adventurers added to the legend of Flight 4422 and its rumors of gold.

By 1998, Marc and I had learned much about the plane, its passengers, and the mountain. In spite of all of the unconfirmed rumors and the inconclusive items we'd found in the glacier, we still thought there was a chance we might learn the truth.

TWO STEPS FORWARD, ONE BACK

"Houston, we have a problem." On February 20, 1998, Marc left devastating news on my answering machine. In attempting to determine the identity of the debris field, he had visited the offices of the Rescue Coordination Center (RCC) at Fort Richardson, just north of Anchorage. There, he learned of another DC-4 crash on Mount Sanford.

On the official RCC pin map of all aircraft crashes in Alaska; two pins were stuck precisely at the point on the 4422 glacier where we had found the debris field. According to the RCC's computer records, a different DC-4 had crashed at exactly the same coordinates on July 1, 1946—almost two years before Flight 4422's demise. The altitude of the supposed 1946 wreck was 4,000 feet. The report went on to state "at times, some of the wreckage is visible."

Marc was stunned by the report. Previously, we found nothing about any another airliner crash around Mount Sanford. Four days after hearing the message, I called Marc to discuss the new information. With our unique knowledge about the site and Flight 4422's history, we reasoned that the lowest altitude of the wreckage we had located was above 5,800 feet and the remainder of the debris field was spread all the way up another thousand feet. The large debris field we located was consistent with the glacier's movement.

The relatively low altitude of the supposed second wreck—4,000 feet— would place it five to six miles to the west of the debris field—more than halfway to the Sanford River. The account of the second aircraft made no sense and the RCC didn't have any more information about it. We decided there was something fishy about the report.

Although I had found a note in the FAA records indicating that NC-95422's engines had been replaced with 2SD13Gs and NC-95422's engines' model now matched the data plate we'd found, we still needed something to confirm the data plate's actual serial number. A positive identification of the serial numbers was the only way to resolve the two-crash mystery.

Marc and I both wondered how the Rescue Center's information could possibly be that far off. On the other hand, if it was correct, why hadn't we seen this other wreckage? *Could 4422 be on an adjacent mountain, or was the information just plain wrong?* Or, had there been some shenanigans somewhere along the line, with someone intentionally placing this bogus information in the RCC's database? But why? What was so important about 4422? It made no sense.

I called Layton and Lou Bennett in Haines, Alaska. They didn't remember any other big airplane wreck on Mount Sanford. They lived in Gulkana during that time and worked at the CAA, so it was their job to know about such things. It was beginning to look more and more like someone had faked the data about the second wreck and placed it in the files of the RCC.

I asked Marc, "Did I tell you that when I was at AFHRS at Maxwell AFB, the original Aircraft Card records of NC-95422 were missing? There were actually two missing files: the original aircraft record card of the plane military ID Serial No. 35966 and the primary backup file. Do you think someone has tried to make the paper trail of Flight 4422 disappear?"

"I don't know," he said, "but there's certainly enough weird stuff associated with this plane for me to believe almost anything."

I mentioned the rumor about the FBI's involvement.

"That's weird, too," Marc said. "We have to figure out for certain if the FBI was called in to investigate, or if that's just a rumor. My first shot was a bust, but I'll try another Freedom of Information Act request through the Alaskan office of the FBI."

We needed to determine the truth about the second wreck, and soon. It was already March and our window of opportunity to visit the site in 1998 was approaching quickly.

Marc proceeded to query the RCC again, but got no more information to support or eliminate the existence of the second DC-4 wreckage site.

With no reference to any military or civilian accident report, no victim information, no news articles, and no information about when or who had input the information, we figured it had to be an error. The second DC-4 wreck existed only in the RCC computer and as a pin on the RCC's map. It was yet another strange twist for 4422.

Meanwhile, I stepped up my efforts to identify engine serial number 107507. I had already been through the drill with the FAA, NTSB, AFHRS, ALPA, and the Smithsonian Institution. None of them had such records. Pratt & Whitney was my last chance.

After unfolding the little note from Frank McAbee, the P & W executive,

I read the telephone number and the name—Mr. Argassi. I dialed the number and Argassi answered. It was P & W all right, and he was on the company's legal staff. I explained that I needed help in identifying a half-century-old serial number. Argassi said he would like to help, but that it would take awhile to locate someone who could find the records, that is, if they still existed. Then an expert would have to review the records. Argassi assured me he would follow up but it would take some time.

In January, I flew to Alaska and visited the RCC in person to get an idea about the aircraft crash distribution around Mount Sanford. The RCC's map showed two other wrecks on the site—a helicopter and a small fixed-wing airplane, both on the east side of the mountain. Unlike the supposed second DC-4 crash, both had information backing them up. In the meantime, P & W was doing its best to help us. Historian Fred Domer of P&W had been in touch with me, and he seemed optimistic that he could get the engine number records for us.

Marc and I agreed that we had to get back to the site as soon as possible. But, due to the circumstances of the treasure rumors and the fact that the debris field we located was in a national park, we also agreed that it was time to hire some legal counsel. Marc suggested an acquaintance of his, Peter Hess.

A resident of Wilmington, Delaware, Hess was a world-class deep-sea diver and admiralty attorney who had worked with the National Park Service in relation to salvaged ships, abandoned wrecks, and sunken airplanes. What's more, he was a member of the Explorers Club, an exclusive organization of some of the world's leading scientists, mountain climbers, divers, nature photographers, oceanographers, even astronauts. They help each other and promote expeditions and leading-edge research throughout the world.

"If this is really Flight 4422, Peter can help us handle it properly. And the Explorers Club might help with our expeditions," Marc said.

Based on our interviews and common sense, Marc and I agreed that it was probable some other searchers may have seen or even recovered some of Flight 4422's debris. Maybe the wreckage had been visible for a while and then, at some point, disappeared into the glacier. There was a lot of heavy snowfall in the '60s, and the deep crevasses in the two sets of huge ice falls were perfect tombs into which the plane may have fallen.

As for the rumored second DC-4, the Bennetts' word was good enough for us. If anyone would have known about a second crash, they would. But proving something doesn't exist is next to impossible. The ghost wreck of 1946 continued to haunt us while we waited for P & W to provide the all-important answers about the data plate. It was our last hope.

RETRACING TIME AND TREASURE

On March 12, 1998, Marc and I planned to commemorate the 50th anniversary of the crash of Flight 4422 by re-flying its route. The only differences from 1948 were that, due to safety concerns, we would fly in daylight rather than darkness, our plane would be much smaller, and our airspeed would be closer to 110 miles per hour rather than a bit over 200. In addition to commemorating the flight and those who lost their lives, we thought there was a possibility we might discover some unknown clue about the crash while flying the same course.

I arrived in Anchorage just after midnight on March 10. Unfortunately, Marc's Super Cub had developed an oil pressure problem. He'd also acquired a Cessna 185 in 1996, but that plane was still equipped with floats. Neither plane was flyable for this trip. Undeterred, I had gotten checked out and rented a single-engine Cessna 172 Skyhawk from a local aircraft service—the fifth light airplane we had used in the project.

Our warm breath lingered in the frosty 5 degree F. air inside the cockpit as I cranked up the four-place 172's preheated engine. It was 10 a.m., 10 hours ahead of 4422's departure time 50 years earlier. The sky was a frigid pale blue and clear, just as it had been back in 1948. With nearly 200 pounds of survival equipment on board, we took off and flew the same ill-fated path and altitudes of Flight 4422.

Frozen rivers passed underneath. Snow covered the ground as we flew over Sheep Mountain and passed just south of Gulkana. It was minus 20 degrees on the ground—nearly as cold as the minus 35 degrees that fateful night in 1948. By comparison, the cockpit of the Skyhawk seemed toasty warm.

Flying a light plane 50 miles into the winter wilderness over a high glacier in Alaska is risky business even in the best conditions. As we passed Gulkana, the last outpost of civilization, I scrutinized the control panel one more time.

"Oil pressure—good. Temperature—OK. Fuel levels—fine. Electrics—good. Flight controls—no problems. Is it a go?"

"The weather still looks good," Marc said. "No indication of wind. Our FAA flight plan is open and our friends know where we are. Let's go for it. Make sure your survival vest is on tight."

We both tightened our seat belts and survival vests. Then we headed east over the northernmost slopes of Mount Drum. We flew at 11,000 feet—the same altitude 4422 had flown—directly toward 4422's impact point on the deadly rock and ice cliffs of Mount Sanford.

In perfectly smooth air, the Cessna approached the cliffs and the huge mountain completely filled the windscreen. Nothing but steep slopes of rock and ice lay ahead as we bored straight to a point just a few hundred yards short of where the DC-4 smashed into the side of the mountain. We realized that at a quarter mile west of the cliffs, at a speed of just over 200 miles per hour, there was no way Flight 4422 could have avoided the collision; there would not have been enough time.

With little time left before what would have been our own impact, I turned the little plane quickly—away from the deadly slopes. We had just gotten a terrifying close-up of what, apparently, Flight 4422's pilots did not see.

Even in the full light of the mid-winter day, it was easy to understand how the DC-4's aircrew could have flown straight into the night-darkened side of the mountain—especially in a cascade of blinding northern lights. There would have been no last-second heroic turns by either pilot to avoid the collision.

Looking down, we could see where the plane and its victims fell, a half-mile beneath us, onto the glacier. I continued to turn the plane another 90 degrees left in a steep bank, then reduced the angle. We departed the cliffs in a slow, reverent turn, just as the memorial flight's DC-4 full of clergy had done several days after the crash in 1948.

Heading back to the west, out of harm's way, we saw a wintery panorama. The entire length of the glacier appeared as a bluish white, undulating carpet. Icy peaks cast long shadows across the snow and ice, and the late winter sun's low rays reflected off silvery sections of wind-blown ice. Occasional patches of aquamarine blue pierced the surface of glacial tarns.

Twenty-foot snowdrifts covered much of the glacier. In the gleaming sunlight, somehow, it seemed kinder and gentler—almost warm. With a few well-placed red and white candy canes it would look like a winter wonderland. As we passed the west end of the glacier, the dark shadow of Mount Drum shattered the dreamscape, quickly transforming it into an unforgiving glacial tomb. Now we were in the shadow, and the air temperature in the cockpit dropped 20 degrees.

"We'd better head on back," I said. "I think we've pushed our luck enough. If the engine quits or something else malfunctions, we could be in trouble."

Marc agreed, and we headed back into the sunset...to Anchorage.

Far away in Delaware, our lawyer Peter Hess, felt the same way as Bruce Collins, the Park Service's aviation director. Hess was adamant that we positively identify the wreckage before we went any further. Also, if it was indeed Flight 4422, we had to know more about the rumors of treasure on board— before the discovery became public.

Hess warned us, "No matter what you do, there will always be questions about your motives and whether or not you found gold or anything else of value on the site. Those kinds of questions come with the territory and there's no way to avoid them. Shipwreck researchers deal with these things every day. Be ready to be second-guessed and be ready with answers. Be ready for questions about the gold, the passengers, and crew. What about the ship, the SS *Sunset*? You'd better know the facts."

"By the way," he added, "if that debris field is indeed Flight 4422, it's now 50 years old, and National Park regulations make it an official, federally protected, archaeological grave site. You are going to have to get a special use permit to legally bring anything out."

Hess also asked if we had contacted the relatives of the victims. I told him no, but that we were working on it and, so far, had information about relatives of 10 of the men. We didn't think we should contact any family members until we were absolutely positive about the wreck's identity.

Hess thought about it, then agreed and said, "Okay, I'll check into the insurance angle and see what, if anything, was paid out after the crash."

He asked Marc to check with NWA and try to find out who the company's insurance carrier was in 1948.

"That ought to be easy," Marc said sarcastically.

All three of us had our marching orders.

The Internet had been an indispensable tool for researching the SS *Sunset*. It had also helped us find information about the plane, 1948 aviation, shipping, and the men on board Flight 4422. We were able to locate archives all over the United States as well as in England and Canada. However, even that didn't provide everything we needed. The records from the Panamanian-registered Overseas Tankship Corporation were nonexistent.

I contacted many agencies and reviewed records from Lloyd's of London, Clarkson's Tank register, "World Tankers" by Norman Middlemiss, the

"Texaco Fleet News," "Victory Ships and Tankers" by Sawyer and Mitchell, and Moody's Industrial news and records. All told, it took three years of research before I was confident we knew the truth about the ship and its rumored payroll.

I eventually flew to Auckland, New Zealand, where I met Bernie Hopkins, the radio operator on the *Sunset*'s sister ship, *Grand River*.

Arriving in a heavy rainstorm after a 14-hour flight from Los Angeles in March 2003, Bernard "Bernie" Newall Hopkins picked me up at the airport. He was a slim and trim man in his late 70s with thinning hair. Although we'd been communicating for several years by phone and mail, this was our first face-to-face meeting. I spent a wonderful five days in New Zealand with Hopkins and his wife, Glenys. He took me on a tour of Auckland, the west side beaches with pounding waves, and the local museum featuring Sir Edmund Hillary, New Zealand's number-one citizen. During breaks in our tour, he explained how the Overseas Tankship Corporation, owner of both the *Sunset* and the *Grand River*, operated in 1948. I learned, in detail, how the pay was treated, how the men on the ship worked in shifts, and the truth about some of 4422's treasure rumors.

Hopkins explained that the radio operator's secondary duty included being the ship's accountant, a task for which he received an extra $25 per month. He also told me that among OTC sailors, he never heard any rumors of any gold involved with the *Sunset* or the *Grand River* until he read the 1960 news article. All of the OTC ships used identical accounting procedures. Hopkins described how the pay records were created and what happened to that paperwork at the end of a cruise.

"We made 12 copies of the final pay sheet—known as a square account. Six copies went to OTC's headquarters in New York City on Flight 4422 with the sailors. Each sailor had one copy for himself, and the other five copies were sent to New York by a different route—by regular sea mail. I know this, because I'm the one who actually hand-made those records for my ships and mailed them," he said. "The task was very time consuming, it was all done by hand."

He continued. "As the radio operator officer, I got paid extra to make the square accounts. Most of the sailors had automatic pay allotments to home."

He explained that although the sailors could have received a small amount of spending money from the ship's cash account (known as a "draw"), OTC sailors were never paid in full until they returned to OTC's headquarters in New York. Upon arrival in New York, usually at LaGuardia Airport, the sailors were paid $50 U.S. Then, they went to OTC's U.S. head office in Manhattan where the payroll office resolved any outstanding issues with each sailor's square account. Each man picked up his remaining pay.

Hopkins continued, "In China, we radioed ahead for a little spending money in local currency. That was a lot of cash at the tremendously inflated rate at the time of 300,000 to 500,000 of Chinese currency to $1 U.S. We left Shanghai three days before the *Sunset* docked."

I was amazed when Hopkins gave me a carbon copy of the 1948 pay document from his own ship. He had saved them for half a century. Then, he showed me how he used to tap out messages in Morse code. This was the same way he'd communicated with other ships long ago when he'd learned of Flight 4422's demise.

I'd located many of the *Sunset's* sailors' probate and lawsuit records. Those backed up Hopkins' statements. The victims' heirs received the pay earned by their relative sailor as shown on the square accounts referred to in legal documents.

While in New Zealand, I also spoke with one of Hopkins' acquaintances, Vic Young. A marine photographer in Seatoun, Wellington, New Zealand, Young had provided us with the only known photos of the SS *Sunset*. Harbormaster Captain Michael H. Pryce, also from Wellington, was an invaluable source of information regarding the history of the *Sunset* and the OTC. Captain Pryce confirmed much of the *Sunset's* past and added some valuable information about a sailor's life on other T-2 tankers. With these facts in hand, I wished my new good friend farewell and boarded my plane at Auckland airport.

After flying back to Colorado, I corresponded with many museums and maritime agencies via email, telephone, and letters. I also got information from the Steamship Historical Society of America, the Independence Seaport Museum in Philadelphia, the Mariner's Museum in Virginia, and the Naval Historical Center in Washington, D.C. All helped us learn the *Sunset's* history. Everything we learned dispelled the rumor of the ship being sold to Chiang Kai-shek after the March 12 oil and ship delivery.

THE *SUNSET* HAD a complicated history that had taken her through four different owners: U. S. government, CALTEX, Tokyo LPG Carrier Co., and the Tanker Leasing Corp. She had four names: SS *Sunset*, *Caltex Lisbon*, *Toyosu Maru*, and finally just *Toyosu*. The *Sunset* arrived in Shanghai in 1948 and then operated from Shanghai for five years. In 1952, the *Sunset* was renamed *Caltex Lisbon*. The next year, OTC ceased operations and all 53 tankers assigned to OTC were transferred to the direct ownership of Caltex. On February 4, 1962, the *Caltex Lisbon* was temporarily stored at Innoshima, Japan.

The *Caltex Lisbon* was finally sold in January 1963 to the Tokyo LPG Carrier Company. The new owners immediately converted her into a liquefied gas and crude LPG oil carrier. The work was done at the Hitachi SB and Company yard at Innoshima, with technical support assistance from Caltex. Just before her maiden voyage as an LPG carrier for Tokyo LPG, on November 10, 1963, the *Caltex Lisbon* was rechristened *Toyosu Maru*. In 1968, the Caltex fleet was abandoned by Texaco. Roughly half of the ships kept their Texaco names. The others received names associated with Chevron.

In 1977, in an unusual circular journey of ownership, the *Toyosu Maru* was transferred to the Tanker Leasing Corp. Overseas—a Panamanian company. The ship was again registered in Panama and flew the Panamanian flag. The Maru was dropped from her name, thus becoming simply the *Toyosu*. In 1977, she underwent one last rebuild and had her engines replaced in Hiroshima.

The *Sunset*, aka *Caltex Lisbon*, aka *Toyosu Maru*, aka *Toyosu*, finally met her end on August 14, 1984, when the *Toyosu* was sold to Taiwanese ship breakers in Kaoshung, Taiwan. The ship was demolished and her metal recycled. In 1984, a new LPG ship took the name *Toyosu Maru*, and a ship in a different company was christened the *Sunset*. Recycled pieces of the original SS *Sunset* were sold and scattered.

All of our research about the SS *Sunset* clearly proves the ship had not been sold in 1948 to Chiang Kai-shek or anyone else in China. And, it had certainly not been paid for in gold in 1948. If Flight 4422 had any gold or other treasure on board, it was for reasons unrelated to the *Sunset*.

However, our research also indicated that at least one of the roots of the story about the ship being sold to Chiang Kai-shek had actually been started by the *Sunset*'s sailors—well before they had even left the docks of Chester, Pennsylvania, in 1947. A few sailors had told their families the *Sunset* was going to be sold to Chiang Kai-shek—and paid for in gold. Following the crash, those families told that story to the news media.

Once in print, the rumor became truth. There was, however, one small bit of truth to the story: Captain Pryce of New Zealand explained that prior to March 12, 1948, some other smaller ships had been sold to China, and many of the *Sunset*'s crew knew about those sales. Once the sailors knew the *Sunset* was going to remain in China, it was no great leap of logic to believe that it, too, was going to be sold and paid for in gold.

The story seemed to be supported by the fact that OTC kept the *Sunset* harbored in China between its oil-transporting voyages after 4422's accident, giving the impression to outsiders that the ship had been sold to China. And gold was a common method of payment in the years immediately after the war, so the story made sense from that aspect as well.

EARLY MAY 1998 found me flying my Cessna Turbo 210 over the long route through Canada, the ALCAN, and on into Anchorage where I would leave it for the entire summer and use it for that summer's expedition. Weather was a problem again. Avoiding two major weather systems, I made it to Anchorage in only two days. Nearing the Canadian-Alaskan border, I flew the shortcut over Mount Sanford in the opposite direction from Snag intersection directly to Gulkana. Of course, I took a quick look at the debris field on the 4422 glacier.

As expected, the site was still covered with snow—dramatically different from its fully winterized condition two months earlier during our memorial flight. I headed to Anchorage, parked the plane, and flew as a passenger to JFK International to work for a few weeks, then flew back to Colorado.

In late June, I returned to Anchorage with my Colorado neighbor, Jon Shallop, who held a PhD in speech and hearing sciences and experimental psychology. Prior to those involvements, he had worked as a professional photographer. Jon also held a private pilot's license and agreed to help photograph the crash site from the air.

After arriving on a commercial flight, we stayed overnight in Anchorage. The next morning, we donned full expedition clothing, climbed in my C-210, and flew to Mount Sanford. At 17,500 feet and 160 miles an hour, we sucked on oxygen and traded off flying the plane while shooting still photographs and videotape of the west side of the mountain through open windows. From that altitude, we got a full view of the mountain and accident site.

Lower, directly over the glacier's surface, we spotted the propellers and ladder. We couldn't see the engine but observed that the debris field was generally still intact. Flying over the landing zone at Cub Valley we saw that it was already clear of much of the snow. We returned to Gulkana, refueled, then flew southeast to Haines where we again interviewed Layton and Lou Bennett.

Evening found us navigating our way up the coast to Anchorage. It was nearly midnight when we met Marc at the F Street Bar and Grill, our normal post-expedition hangout. We discussed the day's events. Marc grilled us like a murder detective about everything the Bennetts had said, as well as the conditions of the glacier. It had been a long one-day trip. Leaving my C-210 in Alaska, Jon Shallop and I flew commercially back to Colorado. But Marc's and my monotonous and seemingly endless archival research continued.

By the summer of 1998, we had determined that the lost airplane had three different registration designations, the ship had four different names, and the crash site was supposed to have two DC-4s, not one. Things were getting complicated. We always tried to go to the firsthand source of information. In this case, Pratt & Whitney wasn't just a firsthand source, it was the *only* source...and luck was with us.

ON JUNE 25, 1998, the day before I was to leave for Alaska to join Marc for our 1998 expedition, after a flight from Moscow, I landed the Boeing 767ER at JFK. After clearing customs and immigration, I checked my phone messages. The very first one delivered the news I'd been waiting for: "Hi, Kevin. This is Fred Domer, Pratt & Whitney. I located the files. The records show that Pratt & Whitney delivered engine number 107507, a 2SD13G type engine, on April 29, 1946, to Northwest Airlines in care of Glenn L. Martin, Baltimore, Maryland. The sales order was No. 63080 and the contract number was No. 28263. I also have the records of 21 other engines shipped to the same address, engine numbers 107525-107545, shipped April 29, 1946. I've mailed copies of all of them to you. I hope this helps."

"I hope this helps"—what an understatement! This was fantastic information for the project—the Holy Grail of aircraft identification. I called Marc with the news. Now we were positive this plane was Flight 4422. Further confirmation came from the fact that the numbers of the other engines shipped to Glenn L. Martin were numerically consistent with the other post-WWII C-54/DC-4s leased by NWA. We were finally making some real headway.

Marc and I rehashed the facts and reviewed our logic. First, the engine in the glacier was indeed an R-2000 style with two rows of seven cylinders each. Second, the engine supposed to be on Flight 4422 was a Pratt & Whitney, two rows, seven cylinders each. Third, Serial Number 107507 was delivered to NWA c/o Glenn L. Martin prior to July 1, 1946. That R-2000 engine was modified by the Glenn L. Martin Company to become a 2SD13G, the model number on the data plate we found. The mystery of the data plate was solved. If there was another DC-4 on Mount Sanford, we never saw any part of it.

I set out to determine why Glenn L. Martin received those engines and what connection the Glenn L. Martin Company had with Northwest Airlines in 1946. This quest turned out to be easy because the answers were right at my fingertips. My father, Frank McGregor, had worked for the Martin Company in the 1950s and '60s and still had many friends from the company. He put me in touch with one of them—ex-Martin aeronautical engineer George McGee.

During an afternoon meeting, McGee told me all about Glenn L. Martin. "He was an aeronautical engineering genius and aviation pioneer. During WWII and the subsequent heyday of aircraft design, research, and manufacturing, the Martin Company was involved in all sorts of engine and aircraft modifications and research. The 2SD13G was a special model number for the civilian modification done by the Martin Company for many airlines. The modifications made the R-2000s more efficient and reliable for commercial use."

To eliminate any confusion, McGee also told me that the man's name, Glenn L. Martin, in practice, was used as the same name as the Glenn L. Martin Company. Sending the engines to the man was the same as sending them to the company.

I showed McGee the engine data plate information I'd received from P & W, and he confirmed that we had made a good match of the Martin modified engine to NC-95422.

Pratt & Whitney's historical record-keeping had helped solve one of Flight 4422's mysteries with the data plate information. Now we were certain the debris in the glacier was from Flight 4422. But the inconsistency of the records in the Alaskan Rescue Coordination Center's files still bothered us.

"Is there something going on here we don't see?" Marc asked.

"I just don't know. But it seems like we've covered it pretty well," I answered.

We planned another expedition to the site, an expedition that was necessary to provide more answers, more confirmation, and more insight into the glacier's movements. We couldn't take a chance of going public without being absolutely, 100 percent certain we were correct. What if everything had reburied itself and disappeared? Glaciers can do that. We had to get back to the debris field.

Like a knight on a white horse, Peter Hess had taken on some of the enormous research load. After learning about Flight 4422, he had also become infected with its mystery. He told us to head back to the glacier and see what else we could find. Meanwhile, he tried to determine if any insurance payouts or claims were ever made regarding cargo, payrolls, or anything else from 4422. I looked forward to getting back to Mount Sanford's sparkling snow and ice—a welcome change from the endless volumes of archives in dark halls and basements. The research seemed to have no end.

I ARRIVED IN ANCHORAGE in July 1998, my third trip to the city that year.

It had been a relatively dry year so we thought we could go to the mountain a little earlier. Marc had the equipment laid out in neat piles, packed and ready to go as soon as possible. But no sooner had I arrived than low clouds and heavy rain began. It poured nonstop, keeping us on the ground in Anchorage for four valuable days. Ducks and other birds were grounded while we waited for five low-pressure systems over Alaska to lose some of their force. Those lows pumped in moisture from the Gulf of Alaska, producing heavy rain and, at the higher elevations, snow. This created havoc with our plans—we had already learned that the landing zone might be too wet and hazardous in such conditions. So we waited.

The delay gave us time to once again conduct our customary packing ritual where we discussed exactly what we had to take and what could be left behind. Marc's Super Cub has extremely limited cargo space, all inside, behind the back seat—my place. More important, in addition to the structural limits, there is a weight limit based on takeoff and landing conditions. That's especially critical at a high-altitude landing zone with a rough surface and only one way in and out. We had to be as light as possible without sacrificing the necessary expedition and safety gear.

We went over each piece of clothing, making certain we didn't take one piece of equipment we didn't need. We actually cut our ropes to the minimum acceptable lengths, counted each day's required food, cast aside all but one set of extra batteries for the photo equipment, and, to my chagrin, carried a minimum number of rolls of film.

The give-and-take was serious but, at times, laughable. Good-natured bantering was an important part of the process.

"I'll leave three rolls of film if you'll go with only one roll of toilet paper," I said.

"No way. That's one thing we can't have too much of," Marc countered. "But I'll leave my extra shoes if you'll leave the three rolls—and one more ice screw."

"Okay, that one's a deal. You leave three packs of gum and I'll leave one empty water bottle."

It went on like this for hours until we agreed on each item.

ONE EVENING DURING dinner at the local Chinese Kitchen, I said, "Marc, this might be the last time we go there totally secretly. Things might change a lot once we announce this. But this has been one fantastic adventure and I thank you for that."

"It's been a great run and I don't think we could have formed a better team," Marc said. "Let's make this year's trip a safe one and nail it down once and for all. It would be irresponsible to keep it secret."

Between courses of Chinese food, we rehashed every detail: Bernie Hopkins' information, the square accounts, the probate files, the true history of the SS *Sunset*, and the fact that at least three of the treasure rumors were not true: The ship was not sold until many years after 1948. Therefore, payment for it could not have been on board 4422. The sailors were not paid any significant amount of money when they got off the ship. They were to receive their final pay in New York. There was no sailors' payroll on board Flight 4422. And, the rumor of any gold in the sailors' pockets was not true other than the possibility they may have been carrying spending money, just like anyone else would.

"What about the rumor of Chiang Kai-shek smuggling gold out of China on 4422?" Marc asked. "It doesn't look like much of a possibility to me. The timing is all wrong."

I agreed. "Chiang was still in power and in pretty good shape in March 1948. He had no reason to be taking things out of China yet. Gold was $35 per ounce in the USA. At the same time, on the black market in China, it sold for $400 an ounce. Someone would want to smuggle gold *into* China, not out."

I had spoken with several Chinese history experts, and they told me there was no indication that treasure had been smuggled out by Chiang in early 1948. But in late 1949, it's clear that Chiang scooped up everything he could get his hands on and took it to Taiwan to start his government in exile, including gold, jade, museum pieces of all kinds, and one of the world's greatest collections of art. He basically looted China. But all of that happened just before Chiang left China in '49, not earlier.

"What about all the stories you heard from the older NWA captains and other crew members?" I asked Marc. "NWA may never admit it officially, but I have talked with many senior and retired NWA aircrew members. Although most all of the stories I heard are secondhand, many NWA pilots told me they really did fly airplanes full of gold, cash, jade, and all kinds of artwork and treasures to Taiwan. They flew out of three different cities in China—loaded to the brink with the stuff. But again, none of that occurred until mid-1949, when Chiang was losing power in China. I never heard anyone indicate that anything from China was on 4422."

"Then how did all of these rumors get started at NWA?" I asked. "There has to be something factual at the bottom somewhere."

"I know," Marc said. "Some of the most credible crew members told me nothing is true about Chiang and Flight 4422, but something of great interest must have been on that flight. It seems no one really knows what it was. One thing for certain, whatever it was, there's no paper trail."

Then I asked Marc about NWA Captain Ed Becker—a pilot who'd been quite adamant there was gold on board the plane and had gone to Mount Sanford in 1989 and 1994 in search of Flight 4422. Marc couldn't explain how or why Becker came up with the story.

We sat in silence for a moment, finishing our egg rolls. Finally, I said, "You know, we can't ever prove a negative. There will never be any way to prove Chiang did *not* have something on board Flight 4422, but nothing indicates there was. Everything we've found indicates there was not."

By then, we were certain that most of 4422's treasure rumors were not true. With that knowledge, we embarked on our 1998 expedition—back to the debris field.

I HAD BEEN ACCEPTED into the Explorers Club in late 1997, and Marc had been accepted several months later. The club puts numbered flags at expedition sites approved by its flag committee; they are returned to the club and used again on later expeditions. Thus, each flag has a colorful record of having been placed at unique sites all over the world. Our 1998 expedition to the 4422 glacier on Mount Sanford was approved and flag number 173 arrived in Anchorage just in time for our trip. We packed it in the back of Marc's Cub—to be flown over the secret site during our 1998 expedition.

We named that year's trek "1998 McCall Glacial Expedition" in honor of Travis McCall, the union steward of the *Sunset's* Merchant Mariners. His wife, Collene, had spearheaded a lawsuit against OTC and NWA. It was McCall's information that I found first with details beyond that in the CAB's report. And, I'd already decided that the first family I would contact would be that of Travis McCall. Of all the men on board the plane, I knew the most about Travis McCall and his family. From what I had learned, McCall took care of the men for whom he served as the union steward and I had gained a deep respect for the man. So, it seemed appropriate to name that year's expedition after him.

JULY 10, 1998, FOUND Marc in the Cub and me in my Cessna Centurion on our way to Gulkana. Once again, we soared over the wild rivers and between the peaks reaching into the infinite blue of the Alaskan skies. Although it must have been the fifteenth time we'd flown the route, we were still infected with the same nervous anticipation and exhilaration of our first flight five years earlier. Gulkana was the point of no return—the place where we accepted or rejected the hazards we knew existed. After that, we were flying back into history—to 1948—into a time capsule encapsulated in ice.

After touching down at Gulkana, Marc shut down the Cub and we strapped into the Centurion then flew to the glacier. Surprisingly, the landing surface appeared dry and acceptable. Returning to Gulkana, we changed planes, repacked the Super Cub, and flew back up to Cub Valley.

The engine ran smoothly as we winged our way over the rivers, lakes, and sub-arctic taiga forest of black spruce, white spruce, aspen, and alder. With only the sound of the engine and rushing air, we continued on to what we thought would be our last visit to the debris field.

Over the years, our emotions had gone from one extreme to the other: The tragic loss of life rivaled the extreme adventure, nature's intense and wild summertime beauty opposed its cold winter harshness, and 50-year-old tall tales were at odds with what we now knew and held so secretly. Soon, we would provide long-awaited answers and allow closure for many relatives.

Heading for Cub Valley's landing zone, Marc spotted several rain showers, including a big one that hung over the zone.

"Not again," he said into the intercom. "We're good on gas; how about we wait a little bit?"

I agreed. This time, I had my glasses on and I really could see that we were okay on gas.

While waiting for the showers to move or dissipate, we flew up the glacier and over the debris field. The two-bladed propeller and the ladder were in view—but just barely. In contrast to the Centurion, the Cub's slower airspeed allowed a much better look.

I could see some significant changes in the glacier's surface. The second propeller was either on or just over an ice cliff to its west, and the engine was not visible. Some intra-glacial surface pools that existed the previous year were no longer evident. The glacial rivers on the surface still flowed, but their courses appeared to have changed somewhat. Thankfully, the ice bridge appeared to be intact.

Fifteen minutes later, the storm moved away and we flew back to Cub Valley. Marc lined up with the landing zone and flew the Super Cub to a bumpy touchdown. The rock-covered surface was still relatively smooth and there were a few inches of water in the little stream.

It was a good thing we had waited the several days in Anchorage—small sand and dirt cliffs along the sides of the stream provided evidence that deep water on other parts of the landing zone had only recently run out. The area was mostly damp, but just dry enough to land. If we had touched down even one day earlier, there was a chance the wheels would have bogged down in the water and mud and flipped the Super Cub tail-over-nose. Things like that happen in the bush all the time.

Large drops of rain began falling just after we landed in Cub Valley at 7:30 p.m. We waited in the Cub for an hour. When the rain diminished to a drizzle, we unloaded our gear, erected our tent, and tied down the Cub. It was Marc's third visit to the valley, my fourth.

Cub Valley seemed familiar now, and comfortable. We knew what to expect of the glacier and wreckage. But the anticipation of being on the site still gave us the familiar butterflies in our stomachs. And although we were convinced that the treasure stories really were just rumors, the thought of some type of riches lingered in our minds—just as it must have for every person who visited the mysterious valley.

We agreed that after this trip, we would make our discovery public. We would no longer be the sole link to the spirits who inhabited the glacier. It was time to share it with the rest of the world and, most important, with the relatives and friends of all 30 men who left this world so tragically.

The resting place of Flight 4422 was special to us. It was a place not only for reflection on the lives of the sailors and aircrew, but for our own lives as well. The project was a child that had grown into an adult. Releasing it into the world on its own would not be easy for us. But we knew it was time.

The night was very cool. In our warm sleeping bags, on the grass and rocks, at the bottom of one of the thousands of valleys in the wide expanse of the Wrangell-Saint Elias National Park, the gentle breeze ruffled the folds of Marc's blue and yellow tent. Gradually, we fell asleep listening to the splash of raindrops in the palm of God's creation, under the umbrella of the infinite arctic heavens. What new revelations would the morning bring? Would everything be in the same place or would the glacier play new tricks on us?

 Mount Sanford, July 1998

CONFIRMATION

It was 7 a.m. The pot's lid quivered and the water hissed as it boiled. A hot, rehydrated, freeze-dried breakfast of oatmeal provided the energy for our hike up the south side of the valley. Under a cold, hazy sky, a thin coating of frost covered the grass, then disappeared as the early morning haze warmed the valley a few degrees.

The sun played hide-and-seek among a few clouds floating near Mount Sanford's summit. Ghostly waves of milky clouds hugged the ridge top and cascaded down from the 8,000-foot south ridge we had climbed in 1996. Carefully examining the expanse of the glacier's surface of rocks and ice, we noticed some ice peaks were gone, while others had popped up elsewhere. We would have to slightly alter our glacial climbing route due to changes in the locations of small lakes and cliffs. This year, we were equipped with high-tech camera gear and a portable GPS receiver. We took our time and made several photo stops.

At Green Point, three miles up the south side of the valley, we located and then crossed the rock-covered ice bridge. The fact that the bridge was intact indicated the glacier had moved little, if at all. Northeast of the bridge was a milky blue 200-foot-long glacial pool barely above freezing. Miniature icebergs floated in the small lake and 1/8-inch-thick surface ice extended two feet from the shore.

We generally followed our 1997 exit route—in reverse, planting wands on the way. We passed the city-block-long, sapphire-blue glacial lake and the volcanic boulder twice the size of a small car. Our route twisted and turned, avoiding dangerous new crevasses. Returning in low visibility would be much safer on our route marked with wands.

Traveling on a glacier can be like walking through a house of mirrors, the reflections changing constantly. Crevasses can form, and disappear, in a matter of days. With a new route marked, we made our way to the debris field.

It was an eerie sight. The blades of the heavily damaged hub with two propeller blades pointed to the sky—two arms of a long-lost friend, consigned to the wilderness. The propeller hub with one blade on its demolished and now seriously rusting hub was buried in rocks 20 feet or so down the edge of a new ice slope to its west. Many more small parts had surfaced on the glacier. Electrical components, small pieces of aluminum in various colors, pieces of wire, and pipes littered the ice. No longer a cliff, nearly 10 feet of ice had melted in just one year. "Where's the engine?" Marc asked. "It has to be somewhere around here."

A 1,600-pound hunk of metal just doesn't disappear. But it wasn't next to the glacial stream where it had been the previous year. We removed our backpacks and Marc scrambled down to look. I climbed back up Propeller Point to search for the engine from above. But it remained hidden. Then I spotted a bump on the hill to Marc's left and I asked him to check it out.

Sure enough, there it was—nearly buried under several dozen fist-sized rocks that had rolled down from the 25-foot hill of ice and rock. Now it was much farther from the stream's edge than it had been in 1997. Using a tape measure, we discovered the engine hadn't moved at all—the stream had. Now we began to understand the dramatic glacial dynamics in action.

Between 1995 and 1998, we had learned a lot about the glacier. It was complex. Most of the glacier's action was in the jumbled mess of rock and ice at its edges where it cut away and moved against the mountain. Melting was significant; at its west end near the Sanford River, there was approximately 20 feet of rock on its surface. At the top of the glacier, near the ice falls, there was as little as six inches. Surface and subsurface rivers of water gushed through and on the surface of the glacier, carrying melted-out airplane parts down into the glacier, releasing others from the ice.

In just one year, the stream near the propeller had sliced its way 15 feet to the south and seven feet down into the glacier. Propeller Point was under attack by the same stream. Sooner or later, Propeller Point would disappear, along with the parts of the plane.

As I stood just north of Propeller Point, I noticed a slightly familiar aroma in the air. Marc smelled it too. I said, "That's tobacco."

"I think you're right. Let's look over there," Marc said, pointing to the west.

Sure enough, lying between two six-inch rocks was a small wad of tobacco in a crumpled piece of red paper. I immediately recognized the paper as being from a pack of Lucky Strike cigarettes—the same brand my grandfather used to smoke. Someone's cigarette pack had remained hidden in the glacier for 50 years—all that was left as a sign of the life someone had once lived.

Then Marc pointed to something reflecting the dim sunlight far off to the northeast. He walked toward it as I guided him, keeping an eye on the object. When Marc reached it, he discovered a twisted, foot-long piece of aluminum. He picked it up and noticed some letters stamped on the bottom: N W A.

"This is obviously a piece of something that was modified specifically for Northwest Airlines," he said.

We had no idea what part of the plane it was from, but it was a second piece of evidence that identified the wreckage as Flight 4422. We were making progress.

Satisfied the glacier would remain relatively stable and the airplane's parts accessible for at least one more year, we returned to Propeller Point and temporarily planted the Explorers Club flag No. 173, commemorating the exploration of Flight 4422.

Then we hiked back to our campsite south of the debris field. Just before getting to the tent, we came across the clip from a clipboard. It was an artifact that could have come from the cockpit, probably not one of passengers, the flight mechanic, or purser. There was no way to tell. Cockpit instruments might have told the truth about the flight's final seconds. Unfortunately, we found none—most likely because they were destroyed in the initial impact. That clipboard piece may have been the only thing that survived from the cockpit.

We arrived at the tent, climbed into our sleeping bags, and went right to sleep. The sound of avalanches falling from the slopes hidden by clouds hardly fazed us anymore.

At 10:10 a.m. beneath a clear sky, we left Flight 4422. Hustling down our well-marked route, we arrived in Cub Valley at 1:15 p.m., reloaded the Cub, and took off an hour later. After refueling at Gulkana, we flew back to Anchorage. The day had started on the remote glacial site of the famous crash, and by 5 p.m. we were back in the big city. It had been our fastest-ever expedition and our information about the site of Flight 4422 was now solid.

We stayed up until 3 a.m. the next morning, discussing what we had learned. We noted the debris positions we had plotted in 1997, a quarter mile below the ice falls where we had located those first three tiny pieces of wreckage. Comparing the locations to the 1998 plots, it was clear there had been no huge glacial movement. But the glacial stream's deepening at least seven-and-a-half feet and other items appearing out of the ice was proof and meant the glacier was melting in place on its surface—in addition to its receding at its bottom, near the Sanford River.

There were two possible reasons why the glacier was giving up some of its secrets. The first was the earth's climate, which was and is undergoing a warming trend. That may have initially caused the glacier to melt and slow its movement. In reviewing NASA photos taken in 1957 and 1972, we saw that the glacier had been forming less in recent years and much of the older snow packs had melted.

A second, more sinister, possibility was heat from the 1964 earthquake which caused a tremendous amount of damage in Alaska. Since the earthquake, the Wrangell Mountains have been steaming away near their summit, possibly from newly formed deep cracks in the earth's surface. The upper parts of some old glaciers that covered large areas on Mount Wrangell just south of Mount Sanford, are now barren of snow with some rocks getting as hot as 180 degrees F. on sunny days. This may have caused a slight local temperature increase, thus adding to a melting effect. There was really no way to know which had caused more of the glacier's demise.

Scientific answers about the glacier would have to come from real scientists and glaciologists with comprehensive data bases, research capabilities, and funding. But our rough-cut field work had resulted in locating 4422. No one could refute that.

Among the newly visible parts in 1998, one hydraulic line near Propeller Point protruded six inches from the ice in 1997; in 1998, its entire three-foot length was visible. It was embedded in the ice at roughly a 30-degree angle, and at least 10 inches of ice had melted away in one year. Overall, to us, it looked like about a foot of surface ice melted away between July 1997 and July 1998.

The NWA ramp agent, Hartmut Pluntke, called it correctly. During an interview in early 1997, in his thick German accent, he told me, "I know that parts are coming out of the glacier now." He, Bob Lowenthal, Bob's daughter Kristi, and Ed Becker with his team of two guide-climbers had been in the right place but at the wrong time—about eight years too early.

Thousands of aircraft parts less than an inch in length or width indicated the aircraft had exploded with a tremendous impact. Debris had spread over an area roughly a half-mile wide. Although it is clear the debris also spread vertically on the cliffs, it was impossible to measure the vertical distribution because we couldn't know exactly where parts landed or fell immediately after the impact. Nor is it possible to know exactly how they were affected by 50 years of glacial movement and travel through two major ice falls. What's more, the site would continue to change.

Now, a new question faced us: Would anyone believe we had found the famous plane? After all, it was a unusual project laced with rumors of treasure, mystery, and intrigue. We had to confirm the site's existence, indisputably and properly by legally recovering identifiable parts. We knew we had to do it right. For that, we learned we had to go to the National Park Service headquarters at Wrangell-Saint Elias National Park. And we needed our attorney, friend, and fellow researcher, Peter Hess, at our side. The site of the wreckage was complicated by the fact it was inside the boundaries of a wild, remote, and beautiful national park.

As of March 13, 1998, Flight 4422's site was federally protected as an archaeological site—even though park officials didn't know it existed anywhere but in legend. Peter Hess warned us that we had to tread carefully or the entire project could be shattered.

Following the directives from Alaska's National Park Service Aviation Director, Bruce Collins, we were ready to present our information to park officials. Our plan was to set up a meeting and simply walk into the park service office, tell them we'd found the wreck, and get a permit to retrieve pieces of the wreckage to legally, 100 percent, prove it existed. We assumed it would be a simple task. Boy, were we wrong.

A LONG COLD WINTER

O ur plan for that year was simple. We wanted to meet with the Park Service officials and get a permit to recover pieces from Flight 4422's wreckage during our planned 1999 expedition. But, due to our hectic lives, we had difficulty coordinating a time to contact the Park Service to set up a meeting.

That winter was a frigid one for Marc and me in many ways. Outside of Alaska, we continued to conduct more research. It was very difficult—harder than anything we had done previously. Drastically different from the demanding hiking and technical flying, for me, it was the emotional aspect of my research that proved to be so challenging. It was new territory.

As a commercial pilot, I flew mostly to the freezing Scandinavian countries and Moscow that winter. It seemed as if every time I went home to Colorado, it too was enduring cold snaps and deep snow. Marc was in Anchorage, New York, and Tokyo much of the time—all cold. In Alaska, large amounts of snow fell, and it was during that winter that the conflict in Kosovo and the U.S. military's role there intensified.

Although I'd retired from the Air Force Reserves in 1997, Marc was still active and constantly on pins and needles, faced with the possibility of being called up to serve full time. That would have meant taking a huge pay cut as well as spending months in the military—far away from Alaska and Mount Sanford. A recall to active duty for Marc would ruin our chances of completing the project in 1999.

As it turned out, Marc's unit was never called to active duty. However, he still had to spend most of his days off at Travis AFB due to the squadron's heavy flying schedule. Meanwhile, all of my spare time went to researching Flight 4422. Marc helped me decipher different facets of the project, including family trees, but the most important thing he could do was to be available for one last trip to the glacier in late July. I didn't want to do another solo flight and climb, especially since the debris field was in the center of the glacier.

Despite all the complications, we were determined to complete the project in the best manner possible. We were not going to let anyone stop us and we were not going to let anyone down—especially the relatives of the 30 men lost in the crash. They had already waited long enough.

In probate courts in New York and New Jersey, I again found myself sifting through old files. In sailor Jackie Jamele's file I found some personal items as well as the documents required to settle his estate. As I turned a page, I saw a copy of a postcard he had sent and I had to fight off that choked-up feeling in my throat. I could almost hear the young sailor's Jersey accent as I read the postcard:

Mr. John Morrisey
764 47th St.
Brklyn, NY USA
Liverpool, Jan 13, 1948
    Hi Ya Unc, How's things? Over here in Liverpool, England and everything is OK. We are having a good trip so far. I ought to be home in about a month if everything goes right. So till the next time I'll say so long. PS: This Liverpool sure is powerful luck (good fortune due to a stopover at an oil terminal very near a major city and all the excitement there). Jack.

Later in the same file, I found a copy of the last letter Jamele ever wrote—to his brother, Vincent, who was stationed with the Army in Germany. I again had a hard time controlling my emotions as I read:

Jan 29, 1948
P.F.C. Vincent Jamele c/o Wolfgang Red Cross
Hanau, Germany
S.S. Sunset Jan 21-48
    Dear Vin, Thought I'd drop you a line so here it is. How've you been big brother? Guess that Jan 30-1948—will be your 22nd birthday. Sorry I can't send you anything, but next year will be different. Maybe we will have a couple beers together. How'd you spend Christmas and New Years? I spent them both at sea. We left the states the 22nd of Dec (Chester, PA). This trip is supposed to last about three months. And the money is pretty good. We draw 200 dollars a month straight wages and 1.50 an hour overtime & 2.50 a day for every day we are in mined

waters. So I expect to make between 6 & 8 hundred this trip. Right now they expect this trip to last only about two months. We've made two ports since we left. We picked up a load of crude at Curacao in the Dutch West Indies and delivered it to Liverpool, England. Right now we are headed for Aden Arabia then to Biriene Arabia. From there, to Shanghai China or Manila. When we finally do get to China we leave the ship there and fly home by plane. So all in all this is a pretty good outfit to work for. Hear you started to send home an allotment. I think that's the best and smartest thing you've done since you've been in the Army. It's just too bad you didn't start earlier you would sure have a piece of dough saved by this time. So what have you been doing with your self? Make any more rates in that man's Army? Hell bent. I'll sign off now hoping everything is all right with you. So till I see you again which I hope won't be long. I'll sign off as ever, your loving brother, Jack. PS: A very happy birthday to you Vini.

Jamele's letter, like other cards and letters I found in a few sailors' files, reminded me of those I had written during my own years of military service, traveling around the world. Apparently my emotions were evident, because the Brooklyn Probate Court clerk asked me if something were wrong. He was astonished when I showed him some of the old news articles and explained the significance of the files and letters. I told him about the project and explained what his archives meant to it. Then he read each letter. When he was done, he said, "I really hope you can find the answers to all of this. I've been here for many years and this is the most meaningful file I have ever handled."

That clerk was typical of the hundreds of understanding, patient librarians, clerks, and archivists who maintain reams of historical documents.

Then, as I continued paging through Jamele's thick file, I made a stunning discovery: reverse-printed, white on black, copies of Flight 4422's passenger and crew manifests. Next to each passenger's name was the weight of his baggage. Could this be the missing manifest? It was almost as though, from beyond the grave, the sailors themselves were helping us discover the truth about Flight 4422.

On other pages of the death file was the proof about their pay. Just as he had advised his brother, Jackie Jamele had allotments going home and the remainder of his salary was paid into his estate. The second set of square accounts had made it to New York by regular mail, just as Bernie Hopkins claimed. Jamele's and other sailors' probate files showed that, without a doubt, none of the *Sunset's* sailors had collected any substantial money upon disembarking from China.

I glanced at my watch. Damn, I was going to be late for work if I didn't leave immediately. The copy machine worked hard, burning copies as quickly as possible. When it was finished, I ran outside and hailed a taxi. I offered the driver a $10 extra tip in advance and we sped through Brooklyn, in and out of traffic, via the Van Wyck Freeway to JFK airport. I signed in for my flight to Frankfurt, Germany, with 10 minutes to spare.

Over the next eight months, I found much of the same story in several other sailors' probate files. Those old pages contained all kinds of information. Dates, locations, and verbiage on letters and post cards helped me map the *Sunset's* journey and bring the sailors to life. What's more, the names and addresses in those files would provide vital information for locating living relatives. We had deliberately decided not to contact the relatives until we had to. We still thought is best not to disturb anyone until we had legally identified the wreckage as that of NWA Flight 4422.

I also discovered lawsuit records archived in Manhattan. Several of the families of the sailors had sued Overseas Tankship Corporation and Northwest Airlines. Many of the suits were settled out of court, but years later, several of the others were tried in court and decided in favor of the airline and ship company. The files contained a lot of information and more clues about where we could locate the victims' relatives.

By January 1999, Peter Hess, Marc, and I had everything we needed to go to the Park Service. We knew the majority of the ship's and airplane's histories. We concluded the CAB report from 1948 was accurate. We also had learned much about the 30 men on board. Their lives were spread before us like an artist's fresco.

IN JANUARY 1999, I finally got a chance to call the Park Service to set up a meeting. I telephoned Jon Jarvis, superintendent of the National Park Service, Wrangell-Saint Elias National Park. He was not there, so I left a message. About an hour later, he returned my call. Jarvis quickly took control of the call and threw up a wall of resistance. He told me, "Every five years or so someone has tried to talk the Park Service into allowing an excavating of the glacier to find the wreck and its fabled treasure of gold, or whatever." He continued, "We have all kinds of rules, protections, and penalties available to the Park Service."

I was stunned, but forged ahead.

Explaining our project, I told Jarvis we were writing a story about the mysterious plane, its legends, myths, and truths. We knew the entire history—an enduring story that was part of the park's history. I tried to make him understand that the project was a historical endeavor, not another gold hunter's quest. But Jarvis ignored me and said, "We want no publicity about the wreck, because that will just bring more."

He obviously viewed us as another group in the parade of Flight 4422 treasure hunters; we would learn later that the park indeed had a chronic problem with such people.

The superintendent continued, "I am not wasting my time for a meeting until we have a proposal and each and every one of the families agrees on it. We'll just have our attorneys sit down and talk with you and it will all be very clear."

Looking at the faces of the sailors and aircrew on my table, I interrupted him. "But what about the history and the lost plane stuck up there in the glacier? What about the men and their families? What about their memories and questions about the crash? Don't they deserve answers? Don't you care about them?"

Jarvis really did care about the relatives—it just hadn't come through that way to me at the time.

WE WENT BACK and forth for about 20 minutes. Near the end, I felt that at least I had explained, very clearly, that Marc and I were extremely serious about it being a true historical project. But I also made certain Jarvis knew these two pilots weren't going to give up easily. And I hid my hole card: I didn't reveal that Marc and I had already found 4422. It just didn't seem to be the right time.

Then the ice seemed to crack just a bit when I said, "We know all about Captain Ed Becker's expeditions and our project is not anything like his. We don't plan on using a helicopter and we have not talked to the news media."

Captain Ed Becker had gone to the *Anchorage Daily News* on August 9, 1989, and told them how he was going to search for the plane and its load of gold. Through some Alaskan contacts, Marc had learned that Becker's actions and the newspaper article had seriously pissed off the Park Service by creating the kind of publicity it did not want.

"Well, that's a start," the superintendent said, chuckling, loosening up just a bit.

The protector, Jarvis, and the researcher, me, agreed to meet on February 2, 1999, at the Wrangell-Saint Elias Park headquarters at Copper Center, Alaska. Maybe we were getting somewhere after all.

PETER HESS TRAVELED from Delaware to accompany Marc and me to the meeting. We desperately needed our Philadelphia lawyer and his expertise in working with various divisions of the federal government, including the National Park Service. Hess had previously helped other people recover entire airplanes and research shipwrecks in various stages of disintegration from lakes, swamps, and mountainsides—major historical projects.

Years earlier, Hess was the attorney in a lawsuit against the National Oceanic and Atmospheric Association (NOAA) in the case of the Civil War ship *Monitor*. The successful action forced NOAA to allow non-NOAA scientific photographic research on the sunken ship before it disintegrated. Prior to the lawsuit, NOAA had placed the *Monitor* off limits to everyone except its own personnel. Hess was on the side of exploration and documentation of historic items before they disappeared forever.

Our own governmental agencies, at times, seemed to hold a view opposed to his and in the case of 4422, to Marc's and my view as well. Unfortunately, it appears that our government sometimes gets tied up in its own red tape and misses the big picture. Having been in the military a long time, Marc and I understood that very well.

Our initial goal seemed simple. We planned to pass along all of our information during the meeting with the Park Service. We also thought we could set up a framework for working with the Park Service at the crash site and possibly arrange some kind of memorial. But we knew we were on unfamiliar legal ground—we knew nothing about permits. Hess was well versed in such matters, so we basically put the matter in his hands. Neither Hess nor we two pilots were going to let any bureaucracy screw it up. The victims and their families deserved closure and to have the project done right.

Disappointed with the results of my first telephone call to the Park Service, we were wary of what might happen once the government became involved. In preparation for the February meeting, we were loaded for bear. With Peter Hess on our side, we couldn't lose.

IT WAS SUPER BOWL Sunday 1999 when I walked out of the terminal at the Anchorage International Airport. Big flakes of snow coated my dark suit and tie. In contrast, Hess showed up 30 minutes later dressed like a gold miner from the Klondike—beard and all. He instantly fit in as an Alaskan from the bush. Marc was already there to pick us up in his white Jeep Cherokee.

The previous evening, Hess and I had attended the annual California Wreck Divers Convention near San Diego, where he was the keynote speaker. He gave an outstanding presentation about famous shipwrecks, various historical projects, treasure hunters, and the status of the United Nations Education and Security Council's latest attempt to lay claim to all the shipwrecks in international waters throughout the world. If that ever happens, we will probably never again hear of the discovery of another sunken ship.

Hess was well built, six feet tall, good looking, and in outstanding physical condition. He could easily free-dive (without air tanks) down to 70 feet—more fish than man. Then in his 40s, he wore Benjamin Franklin-type reading glasses for close-up work. He had a worldwide reputation as a diver and expert on maritime law, particularly as it relates to shipwrecks. As a diver, he had used all of the different gas mixtures, and had dived on many famous wrecks, including the *Andrea Doria*. The prestigious Explorers Club, headquartered in New York, was lucky to have him on its board of directors at the time. There could have been no one better to help us with 4422. But that day, at the Wreck Divers Convention, we learned something else that made us even more guarded about the Park Service.

The convention had a few surprise guests: self-made explorer Gerry Freeman; his brother, Doyle; and Gerry's daughter, Jennifer. They had formed the "Lost 49ers Wagon Train Exploration Team." In the blistering heat of Death Valley and the adjacent area, they'd completed 10 years of research and on-site documentation, retracing the steps of a famous lost wagon train. I listened intently because the Freeman team had recently located a circa-1850 trunk in a remote cave—a cave within the boundaries of Death Valley National Park.

The trunk contained many historical artifacts: photos, gold coins, and the diary of William Robinson, a well-documented member of the doomed wagon train. Their discovery made front-page news and morning news shows—an appropriate tribute to the team's historically significant work. So what did this have to do with Flight 4422, way up in bone-chilling Alaska? The discovery's back story held a warning.

According to Gerry Freeman, National Park Service personnel were not at all happy with his find. He had turned the trunk over to them after a week of studying it. According to Freeman, once they had custody of the trunk, officials told him to play down the value of the find. Then the Park Service hired other experts who proceeded to discredit the discovery.

During a television interview, he was asked, "Why did you turn this over to the National Park Service at all? Why didn't you just keep it?"

He answered, "Because it didn't belong to us. It belongs to you, to your grandchildren, to all Americans."

Freeman was correct. Descendants of William Robinson normally would be able to claim the artifacts. However, since the artifacts had been legally "abandoned," the rules of ownership made them the property of the National Park Service. In short, the Park Service discredited the find. To some, it made Freeman look like a liar.

To me, it made no sense, physically or financially, that Freeman and his team would have faked finding any such items in the remote cave. But they were accused of doing just that. A storm of controversy ensued; questions and criticism arose, the results of which are beyond the scope of this story.

What the Park Service did not know at the time was that Freeman had prostate cancer and would die a year later. He had nothing to hide and no reason to hide it. The so-called experts even criticized him for having apparently glued part of the trunk back together.

I am proud to have met Gerry Freeman and his team. To have heard the firsthand story from a man dedicated to learning the truth about people he never knew was compelling. From my viewpoint, he and his team did a superb job. I believe he was a first-class explorer and researcher. Regarding governmental protections versus the individual researcher, sometimes the pendulum swings too far—in either direction. The question uppermost in the minds of Marc, Peter Hess, and me was this: Just who does the National Park Service work for? And who owns the national parks? Answer: taxpaying Americans.

The Park Service's actions in California had formidable ramifications for Flight 4422. If officials were to similarly discredit our research on NWA Flight 4422 and our discoveries, it would have been devastating to everyone involved, including the families of the crash victims. We had no idea how we would be treated. To get an understanding of how relatives might react, I finally called one family member—Merchant Mariner Travis McCall's son, Andrew. We had a wonderful conversation during which I learned one overwhelming point—Andrew wanted to know the factual information about the crash. He wanted to know the truth, have closure, and to know there was appropriate concern for the crash site. The last thing Andrew McCall wanted was to have a mockery made of our efforts. It was with those feelings that Marc, Hess, and I met with Jon Jarvis and his five employees two days later.

IT TOOK SIX HOURS of driving over ice-and-snow-covered highways to reach Gulkana the night before the meeting. We nearly crashed only once, during a nicely executed 360-degree pirouette on the ice with Marc at the wheel. We left only two pieces of the Jeep's bumper in the hard wall of plowed snow. After spending the night at our favorite hotel, the Caribou Inn, we showed up at 9 a.m. at the Wrangell-Saint Elias National Park headquarters. A U.S. flag flew out front. Several feet of plowed snow created a natural fence around the parking lot.

Like a scene from an old Western movie, the three of us exited the Jeep. Peter Hess snapped his briefcase closed with the sound of a pistol cocking; I slapped stacks of files together, and Marc clicked his cell phone off and stuffed it in his pocket. Like dust in the desert, little whirlwinds of snow spun across the icy surface. Then, we three amigos crossed the parking lot, ready for a showdown at the OK Corral of Alaska.

We checked in with the secretary, who had a quizzical smile on her face as though saying *Do you know what you're in for?* She'd obviously heard remarks in the office about more treasure hunters coming to visit. She ushered us into a large room—the superintendent's office—which had a large folding table in the center. We sat down at the table.

Then our chief protagonist, Park Superintendent Jon Jarvis, entered the room. I thought I heard the jingling of spurs as he walked behind his desk and commandingly sat down. Then Jarvis's compadres walked in one by one, taking their places around the table. The temperature outside was a bone-numbing 24 degrees below zero. For me, the emotional climate inside the office was just as cold.

Jarvis, badge sparkling, boots polished to a high shine, was the epitome of a park officer. In his late 30s, he wore his uniform with a pride that impressed Lt. Colonel Marc Millican and me—now retired USAFR Major McGregor. The four park rangers were equally professional, in complete uniform with guns and enough shiny handcuffs for the three of us.

Across from them, we were armed only with papers, photos, and a story.

A ninth person was present: Geoff Bleakley, the park historian, who sat quietly in the corner. He later proved to have a wealth of park information. He was the one person who exhibited a real interest in the history of Flight 4422. Bleakley even had a Flight 4422 file of his own; the wreck had intrigued him for a long time.

After introductions, the verbal battle began. I launched into the history we had so painstakingly uncovered about the SS *Sunset*, the plane NC-95422, its occupants, and the many rumors about treasure on the glacier. I figured if we accomplished nothing else, at least the National Park Service would now understand the facts behind the legends associated with the plane wreck located in one of the most treacherous areas of the park.

I believe the men of Flight 4422, looking down from their resting place only 60 miles away, would have enjoyed the rhetoric and jockeying for position, and the discussion about any recovery.

Superintendent Jarvis maintained a staunch protective wall, while we three amigos touted the potential positive results of a joint project wherein history would be told, families would have closure, and most likely, an airing of the facts would rid the park of its gold-seeker problem. Our passion was clear.

After the history lesson about Flight 4422, I explained the possibilities of recovering identifying parts of the airplane. Jarvis didn't seem to hear. He stuck to the book and listed the rules about what we could *not* do, and if we did, he again cautioned, "Our attorneys will have a talk with you."

The other Park Service members listened intently, intrigued at the unusual drama. It was probably one of the most interesting meetings they'd attended in a long time. We later learned they were extremely curious about why we had an attorney with us.

Among a laundry list of items, Marc and I were told by Jarvis there was no problem with visiting the area and taking photos. However, he also explained exactly what constituted an archaeological site, what qualifies as lost and found items, and so on. Although Hess had already pointed this out, Jarvis explained that the debris field would have become an archaeological site 50 years after the accident—March 13, 1998.

Marc asked Jarvis to explain the official rules if, say, a person found a piece of paper lying on the surface of the ice.

The chief ranger in attendance, Hunter Sharp, chimed in at this point: "You can photograph it and read what it says. But you cannot touch it, move it, or disturb it in any way. You can't even turn it over to see what is on the other side."

"But this wreck is on and in a moving, changing glacier," Marc said. "That makes no sense at all."

Jarvis stepped in. "Those are the rules."

Marc was perplexed, as was I.

AS THE MEETING WORE ON, it became clear that the Park Service didn't really want anything to do with Flight 4422. Hess continually jumped in, running interference for Marc and me as the meeting became a bit confrontational. The climate in the office seemed to have soared from frigid to super-hot. So we took a break.

I was torn. I was pissed off, disappointed, and close to tears. As the primary researcher for the lost men and their families, I thought about the years of hard work we'd put in and remembered the things I knew about each of Flight 4422's victims. Marc and I decided to become more resolute than ever and decided that no one, including the bureaucracy of the National Park Service, was going to stop us from achieving our goals regarding Flight 4422. The missing men and their relatives deserved better.

Out of earshot of the Park Service people, the three of us discussed what had happened so far and decided this was a cat-and-mouse game. We were the mice and the six cats had all the weapons. Although we didn't feel completely right about it, we made a decision we believed was in the best interest of Flight 4422 and its men: Unless asked directly, we would not reveal the fact that we had already found the wreck. Six months later, events would prove that we had made the right decision.

Throughout the rest of the meeting, we listened carefully. Between the lines, we learned that apparently no one but us knew that remnants of the famous airplane were coming out of the ice. In fact, the Park Service folks were unaware that the debris field existed. But we also became aware that there was a very good reason they wouldn't know: Jarvis and his team had an enormous responsibility managing more than 13.2 million acres of national park and preserve wilderness. The Wrangell-Saint Elias National Park combined with the adjacent park area in Canada forms the largest protected area in the world. There are many old airplane crashes scattered across the area. Sometimes the park's personnel have to make tough calls balancing the wilderness, history, researchers, and wreck hunters. Even today, aircraft disappear without a trace in Alaska and its parks.

Marc and I sympathized to an extent—we are both great supporters of our national parks—but this was a personal battle about 4422. At one point, Jarvis said, "Every few years, something about the Gold Wreck comes up. Among other things, people inquire about the supposed treasure. A year or two ago, we had a guy from Canada who simply walked in and asked how he could get to the wreckage and recover its gold."

It was clear Flight 4422 had been a lingering problem for the park, and to simply not deal with it at all was easier than confronting the problem. In retrospect, one can only imagine how shocked they must have been when we presented our detailed history of the wreck.

I continued with carefully chosen words: "Due to our research, we are quite certain we know right where the famous wreck is. Also, at this point we have not found any documents or other proof indicating there is, or was, gold, cash, or other treasure on the plane. It seems to be an unfounded rumor."

At the time, to have revealed the location of the crash would have only led to a bureaucratic quagmire that would have smothered the entire project. In addition, we were concerned that, once revealed, our hard-won information would be leaked by those in the room. A leak could be devastating; the last thing anybody needed was another "wreck rush."

Our goals remained steadfast: find the truth, provide closure for the families, and commemorate those who had lost their lives. After 50 years, very little information had come to light about the men who died in the crash. It was the stories of gold and treasure that were published and had whetted the appetites of would-be adventurers.

Nearing the end of the tense one-and-a-half-hour meeting, Jarvis and Hess finally got down to brass tacks and discussed what it would take to get a special permit to recover artifacts to positively identify the airplane—that is, assuming we could find it.

Jarvis stated that, among many other archaeological requirements, his only specific guidance was what the previous superintendent had written. That policy stated that a permit would be granted only if we could locate and get permission to disturb the crash site and recover parts of the plane. That permission had to come directly from *all* relatives of the victims. Hess immediately snapped back, "What kind of requirement is that? There is nothing anywhere in the regulations like that at all. Kevin and Marc have already told you the situation and you know it's utterly impossible to comply with your request!"

Obviously, this was new ground for the superintendent. I pointed out that in light of the research already completed, it would be next to impossible to find all the relatives, assuming they still existed for each victim. "We're quite sure we can find relatives for about half of the men," I said, "and I have no question they will go along with the project."

Silence engulfed the room. After a few moments, Jarvis acquiesced in the name of preservation, research, and protection. "I will consider a permit application if you can get half of the victims' families' authorizations and comply with a list we will provide about some other basic archaeological requirements."

One of those requirements to obtain the permit was for us to obtain a $5,000 performance bond. It made absolutely no sense to Marc or me, but that was part of the deal.

That was good enough for us. We had the tiny opening we needed to get a permit. After discussing some other minor items, we left the meeting relatively happy with the new edict in hand. Things were good.

PRIOR TO THE MEETING, I had already spoken with one of the relatives, Andrew McCall. I made a second phone call to Andrew. During that conversation, it became clear that many of the questions about his father's death had been left unanswered. A gaping hole remained in the family's history; there had never been any closure. It made my resolve greater than ever.

Andrew McCall told me that his father's body had never been recovered. Then he invited me to visit him and his wife at their home in Tifton, Georgia. Several months later, I did just that. On a warm Georgia evening, I met with him and several other family members at the McCalls' home. He even took me to see the monument constructed half a century earlier in memory of his father. The epitaph reads: "In memory, Travis M. McCall, He Rests on Mount Sanford, Alaska."

His wife, Collene, rests interred beside the monument. I left a bouquet of flowers at the site.

I felt the conversation with Andrew McCall was a barometer for what we might expect from the members of other families. Prior to the meeting with Jon Jarvis, we had decided to delay talking with any other family members until everything was lined up for the project's final segment. That way, we felt, if we were unsuccessful in getting a permit or the project stalled for some other reason, we would not have created any discomfort for the families. Basically, it was going to be one way or the other: We would either be able to tell them the final complete story, or we wouldn't bother them at all.

But now things had changed. The Park Service's edict required us to contact the families immediately. The project's course had now been set, but we were no longer at the helm. It now lay in the hands of the relatives of Flight 4422's victims. They could easily have put a stop to our effort of 13 years and counting. But, that is not what happened—far from it.

During all the years of researching, hiking, and flying, Marc and I had been looking through a one-way mirror, without anyone looking back. Now a window of opportunity opened through which a stream of information would flow after being hampered for 50 years.

Flying back to Mount Sanford in formation. To improve safety, the explorers used two planes during some of the most risky flights. *Photograph by author.*

Marc Millican looking up into lower ice falls and up toward impact point. *Photograph by author.*

The impact spot high on the west face of Mount Sanford at 11,000 feet. Layton Bennett flew to the site the day following the accident and saw four distinctive black spots where the DC-4's engines' oil splattered against the mountain after impact. This slope is at approximately a 70-degree angle to the horizon. *Photograph by author.*

A dinner knife with the NWA logo was found north and west of Propeller Point and helped to positively identify the debris field. *Photograph by author.*

Marc Millican (L) and author with Explorers Club flag number 173 at Propeller Point in 1998. The glacier that Flight 4422 fell into is in the background with recent snow. *Photograph by author.*

A piece of wood carved with tree and coconuts appears to be from a curio box and may have been purchased by a sailor or an airman overseas. *Photograph by author.*

Attorney Peter Hess worked hard to help the explorers obtain a permit to recover pieces of the plane. *Photograph by author.*

Layton Bennett with Luscombe airplane that he used in search for 4422 in 1948. *Courtesy Layton Bennett.*

Author with Ken Crewdson, the radio operator who was the last person to talk with Flight 4422. *Photograph by Marc Millican.*

Pro Montaineer Vern Tejas (L) with Alice Becker and Northwest Airlines Captain Ed Becker. These men, along with Rick Ford (not pictured), went to Mount Sanford in 1989 to find the wreck of Flight 4422. *Courtesy Al Sebaka.*

Northwest Airlines Captain Robert Lowenthal (L) with his daughter and Hartmut Pluntke (R) tried to find the wreckage of Flight 4422 and its rumored treasure in 1989. *Photographs by author.*

Merchant Mariner Bernie Hopkins, the radio operator and pay record chief on the SS *Grand River*, a sister ship of the SS *Sunset*, helped research the mystery of the treasure possibly on board Flight 4422. *Courtesy Bernie Hopkins.*

Fred Ewan, who with his dog musher partner, Jake Butler, planned to find whatever treasure was on 4422, but canceled the expedition due to avalanche danger. *Photograph by author.*

Author with Helen Cameron who saw flames from 4422 on March 12, 1948. *Photograph by John Shallop.*

1950s bush pilots Cleo McMahan (L) and Jack Wilson get together in 2000 to recount when they flew gold seekers to Mount Sanford. *Courtesy of Sally McMahan Pollen, author of* Papa was a Bush Pilot.

Engine No.	Order No.	Number	T	e m	Purchaser	Shipped	Destination
107500	94455	61770			No. West	4-24-46	No. West Airl. Overhaul Base, St. Paul, Minn.
107501	23141	61020			No. West	4-23-46	No. West Airl. C/o Glenn L. Martin, Baltimore
107502							
107503							
107504							
107505							
107506	73141	63020				4-24-46	No. West Airl. Overhaul Base, St. Paul, Minn.
107507						4-24-46	No. West Airl. C/o Glenn Martin, Baltimore, Md.
		63020			EAL	4-25-46	EAL - Hialeah, Florida
						4-29-46	EAL - C/o Glenn Martin, Baltimore, Md.
		63020			EAL	4-25-46	EAL - Hialeah - Florida
						4-29-46	EAL - C/o Glenn Martin, Baltimore, Md
	3141	63070			No. West	4/24/46	No. West Airl. C/o Glenn Martin, Baltimore, Md.
107520	73141	63020			No. West	4-25-46	No. West Airl. St. Paul, Minn.
107521	73141					4/29/46	No. West Airl. C/o Glenn Martin, Baltimore, Md.
107522							
107523	73141	63070			No. West	4/24/46	No. West Airl. Overhaul Base, St. Paul, Minn.

The wreckage of Flight 4422 was identified by Pratt and Whitney documents showing Serial number 107507 (on the line just above the data plate) as having been shipped to Northwest Airlines in care of the Glenn L. Martin.

Dave Edwins (center wearing tie) was the station manager in Shanghai in 1948 and was in charge of loading the plane used for Flight 4422 in Shanghai. Years later, he would recount for the explorers with what he knew about the flight. *Photograph courtesy of Dave Edwins.*

CONTACT WITH THE RELATIVES

What would a person think when I called and said, "My name is Kevin McGregor and I am trying to locate relatives of John Smith. He was lost in a 1948 airplane crash in Alaska. I am part of a historical research project involving this plane."

Each person handles such things in his or her own way. Hearing stories from the families and details of the lives of the sailors and members of the aircrew was unquestionably the most important part of the project. It was also the most emotionally draining. Even so, we looked forward to conversations and meetings with the relatives, extended families, and friends of the people who were lost so long ago without any chance to say farewell.

After 50 years, just figuring out who those persons were was difficult. Although we had names to go on from earlier research, it took several months to learn where many of them now lived. And despite our best efforts, there were some relatives who escaped our search entirely.

I had started searching for living relatives several years earlier while studying the basic information on the accident report, verifying who was on board the plane. That helped in naming the aircrew, but not all of the passengers. Unfortunately, the passenger manifest was not part of the CAB's summary report. Several 1948 newspapers provided a list of passengers, but those articles were full of misspellings and other incorrect information. Even some official reports had the incorrect number of passengers among other factual blunders, such as the type of aircraft. All that changed when I found Jackie Jamele's probate file, which included the passenger manifest, making my research much easier.

Newspapers from the hometowns of the sailors and aircrew members provided some amazingly detailed and personal information. Old lawsuit and probate archives provided even more. Like a military buddy from the past, Jackie Jamele's probate file offered a plethora of information about the other passengers, their families, the plane, and parts of the *Sunset's* route. Through the Internet, I did a wide search of names, sometimes a thousand or more, and made the closest family match I could.

Then I called all kinds of relatives. Often they were able to lead me to the closest living family members and also provide some details about the crash. When I struck a positive contact, I contacted him or her first by phone, then by follow-up letters and printed information. We quickly learned that getting right to the point worked best.

The first telephone call to each person was the most difficult. Unfortunately, due to the prevalence of sales calls made at the dinner hour and the numerous calls requesting donations, people have become guarded. Caller ID and blocking devices created significant barricades.

Many distant relatives hung up on me. Some said, "Don't call again—I know this is a sales call," or "This can't be true," or "What kind of cruel hoax is this?" or "Who's trying to take advantage of that airplane crash?"

However, for roughly every 40 unsuccessful calls, there would be one associated with the correct family. On those rare occasions when I was right on, not one victim's relative ever hung up.

It was difficult, frustrating, and humbling—all at the same time. There were many conversations with people who immediately said things like, "I'm very happy to finally know someone cares so we can learn the truth" or "By all means, find out everything you can and I want to know every detail" and "We always wondered what really happened."

These conversations became most significant to the entire project and spurred Marc and me onward.

For problematic phone calls I tried several methods. I would wait a day or two, then get a different member of a family on the phone and finally be able to get the message across. Other times I just called right back and started with, "This is not a sales call of any type. Please listen to me for just a minute." Sometimes that worked; other times I got a "click." A few went on like this for several months.

Slowly but surely we succeeded. The information I conveyed to the relatives was as complete as possible and revealed that we were sure we knew where the site was. I told the relatives about the rumors of treasure, the crash investigation, previous expeditions, and whatever else they wanted to know. It was shocking information to some of them, yet rewarding in that they were learning the truth. We followed up with more information via letters, faxes, and emails, and promised to keep them up to date on the project.

We pieced together family trees in an attempt to figure out who was who. Finding relatives for one person is difficult, but for 30 was daunting. It was amazing to see how people's lives changed. Name changes, marriages, divorces, separations, moves, and many other events created confusion. But once we were in contact with direct family members, things got easier.

Opening old wounds was a double-edged sword—it awakened suppressed memories while satisfying long-held needs for closure. Some cried on the phone as they realized someone else cared about their brother, cousin, uncle, or father who, in some cases, hadn't been mentioned in decades. There were many times when I had to work hard to keep my composure as I talked with them. Being the link between the living and the dead was a heavy responsibility.

The many hours we spent on the computer and telephone added up quickly. Marc's and my telephone bills became unwieldy monsters as we did all we could to find relatives of those lost on Flight 4422.

Some relatives had nothing good to say about the CAB's investigation, the ship company, or the airline. A few of the relatives, whose families had been involved in the inevitable civil lawsuits, knew about the legal proceedings. But most did not know why some of the lawsuits were settled out of court so quickly. Others treated the lawsuits as family secrets.

One day the 10-year-old grandnephew of sailor Arthur Eilertsen answered the phone. After I made my opening statement, he yelled, "Hey, Grandpa, someone is calling about Uncle Arthur's old plane crash—about where he died in the mountains."

This was one example of how at least a bit of knowledge of the crash and investigation had been passed down in one family. The men entombed in the ice were never forgotten by their direct relatives. But surprisingly, only a few of the families had any knowledge about the rumors of treasure or the subsequent legendary status of the plane, and they knew almost nothing about what had occurred after the crash. Mostly, though, we heard sincere gratitude from the relatives, and that kept us going. They supported us by immediately sending the necessary letters for the Park Service.

I reached Stanley Comshick, the brother of John R. Comshick. He told me he was thrilled to know that someone cared about his brother. For more than an hour he and I compared then to now, discussing the two brothers' roles in WWII, army food, and military life in general. He told me how much he had missed his brother all these years. They had been very close.

Stanley Comshick was the first to send his project approval letter. I only wish that he could have seen the project's completion. He passed away in April 1999. At least he left the world knowing that someone outside the family cared about his long-lost brother. Such experiences are priceless.

Merchant Mariner Jackie Jamele's sister-in-law, Gwendolyn Jamele, phoned us often with more details and thanks for what we were doing. Daniel Rice's relatives sent us emails with information, photos, and appreciative notes.

Following the telephone calls, in which I explained the Park Service's requirements, I sent project approval letters for the relatives to sign. Years later, we learned some of them had actually checked on us by calling the Park Service to verify we were telling them the truth. Good for them.

Tracking down relatives was often extremely difficult. Such was the case of Wilfred Beswick, who was originally from Seymour Grove, Old Trafford, England. I had no success during my research in English archives, so I placed an advertisement in the *Manchester* (England) *Evening News*. Three months later, I was amazed to receive a letter from a Mrs. Margaret Price, who had seen the advertisement. Her brother, Reggie, had been the best friend of one of Wilfred Beswick's brothers in the 1940s. Through Mrs. Price, we contacted Wilfred's family, who had moved to Canada decades earlier.

The family of Howard Davidson was caught completely off guard by my first call, although there was an element of déjà vu for them. In the late 1950s, two men had knocked on the door of Davidson's parents' house and said, "We want to find the lost plane. Is it okay with you if we take anything of value we might find that belonged to Howard?"

Leroy Davidson, one of Howard's brothers, remembers his parents stating unequivocally, "To hell with whatever of value might be on that plane, by all means go and find out what happened!"

But they never heard from the men again and no one remembers their names.

The Davidson family was hard to convince of our sincerity and required many letters and telephone calls. They even asked to see photos of the mountain before they signed a letter of approval. But once convinced, the Davidsons became strong supporters of the project. Through letters and emails, the Davidson family let us know how much they appreciated what we were doing.

By May 1999, we had contacted more than 70 relatives of those who had perished. We were exhausted, but excited, when Peter Hess sent in the official request for a permit, accompanied by the huge stack of approval letters. "Jon Jarvis is in for one hell of a surprise," I said, as our attorney-friend put the finishing touches on the envelope.

Many of the approval letters actually came from people in elder care centers, some overseas, and one in a convent. Sister Aileen Rice, sibling of Merchant Mariner Daniel Rice, sent us many wonderful letters of support and thanks. With that kind of backing, Marc and I figured we couldn't go wrong.

We never did determine exactly how many direct relatives were finally aware of the project; it was hundreds, probably closer to a thousand. Their support was overwhelming and satisfying. The relatives were surprised, but glad to learn about the wild treasure stories, the details of the *Sunset*'s cruise, the plane's route, our expeditions, and other explorers.

That list of relatives became the most coveted treasure for Marc, Peter Hess, and me. We protected it as though it were made of gold, because, for us, it told the story.

The Park Service had set the bar very high for us to obtain the special permit. But we met the challenge. In addition to the letters of approval, we put up the $5,000 performance bond as required. Then Hess, through a sort of legal tug-of-war, obtained the limited, one-time, special-use permit.

In mid-July, 1999, the Wrangell-Saint Elias National Park's Acting Superintendent, Chief Ranger Hunter Sharp, issued a "Special Use Permit to recover identifying artifacts from Flight 4422, which crashed March 12, 1948." I was recognized by the Park Service as qualified to collect artifacts and document the site via still photos, video, sketches, and GPS coordinates.

Hess had done his job well; now it was Marc's and my turn. All we had to do was get to the site one more time, document it properly, and bring out enough items to prove to the world once and for all that Flight 4422 was really there. It seemed like a relatively easy task. But the mountain was not going to give up its secrets easily.

Mount Sanford, July 1999 **26**

WE'RE GOING FOR IT

I arrived in Anchorage just before midnight on July 19, 1999. Marc picked me up and we immediately started going over plans for our expedition to Mount Sanford. It was to be our last expedition, but the pieces were not coming together as they normally did.

The whole year had been the most challenging yet. Making the family contacts and obtaining letters of approval had been a monumental task. Getting the permit from the Park Service had been very difficult. Then we had to come up with the $5,000 bond. Even getting time off from work was problematic; it wasn't until the last minute that Marc was able to finagle the necessary time off from NWA. Juggling schedules, emotions, and expedition requirements was almost too much for us.

Now, the weather was bad—rain and more rain. Then snow fell in mid-July. An unusual midsummer cold snap had dumped heavy snow down to 5,000 feet on the mountains east of Anchorage all the way to the Canadian border, which included Mount Sanford. Of course any snow cover at the 6,000-foot level on Mount Sanford would greatly complicate, if not preclude, an expedition.

After all our work, neither Marc nor I wanted to even imagine a cancellation, or non-completion of the expedition. That would be disappointing to the families and potentially devastating to the entire project.

To complicate matters further, the Air Force recently had initiated a controversial, mandatory anthrax vaccination program. A hearing had been scheduled in Washington, D.C., for July 21, and Marc was required to attend. He planned to immediately fly back. After my arrival in Anchorage, we spent just two hours discussing the project before he started packing for D.C. I dropped him off at the airport in the early morning hours of July 20. Then I drove to the Park Service's Copper Center headquarters to pick up the permit Peter Hess had skillfully arranged.

Heavy rain formed little rivers in the street as I left Anchorage. Low clouds and moisture totally obscured the mountains in every direction—not a welcome sight. My heart felt heavy as I drove down the highway on the verge of hydroplaning. It was the same road I'd traveled many times during the project, directly under the path the DC-4 had flown 51 years earlier. Five hours later, I was in Gulkana. Looking east, neither Mount Sanford nor Mount Drum was in view—not even peeking out. Dark clouds with heavy rain reached all the way to the ground.

I turned south and drove to Copper Center. At the park's headquarters, the cold water poured off the roof while I spent nearly an hour bringing Anne Worthington, the park's archivist, up to speed on the project and the history of Flight 4422. She had not been available during our February meeting and was fascinated with the history of the ship, the plane, and the men on board; her excitement helped perk me up. It was a pleasure to again tell the intriguing story of the lost men. As protectors and curators of history, Worthington and Park Historian Geoff Bleakley made me feel better because both genuinely cared about Flight 4422.

With the all-important permit in hand, I headed back to Anchorage. All we needed now was a little luck and good weather.

As I neared Gulkana, the rain stopped and the clouds parted just enough to allow me a peek at Mount Drum and Mount Sanford. I gasped—the mountains were solid white, every slope covered with snow, all the way down to 5,000 feet. The snow must have been more than a foot deep at the higher levels. It was a disaster for our project.

Not now, I whispered. Our equipment was already packed, we had the hard-earned special permit in hand, and, most important, we had the strong, unwavering support of the relatives. Everything was in place—everything but the weather, always the weather.

Late the next evening found me helping Marc toss his bags into his soaking-wet Jeep. He had flown straight back from Washington, D.C., so we could get to the glacier as soon as possible. My spirits were dampened by the weather, and the forecast indicated no change.

But the next morning brought a ray of hope: The new forecast showed a slight chance that the moisture-laden cold air mass might move out of the Copper River Basin over the next few days. If so, there might be some clearing over Mount Sanford on the basin's east side. This could melt the snow at the altitude of the 4422 debris field.

It would be a gamble because there was no weather station actually on Mount Sanford. Gulkana was the closest station, 50 miles away. We would only know the local conditions by actually being there. This is where our combined 50 years of military flying, general aviation, weather experience, and Marc's in-depth knowledge of Alaska would pay off.

After one last good night's sleep, I again drove Marc's Jeep over the rain-soaked roads while he flew his Piper Cub through the showers to Gulkana. Light rain continued to fall as we arrived at the Caribou Inn on July 22 at 5 p.m. To the east, between occasional breaks in the clouds, we could still see much snow cover at 5,000 feet and higher—not good. The extended forecast indicated another weather system would come in three days later. That didn't leave much of a window in which to work. We decided to wait until the next day to make a decision.

In the meantime, we checked in at the Caribou Inn, had a huge dinner, rechecked our equipment, and hit the sack. The young man at the check-in counter had aspirations of becoming a park ranger and had noted our unusual backpacking and photography equipment. He asked a few probing questions. Without divulging any details, we told him we were involved in a documentation project in the park. "A glacier project," we admitted. The would-be park ranger was intrigued. We were impressed by his interest, but could say no more. The young man would be there to witness the events in the days ahead.

After a restless night, I was up at 5 a.m. I got dressed, went to the Jeep, and drove two miles west, where I filmed and carefully observed Mount Sanford and Mount Drum. Dark blue and gray mid-level clouds covered the sky. I couldn't even see the ridge above Cub Valley. Whether or not we could land at the upper strip was a big question. In fact, it was questionable if we could complete any part of the expedition.

Marc got up around 7 a.m. After completing our usual pre-expedition checklist, we stood on the porch of the restaurant. It was decision time. For 30 minutes, we carefully assessed all the factors. Was it worth it? Finally, we decided to give it try and departed Gulkana at noon on July 23 after leaving a phone message for Acting Supervisor Ranger Hunter Sharp: "We're going for it."

ONLY THE PARK SERVICE, our bush pilot network, and Peter Hess knew what we were doing. There were no calls to the press. Even the relatives of those lost did not know the specifics of how and when we would attempt to reach the site. But the families were with us in spirit. Flight 4422 was waiting for us beneath a blanket of snow.

Marc piloted the Super Cub, stuffed with all of our equipment, up into the iron-blue and gray sky. The low clouds were not good. But high above us alto cirrus clouds lined up in waves, signaling a change.

As usual, we flew east, following the ill-fated course of the DC-4, NC-95422. We were nervous because we were certain this would be our last trip to the special glacier, and we also knew the chances of something bad happening were at an all-time high. All the chips were on the table now: our reputations, our lives, and the entire project. We circled Cub Valley twice at 12:45 p.m. The landing area was completely flooded with water. "No way, José. We're on wheels, not floats," Marc said.

The small stream in the center of the landing area had changed course slightly and now sliced through the middle, making two very short landing zones instead of one. I echoed Marc's sentiments as we flew farther up the glacier to take a look at the debris field. Even down close, we couldn't see any aircraft debris from the air; the glacier was covered in snow, just as it was in the middle of winter, reducing the possibility of locating any artifacts. Things were not looking good at all.

I took a quick look at the Super Cub's outside air temperature gauge.

"Marc, look at this," I said. "The freezing level is all the way up at our current altitude—7,000 feet. The temperature is rising just a bit. I think there might be a slight inversion—where we're warmer up here than down in the valley."

Marc peered at the little gauge. "I think you're right. Let's keep an eye on it. We still might have a chance, but we certainly can't land in Cub Valley right now. We'll have to land way down back at the Sanford River and hike the entire glacier. Are you up for it?"

I chuckled. "Of course I'm up for it. And, it's about time you had to hike to the whole glacier anyway. You've been skating during the last two trips."

The increased temperature indicated by the outside air temperature gauge was good news. But we had to fly all the way back down to the Sanford River and land on the backup strip where I had landed in 1995, and where we had diverted in 1997. That meant a grueling 16-mile climb from the landing zone all the way up to the icefalls on the glacier.

A few minutes later, we made a short, bumpy touchdown on the backup strip. Marc brought the Cub to a stop, taxied to the north end, whipped it around, and shut her down.

The quiet serenity of the huge valley was quickly broken by the sound of mosquitoes zooming toward us in search of blood. Mosquito net hats and another thick shirt were the clothing of the day. At the 3,000-foot altitude of the landing zone, the temperature rose to 50 degrees F. The altimeter read 30.04, just a little higher than the standard setting of 29.92. That meant at least a little higher pressure was moving in and should bring clearer skies.

We decided to climb to the site with the hope the snow would melt during our two-day climb and allow us to collect artifacts that would prove the site was that of 4422. Even just two or three degrees of warmer temperature would make a difference. But it would be another ball-buster of a hike. With heavy packs, we started east from the Sanford River landing zone at 3:30 p.m. on July 23, 1999. We walked over ankle-wrenching rocks on the flats, passed safely through the 15-foot-tall bushes, and took one last look at the Super Cub as we started up the glacier. Four years had passed since I had hiked this area. The climb seemed more difficult this time, and the route had changed dramatically due to the glacier receding about 200 feet.

At the subsurface stream's exit point, the water roared into the open. Thousand-pound boulders occasionally melted out of the glacier, falling from the walls of ice into the stream with a thundering *kaboom* and *splash*. Marking our route carefully with wands, we negotiated the cliffs of ice and marble-like piles of rock—which slid at the slightest touch.

We generally retraced my 1995 route to a point just above Cub Valley. There, we dropped our packs and set up camp at 9 p.m. Light rain fell, but no snow. On the way, we'd stopped at the old campsite at the west end of Cub Valley. Nothing had changed among the old cans, broken glass jars, bowls, and other items. The five-gallon gas can stamped 1951 was still there. Midnight found us in our warm sleeping bags. Under a misty night sky, the tent was damp, the temperature 43 degrees F. We spent a restless night, wondering what the next day would bring.

A WET MORNING with an overcast sky hid the sun, but only a few raindrops fell. It was a toss-up as to whether the crash site would be clear of snow. After a quick breakfast of granola bars, we packed up and left Cub Valley at 8:50 a.m. on July 24. We could see that a lot of snow had melted during the relatively warm night; the snow level now appeared to be nearer to 6,500 feet. Maybe we would get lucky.

Light rain mixed with some sleet fell as we clambered over the ice bridge and onto the glacier. We again used wands to mark a new route. With a clear goal in mind and relatively lightweight packs, we moved quickly, making no photo stops. Arriving at the debris field just before 11:45 a.m., we had hit it perfectly. Just enough time had passed so that the light rain and higher temperature had melted most of the new snow. The north-facing slopes still had several inches of snow, but most of the site was in acceptable condition to collect artifacts. One day earlier would have been too early.

Tired and wet, we set up the tent a quarter mile west of the debris field, rolled out the sleeping bags, and rested for two hours. The familiar pitter-patter of raindrops continued as we drifted off to sleep just a few hundred feet from the resting place of 30 men. At 2 p.m., as light snow fell a thousand feet higher on the mountain, we tumbled out of the tent and began the documentation and recovery portion of the expedition. Thousands of metallic pieces were strewn over a one-mile-long, three-quarter-mile-wide field of debris. We would recover only enough pieces to positively identify the wreckage, disturbing the site as little as possible.

After 50 years, the truth about Flight 4422 had come full circle. Now all we had to do to close that circle was to carefully complete the mission and not screw it up by doing something stupid, like getting hurt.

At 3 p.m., Marc jumped across the raging glacial stream and clawed his way back up the other side. I followed, but the small ice point from which we jumped broke underneath me. I swung my ice axe hard, jamming its sharp end into the ice on my right side. Luckily, it held. Stepping back, I regained my balance. Moving upriver a hundred feet, I crossed safely and joined Marc at the propellers. Although the glacier had changed and aircrafts parts had moved, we found the engine, the propellers, and hundreds of other small aircraft parts.

The blade with the identifying numbers was still visible on top of the ice—Model 6507-A-0, with the stenciled serial number RR L6377. The numbers were faded somewhat since 1997—the bright summer sun had taken its toll—but still legible. We would have liked to recover the propeller blade with the stenciled numbers, but the blade was just too heavy to carry out of the valley.

Meanwhile, the cold weather and 100 percent humidity again wreaked havoc with our cameras. Film jammed in one of the still cameras and two rolls ended up ruined by the humidity. Our video cameras also had trouble with the high humidity—one intermittently displayed a humidity error code and the other simply stopped working.

We recovered the engine data plate. Using the handheld GPS receiver and basic quadrangle charts, we noted its precise location and GPS coordinates. After photographing and making a sketch of the data plate, Marc and I returned to Propeller Point. At the top, we planted 30 small American flags and a three-foot-tall white cross with the names of the 30 men written on it. A gentle rain fell as we held a short memorial ceremony for the men of Flight 4422. I read several poems by Navigator Wayne Worsley. Then, Marc said a few words. With a final salute, we removed the flags and the cross.

Continuing with the last bit of our survey and recovery, we found the landing gear strut lying on top of the ice just east of Propeller Point. Its chrome still reflected the cloudy day's light, but now there was a hint of rust on the exposed steel. Unfortunately, it also was too heavy to carry. A little farther to the northeast, on the south edge of the surface glacial stream, I picked up a small piece of brown fiber-like material, a piece of either a floor or wall.

After photographing each artifact, we carefully noted its location and made a detailed in situ sketch. Then we placed each item inside its own artifact bag. As a nonartist, I was proud of the sketches I drew on waterproof paper high up on the glacier, in the cold rain.

No bars of gold were strewn about the debris field, nor were there any indications that such items ever existed. There were no broken wooden crates and no coins reflected in the dim rays of the sun.

Twenty minutes after holding the memorial service, Marc and I were scrambling up the south side of a 50-foot depression that had been melted out by water running down the glacier's surface. We had accomplished just about everything we needed to. Loaded down with the documentary equipment, I was 10 feet behind Marc when he abruptly stopped and exclaimed, "Oh, my God!"

Marc's unusual, serious reaction hinted to me this could mean only one thing—the one thing we did not want to find.

I said, "What is it, human remains?"

"Yes," he answered.

THE HUMAN TOUCH

There, lying on the ice, was an arm and hand. It must have melted out of the glacier within the past few days or, at most, weeks. The index finger pointed slightly west of due north. The other three fingers were almost closed and the thumb was relaxed. Having just been released from the icy grip of its lonely tomb after 50 years, the human remains were remarkably well preserved. No animals or birds had yet found it. Marc and I stood over it with both shock and sadness on our faces.

Upon closer inspection, we could see it was a human left hand and forearm—pale white with a tinge of yellow in places. The fingernails of its long, strong fingers, which were well manicured and without jewelry, at first glance appeared to be extremely long, extending about three-eighths of an inch beyond the end of the finger. The nails had not grown—rather the tissue of the fingers had receded, making it appear as if the nails had lengthened. The ridges on the pads of the fingers, forming fingerprints, couldn't be photographed due to the position of the hand. Although trained to do so, I wasn't allowed to take fingerprints due to the park permit's restrictions. The skin of the arm and the hand was intact, but there was no longer any hair. The skin appeared to be soft, but we were not allowed to touch it.

The hand obviously had hit something with tremendous force, as evidenced by deep contusions on the knuckles. Known as boxer's fractures, the blunt, severe blows shattered the fingers in several places, ripping through the skin.

We spotted a hint of green bacteria or fungus where the arm disappeared into the glacier. We couldn't determine if it was attached to any other still-buried human parts because we were not allowed to chip any ice to find out. Our Special Use Park Permit stated specifically, "If any human remains are located, they are to be fully documented but not disturbed in any other way."

The discovery caught us off guard. We had come to believe that all of the men on board the plane probably were cremated in the well-documented inferno following the crash; or that any human remains were simply buried too deep in the ice to be found.

The lonely and forlorn piece of someone wasn't macabre at all to me. We had always known it was possible we might encounter such remains. Since the arm was located right in the middle of Fight 4422's debris field, common sense dictated an extremely high chance it belonged to one of the 30 men.

We knelt beside it and took careful notes on the only human remain ever found from the crash of Flight 4422. Amazingly, there was only a faint odor from the deteriorating flesh. Other than fingerprints, there were no other identifying marks: no tattoos or scars. There was no watch, no ring, and no evidence of such having been worn by the victim.

We carefully photographed, videotaped, and measured the arm and hand. It was 17 ¼ inches from the fingertips to the accessible end of the elbow. I was still kneeling, studying it closely with amazement, when all of a sudden, Marc stepped back, shocked.

"We're leaving this place right now! This wasn't in the cards and I've had enough!"

I tried to calm him. "Marc, we can't leave now. There's still more documentation we have to complete."

"Nope, I'm done right now. We're leaving this place."

"I can finish it by myself," I said, "but it wouldn't be very safe. We also have a duty to finish this right—a duty to the Park Service, the families, and the project. Not only that, we have to finish it right to keep our own credibility. There's just a little more to do and it shouldn't take more than an hour or so. What do you say?"

The human arm had obviously shaken Marc. But after thinking about what I said, he finally agreed to stay with me.

"Just so you know," he said, "I'm not comfortable at all with this. I'll do it, but then we have to leave right away."

"It's a deal," I said.

Marc had never been around human remains, so he was understandably not comfortable. I had been involved with the investigations of a few fatal auto and airplane crashes, so I was somewhat accustomed to such gruesome scenes. I learned to just deal with it.

To mark the location, we set up a three-foot-tall climbing wand. We secured it with several large rocks on top of a four-foot-high boulder. Then we attached a foot-long strip of orange survey tape to the top of the wand that could be seen from the air. That would make it easy to spot if the Park

Service or some other authority needed to locate it. After videotaping, photographing, and making a pencil sketch of the arm and hand, we left the area and continued collecting items that would offer proof of the plane's identity.

Some 570 feet east of Propeller Point, Marc saw a flash of something among three fist-sized rocks. It was a cigarette lighter. The wet, chrome-plated body, which appeared as good as new, glinted in the arctic sun. The mechanism was rusty, its spark wheel was locked solid, and its fuel was long gone. No initials, inscriptions, or brand name adorned the lighter; nothing indicated who might have owned it. After the usual photographing and sketching, Marc put it in an archival sack and marked it on the outside.

Twenty feet back to the west, I relocated the metal clip from some kind of clipboard. It was the only piece of debris we located that might have been from the cockpit of the DC-4. Just a few feet to the south, I noticed an unusual four-inch piece of aluminum that still had chips of red and blue paint—Flight 4422's colors in 1948. I documented and bagged it.

A quarter mile to the east, Marc recovered the two pieces of plexiglass, each roughly three inches long. One was consistent with the thickness of a DC-4's windshield, and the other, thinner piece was apparently from a passenger window and its outside, convex side was burned. It made sense that this piece could be from the plane because we knew there was an intense fire where the DC-4 hit the mountain.

Searching for more artifacts, we hiked northwest and then descended to where we crossed the glacial stream, putting us on the north side of the stream. A half mile to the northeast we picked up a crumpled piece of aluminum stamped "NWA" on its edge, lying in a flat area 300 feet northwest of the stream. A few feet away we found two dinner knives. One had "NWA" stamped on its handle, and the other had no handle at all. Both blades were inscribed with the manufacturer's name, "INSICO," near the handle.

After completing the data and parts collection requirements, we headed southwest, toward the tent. On the way, we rephotographed the ladder, the climbing rope, and the engine. We had intended to note the engine's new distance from the surface glacial stream, but the stream was gone. In just one year, the surface stream had mined its way southerly and now was somewhere underneath the glacier. Although many other aircraft parts had disappeared, the huge radial engine was now high and dry.

A hundred and fifty feet south of the ladder, near the stream, an engine control unit with "Stromberg" stamped on its data plate sat on top of some rocks. It was the type used on old radial engines and the black paint on the unit was as good as new. The ID tag—parts list no. 390727, ser. 886216A—was still riveted to the body. It was quite heavy so we left it. Thousands of small pieces of aluminum littered the area near the stream, further evidence that the DC-4 had been demolished. No other pieces we found had any identifiable markings. This was not only the grave of 30 men, but the resting place of a magnificent airplane as well.

It was 11 p.m. when we finally reached the tent, just outside the debris field. We were exhausted, physically and emotionally. I wiped moisture off the water-resistant pages, then completed the sketches and wrote some notes in our logbook. Marc fired up the gas stove. It soon hissed with boiling water. The hot chocolate was first, followed by a freeze-dried dinner of spaghetti. We rehydrated with two quarts of water each while discussing the day's events.

"I'm very glad to be out of the debris field," Marc said. "You might be comfortable with human remains, but I'm not. I'll never step foot in there again."

I was quiet for a few moments, and then replied, "I know what you mean. I just mentally put it on the side and will deal with it later. That's how I have to handle these kinds of things. Those NTSB investigators deal with this all the time. They really have a tough job."

I was intrigued by our discovery of the arm. It was almost surely from someone on Flight 4422. I tried to picture who and what the hand had last touched. I wondered what situations it had been in. Had the fingers pulled a trigger during WWII? Did it have the skill of artist and teletype operator Robert Haslett, the purser on board the plane? Was it one of the pilots? But, it seemed that only fingerprints, and possibly DNA, could provide an identity. That would be a tough job.

We both knew that finding part of a person would completely change the complexion of the project. To what degree, we didn't know. Instead of just recovering identifying artifacts to prove the debris field was that of the legendary DC-4, this area was now, undeniably, a real grave site. All of our homework had been worth it.

The discovery also indicated that all of the human flesh had not been consumed by the post-impact fire and explosion. That fact added an uneasy feeling to the site. We knew it would be at least equally as disturbing to anyone else. It would also make it harder when informing the relatives. The arm could belong to any of the 30 men on board Flight 4422. Would anyone other than the families care? We discussed the best way to break the news to the families and the world. As it turned out, that was one thing we didn't need to worry about.

Pointing to the west, Marc said, "It's Saturday night. Look out there. I can see the lights of Glennallen flickering between the clouds. It sure looks nice and warm down there. I've never felt this kind of cold before. I'd like to start back down first thing tomorrow."

After a few moments, I said, "Just think, these 30 guys have been up here all this time. So far, they've missed about 2,600 Saturday nights."

We agreed that starting down first thing in the morning would be best. If we hauled ass, we could make it all the way down, fly out, and inform the Park Service of our discovery the same day.

Only the sound of rain disturbed the silence as we drifted off to sleep sometime after midnight. Higher up, on the sweeping slopes of Mount Sanford, small avalanches slid down narrow ravines carved in the rock and ice, just as they had for centuries. Soon a thick fog formed and visibility dropped to less than a hundred feet on the glacier. As darkness fell, our tent and the resting site of Flight 4422 were completely covered in fog, hidden from the world one last time.

EVERYTHING WAS SOAKED as we hastily packed up the next morning. Thankfully, the snow level had remained above us at about 7,000 feet. The temperature at the tent hovered just above freezing. I took one last short walk and came upon a small piece of wood about a hundred feet northwest of the tent. It was unusual, about two by eight inches long, hand-engraved with palm trees that dovetailed at both ends. It looked like a piece of a curio box. After carefully noting its location, I sketched and photographed it, then placed it in an artifact bag.

Marc joined me and noticed a small piece of a bowl or plate about 200 yards northwest of Propeller Point. Printed on the bottom of the two-inch piece of plastic was "BAKE IN THI" and "PLAS." It was obviously made of Bakelite, a material popular in the 1940s and '50s. That was the last piece we recovered from Flight 4422.

With enough items in hand to clearly identify the debris field as that of the missing DC-4, we broke camp at 8:50 a.m. A thousand feet to the east, the orange survey flag flapped at the top of the wand, marking the remote location of the human arm. Neither Marc nor I had any idea if we would ever see it again. We didn't know if it would be recovered, or if it would remain on or in the ice forever.

We hiked quickly, following the wands and retrieving them as we passed, then placing them like arrows into a sort of quiver in my backpack. After crossing the ice bridge, we traveled from Green Point down the lush valley to

Cub Valley, arriving just before noon. We dropped the heavy packs from our aching shoulders and took a short break.

We started hiking again. Fifteen minutes later, we stopped at the old campsite we'd located before at the westernmost end of Cub Valley. After snapping a few more photos, we ignored the pain in our legs and shoulders and continued down the south side of the glacier. After several hours, green bushes came into view and a few bugs buzzed around us, signaling our reentry into the world of the living.

The last one-and-a-half miles were a grueling climb back into the center of the glacier. Again, wand to wand, we retraced our route across the glacier's westernmost hills, occasionally slipping and sliding on the rock-covered ice. Gradually, the trail evaporated behind us and, as we removed the wands, the glacier returned to its natural condition. Other than the wand marking the arm far to the northeast, nothing but footprints remained of our visit.

Finally, we climbed down the terminus of the glacier, where the stream shot out and washed over rocks and boulders, then flowed to the Sanford River. A hundred feet to the west of the terminus, a bloody set of sheep's horns indicated another fresh kill. Marc thought it was a bear kill, but we didn't have the desire or time to investigate. He paused and rechecked his .44 Magnum.

It was 3:30 p.m. and there was no time to lose. To the south, dark clouds gathered, signaling another weather system moving in. Strong wind already was blowing plumes of snow off the ridges on Mount Drum. Incredibly, we were in yet another race with the relentless weather.

We were tired, but we moved quickly, scrambling over the rocks, tromping along the boulders on the river's edge, then through the wash of the raging glacial river. In order not to startle any bears, we made a lot of noise crashing through the thick bushes. For three days, Marc and I had pushed ourselves to the limit and now we were sore, dirty, exhausted, and ragged. We hiked to the Cub, our best friend in the wilderness and lifeline to civilization.

The little plane was still in good shape—its big balloon tires had stayed well inflated. We breathed a sigh of relief but took no time to rest as the wind started picking up. Five miles to the south, we could see gusts whipping up plumes of dust, just as they had in 1994. We could smell the moisture in the air. Then large drops of rain began to batter the Cub. With dark clouds now covering the sky 10 miles farther south, we loaded our gear in record time.

I stuffed myself into the back seat as Marc started the 150-horsepower engine. It roared to life—music to pilots' ears. He wasted no time taxiing the metal and cloth plane to the northwest end of the makeshift runway, then spun it around by pressing one brake, thus turning the tail wheel. Now the plane's nose pointed southeast, into the wind, which blew a steady 20 miles per hour.

With full power, the Cub's tail came up immediately. We were airborne in five seconds, using less than 200 feet of the takeoff zone. It was exactly 4:30 p.m. To prevent any repeat of the 1994 incident, Marc held the plane down, close to the surface, and increased the airspeed just in case a gust arose. Everything remained stable as he turned us to the right. Climbing out, we encountered moderate turbulence. He kept the plane's airspeed close to 80 miles an hour as we bounced and rocked while turning back to the northwest.

As we passed the bottom of the 4422 glacier, only its lowest part was in view due to heavy rain and wind gusts now raking its surface. Plumes of loose dirt flew high into the air as we flew to the northwest.

Mount Sanford disappeared from view. Marc and I said one final goodbye to the 30 men—men we had come to regard as friends, colleagues. Our documentation complete, we were both certain we would never be on the crash site again.

With plenty of fuel, Marc flew the Cub low and fast, 1,500 feet above the ground, just below the clouds. Once out of the valley, it was a smooth and peaceful but melancholy flight as the two of us reflected silently on what we knew would no longer be our secret—one held between the living and the dead. This flight would be the beginning of the end of many years of research, expeditions, and hard work.

Marc finally broke the silence. "Let's just keep this last part safe and take it easy. We have just a little way to go. It looks like we might make it back by 5 o'clock, just before the Park Service closes."

I looked at the fuel gauges, "The gas level looks pretty good this time."

In continuing silence, we soared one last time over the Alaskan wilderness. Beautiful trees, swamp-like tundra, moose, and lakes with trumpeter swans passed beneath us like a movie in slow motion. Within a week we would both be flying big jets to Bombay or Tokyo.

We felt lucky to have spent a special time in such a pristine and beautiful place. I knew I would miss its splendor and the private trust I had with Flight 4422. The last thing to do would be to provide closure for the relatives, who had been yearning for answers for more than a half century. My pilot buddy and I were the only real link between the men in the glacier and their families.

OVERCAST SKIES DARKENED the afternoon and light rain fell as we landed at 4:50 p.m. Marc landed and briskly taxied onto the parking ramp. I saw Park Ranger Hanna closing up the Park Service's hangar. So, while Marc tied the airplane down, I hustled across the tarmac and spoke with him. At first, he didn't know who I was. Marc joined us a few minutes later. The next day Hanna would tell us, "You guys looked pretty darn rough, with scruffy beards, dirty clothes—all haggard. That's why I didn't recognize you."

We briefly explained to Hanna how we had recovered identifying artifacts from the wreckage of Flight 4422 and that we also had found a well-preserved human forearm and its hand. He wrote down the information and made some phone calls. Within a few minutes, we had scheduled a noon meeting the next day at the Park Service headquarters.

We immediately called Peter Hess and filled him in. He would start notifying the relatives immediately the next morning.

After putting the Super Cub to bed, two exhausted and rough-looking pilot-researchers loaded up the Jeep and again headed to the Caribou Inn, our home away from home. The young man behind the counter recognized us from many days earlier and asked, "Did you guys find what you were looking for?"

At first we were speechless, uncertain what to say. Finally, I said, "Yes, we did, and you might be hearing about it sometime soon. But we still have a lot of work to do."

The young man seemed to understand our evasiveness. He checked us in without asking any more questions.

After long, warm showers, a shave, and clean clothes, we headed to the inn's restaurant and enjoyed a big dinner of steak and potatoes. We had no idea this would be our last bit of peace and quiet for several weeks. All hell was about to break loose.

We stayed up until midnight, putting together a detailed video briefing for the Park Service. We slept well, woke up at 9 a.m., and drove to the Park Service headquarters at Copper Center, a 15-minute drive south of Glennallen. At precisely noon, Acting Superintendent Hunter Sharp and his staff welcomed us. Sgt. Rodney Dial, the Alaska State Trooper representative, also was there. Superintendent Jon Jarvis was out of town. The climate was completely different from the February meeting. Not only was this an exciting discovery for everyone, it seemed that we had proven ourselves worthy in the eyes of the park officers. In fact, we almost felt as though we were part of the Park Service team.

We described the site and showed them the recovered artifacts. I could hear a pin drop when we showed the short videotape close-up of the arm and hand. Everyone moved closed to the video monitor to get a closer look. But there was no queasiness among anyone in the group; these were professionals. At the end of the meeting, we all agreed it would be best to keep things quiet for several months until the snow fell again and covered the site, thus thwarting any gold seekers' or wreck hunters' attempts to get to the site in the immediate future. Everyone agreed that the information would be handled with care.

Marc voiced his concerns about being able to notify Northwest Airlines in the most appropriate manner. It was too late and he would have to call them the next morning. We agreed that we would immediately contact the families and let them know what we had found. In addition to the Park Service, there were other notifications that needed to be made because a human remain was involved. Those notifications, it turned out, would change everything.

At the end of the noon meeting, Sergeant Dial informed the group that Alaska State Trooper Bob Larson would fly the State Troopers' Long Ranger turbine helicopter to Gulkana the next day. They would put together a team, fly to the site, and recover the human arm. The plan was for everyone involved to meet at the National Park Service's hangar at 7:30 a.m. Tuesday. There, they would make the final plans for the recovery.

Meanwhile, back in Delaware, Peter Hess and his staff had been busy informing the relatives about our success. He also told them we had recovered identifying parts from Flight 4422, and that we had found an unidentified human arm and hand.

Marc and I felt the control of our project slipping away. It was unnerving. We no longer knew what lay ahead and we no longer were making the decisions about our 10-year project. That evening, we decided that if one of us was asked to go to the site in the helicopter, it would be me. Marc needed to concentrate on the delicate task of notifying Northwest Airlines.

In Glennallen, heavy rain fell all night and into the next day. But on Mount Sanford, as the temperature dropped in the early morning hours, the rainfall changed to snow. The site and the arm and hand were again in danger of disappearing beneath a mantle of white.

RESCUE AND MEDIA BLITZ

The alarm rang at 6:30 a.m. It didn't matter. Marc and I were already up, but not in top form, having slept poorly. In Glennallen, the rain came down in torrents. Water gushed off the roofs, overshooting the gutters. Six-inch-deep streams flooded the Caribou Inn's parking lot.

Marc telephoned the Park Service hangar to check on the progress of the helicopter. He was told that it was stuck at Gun Sight pass, a high point on the highway halfway between Anchorage and Gulkana. Even for the Alaska State Troopers' multi-million-dollar search-and-rescue helicopter and its top pilot, Bob Larson, the weather was too bad to fly. He had landed the helicopter adjacent to a hotel-gas station facility. Telephoning the Gulkana Troopers' office, Bob said thick clouds were right on the deck at Gun Sight and rain and fog cut visibility to zero. He would just have to wait it out.

Marc and I, still exhausted from the climb, planned to relax and recover from the physically demanding expedition. We thought it also would be a great opportunity to put together more information for the Park Service. Unfortunately, we never got a chance. The day had started pretty badly with the poor weather, and then it got worse.

WATER FLEW FIVE FEET into the air as the pickup truck driven by Sergeant Dial parted the small ocean in the Caribou Inn parking lot. He hopped out of the truck at precisely 7:15 a.m. and splashed his way across the 20 feet between the truck and the hotel. Meeting Marc and me just inside, he dropped the bomb.

"The cat's out of the bag!" he exclaimed.

"What do you mean?" Marc and I shot back at the same time.

"At 7 a.m., in its lead story, one of the radio stations in Anchorage announced that the famous DC-4 Gold Wreck on Mount Sanford, missing since 1948, had been discovered," the sergeant replied.

Neither Marc nor I could believe our ears. What we thought had been so carefully and quietly orchestrated and kept secret for many years had been blown sky high.

"Are you kidding me? We all agreed to keep this absolutely quiet," Marc said.

"I can't believe it, either," Sergeant Dial said. "I don't know who blew it."

"So, the cat's out of the bag for real?" I asked.

"Yes, for certain," Dial answered.

"Holy shit," I said.

Marc was livid. Uncharacteristic four-letter words came out of his mouth faster than an auctioneer's words at a cattle sale. He was pissed because more was at stake than just the project. This could mean his career. As a pilot for NWA, he felt it was his solemn duty to treat Flight 4422 correctly, and we had done so to the utmost possible extent. The plan agreed to with the National Park Service was to quietly confirm the identity and location of the site, notify the relatives, wait a few months for the snow to fall, and then put together a joint press conference and news release. Obviously, that was no longer possible.

"Calm down, Marc," I said. "We have to play the cards we've been dealt."

He snapped back, "What do you mean, calm down? Some jackass released the information against our wishes and against our agreement. This is *our* project and no one else has the right to ruin it."

"It's not just our project anymore," I said. "Now it belongs to the world."

AT LEAST ONE THING had gone right. The preparation by Peter Hess had been a good idea. By Tuesday morning, all the known families of 4422's victims had been contacted, well ahead of the unfortunate and untimely leaked news. None of the known relatives were caught off guard. However, we still hoped other relatives would hear the news and contact us. We had always been intent on finding relatives of *all* the men. But this was not the way we'd wanted it to happen.

Marc telephoned Northwest Airline's headquarters in Minneapolis and learned the news had already been broadcast in Minnesota and the rest of the country. The last official message from Alaska to Minneapolis regarding Flight 4422 had been transmitted in 1948 by relatively tedious Western Union teletypes to specific, individual stations. In 1999, news of our discovery zipped electronically around the world within seconds.

The remainder of the day was a nightmare for all of us—the National Park Service, the Alaska State Troopers, Peter Hess, Marc, and me. We were inundated with phone calls, emails, and faxes from news outlets, local and national. Each one wanted its own scoop and all but one wanted to be the first to tell all about the rumored gold. NWA got calls from the media as well as calls from relatives of people lost in other long-ago plane crashes.

NWA's public affairs officer called Marc and asked him to fax copies of the crew and passenger manifests as well as a brief history of the accident so NWA could determine exactly who was on the flight and answer questions appropriately. The public affairs person reiterated that the company had absolutely no records regarding Flight 4422. I guess that's when I finally became convinced that NWA had been telling us the truth about not having records of the crash.

Although we never learned for certain how it happened, we later understood the leak had occurred something like this: The Park Service notified the Alaska State Troopers because human remains were involved. The State Troopers notified the National Transportation Safety Board because it involved an airplane wreck. The NTSB somehow contacted the FAA, possibly via an automatic online link. Supposedly someone, somewhere in the link, was married to a news person. Unfortunately, that person decided to release the news. It's hard to keep a secret anymore.

This leak really screwed up what Marc and I, the National Park Service, and the State Troopers had in mind: an appropriate, well-planned and complete information release at a press conference. It was sad how some callous people in the media put achieving a scoop ahead of more important concerns.

Flight 4422 had made the news again. While the helicopter was stuck at Gun Sight, we were bombarded by the news media via cell phone, the hotel telephone, and emails. Some of the media outlets who contacted us were the television programs: Unsolved Mysteries, Extra, WCCO in Minneapolis, ABC News, ABC Nightline, CBS, CNN, A & E, History, King 5 TV Seattle, NPR, and three local Anchorage TV stations.

Newspaper reporters from the *Anchorage Daily News*, *Fairbanks Daily News Miner*, Reuters News Service, *Washington Post*, *Minneapolis Star Tribune*, and *London Times* called. But there was one news source that handled things differently; it was a real breath of fresh air when a producer from NBC's Dateline called. Shane Bishop's first questions were about the people and their relatives. That made all the difference to Marc and me. Bishop suggested we let things quiet down and he would get back to us in a week.

Operating without a secretary, we were overwhelmed and lost track of exactly who called and when, but we handled as many calls as possible.

Our number one goal remained to communicate as much as possible with the families of the men who lost their lives. Sure enough, several previously unknown relatives of the lost men contacted us. We responded to those calls immediately.

That morning was absolutely crazy. In Anchorage, Jane Ahern, National Park Service media relations supervisor, worked feverishly with Marc, Peter Hess in Delaware, and the Park Service's Acting Superintendent, Hunter Sharp, to coordinate an accurate news release. Meanwhile, we stood by for the helicopter as the rain continued.

It was 1:30 p.m. when the weather finally let up enough for Bob Larson to take the helicopter into the air above Gun Sight. Half an hour later, the unmistakable staccato *wop-wop-wop-wop-wop* pounded the air over Glennallen as the six-place, turbine-powered, Bell Jet Long Ranger helicopter arrived under thick clouds. Larson landed the Ranger at Gulkana's airport with plenty of time to make it to the site and back. Thirty minutes later, Larson and NTSB investigator Scott Erickson walked into the State Troopers' Gulkana office at the intersection of State Highways One and Four.

After a few quick introductions, Marc and I briefed them on the details of the site and what we had found, and showed them the videotape of the DC-4's wreckage site, which included the arm and hand. Because we were the experts about the area and had the most detailed information, we also carefully reviewed our site maps, including emergency egress routes from the site and rendezvous points in case of an unplanned landing. This was serious business.

After we distributed copies of the maps to the team, we waited for the heavy rain to subside somewhat. After two hours, Larson decided it had let up enough to attempt accessing the site. Then he, Scott Erickson, Geoff Bleakley, Sergeant Dial, and I headed out to load the helicopter, which was sitting in the rain. Several bright orange bags of survival equipment accounted for most of the cargo. Cameras and investigatory tools made up the remainder.

After a thorough preflight, Larson secured the doors and strapped himself into the pilot's seat on the right side. Sergeant Dial sat in the left seat. Park Historian Bleakley and NTSB Investigator Erickson took their places in the passenger compartment. I sat next to Erickson.

The blue and white, multi-million-dollar helicopter was loaded with first-class navigational equipment and a first-class pilot. After half a century, the first official search-and-rescue mission to Flight 4422's actual ground site was ready to go.

Larson started the large turbine engine in virtually the same sequence

Marc and I follow to start our big jets' engines. At first, there was just the increasing sound of airflow. Then he switched on the fuel and ignition. Soon the low blast-furnace drone of the turbine sections' burning jet fuel filled the air. A few moments later, it sounded just like an airliner's jet engine with one difference: During the sequence, the helicopter blades started turning, cutting huge paths through the air. It was loud, so we all wore headsets with intercom. A hint of the odor of jet exhaust filtered into the cabin.

I hadn't been in a helicopter since 1982 during Air Force survival school, when trainees were practice-rescued and lifted hundreds of feet above the forest. This was much different. As the engine started, my thoughts drifted. I had been all over the world, but this made me appreciate the good ol' USA. There aren't many governments that would spend so much money and personnel time recovering a small human remain from the clutches of a remote and dangerous glacier. I thought about the incredible feats of the personnel at JPAC (Joint Pacific Accounting Command) who recover and identify people missing in action (MIAs). I also thought about Arlington National Cemetery and the respect we have for our soldiers, sailors, airmen, and their families.

THE HUGE HELICOPTER slowly lifted into the air, its blades thumping, batting down the gold and green grass between the taxiway and runway. Larson turned it east under a dark and wet sky, with visibility less than five miles. We followed the Sanford River—on the same route Layton Bennett had flown in his low-tech Luscombe back in '48.

The helicopter's racket spooked the animals below. Caribou scattered and a grizzly bear ran from a clearing near the river. Inside the chopper, no one said much. In the Super Cub, Marc and I had always flown at a much higher altitude, usually several thousand feet. And our airspeed was considerably faster than the helicopter's. Looking out the window now, I got a slow, breathtaking close-up of the landscape. It seemed different—wilder, and more remote and dangerous than before. At the same time, it was all familiar territory.

The lower slopes and cascading glaciers of Mount Drum passed far off to our right, partially hidden behind shafts of rain and sleet coming down from the clouds. I felt strange; the emotional shield I'd used for so long was no longer in place. I felt vulnerable and struggled to keep a steady face.

I didn't know exactly why I felt that way; maybe it was because this was the first time I'd gone to the glacier in recent years without Marc, my steadfast friend. Maybe it was the release of the long-held secrets and the heavy burden

I felt on behalf of those lost and their families. Or maybe it was simply the exhaustion of our expedition and unbelievably hectic last few days. And then there was this superb flying machine and the exceptional onboard team that had joined Marc's and my quest. It was humbling and overwhelming.

My intercom headset and eyeglasses helped hide my face from the others. Geoff Bleakley sat across from me, but he was watching the beauty of the wilderness pass beneath us.

In the adjacent seat, Scott Erickson's emotional shield was well in place. He was strictly business. NTSB investigators are among the most respected people in the aviation industry. Using the bits and pieces of aircraft and people, they study transportation accidents to find out what went wrong and try to prevent them from happening again. Aircraft and training improvements suggested by the NTSB over the years have saved many lives. Captain Chesley "Sully" Sullenberger's successful ditching of a jet in the Hudson River in January 2009 is a testament to such improvements.

Despite his businesslike mien, Erickson was compassionate and understanding. If anyone on board the chopper understood my feelings, he did. We both knew that this wasn't just any crash—it was Flight 4422, the legendary Gold Wreck.

As we neared Mount Sanford, the rain came down harder. If we had been flying the Super Cub, we would have already turned around. But the Long Ranger continued its stately journey just above the surface. Over the intercom, in my most controlled and serious voice, I pointed out the correct glacier. Larson marked the position in the Global Positioning System and guided the helicopter up the centuries-old glacier.

There is no one else I would have wanted at the controls. Our lives, quite literally, were in Bob Larson's highly skilled, mission-hardened hands. The other four of us were along for the ride, viewing the natural sights with awe, photographing and videotaping the scene below.

Everything outside was soaked, and fog formed in the low recesses of the glacier as the visibility on its south side suddenly dropped to near zero. Larson simply maneuvered the helicopter over to the north side, which took about 30 seconds. If we'd been climbing on the surface, that action of crossing the glacier would have taken many hours of dangerous technical ice work.

As Sergeant Dial kept an eye on the spires of ice and glacial ponds, dime-sized raindrops splattered against the helicopter's bubble windshield and observation side windows in the back, and streams of water ran across them like spider webs. The center of the glacier looked entirely different as I viewed it from less than a hundred feet in the air. I got on the intercom again and, with a lump in my throat, I pointed out the familiar landmarks.

As we flew farther up the glacier, the weather worsened. It felt like we were cheating; each time Marc and I had accessed the site on foot, we had to pay the penalty of hazardous flying and then physically demanding and risky climbs.

I also knew how the helicopter sounded outside. The pounding *wop-wop-wop-wop-wop* of its blades echoed off the slopes and glaciers of the valley, disrupting the serenity Marc and I knew so well. But it was a rare and beautiful experience to pass so slowly over Mother Nature's ice sculptures.

We passed by Cub Valley and the old camp site from the 1950s. Then we continued on past Sheep Ridge and Green Point. Thoughts of each of the sailors and aircrew passed through my mind as we flew toward the debris field. In just a few minutes, the secret friendship Marc and I held with the 30 men would be broken. Then, someone else, barely familiar with the men and their history, would invade and investigate the site. I began to second-guess our decision, wondering if we had made the right choice in making the site public. Of course it was the right one…wasn't it? I fought hard to keep my emotions inside.

As Propeller Point came into view, the rain changed to sleet, then to snow—extremely dangerous flying conditions for a helicopter. Nothing comes easy on Mount Sanford and its glaciers.

I pointed out Propeller Point. Larson flew directly over the point several times before he and the others saw the propeller blades hidden among the volcanic rocks, along with some of the other aircraft debris on the glacier. Larson punched the present position button, permanently storing the GPS coordinates of the debris field. That was the moment that Flight 4422's location ceased to be secret, no longer known only to Marc and me. Now, it was officially documented.

Over the intercom, everyone discussed the glacier's incredibly rough, undulating, moonlike terrain and how impressed they were that we had found anything at all. Then they all saw the 16-foot aluminum ladder. From the low altitude, it stuck out like a sore thumb.

Someone asked me, "Is that yours?"

"Nope," I said, "it's not ours and we don't know for certain who it belongs to. But we do know many others were here before us."

Unable to hover in one place, we had to keep moving due to the altitude, wind, and other conditions. People think a helicopter can land anywhere. Not true. There are many physical and aerodynamic limits, and the pilot's skill determines the rest of its capabilities.

We circled the area at a low speed and altitude. As we did, an unnerving thought occurred to me: What if someone or an animal had come up during the past two days and removed the arm? What would everyone think of Marc and me? Was it some kind of hoax? Were we nuts? Just then, we passed about 30 feet south of the arm. Sergeant Dial called out, "There's your flag." The green bamboo wand and its orange survey flag was in full view, blowing in the wind. It would have been toppled by the wind gusts had we not anchored it so well. Everyone in the helicopter saw the flag, but patches of snow made it impossible to pick out the arm.

Turning the helicopter to the right, Larson headed southwest to prepare for a landing on the rock-covered glacier. A gust of wind caught the chopper's tail rotor, and started to turn the aircraft much quicker and farther than he expected. With his years of experience, he knew just what to do—get out of there—quickly!

In the rain, snow, and wind, he poured on the coal, demanding full power from the turbine engine. Gingerly adjusting its flight controls, he kept the helicopter under control, but this obviously was dangerous business.

We moved gently forward under full power as the light snow flakes changed into bigger ones. The temperature was near freezing and the humidity was nearly 100 percent. Larson said, "I think we might be picking up some rotor blade icing."

Later, in his usual steady voice, he told me, "That was the time to get the heck out of there."

The unpredictable, gusty winds had created a very hazardous situation, which could have resulted in his losing control of the tail. Had we stayed only a few more seconds in that specific situation, we might have smacked the glacier and at a minimum, damaged the craft. Additionally, there are all kinds of problems associated with icing and helicopters. Of course, in Alaska, icing is a year-round hazard.

Larson decided to abort the mission. He picked up speed and headed back down the glacier as the incessant gales gusted even stronger. Then there was another surprise: The visibility down the glacier was even worse. Now clouds were right on the surface, all the way across the glacial valley. Some of the ice spires disappeared into the low clouds.

At times, Larson flew less than 50 feet above the surface, actually climbing slightly from time to time, narrowly missing the towers of ice and rock. This shocked me; I was used to flying thousands of feet in the air.

Then, over the intercom he said, "We'll have to come back on a better day. It's just another wreck."

He delivered the statement in a dry, emotionless voice. I couldn't believe my ears. "Just another wreck"? My feelings were hurt. To Marc and me, this had become almost a sacred quest—something extremely important personally, a piece of history, and a chance for closure for many families. How could anyone call it "just another wreck"? But if I were honest with myself, I also knew Larson was correct. All the others on board the Jet Ranger knew it, too. In the cold, harsh terms of reality, Flight 4422 really was just another wreck.

I realized that I was too emotionally involved and could no longer see things as clearly as I should have. The combination of the physical fatigue from the expedition, the recent nights of little sleep, and the shocking way the news had leaked had taken its toll. Maybe it was true, as someone had suggested, our passion for 4422 had gone a little too far—maybe it had reached the level of a near-obsession. And obsessions can be dangerous.

The snow continued to fall in the frigid air above the glacier and the potential for rotor blade icing was still a concern. I volunteered to be dropped off at Cub Valley, which was at a lower altitude. My thinking was that if they dropped me off, with the lighter weight the helicopter could maneuver better and they could fly back up the glacier, land at the site, and pick me up on the way out. Larson thought about that for a few seconds and replied, "No, we all came out together and we'll all go back together."

Again, he was right. Pilots have a saying: There are old pilots and there are bold pilots, but there are no old, bold pilots. Larson had taken the appropriate action to abort the entire mission due to the bad weather at the site of 4422. There was no more discussion.

We continued flying down the glacier in the rain, traveling even slower due to the reduced visibility.

The bottom of the glacier finally came into view, and we followed the outflow stream to the Sanford River, then flew a direct course to Gulkana.

We touched down in a deluge of rain. Neither Mount Sanford nor Mount Drum was in sight. But inside the Park Service's hangar, good news awaited: The weather was forecast to change dramatically, and the next day would be clear and beautiful. Alaska is like that.

Although we hadn't landed at the site, this first 1999 recovery mission was a success. Larson and the team now had a positive GPS fix on the wreckage site. Now there was no question about its existence or Marc's and my credibility. And we could easily retrieve the arm if it was there when we returned.

After unloading the helicopter, I looked back to the east. Once again, I felt certain I would never again be on the site of Flight 4422. Marc and I decided that if one of us were asked to go along again, this time he would do it. Back in Gulkana, he had been busy keeping the media placated, communicating with NWA, and trying to keep the story straight among the various government agencies and news outlets.

Then the Park Service Headquarters and the State Troopers both contacted us and told Marc and me that we must go to Anchorage as soon as possible and arrange a news conference. It was our job to give the media the facts of our discovery. In retrospect, had the discovery been kept secret, even for a few days, it would have been much easier, better handled, and more accurate information would have been distributed.

The next morning, Marc and I awoke to the familiar sound of the helicopter, taking off and heading east to the site under perfectly clear skies. We headed west. Neither of us had been asked to go along. After checking in with everyone, Marc flew the Cub to Anchorage, while I drove the Jeep.

Bob Larson and the Park Service's team had no problems landing at the debris field, and they recovered the arm and hand. Sergeant Dial had dug a 15-foot-wide, five-foot-deep exploratory pit around the arm. It proved to be the only body part found on the site, but he also discovered a ring just below the surface of the ice, roughly five feet from the arm. The ring was silver, with a diamond-shaped, black rendering of what appeared to be a minaret. On one side of the diamond shape was inscribed "1946," and on the other "IRAN." Other than a few fragments that Sergeant Dial thought might have been the bones from a human foot, no other human remains were found. I would have loved to have been there for the recovery.

The team searched the area on foot then flew the helicopter all over the valley and up and down the cliffs, completing another extensive search. They found that all the wreckage was confined within the area Marc and I had described. Now, officially, there would no longer be any lingering rumors about the DC-4's location or what was really there. They didn't find any gold or anything that even suggested the existence of treasure. Most of the wreckage was still buried deep in the glacier.

The sun was low on the horizon when the helicopter swooped back into Gulkana. Other than the ring, the arm with its hand, and the 12 items Marc and I had brought out, everything stayed right where it was on and in the glacier, undisturbed. The mission was a complete success.

Late that afternoon in Anchorage, Marc and I held a press conference where we displayed the 12 recovered artifacts and told our story to an audience of television and newspaper reporters. We made copies of some of our site footage and gave them to the media people, who rushed off to file their stories about the discovery of the lost airplane. It aired on three Alaska TV stations as well as CNN, which broadcast a three-minute piece that included some of our video.

Eventually, the story was broadcast on National Public Radio and many other radio and television stations throughout the United States and other parts of the world. The story of Flight 4422 seemed to intrigue everyone. The next year—2000—with assistance from Marc and me, Eric Riddle from Seattle's King 5 TV produced a poignant 10-minute piece for the station's evening news show. Seattle had been home to 4422's purser, Robert Haslett. The program—professionally and sensitively done—would air many times.

NBC Dateline would air the story in 2002. That piece was later sold to the National Geographic Channel, re-edited, and shown in 2004. Tragically, in 2001, two years after his flights to the site of 4422, Bob Larson would lose his life in a helicopter crash in bad weather over the Cook Inlet, near Anchorage. The death of this skilled pilot was evidence once again of the hazards of flying in Alaska.

With all the media attention, and most of the mysteries solved, people thought the Flight 4422 project was complete. Not by a long shot.

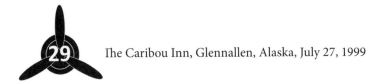

CLOSURE

On July 27, 1999. Cindi Chandler was listening to a music station as she zipped down the freeway 10 miles from her home in Charlotte, North Carolina, when the music turned to static. Adjusting the tuner to a couple of her favorite stations, she could find only garble. She pushed the automatic scan button. When it stopped, she heard, "Alaska's fabled gold wreck has been found. The crash with 30 persons on board occurred in 1948 on Mount Sanford, Alaska…." Shocked, she pulled to the side of the highway, picked up her cell phone, and called her mother, Jan Davis. "Mom, I think someone found Uncle Jehu's plane. Turn on the radio—NPR!"

Jan Davis was the niece of 4422's copilot, Jehu Stickel. In 1948, the 16-year-old girl had promised she would find her favorite uncle, who had disappeared somewhere in the mountains of Alaska.

The day after the radio broadcast, July 28, 1999, Davis contacted us through NPR. She was extremely thankful to learn about our expeditions and research. She now had peace in knowing what happened to her uncle.

By 1999, the years of searching for relatives had resulted in our finding, then contacting, living relatives of 18 of the lost men. Now, when the news of the discovery was released and transmitted over the airwaves and newspapers, we were contacted by relatives of six more of the men for a total of 24 out of 30.

Nearly all the relatives were thankful to hear the truth about Flight 4422. Knowing what happened to the men was a relief and closure to long-held family stories about their legendary relatives lost on a faraway mountain covered with snow and ice.

One of the new contacts was Liz Adler, who learned about 4422's discovery while watching CNN's three-minute news report. The crash occurred six months before she was born, and she never knew much about her father, Eugene. Her mother could never talk about him—the loss had been too much for her. Adler later told me, "Knowing these things about my father and his fate has filled a huge void that has always been with me."

For Marc and me, those words alone made the entire project worth every minute and every dollar.

Retired Canadian Militia Major Randall Haslett, the son of Flight 4422's purser, was a year old when his father perished. He was astounded to learn of the DC-4's discovery through his cousin in western Canada, who had heard the news. After an Internet search, Haslett was soon talking with Marc.

Also in Canada, Pearl Ault and her siblings were relieved to finally know what really happened to their brother, Wilfred Beswick. She could now put to rest the haunting image of his last goodbye wave as he turned the corner in Old Trafford, England, decades earlier.

In London, Polly Rector Logan, the daughter of Flight Mechanic Donald Rector, learned about the discovery from her aunt, who lived in the United States and had heard a radio report about the discovery. I met Polly and her husband, Richard, while I was on a trip to London. I was the copilot on an airline trip which landed at London's Gatwick International Airport 30 minutes ahead of schedule. After clearing customs and immigration, I converted some U.S. money to English pounds, then rode the train into the London Bridge terminal. I rang up the Logans and let them know I would be at the Costa coffee bar; they met me there about an hour later. She was stunning in a long white dress; he was handsome, six feet five, a design engineer with knowing eyes.

They promptly took me on a whirlwind tour of the sites of London while we discussed Flight 4422; Polly Logan's father, Donald Rector; and the rest of her family.

Throughout the afternoon, as the three of us became more comfortable with the subject and each other, Polly explained that her father had always had an interest in mechanical things; so much so that Donald's uncle helped fund his education at a vocational school specializing in mechanics. Then she told me the rest of her father's story.

A true example of love at first sight, Rector had met his future wife, Mary, in Chicago, and they were married shortly thereafter. Five feet ten inches tall, with broad shoulders, he had curly blond hair that stood out against his dark Northwest Airlines uniform. But his trademark was his hands—seemingly permanently stained from grease and oil.

Mary Rector also found work with Northwest, becoming the first female ticket agent for the airline. Soon, the couple settled down in St. Louis, Minnesota, with two children, Polly and Paul, who became the delight of their lives. Prior to her husband's departure for his 12-day trip to Alaska that included flying Flight 4422 from Anchorage to Edmonton; Mary had an uneasy feeling about it. The day after he left, after washing all of his white work shirts and hanging them out to dry, she went back inside the house. For some reason, she decided to look out the window and count the shirts. There were 13 of them, flapping in the breeze. It was a memory still vividly etched in her mind when the telephone rang on Saturday, *March 13*, 1948. Flight 4422 was missing and believed to have crashed.

She was devastated by the loss of her husband, but the ensuing investigation upset her even more. A constant barrage of questions from government officials intruded into the family's life. It wasn't just one interview; there were many visits and questions from several government agencies. And they all seemed to ask the same questions in different ways, over and over. The questions would have most likely included things related to sabotage or hijacking, alcohol, smuggling, and the couple's assets. Although she had nothing to hide, the inquiries and interrogations scared the hell out of her. She became convinced there was something very out of the ordinary about Flight 4422. What, she didn't know.

She was so shaken by the ordeal that, soon after the accident, she left her well-paying job at NWA. It took a lot of guts for a single mother with two young children to move far away—all the way to in Santa Fe, New Mexico. At the time, Santa Fe was a small, peaceful, relatively unknown place hidden in the mountains of the Southwest. It was a great place to raise her children—far away from Minneapolis, the airline, and the dark memories associated with the accident.

Mary Rector never remarried, and she and her children became very close. They grew to love Santa Fe, and they built new memories there. As her son got older, he worked on anything mechanical, and it was evident he had inherited some of his father's skills.

My visit with the Logans was wonderful. She was grateful to know the truth about Flight 4422—that it had really crashed, that no one survived, and no one suffered. The treasure rumors and the plane's status as a legend were new to her and her husband.

Before we parted, she took from her purse one of her mother's last letters and shared it with me. Mary Rector had written, "I hope someone will finally investigate the crash and learn the truth."

Although it was several years after she passed away, she got her wish when we found 4422. For her daughter, Polly, that chapter of her life was finally closed.

MARC AND I NEVER knew what to expect in meetings with the relatives of the Flight 4422's victims. Speaking with them in person was much different from letters and telephone calls. Some wanted to know the facts immediately. Others needed warming up before they were ready for the entire story. A few appeared to not want to know anything about the most basic facts of the crash, yet subconsciously they seemed interested in the details. A conversation may have been superficially about the economy and weather, but questions about Flight 4422 would sneak into the discussion. We listened carefully to each relative and went with the flow. In the end, all of them learned all the facts they wanted to know.

One day, we learned that a relative of one of Flight 4422's victims lived only a few miles from Marc's house in Anchorage. Dorothy Denman heard the news of our discovery in July 1999 and had contacted the local news media before she was able to talk with Marc or me. For some reason, she had decided that she was not happy with our discovery. Denman's favorite uncle, August Koistinen, was one of the sailors lost in the crash.

After a story about Denman and her uncle appeared in the *Anchorage Daily News* on July 31, 1999, Marc spoke with her and brought her up to date on the project. He gave her the details about the location of the debris field and told her no one had suffered, but this didn't comfort her. She said she would rather have remembered the men as though the plane was still intact with all of them still in their seats. Each person handles such things in his or her own way.

Arthur Eilertsen's relatives had a completely different reaction from Dorothy Denman. Eilertsen and his brother-in-law, Frank Oravetz, had been best friends throughout WWII. Oravetz was incredibly happy to learn the facts surrounding the accident. In the fall of 1947, Oravetz had helped Eilertsen get the job on the SS *Sunset*. They planned to sail the world together, but at the last minute Oravetz called OTC and canceled. It seems that his wife, Anna (Eilertsen's sister), absolutely would not let her husband get on the ship. So Arthur sailed without his best buddy.

After the crash, Eilertsen's mother blamed Oravetz for her son's death. The pain from the improperly placed blame remained with him for 51 years, and in response he buried the memories of the wonderful lives he and Eilertsen had shared.

In 1999, during an hour-long, extremely emotional phone conversation, Oravetz shed tears from a half century of misplaced guilt. I told him what had happened in other families, like the Davidsons, and tried to explain that there was no way Eilertsen's death was his fault. That's called closure and for me, it was a wonderful thing to be able to give another human being such relief.

Although we wouldn't know it for several years, after the telephone conversation Oravetz began to change for the better. Fond memories of his brother-in-law returned. He told his son, Ron Oravetz, and his grandchildren about their Uncle Arthur, their lives together, and incidents from their trips throughout Europe and Asia. They'd shared life-and-death experiences during WWII. He talked about teaching Eilertsen how to make rings.

The relatives of Robert Rabich called Marc. It was a local call; Rabich also had relatives living in Alaska. Most of them were interested in the plane and glad to know it finally had been found. From the bits of information they remembered about their legendary Uncle Robert, we learned that he had cleaned out his savings account to buy things on the trip. He was a sharp entrepreneur.

After departing Pennsylvania in November 1947, the *Sunset*'s first stop was Curacao or Aruba. At that time, the northern tip of South America was one of many places where one could buy uncut diamonds and gems at a super-low price. Just like crew members do today, sailors on the *Sunset* may have bought them. This may have been one source of the rumors of diamonds on board Flight 4422.

THE DISCOVERY OF THE wreck received more press in 1999 and 2000. Helen O'Neill of the Associated Press wrote a magnificent two-part article that appeared in many papers. British writer Barry Wigmore flew to Canada and interviewed Pearl Ault, then wrote a touching story in the *London Times Two* weekend newspaper. The article focused on Wilfred Beswick, the only British sailor on the *Sunset*. Thanks to these two articles, the world learned much of the truth about Flight 4422 and its men.

One afternoon in 1999, Shane Bishop, a producer for NBC's Dateline, called again. Bishop had taken a different approach from the other media callers by asking me first about the people on Flight 4422, not the rumored gold. Those were the questions Marc and I were waiting for someone to ask.

In the summer of 2000, Bishop, Dateline reporter John Larson and their film team came to Alaska. They conducted interviews and flew in fixed-wing planes and a helicopter, putting together a half-hour special about 4422 that took nearly a year to produce. Scheduled to air on September 14, 2001, it was postponed due to the disaster of 9/11.

The program finally aired several times in the fall of 2002 on NBC. It was then sold to *National Geographic*, where it was modified, rebranded, and aired as part of the Living Dangerously series in 2004. The programs told the story about 4422 and helped promote our goal of locating even more relatives.

Much of our Flight 4422 project was effectively frozen for several years while the United States suffered through the aftermath of the attacks on the Twin Towers and the Pentagon. Many airlines plunged into bankruptcy. Northwest and Delta filed for bankruptcy on the same day. Despite the resultant havoc in our schedules and huge pay cuts, we quietly continued our attempts to identify the arm and hand.

Our research revealed the sad and messy business of the inevitable, complicated lawsuits that follow major accidents. Many survivors of the sailors filed actions against Overseas Tankship Corporation. In particular, Travis McCall's widow filed a suit known as Collene W. *McCall, as Administratrix of the Estate of Travis M. McCall vs. Overseas Tankship Corporation, vs. Northwest Airlines, Inc.*

The suit lasted seven years in New York courts. On May 7, 1954, Judge Edward A. Conger, United States District Court, Southern District of New York, wrote in part, "I feel the plaintiff has failed to make out a case against the defendant, Overseas, under the Jones Act. I also hold that neither Northwest Airlines nor the crew of the plane were officers, agents, or servants of Overseas Tankship Corporation at the time of the accident."

Ruling on the appeal, on May 10, 1955, Judge Learned Hand, United States Court of Appeals Second Circuit, upheld the lower court's decision. Judge Hand wrote, "Since we are all agreed that the airplane company was an independent contractor, whose negligence is not to be imputed to the defendant, it is not necessary to decide whether McCall was still in the employment of the defendant when he was killed, and I prefer not to do so."

These rulings in essence absolved OTC from any liability for damages. When considering NWA's liability, there were two laws that limited its damages: In 1948, the Warsaw Act limited all international flights' liability to approximately $8,300 for each passenger. And, the Complied Laws of the Territory of Alaska, 1933, section 3845 titled, "When Death Ensues From an Injury," limited wrongful death damages to $10,000.

Each sailor on board the plane had been provided a $25,000 insurance contract purchased by NWA as part of a charter contract with OTC. Through probate records, I confirmed these contracts' proceeds were paid to the heirs. In addition to the $25,000 payouts, some heirs received less than $10,000 each from out-of-court settlements; others received nothing.

Regarding the aircrews, the relatives I interviewed told me they did not receive any insurance payouts other than that purchased privately.

With Flight 4422's debris field identified, relatives knowing much of the truth, and knowledge of the site public, two questions lingered: Whose arm and hand had we discovered? And what was the truth behind the rumors of treasure?

Although we did not know it at the time, what had begun a decade earlier as an adventure to solve the mysteries of a lost plane in the Alaskan wilderness was about to take us to the limits of leading-edge science. Our investigation about which person the arm and hand belonged to had become a forensic investigation that would rival any CSI-like fictional case.

THE COLD CASE FILE

In the 21st-century world of high-tech computers, satellites, and advanced DNA science, it may seem that identification of the arm and hand would be quick and easy. That might be true of something that happened yesterday, but not for this relatively ancient case. Identifying human remains recovered from a 50-year-old frozen accident site proved to be a long, tedious, and often exasperating challenge.

Assuming the arm and hand was from someone on the ill-fated flight, there were 30 possibilities: 24 sailors and six aircrew members. There were five clues that could lead to its identity: fingerprints, the unusual "Iran 1946" ring, the remnants of a pack of Lucky Strikes, a silver cigarette lighter, and, just maybe, DNA.

Any attempt at making a DNA match would be an expensive and difficult process. It required sequencing, or deciphering, the DNA from the arm and hand, then finding appropriate DNA donors among the living relatives of most, if not all, of the lost men.

In 1999, after Sgt. Rodney Dial had retrieved the arm and hand from the crash site, Bob Larson flew it to Anchorage where Alaskan medical examiner Dr. Michael Propst took custody of it. Using the standard technique of rolling the fingers' pads across an ink pad, then rolling them across a fingerprint card, Dr. Propst did his best to obtain fingerprints.

He determined the arm had been severed just above the elbow by something very sharp. X-rays indicated the arm's radius and ulna had been fractured in numerous places. He also concluded the damage was consistent with an airplane crash.

Other than fingerprints, there were no other external identifying marks. Using the fingerprints, Alaska State Department of Public Safety fingerprint specialist Sue Blei took on the task of finding a match. From her office in Anchorage, Blei entered the fingerprints into the latest fingerprint-matching computer systems, which compared the prints with the FBI's files and the California-based nationwide file of millions of fingerprint records. Blei found one very close match. Unfortunately, those prints belonged to a person still incarcerated at a federal prison. She found no others.

In an attempt to find out if any fingerprint files were available from the sailors on board Flight 4422, I contacted Bill Chubb at the National Maritime Center in Arlington, Virginia. Astonishingly, after several months of painstaking research, Chubb located the archived fingerprint files for 22 of the 24 sailors. The Merchant Mariners had been fingerprinted when they signed up in the 1940s. None of the available fingerprint cards had ever been scanned or computerized, so there was no way Blei could have come across them during her initial search.

Blei and her fingerprint team worked hard, attempting a one-to-one match with the Mariners' fingerprint files. Although Dr. Propst had done a remarkable job of obtaining latent fingerprints from the half-century-old fingers, the prints lacked detail, making them difficult to read. At the time, there was no certain way to obtain better latent prints. Blei and her team used specially lit magnifying glasses to examine several of the Merchant Mariners' records to make certain they were not matches. She found four files she thought should not be ruled out, but none of them was conclusive as a match.

After nearly two years of Blei's work, we decided to concentrate on those four files, plus Everett Jenkins (with only thumbprints on file), Eugene Adler, and the six aircrew members—for whom we could find no fingerprint records. Although the process was excruciatingly slow and produced no irrefutable identification, we felt we were making progress.

THE RING STAMPED "Iran 1946" provided a possible avenue for identifying the arm and hand. Although not actually on the hand at the time of its discovery by Sergeant Dial, its proximity to the hand, roughly five feet, suggested that it might have been on one of the fingers at some point. Maybe a family member would recognize it.

We sent photos of the ring and a letter of inquiry to all the known relatives and asked them to try to identify it. They queried older relatives, who in turn studied old photographs in an attempt to find any images resembling the ring. Their replies indicated that 11 of the men did not wear rings, while three definitely wore rings, and two might have. There was no ring information regarding the other 14 men.

The three men known to wear rings were Merchant Mariner Arthur Eilertsen, Flight Purser Robert Haslett, and First Officer Jehu Stickel. Two men who may have worn rings were sailors Carl Sigmund and Stanley Wilkowski. Although the other men on the plane could not be discounted, at least this gave us a little more to go on. Of course, it was also possible that anyone on board Flight 4422 could have bought, traded for, or otherwise obtained the ring for a gift or some other purpose.

Wilkowski and Sigmund had been among those men previously eliminated by Sue Blei as matches, based on the fingerprint analysis. Of the two sailors not eliminated via fingerprints, Merchant Mariner Everett Jenkins, according to his relatives, did not wear rings. No one knew if sailor Eugene Adler wore rings. Of the aircrew members, Navigator Wayne Worsley and Capt. Robert Petry did not wear rings. First Officer Jehu Stickel and Purser Robert Haslett did.

At one point, we thought we might have found a match when Arthur Eilertsen's nephew, Ronald Oravetz, located a photograph of his uncle wearing a large, unusual ring on his left hand. When the image was enhanced, everyone agreed the rings didn't match. However, the 1946 ring appeared to have been made in a similar fashion to the one in the photo, which had an etched image of an anchor on its face.

Another possibility, put forth by Randall Haslett, was that "IRAN" actually stood for "I-RAN" or "1-RAN." Randall theorized that maybe his father, Robert Haslett, had the ring made for him, "Ran" Haslett. In a wedding photo, Robert Haslett wore a large ring on his left hand. But neither theory of identification was conclusive at the time. And, at the time, no other families produced any claims on the ring.

We also tried to determine if anyone on the plane was in Iran in 1946. Although detailed location records of each man were not available, a general study of the merchant ships' voyages, military locations, and the NWA's trip schedules indicated that nearly all of the men on board could have been in Iran. NWA had been heavily involved in transporting WWII soldiers back to the United States from all over the world, and many of the sailors had been active military men during the war in Europe. Most of the other men, as Merchant Mariners during the war, also had opportunities to have been in Iran in 1946.

Having exhausted all reasonable efforts, we had to admit failure, and we abandoned our attempts to learn the arm and hand's identity via the ring.

AN EVEN MORE REMOTE clue was the crushed partial pack of Lucky Strike cigarettes we had found a few hundred feet from the arm and hand. A survey of the families was inconclusive. Of the six certain responses from relatives, four sailors smoked, two didn't smoke, and no one was certain about the others. Jackie Jamele's sister-in-law was adamant that he smoked Luckies, one of the most popular brands of the time. Maybe the cigarettes in the glacier were his, maybe they weren't. There was no way to know.

No relatives commented on the silver-colored cigarette lighter we found near the arm and hand. It had no identifying marks. The lighter remained in the National Park Service archival vault in Alaska.

After the attempting identification via fingerprints, the ring, the cigarettes, and the lighter, we were left with 12 men who could have belonged to the arm and hand.

By 2002, we had exhausted all possibilities except the most expensive and difficult: DNA analysis.

IN 2001, I located a DNA analysis company in Houston, Texas—Identigene. Dr. Propst promptly sent tissue samples to them. After six months of attempting to sequence the DNA, the company gave up. In her final report, Identigene's Dr. Laura Gahn stated: "No quantifiable DNA was obtained. Due to the lack of DNA in this sample, no further analysis was performed."

In subsequent conversations, Gahn told me the biological material of the four samples had been degraded to a point where the DNA strands were too small to get legible results. She said natural events most likely caused the strands to break down into smaller pieces, making them unreadable.

We were very disappointed, but not discouraged. Next, we tried to get the military involved. But because the plane was not engaged in any type of military service when it crashed, they were unable to help us—at least at that time.

We next queried several other commercial forensic companies. None would even consider attempting to read the DNA. We got the same result from other government agencies. Absolutely no one would touch it. It became clear that this was an extremely difficult scientific endeavor that might end up as an expensive failure.

In a last-ditch effort, we again sent a letter to all of Flight 4422's known living relatives describing our attempts and listing the various identification avenues we had tried unsuccessfully. We wrote that we were out of ideas and resources. Quite simply, we needed help.

The relatives responded by offering superb support and a half dozen good ideas. We followed up on each of them, but to no avail. Then we received one more opportunity, one that led to the most tedious, labor-intensive, and frustrating part of the entire project, sending us down another twisting road of investigation that would again change the fate of 4422.

Flight 4422's purser's son, Randall Haslett, made this next segment of the project possible, and it involved all of the families. Our attempts at identifying the arm and hand had come full circle and now lay quite literally in the hands and blood of the relatives: They would supply the necessary DNA.

WHO AM I?

M arc and I met with Dr. Francis G. Fallico on a cold and snowy November afternoon in Anchorage. A staunch supporter of our 4422 project, Dr. Fallico was Alaska's new medical examiner, taking over for the recently retired Dr. Propst. Outside, steam rose and lingered in the cold air above the aluminum-colored Health and Science complex. The sterile examination room was even colder, as he carefully removed the arm and hand from the human-size freezer. Behind Marc and me, on another table, lay the charred corpse of a man who had died in a house fire.

Dr. Fallico removed the sterile wrappings from the arm and hand, giving us our first view of it since we left it in the glacier in 1999. Marc was quiet as we examined the wrinkled, dehydrated, black-blotched specimen. The fragile human arm now looked more like something recovered from an Egyptian tomb. To some, it would have been a macabre scene from a horror movie. To those of us familiar with Flight 4422 and advanced forensic and DNA science, it was a priceless human artifact containing many secrets.

"Do you think there is any way we'll ever determine who this is?" I asked.

"Sure," Dr. Fallico said. "It's difficult, but possible. The only way we'll find out is to try. Let's get this to your DNA specialists and give it our best effort."

After carefully rewrapping the arm and hand, he placed it in a cold-packed, sterile shipping container. It rode in obscurity on commercial jets to DNA expert Dr. Ryan Parr, PhD, suggested by Randall Haslett, at the offices of Genesis Genomics in Thunder Bay, Ontario, Canada, which specializes in leading-edge research on the prevention of cancer and other diseases through the use of DNA technology. Its scientists are also experts in the study of ancient and degraded DNA.

The route of flight, with a bit of irony, followed much the same flight path as Flight 4422, easterly from Anchorage. Slowly but surely, the arm and hand was making its way home. The question remained, whose home and where?

MARC AND I ARE FREQUENTLY asked why we felt so compelled to identify this arm and hand that was almost certainly from a person who died during Flight 4422's crash into Mount Sanford more than 50 years ago. Many times, we asked ourselves the same question. The short answer is that we were stubborn and wanted an answer. At first, we thought it would be easy—just examine the fingerprints and make a match to existing records. We thought that would be a nice closure to the entire project. But it wasn't that easy and as it became more difficult, we worked even harder. We also thought it was strange that from the 30 people on board the plane, this was the only human remain ever found. If we'd found remains from several people, or located some personal identification—such as a wallet or dog tags—we would not have gone so far. Using pieces of metal to identify the DC-4 was one thing. Positive identification of a human on the plane was an entirely different task.

And there was no proof that the arm and hand actually belonged to one of the 30. As our research revealed, there had been many dangerous expeditions looking for Flight 4422. It was possible someone from one of those expeditions died during a search on the glacier. There was also the possibility someone not documented on the manifest was on the plane.

When the first fingerprint study failed, we became even more resolute in our efforts to find an answer. What's more, the family members of those lost on 4422 urged us on. We would get a phone call or email weekly inquiring about our progress. And it wasn't just Marc and me—everyone involved with 4422 wanted an answer. So we forged onward, having no idea how difficult it was going to be but resolved that we would not give up until every possible avenue of discovery was exhausted.

I was disappointed when the first DNA test came back as impossible to read. Then I was even more disappointed when we learned the U. S. military wouldn't help us, even though most of those on board were ex-military.

The synergy and energy among the members of our team grew as more people became involved. Each new member became hooked by the mystery of who the arm and hand belonged to, as well as 4422's other mysteries. We were all infected with the passion of the quest.

ONCE RANDALL HASLETT got involved, the fervor for making an ID increased. He and his wife, Carole, live in New Brunswick, Canada, where he works as an investment advisor. Haslett was 15 months old at the time of the crash. Throughout his life, he has researched Flight 4422, attempting to find answers about his father's death. His own plans for an expedition to the crash site in 1997 were canceled when his mother suddenly became ill and died. Despite this loss, he still wanted to learn everything he could about the crash. The coincidence of his expedition plans to our 1997 expedition was interesting.

Through CNN and the Internet, Haslett contacted us in 1999 after our discovery was made public. He subsequently supplied an infusion of spirit and inspiration at a time when it was needed most. In search of help for our project, he made the contact with Dr. Ryan Parr at Genesis Genomics. At the time, Dr. Parr was working on a private project, attempting to decode the identity of an unknown child-victim's body recovered immediately after the sinking of the *Titanic*. Marc and I were elated when Haslett informed us that Dr. Parr had agreed to help us. It was during a conference call among Marc, me, and Drs. Fallico and Parr, we decided to ship the arm and hand to Dr. Parr. Now, it was there.

WITH LIVING TISSUE, or that of recently deceased persons, a quick identification using DNA technology may be possible. Discovering the identity of a long-deceased person, however, is often not nearly as easy as shown on TV, where the entire story is compressed into an hour. This is now known as the "CSI effect" and is the bane of real-life investigators and prosecutors. In the real world, it may take several months or even years of difficult research to analyze ancient or degraded DNA. Sometimes, the DNA is in such bad condition it can't be successfully analyzed.

Parr's first goal was to determine if any DNA remained that could be analyzed. He explained the fascinating, complicated, and laborious process to me. Many procedures are used in analyzing DNA: extraction of samples from specific areas of the body part, chemicals, electronics, heating, cooling, centrifugal spinning, and specific fluids mixed in at various periods of time are just part of the process.

Parr pointed out that there are two kinds of DNA typically used for identification purposes: Y-DNA (nuclear) and mitochondrial DNA (mtDNA). Y-DNA is handed down along the direct male line of the family, from father to son. All males who can be connected along the exclusively male line of a family will have the same Y-DNA. There is a problem, however, in trying to use Y-DNA in what is considered an ancient project like Flight 4422. In Y-DNA, there is only one Y-chromosome per cell, and it is 50 million "bits" long. In the case of highly degraded remains, there can be little chance of harvesting enough of the right kind of Y-DNA to determine its identity. And although not a specific problem for our project, Y-DNA is not useful for identifying females. The bottom line: Y-DNA was not suitable for this project.

Mitochondrial (mtDNA) is passed along the direct female line of the family. mtDNA is present in small inclusions called mitochondria outside the nucleus of a cell. For the purposes of our research, Dr. Parr gave me some examples of how the mtDNA rules apply. A mother passes her mtDNA to all of her children, but only her daughters pass it on to the next generation. My own sisters and brother and I inherited the same mtDNA from our mother, but only my sisters' children will inherit it in the next generation. If my brother had children, they would inherit their mtDNA from their mother.

The mitochondrial genome is approximately 16,500 bits long—very small compared to the Y-chromosome. However, each mitochondrion can contain up to 10 copies of its own genome and each cell can contain up to 1,000 mitochondria. Therefore, up to 10,000 copies of the mitochondrial genome may exist in each cell.

Since mtDNA is so abundant compared to Y-DNA, and because the mtDNA genome is so much smaller and can be used to identify both males and females, it is the kind of DNA most often used to identify highly degraded remains. In regard to Flight 4422's victims, we needed to study mtDNA.

Dr. Parr removed the sterile wrappings from the arm and hand, which still looked like something from an ancient crypt. Some pieces of the arm were missing, removed earlier as samples during our first failed DNA test. Most likely, this was our last chance for identification.

The Genesis Genomics team quickly discovered a problem: formaldehyde. Immediately after the arm and hand arrived at the medical examiner's office in 1999, unbeknownst to Marc and me, Dr. Propst had soaked it in embalming fluid that included formaldehyde. Parr explained that, unfortunately, formaldehyde makes DNA very difficult to sequence. The DNA cross-links to itself, similar to how duct tape sticks to itself, forming a messy wad. Just a few years earlier, the damage caused to DNA by formaldehyde would have been deemed permanent. Now, due to recent scientific advances, that was no longer necessarily true.

When Propst took possession of the arm and hand after the State Troopers brought it out from the glacier, he had no idea we would go so far as to study the DNA. This arm and hand recovery was not related to a recent crime, so embalming had seemed to be the best choice. In the case of 4422, the arm and hand's embalming eventually turned out to be fortuitous.

Then the team discovered another problem: The arm was contaminated with bacteria and fungi that grow in Alaskan glaciers. When the arm and hand melted out of the glacial ice in 1999, it became partially unfrozen for a week or two. This allowed an acceleration of growth of the bacteria and fungi, which invaded much of the soft tissue, skin, and muscle and part of the bone. This growth was slowed or stopped by being refrozen in the sterile freezers of the medical examiner and subsequent scientists. But some irreversible damage was done.

Although DNA deteriorates on its own (depending on the heat and humidity of its environment), the presence of fungi and bacteria causes it to deteriorate much more quickly, making it even more difficult to extract enough DNA for analysis. In the case of 4422, considering the damage done by the embalming, temperature, humidity, fungi, and bacteria, Dr. Parr had his work cut out for him. It was a difficult, slow process. But he and his team had become passionate about Flight 4422—just as we were. They persevered.

After more than a year of hard work, the team was finally able to extract just enough DNA to begin ruling out potential matches. They referred to this as a partial DNA profile. It was like trying to drive somewhere using a faded roadmap in which not all the details are clear. This was new, evolving science—a journey into the unknown. Sooner or later, we realized, Dr. Parr would need help.

A DNA profile on its own is not useful. For identification purposes, the profile must be compared to the DNA of a family member—the "family reference." If it matches, you have positive identification. When Y-DNA is used, the reference must be a male related to the candidate along the direct male line of his family. When mtDNA is used, the reference can be either male or female, but must be related to the candidate along the female line of the family.

In the case of Flight 4422, we had to use mtDNA. This presented another challenge: finding at least one family member whose DNA would match the DNA of the remains—that is, if the arm and hand really did belong to one of the people on the plane.

We began contacting relatives to obtain DNA samples, and by early 2005 Dr. Parr had the first family reference samples from relatives of three of Flight 4422's aircrew members. After either swabbing their cheeks for DNA tissue or pricking their fingers for blood, the relatives mailed the samples to Dr. Parr. The Genesis Genomics team read the reference samples and compared them to the mtDNA profile. Dr. Parr called me a week later with the bad news: "Sorry, no match—not even close."

"Back to the drawing board," I said.

We had to find family references for more of the men who died in 1948.

Even though we were still in contact with many relatives of all the aircrew members, it wasn't easy locating the correct relatives—female relatives with a direct link to each decedent's mother.

Time had been marching on; people had passed away, some changed addresses, others changed phone numbers and email addresses. But with wonderful help from 4422's relatives, we finally located family references for five more victims.

There was one very interesting saga. In the late 1990s, I'd located a cousin of Capt. James Van Cleef. He told us the captain had a brother living in the state of Washington, but I had been unsuccessful in contacting him. In 2005, I again telephoned the distant cousin in Nampa, Idaho, and explained the desperate need for a family reference. After some research, the cousin learned that Van Cleef had a sister, Benita. He thought she had moved to Idaho many years earlier.

Grasping at whatever straws I could find, I called the Twin Falls, Idaho, courthouse. It only took two hours for the amazing staff to determine exactly who Benita was. They figured out that her name was actually Venita, not Benita. She married Charles Beglan in 1932 and gave birth to one son, Matthew, and one daughter, JoAnne, who had several children. On March 3, 2005, I spoke with Matthew "Brick" Beglan. Among many details of James Van Cleef's life, Beglan told me, "I clearly remember that a million dollars of gold was rumored to have been on that plane."

Five days later, I spoke with Beglan's sister, JoAnne, who also recalled that there was supposedly millions of dollars of gold bullion on the plane. Neither ever heard why it was on board or to whom it belonged. I also spoke with Joanne's daughter, Katie, and arranged to obtain a DNA sample from her.

Katie and I also discussed the history of the legendary DC-4. An hour into the conversation, the hairs on the back of my neck rose when she told me, "This is certainly strange. Last weekend, after decades of doing nothing with it and for no reason in particular, we pulled Uncle Jim's old green 1948 Studebaker out of the garage and started restoring it. Seems kind of strange, doesn't it?"

I was speechless.

Indeed, several weeks after the 1948 crash of Flight 4422, a family member had retrieved Capt. James Van Cleef's Studebaker from NWA's Minneapolis parking lot. The brand-new vehicle had been stored by various family members for half a century. As the latest caretakers, Katie and her husband had pulled the car out into the sunlight and started restoring it the weekend of March 4, 2005—one day after I located descendants of Van Cleef's sister, Venita. The timing was just one more inexplicable coincidence associated with Flight 4422.

OVER THE NEXT MANY months, I made contact with several more relatives: Capt. Robert Petry's sister; Jehu Stickel's mother's sister; Eugene Adler's sister's daughter; a female cousin of Everett Jenkins; Polly Rector Logan; and Wayne Worsley's sister. They all were cooperative in providing Dr. Parr with DNA samples. However, none of their samples matched the arm and hand, thus eliminating five of the six aircrew members as matches.

Finding an appropriate relative for Robert Haslett was a big problem. Randall Haslett and his wife, Carole, worked feverishly trying to locate a DNA donor. They wrote letters to Germany and even hired a German genealogist, but got nowhere.

Haslett finally located information about his Aunt Louise, who died of cancer in 1988. She would be a perfect DNA donor. A search of hospitals for biopsy and other potential DNA material was fruitless. We even discussed having Aunt Louise's body exhumed. That idea seemed pointless when Haslett learned she had been cremated. However, Dr. Parr explained the charred remains might still contain viable DNA, depending on the temperature of the cremation. It seemed that all we needed to do was to find her ashes.

Then, one afternoon I received an email from Haslett that apparently ended the saga of Aunt Louise: "I finally found my Aunt Louise…in Puget Sound."

Haslett had discovered that her ashes had been consigned to the waters of the Pacific, there to drift forever.

Unbelievably, in late 2005, I telephoned Genesis Genomics for an update. An excited Dr. Parr said, "Guess what? We received the envelopes from Randall Haslett."

"What envelopes?" I asked.

"Oh, I guess you didn't know about this. Haslett had found a few envelopes sent to him from his Aunt Louise. The areas where she licked them closed may contain her DNA. We're going to use a new process called Laser Capture. If it's successful, that might be the last sample necessary to make a match. Let's keep our fingers crossed…no guarantees."

But then, a few months later, a disappointed Dr. Parr telephoned me with the news: His team had not been able to isolate the DNA on the envelopes. It seemed that over the years too many people had handled the envelopes and they had become contaminated. This time, it was certain: We had come to the end of the hunt for Aunt Louise's DNA.

Then Dr. Parr surprised me with some very good news. Two other top DNA researchers had joined the team: Dr. Odile Loreille, PhD, at the Armed Forces DNA Identification Lab (AFDIL), and Dr. Dongya Yang, PhD, at

Simon Fraser University, Burnaby, British Columbia, Canada. Dr. Loreille would join us as the primary DNA expert and Drs. Yang and Parr would back up her research by duplicating the tests. They soon became passionate researchers for Flight 4422. But, there were many reasons for this that went way beyond just helping with identifying the arm.

IT WAS IN 2006 that Dr. Odile Loreille, a scientist who specialized in ancient DNA, moved from France to Rockville, Maryland, to begin working at the AFDIL. Dr. Loreille is among the world's top paleo DNA scientists. One of her claims to fame is that she sequenced the DNA from a 100,000-year-old cave bear. That's right—a 100,000-year-old cave bear. She came to Rockville to work on a special project aimed at removing the "un" from unknown by attempting to analyze and sequence the DNA of the embalmed U. S. Korean War soldiers interred at the Punchbowl, a cemetery in an extinct volcanic crater high above the beaches of Honolulu, Hawaii.

During the Korean Was of the 1950s, a war that has never officially come to an end, many U.S. soldiers died. Although most were identified, hundreds remained unknown. They were initially consigned to an ex-POW camp in northern Japan named Kokura, a makeshift morgue and temporary holding place for their remains. For preservation, their bodies were soaked in formaldehyde for several days, after which they were placed in storage. Years later, the men were transferred to the Cemetery of the Pacific, also known as the Punchbowl.

From its magnificent perch high above the beaches of Honolulu, the Punchbowl offers a beautiful view of a hundred miles or more across the Pacific Ocean, including Pearl Harbor. The Punchbowl is a botanical garden, with a tropical abundance of life. In the northeast corner of the cemetery, above carefully manicured grass and Plumeria, narra, Formosa koa, monkey pod, and tecoma trees, is the area known as Section U. Here, under flat, gray stone markers stamped with the word "Unknown," 867 U. S. soldiers from the Korean War were buried. Although a few have had been identified by various means over the years, most of their names remain known only to God—for now.

AFDIL works directly with JPAC (Joint POW/MIA Accounting Command), at Hickam Air Force Base, Hawaii. In a quest to identify every U. S. soldier lost in military service, JPAC studies all available data, including such things as bone structure and personal items, whereas AFDIL specializes in DNA. Recent advances in DNA science offer new techniques to identify these men. This developing science also results in all kinds of scientific spinoffs in terms of research into the world of DNA and the human body.

I was already familiar with and had visited the Punchbowl and JPAC because I'd flown a mission involving JPAC (then known as CILHI-Central Identification Lab Hawaii) in the late 1980s while flying C-141s in the Air Force. Now, due to the connection with 4422, I would visit the Punchbowl many times.

Following a DNA conference attended by both Dr. Loreille and Dr. Parr, he contacted Dr. Loreille at the AFDIL and asked if she could help with the 4422 project. The AFDIL at the time was under the direction of Dr. Mike Coble. He granted her permission to participate.

AFDIL's involvement and study of the arm was made possible due to the potential advances in DNA science. The arm and hand from 4422 was nearly a decade older than the soldiers from the Korean War and it had been recovered from the ice immediately after our discovery. Within hours, it was placed in cold storage, then preserved using fluids (including formaldehyde) during several days, similar to the treatment of the remains of our Korean War soldiers. Thus, the formaldehyde-embalmed specimen from Flight 4422's glacier was unique and offered a rare intermediate scientific opportunity that could advance DNA knowledge.

AT THE TIME, many non-DNA factors tended to indicate the arm and hand belonged to Robert Haslett. As the purser, he might have been standing at the time of impact rather than belted in his seat. The fingernails appeared to be fairly well manicured, and the hand did not appear to be greasy or oily—like a sailor's might be. Exhibiting no burn marks, the arm and hand had apparently been thrown free of the impact's ensuing fire ball.

Randall Haslett was continuing his search for a family member who could supply an mtDNA sample. If he could not find one, it would be necessary for Drs. Parr and Loreille to try to analyze the highly degraded Y-DNA and attempt a match with Haslett's own Y-DNA.

After Loreille tested a few samples from the arm and hand, Parr shipped the entire human arm to her at AFDIL in August 2006. At that point, Dr. Loreille effectively took over the DNA project and became the new primary driving force behind Flight 4422's DNA research. She worked late into the nights and sometimes on weekends developing new protocols. She extracted uncontaminated samples of DNA hidden in the deepest recesses of the bone of the "John Doe" arm and hand. Finally, late one night in September 2006—success!

At eight o'clock the next morning, a very excited Loreille called all our team members and informed us that she had been able to obtain and sequence a large enough amount of noncontaminated DNA to read the entire DNA sequence necessary for identification. She also quickly confirmed the earlier partial DNA sequence accomplished by Parr and his staff. Now equipped with a clear, detailed road map, we could forge ahead with confidence, attempting matches with more family members' DNA.

On the heels of this good news, a few days later Loreille dropped a bomb on Marc and me during a conference call. In her charming French accent, she said, "Now we need to go back and get mitochondrial DNA references from the relatives of the rest of the 30 men."

"Didn't we already rule out many of them," Marc asked, "with the fingerprints?"

"Well, not quite," she replied. "The fingerprints never provided completely reliable eliminations due to the lack of detail. The 1999 study provided some general, nonspecific eliminations based on the rough data Susan Blei had to work with."

After a pregnant silence, I said, "So you mean we have to find 22 more female relatives?"

"That's right," she said. "We'll need to eliminate the rest of them one by one, at least until we have a positive match. A son of one of those females will also work. We can continue by using the general guidance of the results of Blei's fingerprints analysis. Of course, we can also rule out the eight victims already studied by Ryan and me. We must go through all the rest, one by one, with absolute certainty."

Over nearly a decade, Marc and I had done our best to maintain contact with the relatives of those lost on the plane and keep them updated with phone calls, emails, and notes included in Christmas letters. But it was difficult for us to go back and again ask for more help. It wasn't the task itself that was hard—it was the need to discuss all the details again. The relatives were much older now; some had even moved to elder care facilities. Marc and I were older, too. Flight 4422 had taken its toll on us by requiring much more time, work, and expense than we'd ever anticipated.

We knew most relatives would read an update letter, hand it to a niece or nephew, and ask for a summary, or simply put it aside until the proper moment. But we also felt that asking for DNA samples and more in-depth family history pushed the limits and gave us an uneasy feeling. Unlike police investigators, we were a private team with no power to obtain warrants. We had no way to force anyone to give us a DNA sample. The power of persuasion and the relatives' desire for answers were our only tools.

Despite these possible roadblocks, we went to work and located several more DNA family references. But after finding the first individuals, it was clear it was going to be very difficult to locate more. Loreille contacted genetic genealogist Terry Barton in Georgia to get help from the genealogy community. Barton in turn contacted an expert forensic genealogist in California, Dr. Colleen Fitzpatrick.

Dr. Fitzpatrick, as it turned out, is another relentless professional. A retired optical and laser scientist with a degree in nuclear physics, she now works as a forensic genealogist, specializing in DNA identification. Her business associate, Andy Yeiser, works with her and assists in her research. As much a scientific skill as an art, forensic genealogy takes a dedicated, well-trained mind. Fitzpatrick explained to us the difficulties involved in tracing specific members in a family's history—difficulties further complicated in our case by the fact we that had to find individuals with the proper DNA.

Since mtDNA would have to be used, we would have to trace a relative linked along the female line. So, the family reference could be the victim's mother, his brother or sister (linked through their mother), his maternal aunt (linked through his mother and his maternal grandmother), or a son or daughter of his maternal aunt (his first cousin on his mother's side).

But since a woman may change her name when she marries, the family name of the sought-after relative can be any name. Because the victims of the accident died so long ago, many of their immediate family members also were deceased. We needed to do research into more distant family members, and trace their descendants.

For each generation further in the past that a genealogist needs to trace, two additional family names have to be identified and included in the family research. When a genealogist finds one additional name up the family tree to a common ancestor, a second name then must be traced back down to a family member alive today—a very complicated process.

Now, with a complete mtDNA profile, we began to work on obtaining mtDNA from appropriate relatives of 22 more men. We began making calls and mailed many letters to relatives of the men lost on 4422.

Fitzpatrick went right to work and began locating distant relatives of several more of the men. The first family she worked with was that of Olan (aka Olav) Jacobsen, a cook on the *Sunset*. We only knew that he had a brother named Carl and his mother was Amelia. Even though Fitzpatrick was in Guatemala at the time, it took her less than an hour to locate information about the brother. Subsequently, we located a living niece, Carla. Ironically, she lived very close to AFDIL's Rockville headquarters. A few weeks later, we located Olan's aunt's son, a minister in Staten Island—a perfect mitochondrial

DNA donor. Loreille sent him a DNA test kit.

Using information from many sources, we built family trees to assist us in identifying potential DNA donors. Just when we needed even more help with this time-consuming work, yet another researcher/genealogist joined the group: Christine Lyon.

I met Lyon through my writing work with another project: NWA Flight 2501, a DC-4 that plummeted into Lake Michigan on June 23, 1950. Although some pieces of the plane were recovered, no one knew why it crashed. Michigan Shipwreck Research Association (MSRA) and its director, Valerie van Heest, are dedicated to finding Flight 2501. MSRA teamed up with famed adventurer-researcher-author Clive Cussler and his world-renowned research organization, the National Underwater and Marine Agency (NUMA), in conducting a deep water side-scan sonar search of Lake Michigan. Lyon was a member of the MSRA 2501 team. Upon learning about Flight 4422, she offered to help—and proved to be one more tiger. She took up the task of searching for relatives of Merchant Mariner Morris Brooks, one of the more difficult efforts.

Loreille led the DNA team, while Fitzpatrick directed the genealogical research. Lyon worked with both. As though affected by a magical spell cast from the Alaskan glacier, each person gave his or her all for 4422.

Over several months, thousands of emails zipped back and forth among all of our team members. I would land from a week-long international flight and try to catch up to my overloaded email inbox. Slowly, one at a time, appropriate DNA donors were located by Lyon, Fitzpatrick, and Loreille. They gave me the contact information and I made the initial phone calls to family members, confirmed the family links, and coordinated DNA sample shipments. Loreille and the AFDIL team received the samples, sequenced them, and compared them to that of the arm and hand. Those results were verified by Parr's team and Yang. Although occasionally frustrated, we were making good progress.

Through this tedious process, we eliminated each sample as a match, narrowing the possibilities. Randall Haslett's father was eliminated by using Randall's own blood for nuclear DNA (Y-STR) comparison. He was finally comfortable knowing much more about his father's life and the fact that his father rested entirely on Mount Sanford.

One day Fitzpatrick called and said, "Okay, what about Francis Van Zandt?"

Francis Joseph Van Zandt was one of four Merchant Mariners for whom we had very little information.

I faxed her the little data I had, and she called again.

"Okay, that wasn't much at all," she said. "Now send me what other Van Zandt information you have—every possibility, even far-fetched guesses. I need every note. By the way, I already found some information from a personnel file about a Van Zandt who had a scar on his right hand. Which hand did you find?"

"We found a left hand."

She said, "Shoot, this could have been easy, but I guess not."

I mailed her several pages covered with scribbled notes of inconclusive possibilities and dead-end contacts I'd made over the years and one article from the March 14, 1948, issue of the *Roanoke Times* that indicated Van Zandt had lived in Roanoke, Virginia. Using that information, I had not been successful in finding anyone remotely associated with Francis Joseph Van Zandt.

Meanwhile, with the number of DNA match possibilities dwindling and the difficulty of locating more mtDNA donors increasing, Loreille suggested we give the fingerprints another try. She asked me to get the original John Doe fingerprint card from Alaska. I agreed to check and said I would also review the fingerprint and results from Sue Blei's study six years earlier. This would be yet another rehashing of the old research, but it had to be done. Loreille then called Forensics Professor Ted Robinson at George Washington University in Washington, D.C. He jumped at the opportunity to work with the famous arm recovered from the Alaskan glacier. But he did more. He contacted ex-FBI agent Mike Grimm, Sr., a retired Virginia fingerprint expert who works with his son, Mike Grimm, Jr.

Loreille's goal was only to achieve a positive identification by any method. Involving fingerprint experts served as the shot of a starter's pistol for what became a professional race of sorts between DNA and fingerprint experts.

We now had two all-star teams working with us. I assisted wherever I could and was amazed at the incredible fortune bestowed on our project. It now had been nine long years since we found the lonely arm and hand frozen on the glacier, and 59 years since the crash in the desolate Territory of Alaska.

Mike Grimm, Sr., had recently retired as Virginia's latent fingerprint examiner. He operates EVIDENT Crime Scene Products, which supplies law enforcement with the latest forensic equipment and technology. Prior to working for the state of Virginia, he was an FBI agent and continues to be involved with unusual and difficult forensic cases.

When Professor Robinson made his first call to him, Grimm was in Cape Town, South Africa, working on a case. When Robinson began to describe our 4422 project, Grimm immediately recognized the story because his father, Roy Grimm, was a trucker in Alaska at the time of 4422's crash; he had listened to the radio programs, read the newspapers, and heard the rumors about some kind of treasure being on Flight 4422. Years later, he told the legendary story to his son.

Because of his knowledge of the legendary wreck, Grimm, Sr. was immediately excited to be part of the project. Along with him, we got his son, who has a high level of photography and imaging skills. The Grimms seemed to be just another wonderful coincidence. But of course, there were more.

Behind Cape Town, Table Mountain rises majestically, providing a stunning background for photography. Prior to Robinson's phone call, and knowing nothing about the 4422 project, Grimm, Sr., snapped a photo of Table Mountain from Cape Town's harbor. Upon returning home to Union Hall, Virginia, two weeks later, he opened the email file I had sent. It included a copy of the only known photograph of the oil tanker, SS *Sunset*. Goose bumps popped up on his arms as he looked at the photo I'd sent. There, in the background, was Table Mountain. Where Grimm, Sr., had snapped his photo a few days earlier was the exact same spot from which the photo was taken of the *Sunset* half a century earlier.

The Grimms joined Robinson and spent a full day at the National Maritime Center in Arlington, Virginia, reviewing the available fingerprint cards. This time only 14 fingerprint cards of the 24 Merchant Mariners could be located, versus 23 that were located in 1999. Apparently the missing files had been misplaced and could not be found. Just as in 1999 and 2000, and using my 1999 photocopy of the John Doe arm and hand's fingerprint card, Grimm was unable to make any matches from the fingerprint records but continued to make some eliminations based on general patterns. To make it more difficult, the original fingerprint card Dr. Propst created in 1999 could not be located in Alaska. Mike Grimm, Jr., photographed all the available 4422 Merchant Mariners' fingerprint cards for later study.

Robinson made several trips to AFDIL to study the fingers of the arm/hand, and soon determined there was no way to obtain new latent fingerprints by using standard techniques. The shriveled, desiccated skin was nearly smooth; the ridges, islands, and whorls normally seen on the epidermis were long gone, having naturally sloughed off and disintegrated. Now only the skin's smooth underlying dermal layer remained. Each day, more cells naturally came off the fingers' pads. Soon there would be no fingerprints. We were in a race with time.

Back in his Virginia office, Mike Grimm, Sr., used my copy of the original

1999 fingerprint card, photos of the fingerprint cards, and a magnifying glass to isolate several unique ridge details. Using these clues, he eliminated several more of the Mariners' prints from being a match. This narrowed the field of possibilities to just four cards. He called Robinson and told him if he was to make any more progress, he needed better prints.

In his Washington laboratory, Robinson thought long and hard and about how one might obtain new fingerprints from what was now considered ancient human tissue. One possibility was rehydrating the dermal layer—the layer of skin underneath the epidermal layer.

Burning the midnight oil at the AFDIL lab, Robinson and Loreille tried several methods to rehydrate and rejuvenate the prints. They used extreme care because it was a one-shot game—there was always the danger of completely destroying the fingerprint tissue. Nothing worked. Then, Grimm, Sr., suggested trying a new product called ID Enhancer. This is a patented, confidential mixture of chemicals manufactured by KDL Solutions and distributed by EVIDENT. It's used to rejuvenate ancient human tissue to a point where fingerprints almost magically raise up from the dermal layer.

Again late at night, Robinson and Loreille worked on the fingers, using the ID Enhancer. Finally, the ridges, islands, and whorls created by living tissue temporarily rose from the flattened skin. Then, using a special silicone, Robinson made a cast of the new prints to permanently preserve them. The fingertips pads were then removed from their fingers and again soaked in the solution. Even better print details were achieved.

The second set of raised prints was again cast in silicone, then a positive impression was made using a Dental Stone hard casting material. After drying, then dusting with fine fingerprint powder, the positive cast prints were photographed by Mike Grimm, Jr. Using macro photography and enhancement techniques, he created a set of incredible photographs with fine detail of contours, islands, ridges, and scars of each finger and the thumb. The Grimms and Robinson now had to go back and compare the new images to four files archived at the National Maritime Center.

On September 5, 2007, I flew into Washington and went to the nondescript AFDIL headquarters. Fitzpatrick and her associate Andy Yeiser, had flown in from California. We were scheduled to give a presentation about Flight 4422 to the members of the forensic team at AFDIL at noon the next day. Fitzpatrick surprised me with the names of the relatives of two more of the sailors—a niece of Morris Brooks and a niece and nephew of Francis Joseph Van Zandt, both sailors on board Flight 4422. Melva Paine Murray of Bedminster, New Jersey, was the daughter of Morris Brooks' sister,

Gertrude. I contacted her that afternoon. Murray was only vaguely aware of 4422's crash and Brooks' death. The last family contact with Brooks had been in 1941. But she was happy to assist, so we sent her a DNA kit. The Van Zandt contact would take more time.

I spent the afternoon in the lab with Loreille, the AFDIL team, Fitzpatrick, and Yeiser, learning more about DNA. Due to the DNA work accomplished so far, combined with Mike Grimm Sr.'s, fingerprint study, we now concentrated on four persons: John Elkins, Edwin Mustra, Travis McCall, and Francis Van Zandt. We were closing in—we could all feel it. I went to sleep that night believing we were at another turning point for the DC-4 and its men.

END GAME

Early the next morning, I met Professor Robinson and Mike Grimm, Sr. and Jr., at the National Maritime Center in Arlington, Virginia. The office doors opened at exactly 8 a.m. Ten minutes later, the four of us were seated at a large conference table.

Laid out before us were the fingerprint and personnel files of four Merchant Mariners who had not been eliminated by DNA or by fingerprints. However, the files in front of us also contained many archived sets of prints we hadn't seen before.

In the center of the table, Mike Grimm, Sr., laid an 18-inch-wide photograph taken by his son of the newly acquired fingerprint images Robinson and Loreille had obtained from the hand. Amazingly, for each single ridge normally found on the epidermal layer of fingerprints, the dermal layer underneath actually consisted of two ridges. That's where Grimm, Sr.'s, years of experience paid off.

He opened the first folder—Van Zandt's—and his eyes lit up like a Christmas tree. In front of him lay several sets of full, perfectly legible fingerprints inked in 1943. After having spent so much time studying the recently cast prints from the hand, the retired FBI forensic specialist knew immediately that these prints were an unquestionable match! That was it. We had just made the first official identification of the arm and hand—by fingerprints.

With an official voice, Mike Grimm, Sr., sat back in his chair and said, "This has been the most amazing and rewarding project I have ever been involved with. I have matched these fingerprints with those of Merchant Mariner Francis Joseph Van Zandt. This identifies the arm and hand as belonging to Francis Joseph Van Zandt, to the exclusion of all others. These are a perfect match."

Mike Grimm, Sr., had just made the oldest known postmortem

identification via fingerprints in history.

It really was that quick. We all began a mini-celebration right there around the conference table. We all stood, shook hands, and raised our cups of sodas. I toasted, "To Francis Van Zandt and all the others on 4422!"

Four of the office employees came in and looked at the prints and photos, and they too took part in our celebration. They had worked with us since 1999 and were equally fascinated by the match. I called Dr. Loreille and told her the news. She was astonished and passed the information to Dr. Mike Coble (AFDIL chief), Dr. Fitzpatrick, and Andy Yeiser, but told no one else.

We four spent two more hours double-checking all the other data in Francis Van Zandt's file and the files of the other three Merchant Mariners. Each file contained excellent prints, making it relatively easy for Grimm, Sr., to eliminate each of them. We departed the National Maritime Center in time for me to present the Flight 4422 program at AFDIL. My audience was in for a big surprise.

ON THE DRIVE BACK to AFDIL I called Marc and told him the news. He was surprised and very happy we had actually made a positive identification. We discussed the fact that this finding not only identified one of the 30 men on board the plane, but that the identification provided a fourth confirmation that the debris in the glacier was that of 4422. Although there was still much work to do, those few hours at the Maritime Center marked the beginning of the end of our 19-year journey.

Our success also marked the end of the race of identification between fingerprints and DNA. In the world of forensics and identification, there is a bit of a professional rivalry between the group that feels DNA is the most accurate identifier and those who feel that fingerprints are better. The truth is that both are necessary and each has its advantages, depending on the situation. In this case, identification by fingerprints happened first. But it was Loreille's DNA study that had narrowed the field significantly and led us back to the study of the fingerprints, which had been set aside as unsuccessful and impossible eight years earlier. Each discipline supported and substantiated the other.

After my 40-minute program at AFDIL, Professor Robinson and Mike Grimm, Sr., took the podium and gave a brief talk about fingerprints and, in particular, those from the hand. This was unusual because the audience was made up of DNA scientists and their assistants. They were involved strictly with DNA and were all expecting some kind of DNA information associated with 4422 rather than anything to do with fingerprints. The presence of

Grimm, Sr., was a bit like having a fox in the henhouse. He explained the details of our fingerprint study. Then, with no fanfare, Professor Robinson joined him and caught the group completely off guard by calmly announcing that we had just made the first official identification of the arm and hand—by fingerprints.

"The arm and hand," Robinson said, "belongs to Merchant Mariner Francis Joseph Van Zandt."

Gasps, murmurs, and finally applause came from the audience of 20 DNA specialists. They were gracious in congratulating all of us. But while they applauded our hard work and what we had accomplished, they also were slightly dismayed. They were somewhat placated when Loreille took the podium and explained that more work lay ahead: To further validate Van Zandt's fingerprints, we had to find an appropriate mitochondrial DNA donor whose mtDNA matched the arm and hand.

I left Maryland late that afternoon. On the way back to Washington's Reagan National Airport, I stopped by Arlington Cemetery. The summer had ended slightly early that year and the leaves had already begun to fall. As I stood at the cemetery, I heard the familiar sound of timelessness. Among the long rows of white markers, a gentle wind blew the loose leaves to and fro, rustling and whispering at the commands of the wind. In the distance, a bugle played a solemn Taps for the latest interment.

It was the same familiar wind I'd heard in the American cemeteries in Normandy and Verdun, France, at the Punchbowl, and on Mount Sanford in faraway Alaska, where the remains of 30 men and the wreckage of a DC-4 moved slowly in a glacier. It was the sound of eternity—nature's solemn reminder of how helpless we humans are compared to the relentless march of time.

AS WE CONTINUED our DNA study, we now focused most of our attention on the relatives of Francis Van Zandt—one of the most difficult cases. Lyon took my information and studied birth and death records from Vermont and New York. She also contacted Laurie Van Sandt (many immigrants changed the spelling of their name upon immigration to the United States) at the Van Zandt Historical Society in Horsham, Pennsylvania, where she learned that the Van Zandts were closely connected to the Conway family, many of whom immigrated to this country from Ireland. She also determined there were still many Van Zandts and Conways living in and around Troy, New York.

Using the Internet, census records, and telephone directories, Lyon located several more members of the extended Van Zandt family in northern

New York. Armed with those potential contacts, I traveled to several cities in New York and interviewed many senior members of the Conway and Van Zandt families. I also visited several graveyards in New York and obtained information from headstones and cemetery archives.

Through research by contacting churches and priests in Bennington and Arlington, Vermont, we obtained a copy of Francis Joseph Van Zandt's birth certificate. It showed that he was born in 1911 and his parents were Orville Van Zandt, Sr., and Margaret Conway. In search of more information, Fitzpatrick contacted archivist Bill Budde of the Bennington Archival Museum. Budde located church archives from the early 1900s that provided background on the local Irish/German community and four important documents: a second version of Francis J. Van Zandt's birth certificate; a birth certificate for his older brother, Orville, Jr.; a marriage certificate for their parents; and a receipt for a coffin for another brother, Peter, who died at age three. With this information, we knew we were on the right track.

This was our first big break in learning the genealogy. That second version of Orville, Jr.'s, record of birth indicated that his and Francis Van Zandt's mother, Margaret Conway, was from Timerick, Ireland. Fitzpatrick immediately identified this as a typo or misprint.

"There is no Timerick, Ireland," she told me. "The T had to have mistakenly replaced an L at some point in the past, a transcription error." She continued, "Ireland has 32 counties, and you have to be familiar with Ireland to know that."

Being of Irish heritage, Fitzpatrick had visited Ireland numerous times, studied there, and was familiar with the country and its families' genealogy. Looking back, she said, "It's amazing how one word, written many years earlier, could be so important."

Ireland's Margaret Conway was now the key to the genealogy.

The Conway and Van Zandt relatives, in addition to members of the extended families Jubic and Bolster in upstate New York, helped us tremendously. Through them, we got our second break when we learned the names of two Conway sisters and one brother who arrived in America in the 1890s, and the name of another brother who got lost in transit. Now Lyon's list of names on the family tree puzzle was beginning to make sense.

In search of Margaret Conways in Ireland around 1890, Fitzpatrick went through the Irish birth registration indexes at her local Family History Center and used their website. Among several possible Margaret Conways, she found one whose siblings matched those on the list made by Lyon. This third critical genealogical step indicated these siblings were the children of

John Conway and Ellen Drumm in Ireland. That gave Fitzpatrick what she needed to begin the search in Ireland.

Packages containing DNA test swabs from Morris Brooks' niece and the son of Olav/Olan Jacobsen's aunt arrived at AFDIL. Loreille ran tests on both even though there was no expectation of a match; neither mtDNA sample was a match. During the process, however, Olav's niece, Carla, and her family became staunch supporters of our project. We located Edwin Mustra, nephew of Merchant Mariner Edwin Mustra. He provided a DNA sample that resulted in Mustra being the 13th Merchant Mariner eliminated from being a match through DNA. Of course, Edwin Mustra's fingerprints had already been ruled out as a match. We left nothing to chance.

After making inquiries to many Van Zandt family members, we finally located, then contacted, John Van Zandt, the son of Francis Joseph Van Zandt's brother, Orville Jr. To make certain we were on the right track, Loreille obtained a DNA swab from John Van Zandt. His nuclear (Y-STR) DNA was consistent with the DNA from the arm and hand. But that alone could not have been used to make a match. Lyon and Fitzpatrick soon found a few more close Van Zandt relatives in the United States, but none of them were appropriate mtDNA donors. So, the extended family we studied had grown larger.

Now, we had a complicated extended family tree consisting of 48 names from the Conways, Van Zandts, Jubics, Bolsters, and Burkes. To study the family in Ireland, we had to understand everything we could in the U. S. The key, however, would be to connect the family dots to Ellen Drumm from Ireland.

As bits and pieces of Francis Joseph Van Zandt's life emerged from dusty archives and the faded memories of only a few people who knew about the man, we learned his story. Nephew John Van Zandt had only met his uncle once. John's father, Orville, Jr., and Francis had grown up in a difficult situation.

Their mother died around 1911 when the brothers were infants. In 1920, when Orville was 10 and Francis nine, their father died. They also had a sister, Elizabeth, born in 1900, but Fitzpatrick's extensive research uncovered no record for her after 1910—as though she had vanished. Had we located her, perhaps her children could have been mtDNA donors. The boys were taken in by their cousins and raised as just two more children in the family. But at the earliest possible time, they left home to live their own lives.

The brothers were close, but as they got older, the time lengthened between their get-togethers. Francis Van Zandt spent WWII working on several Merchant Marine ships. Once the war was over, he married Lottie Snow. She stayed with her mother in Roanoke, Virginia, while her husband remained at sea most of the time. After the crash of Flight 4422, several years passed before Orville, Jr., learned of his brother's death.

Now concentrating on Ireland, Fitzpatrick studied detailed maps of marriage customs and naming patterns to zero in on particular towns and counties to determine where Ellen Drumm came from. This was a particularly difficult process considering that there are no Drumms listed in local registries as living in or near the county of Limerick today.

Although we located 54 living descendants of all the Conway siblings living in the United States, none was an appropriate mtDNA donor. Through relentless research, Fitzpatrick learned that the Van Zandt brothers' mother, Margaret Conway, had immigrated to America in 1893 and that she had five sisters and four brothers. Many of her siblings also came to the U. S., but a few returned to Ireland.

Over several weeks, Fitzpatrick made scores of phone calls to churches and possible Conway relatives in and around county Limerick. She had nearly exhausted all the possibilities when she was directed to Maurice Conway, of Askeaton, southwest of Shannon, Ireland. He was one family member believed to be knowledgeable about local Conways.

Fitzpatrick called Maurice, and when he answered, she said: "Hello, is this Maurice Conway?"

"Speaking," he answered in a thick Irish accent.

"My name is Colleen Fitzpatrick. I am a consult for the U.S. Armed forces DNA identification laboratory. We are trying to identify a frozen arm and hand found in a glacier in Alaska. We think you can help."

After a long pause, Conway replied, "Can you run that by me again?"

Fitzpatrick had called Conway's cell phone, and he was walking down the street on his way to pick up some milk when he answered. Conway was certainly surprised receiving this unusual call. At first he didn't recognize the names she mentioned and he had no idea about Flight 4422. He asked her to call him back at home in an hour.

Sure enough, an hour later, after talking to his wife to discuss the unusual call, Conway answered. During a 30-minute conversation, which included information about the plane crash, he still did not recognize the names Fitzpatrick mentioned, except one—Drumm.

He said, "I am nearly certain my great-great grandmother was a Drumm."

And even more exciting to Fitzpatrick was that, as Conway recited his genealogy, it seemed that he was related to his great-great grandmother along direct female lines of the family. This raised the possibility that he could be the mtDNA donor we sought.

Maurice Conway was more than willing to help. He asked Fitzpatrick to email him a list of her questions. At first, he was a bit mystified about the urgency because he was unaware of 4422's discovery. The next day, she called him again. During this hour-long call, Fitzpatrick learned that Conway was the only person on earth who had the answers we sought. He also revealed that he was the caretaker of the Mount Pleasant Cemetery near Askeaton and thought there might be some important information there. One could say he had the answers to our questions in his blood.

IN AN ATTEMPT to understand his own genealogy, Conway researched all kinds of church records, local archives, and verbal family history for Fitzpatrick, compiling a huge amount of information. While he worked in Ireland, she worked from Los Angeles via the Internet, family libraries, and archives available to her from the states. She made many more phone calls, and again visited her local Family History Center, where she reviewed microfilms of the Irish birth registration index. Lyon assisted from Michigan, filling in many of the blanks.

Conway contacted his godfather, Patrick Joseph Dundon, of Askeaton. As the family historian, Dundon confirmed that Conway descended from the Drumms. J. M. Feheney, a Brother at the local Catholic church, was a local historian and also helped research and confirm the family tree. That was good enough for us. Although we were still not certain Conway would be a match, Loreille sent a DNA swab kit to him. As soon as he received it, he swished the swab on the inside of his cheek, placed it in its holder, closed and sealed the kit, and mailed it immediately.

The day before Thanksgiving, 2007, an excited Loreille called me to report that Conway's DNA was a positive match to the DNA of the arm and hand. We informed the other members of the team and decided it was appropriate to have Fitzpatrick give him the good news. The next day, at 11 a.m. in Ireland (3 a.m. in California), she called Maurice Conway.

When he answered the phone, Fitzpatrick said, "It's a match! It's a match!"

Conway replied, "That's fine, that's okay, grand job. Goodbye."

Fitzpatrick replied, "No, no, wait. Now we have to prove why you *are* a match."

Despite all the work we had done, there was more to do. At Mount Pleasant Cemetery, many of the members of the Conway and Drumm families rested in peace but held secrets. Over several months, Maurice Conway traveled throughout southwest Ireland, finding more clues to his ancestors and their stories. He made phone calls to relatives and friends, young and old. He spoke with priests, historians, librarians, and archivists in search of his past. Slowly, the pieces of the puzzle came together and he found the answers.

But it was in Mount Pleasant Cemetery, right where he had worked for years, that the answer lay in wait—not on paper, but on a gravestone. Conway wrote down the information engraved on several of the gravestones. One provided the data that proved to be the missing link in the Conway and Van Zandt family trees. Margaret Conway had five sisters. We knew one had died. An inscription on one of the tombstones gave us the final link in the genealogy. The inscription reads:

Erected by John Conway
Mount Pleasant
In Memory of His Dear Father and Mother
Who Died July 1853 aged 53 yrs
Also his wife Ellen
and his children
Michael and Lizzie

After Conway sent the inscription to her, Dr. Fitzpatrick told me, "There are very few times in one's life that one never forgets. This is one of them."

This was the clue we needed. The inscription, including John Conway, his wife, Ellen, and the children's names, Michael and Lizzie [Elizabeth], linked the family together. These four names on the tombstone tied the Conway family in Askeaton, Ireland, to the Conway family in upstate New York, via the records in the Family History Library in southern California.

Through the excellent genealogy research accomplished by Maurice Conway, Fitzpatrick, and many others in Ireland, we learned that Francis Joseph Van Zandt's grandmother, Ellen Drumm, had a sister, Elizabeth Drumm. She had married an O'Shea. Elizabeth Drumm was Conway's great-great-grandmother. In other words, Elizabeth Drumm was Francis Joseph Van Zandt's grandmother's sister—his great-aunt.

The married names in the female line in Maurice Conway's direct mtDNA path are Maria McNamara, Elizabeth Drumm, Ann O'Shea, Bridget Sheehy, and Cathleen McNamee (his mother). Therefore, he was a perfect mtDNA donor, holding the answers to an arm and hand found in a glacier in Alaska. Out of more than six billion people on Earth, Maurice Conway was not just a perfect mtDNA match, he was the *only* one.

Ultimately, we eliminated 13 Merchant Mariners and all six aircrew members as matches through DNA. Fifteen other Merchant Mariners were eliminated by fingerprints. Only five of the sailors were eliminated as matches by both fingerprints and DNA.

Francis Joseph Van Zandt was legally identified by fingerprints, supported by mtDNA, and further supported by nuclear (Y-STR) DNA from Maurice Conway and John Conway. We had solved the identity of the arm and hand. But one big mystery remained—the gold.

WHAT ABOUT THE GOLD?

A lthough the human side of the accident, especially the identification of the arm and hand, was the most important aspect of Flight 4422 and took precedence over everything else, we never lost sight of the importance of getting to the bottom of the rumors of treasure on the plane. After all, that's what made Flight 4422 famous.

By 1999, both Marc and I had been convinced there was no treasure of any kind on the plane. We had researched every way we could to verify any possibility of gold, silver, diamonds, or cash, and we turned up absolutely no evidence that there was treasure on the plane.

The first gold rumor held that the *Sunset* had been sold to China and paid for in gold. The T-2 tanker SS *Sunset* was owned by the Overseas Tank Ship Corporation. It was never sold to China or Chiang Kai-Shek. In fact, it was not sold to anyone until 1962. However, we discovered two roots of this rumor.

Bernie Hopkins put me in touch with Captain Mike Pryce, a harbormaster in New Zealand. Captain Pryce is an authority on the old tankers. I spoke with him about the SS *Sunset* and T-2 tankers in general. He told me that many T-1 tankers (smaller than the T-2 tankers) had been sold to China in 1947 and 1948. These sales were common knowledge among sailors. But there is no way to know exactly how the payments were made—OTC records disappeared long ago. Payments might well have been in gold.

Another source of the rumor is that, according to newspaper reports in 1948, the *Sunset* had been delivered to purchasers in China. Indeed, a few relatives of the sailors said that the sailors had told the media the *Sunset* was going to be sold to China. Although there is no validity to this rumor, the gold-for-ship tales whetted the appetite of the media, which reported them as fact. This rumor is false.

CLEARLY, THE MOST COLORFUL story of treasure on the plane is that of gold bullion, jade, and artwork being smuggled out of China by Chiang Kai-shek. Layton Bennett had mentioned that possibility the night of the crash in 1948. But, Northwest's station manager, Dave Edwins, told me nothing like that was on NC-95422, at least when it left Shanghai. Historical fact indicates Chiang Kai-shek did take treasure out of China and shipped it to Formosa (now Taiwan) in 1949, but not in 1948.

I discovered some interesting facts and compelling evidence about Chiang, gold, and the United States. During WWII, as with many other countries, the U.S. did send aid to China under the lend-lease program enacted March 11, 1941. $1.6 billion worth of supplies was shipped to the Republic of China. According to the U.S. State Department, America also made post-WWII payments to Chiang Kai-shek, but they were made as "payments in kind." These were "credits" China used to buy arms and similar items from other countries, basically putting the purchases on America's tab. Despite a thorough search, we found no indication gold was shipped as official payment of any kind either to or from the United States or China at the time of Flight 4422's demise.

Furthermore, Flight 4422 was flying *from* China *to* the U.S. In 1948, gold was selling for around $400 per ounce on the black market in China. In America, it was selling for around $35 per ounce. It made no sense for a person to smuggle gold *out* of China to the U. S. Shipping it *into* China would have made sense. But there was more.

Over the years, Marc and I interviewed many senior NWA pilots who knew older pilots that had been copilots on DC-3s, DC-4s, and perhaps some other planes, in 1949 on flights from China to Formosa. Retired Capt. Robert Lowenthal flew with many of those pilots, who told him the planes, complete with armed Chinese guards, were heavily loaded with gold, art, jade, and other treasures during the time when the deposed Chiang Kai-shek fled from China to Formosa. One pilot recalled looking in the back of his DC-4 and discovering it was packed with items from wall to wall, as tight as could be. According to *Wikipedia Encyclopedia*, those shipments began on December 22, 1948. A total of 2,972 crates of artifacts were moved to Taiwan. In 1991, I saw many of the 693,507 pieces of ancient Chinese artifacts on display in Taipei's National Palace Museum.

The stories of the flights to Taiwan were true. However, there was more evidence for the rumors: Years after the crash of 4422, the factual story of gold smuggling in a NWA DC-4 at Hong Kong added quite a bit of fuel to the fire and some credibility to 4422's rumors. Retired NWA Capt. Warren

Avenson told me, "One of our DC-4s landed in Hong Kong and had small finger-size pieces of gold taped all over the inside of the tail section, and were found by mechanic Claude Pugh."

This story was confirmed by 1948 NWA Shanghai station manager Dave Edwins when I interviewed him on February 3, 2001. Additionally, Captain Avenson told me, "As a copilot, I flew a flight from Japan to Manila that was full of gold for war reparations."

I also interviewed retired NWA Capt. Vince Doyle on December 31, 2000. Regarding the late 1940s, he told me, "Everyone knew the Chinese government was smuggling gold out of China every chance they got."

Although this information was interesting, neither Marc nor I ever located any paper documentation of such cargo or the flights referred to by any of the NWA pilots.

In an interview with writer Helen O'neill in 1999, NWA Captain Ed Becker said there were three kegs of gold on board Flight 4422. Each keg contained seven bars of gold that weighed 82 pounds apiece. We never found any proof of this and don't where he got the information. I tried to interview Captain Becker many times but never succeeded.

There is a story about a Pan Am airliner in the early 1950s with gold hidden in its wing. During a 2004 interview at Conifer, Colorado, ex-NWA mechanic, later a mechanic for Pan Am, George Holm told me, "A Pan Am DC-6 had lots of gold hidden inside the left outboard auxiliary fuel tank in the left wing. The plane was written up for using more fuel out of that tank than the others. One of my good mechanic friends opened up the tank to work on it and pulled out several large rubber bags full of gold."

Holm thought the plane was in Bangkok, but it could have been in Hong Kong and he never learned exactly how much the gold was worth.

Another example of gold being shipped on airplanes involves KLM, the Dutch airline. An *Associated Press* article in the May 2, 1948, *Anchorage Daily Times* describes the theft of two million dollars of gold from a Macau-bound KLM plane parked overnight in Bangkok, Thailand. A shipping truck, carrying 38 boxes of gold from the plane for safe overnight storage at a customs house, was halted by bandits posing as police and soldiers. Most of the gold disappeared. The police recovered only three boxes.

These kinds of stories certainly spiced up the legends and added to the rampant speculation. It's impossible to prove there was never any gold on board Flight 4422. But, we found nothing that proved there was. The rumors of smuggled gold bullion, jade, and artwork were endless, but we never confirmed a solid basis for any of them being on Fight 4422.

ANOTHER TALE OF TREASURE was printed in the *Copper River Country Journal* on February 4, 1988. In it, bush pilot Jack Wilson is quoted, "They were paid off over there and the crew returned to America on the transport. As far as I know, the only gold on board was in the sailors' pockets."

A local hunting and fishing guide, pilot Jack Wilson flew many people over the crash site of Flight 4422 in the 1950s and 60s. He even dropped off members of the Whaley climbing party near the glacier in 1960. Over many years, Wilson heard all kinds of treasure stories from his passengers.

This rumor actually began in 1948 when people believed the sailors had been paid when they got off the ship in China—and that the payments had been in gold coins. In the 1950s, one treasure seeker told bush pilot Layton Bennett, "Those sailors were paid in gold in China when they got off the ship. I'm going to go up there and get that gold off them."

NWA mechanic Holm heard the same rumor being discussed outside of the hearing room during the 1948 accident hearing in Minneapolis: "[The sailors] were loaded down with either money or gold."

Despite all the stories, this rumor is not true. We had confirmed this through information from Bernie Hopkins, the sailors' probate files, and from facts in the lawsuits filed by the sailors' relatives.

REGARDING THE WWII surrender documents signed in Tokyo Bay, I spoke with Timothy Nenninger, chief, Modern Military Records, at the National Archives in College Park, Maryland. In a June 1998 letter to me, Nenninger wrote, "The two originals (one for the Japanese and one for the U.S.) were never missing, destroyed or recreated."

He even sent me a copy of the custody file. It clearly shows that well before March 1948 those surrender documents were transported on a DC-4 through the Pacific islands of Wake, Midway, and Hawaii—nowhere close to Alaska. There is no way those documents were on 4422.

We never determined exactly how rumors about the surrender documents or a sealed military container began. In the frozen miles of lonely ice, rocks, and debris, we never found anything remotely resembling documents or a container. Although the small piece of wood we found in the debris field could have been part of a box containing documents, the engraving of the coconuts and palm tree, along with the fluted ends, certainly seem to make it nothing more than part of a curio box.

Regarding the CAB report and any military files, Nenninger wrote, "Nor is there any information that would clearly link the events to any military records in our custody." He continued, "If there were any military documents on board, they were not of any historical significance."

IF ORIGINAL TAPE RECORDINGS of meetings between President Franklin Roosevelt and Chiang Kai-shek were on the plane, they would be priceless. The earliest reference we found to this story was a March 11, 1957, United Press International article that said, in part, "According to another rumor, the ship is supposed to have on board a tape recording of a conversation between President Roosevelt and Chiang Kai-shek."

I contacted Robert Parks and Mark Renovitch at the President Franklin D. Roosevelt Library in Hyde Park, New York. Both men said there were no such recordings. Randy Sowell at the Harry S. Truman Library in Independence, Missouri wrote to me in part, "I have found no information concerning documents or recordings of conversations between President Truman and Chiang Kai-shek that were allegedly lost in this crash." Based on this documentation, Marc and I consider this rumor to be false.

Although we were convinced these five rumors were false, we had been unable to disprove the existence of gems or uncut diamonds, or a payroll, other than for the sailors, on the plane.

"FORGET THE GOLD. What about the diamonds?" This made a wonderfully rich headline for a 1988 article in the *Copper River Country Journal*. How could one not be captivated by that possibility? We can't refute it because it may actually be true.

Although exaggerated in the article, the story was based on fact. A logical scenario would be that the sailors and aircrew members, as international travelers, could have purchased gems or diamonds just about anywhere in the world. In fact, many of the 4422's sailors and aircrew bought curios, trinkets, and jewelry overseas, just as crews of airplanes and ships do today. Sailor Travis McCall had purchased a roll of silk in China for his cousin's wedding dress. Wilfred Beswick planned to buy a special doll for the daughter of his Staten Island landlords, and Donald Rector is known to have purchased motors and odds and ends overseas.

The sailors were not rich. Probate, lawsuit records, and the sister ship's pay records show that most of them earned roughly $200 per month and that most of them had allotments from $50 to $150 per month sent directly to their families. This would have left them with relatively little cash.

In China, the U.S. dollar was incredibly strong. The country was full of refugees from all walks of life and from several countries who had gold coins that they often traded for U.S. cash. In fact, American dollars were sometimes referred to as gold.

The sailors would have had some cash, but it's unlikely any of them (or the aircrew) made a huge purchase of gemstones or jewelry. It seems that most of them simply did not have the financial resources to do such a thing. However, this rumor might have been true.

Just before Christmas 2006, I visited Ron Oravetz in Xenia, Ohio. After he recovered from a long stay in the hospital, he invited me to visit him to collect a sample for our DNA study. After I obtained two swabs of DNA from him, Oravetz and I stayed up late discussing his late father, Frank Oravetz—Merchant Mariner Arthur Eilertsen's best friend, WWII buddy, and brother-in-law.

Oravetz told me, "After you spoke with my father in 1999, he began to open up. Growing up, Dad never talked to us about Arthur, WWII, or what happened after the plane crash. He had locked it out of his mind due to the badgering he got from his mother-in-law, who blamed Dad for her son's death. As you know, Dad had gotten Arthur the job on the *Sunset.*" He continued, "But then, Dad opened up and told us about his driving the landing craft troop carriers onto beaches under gunfire and his association with Arthur. He told us how he taught Arthur how to make rings. They made them out of coins in their spare time, using the equipment in the Navy machine shops. They made all kinds, etching some and stamping others with dates and names. Some even had gems in the rings' faces. Dad and Arthur sold some and gave others away as gifts. Arthur had five of the rings with him on board the *Sunset.*"

As identified by Frank Oravetz, the ring stamped "Iran 1946" that was found on the glacier belonged to Arthur Eilertsen. The two men had traveled all over Europe and other parts of the world during and after WWII, and they had been to Iran. Although DNA analysis ruled out the arm and hand as Eilertsens's, the ring was not on the hand when it was located—it was five feet away in the ice.

There is no question the ring belonged to Eilertsen. In fact, Ron Oravetz told me, "Just before Dad passed away, he told me he was certain that was Arthur's ring. He also told me that Arthur had phoned him [Frank] from China or Alaska in 1948. He said that he had bought many gems or diamonds—so many that he had to hide them all over the ship to keep them safe. Dad told me, 'Arthur said they were worth a whole lot of money and that a few other sailors had done the same thing.'"

Ron said, "He bought them so Dad and Arthur could put them into the rings."

Indeed, the construction, inscriptions, and coloring of the Iran 1946 ring are consistent as being the same type of ring in a photo of Arthur Eilertsen. What we do not know is where Arthur purchased the gems and/or diamonds. The *Sunset* stopped in South America, a great market for such items. The Middle East also afforded such opportunities, and in China anything was up for grabs for U.S. cash. In fact, Eilertsen and the other sailors could have gotten great deals almost anywhere during their cruise.

Regarding the legend of Flight 4422 having gems or uncut diamonds on board, we believe this is very possible—based on the statement of Eilertsen's family. However, we found no paper trail nor did we find any such items in the glacier, other than the ring.

WE WENT TO GREAT LENGTHS to get to the bottom of all the rumors associated with supposed treasures on board Flight 4422. The one story that had a life of its own was the one about some kind of payroll or payment—cash, gold, or maybe silver. We were certain the sailors didn't have their payroll with them. But, that doesn't mean a different kind of payroll was not on board. We couldn't kill it. Everywhere we looked, this rumor kept showing up like a bad penny.

During a second visit to AFHRA at Maxwell AFB, I searched carefully, but found no records of any missing military payroll around the time of 4422's crash. However, I did run across an archived report written in 1948 about Nome Air Force Base, Alaska, by its base commander, Lt. Col. James Williams.

I decided to contact now-retired Lt. Colonel Williams to see what, if anything, he remembered about 4422. If there was a military payroll on board, maybe he knew about it. I found his phone number and gave him a call. He remembered the crash of Flight 4422 very well and recalled that his civilian construction superintendent, Wilson Russell, had stated unequivocally that a payroll was on board the plane. He wasn't certain whom it belonged to, but he thought it was the Morrison-Knudsen Company, a big military contractor.

In March 2003, I located Bill Lofholm, who was the paymaster for Morrison-Knudsen (M-K) in 1948. During our hour-long phone conversation, Lofholm confirmed M-K was the largest contractor in Alaska in 1948 and that he was in charge of all of the company's pay. He said employees were paid via checks—precisely to avoid losing cash in one of the too-frequent plane crashes in Alaska. "There was no way Morrison-Knudsen had that payroll on Flight 4422," he said. "I'm certain of that because I am the one who wrote all those checks."

With that, I closed the books on any M-K connection with Flight 4422. However, Lofholm went on to say that he also had heard there was some kind of payroll or payment on Flight 4422. There was no question about it, but no one seemed to know to whom it belonged or why it was on board.

There was another aspect about a possible payroll on board Flight 4422. NWA ramp agent Tiny Eglund, good friend of ramp agent and mountain climber Hartmut Pluntke, was part of the ground crew that worked on Flight 4422 the night it left Anchorage in '48. Pluntke told me that Eglund had told him that he'd seen "something in the cockpit with 'Payroll' stamped on it."

Maybe what he really saw was an envelope containing the *Sunset*'s sailors' payroll records. NWA management's consistent answer over the years has been that they had no knowledge of anything of value being shipped on Flight 4422. After 50 years, there may have no longer been any reason for the company to hide anything.

IN 2007, I SPENT a day with Roy Grimm, Mike Grimm, Sr.'s, father. He told me, "While I was working as a trucker in Alaska back in 1948, I heard on the radio that the crashed plane on Mount Sanford had a $55,000 or $65,000 payroll on board. I heard that with my own ears."

Documentation of any treasure on board Flight 4422 eluded us despite years of archival research. Yet, in March 2012, long-time Alaskan aviator and airline owner Al Wright told Marc and me, "I went to Copper Center (30 miles south of Gulkana) in '48 and personally saw the coroner's report, which clearly stated Flight 4422 had $20,000 of gold certificates on board. I saw it with my own eyes, but figured those certificates had to have burned up in the crash."

We certainly believe Al Wright. However, in again conferring with the Alaska archives experts in Juneau and Anchorage, and spending two days in June 2012 personally searching the Alaska State Archives, I found no such items—no commissioner's reports about 4422 or gold, and no coroner's reports. That doesn't mean those documents never existed, it just means we haven't located them if they still exist.

In her November 15, 1999, major news article about Flight 4422, "Glacier Gold," *Associated Press* writer Helen O'Neill finished with, "Just rumors of about 27 bars of gold—82 pounds apiece—being smuggled aboard the plane in the dead of night."

Everywhere we turned during the first 10 years of research, the rumor of a payroll lingered, but there was never any solid evidence. The fact that 4422's original aircraft card and backup record were missing at Maxwell AFB still bothered me. And the fact that the second Mount Sanford DC-4 crash was in the records at the Rescue Coordination Center at Fort Richardson in Anchorage just didn't make any sense to us. Then, like a bolt of lightning, new information surfaced about the treasure on board 4422. And this one blew us away.

Marc and I accepted an invitation to speak at the Alaska State Aviation Trade Show and Conference in May 2002, the largest aviation gathering in Alaska each year. In the Fed Ex hangar on a beautiful spring day, we told our story about Flight 4422 to an audience of 50 aviators. We finished with our conclusion that we had found no evidence that gold was on board. After the lecture, private pilot Bill Diehl, approached us and said, "I have a hunting buddy you guys need to talk to about this crash."

Marc asked if he could tell us more.

"Nope," Diehl said. "You need to talk to my friend about this. His name is Al Renk. Here's his number."

I pressed him for a hint as to what his friend might tell us. "You need to talk to Al," Diehl said again. "He knows something he has kept quiet for a very long time."

The next day, just after noon, Marc and I knocked on the door of well-known retired trucker Al Renk. A bright orange pickup truck sat in front of his ranch-style home in southwestern Anchorage, only a few miles from Marc's house. After formalities, we explained the basics about our 4422 project. Then Renk told his story—a story we could hardly believe we were hearing.

COLD CACHE

Al Renk sat in a garden chair on the back porch, his large shaggy dog at his side. His wife, Emily, brought out some iced tea, and then went back inside the house. I set up my video camera. It hummed quietly under the bright afternoon sun while Renk told the story of his trucker friends who had made it to the 4422's crash site in 1957.

The team was led by Archie "Dutch" Berck. He was indestructible. In the 1930s, Berck had been in a mining accident that cost him two fingers, an eye, and some other body parts. Doctors spent two hours reattaching many of them. Then, on January 6, 1954, he had a horrible semi-truck crash, sliding off a bridge near Seward, Alaska. He was pinned under the trailer for several hours. In the hospital, the doctors said he would never walk again. But with his iron-like will, he recovered from the near-fatal injuries, walked, and even drove trucks again. His doctors had been surprised he survived.

The other men Renk described—all of whom worked for Alaska Freight Lines—were engine and general truck mechanics. John Henniger was reputed to be the best mechanic in Alaska. He could fix anything—just the man for a wilderness trek. All the men were in their 30s and 40s and saw Flight 4422's treasure as their chance to hit the jackpot. They studied maps and the terrain of eastern Alaska, including its glaciers and weather.

Renk learned about their adventures only after noticing they had been absent from work for two weeks. By itself, that was not unusual. Alaskans often take weeks off at a time to go hunting and fishing. But strangely, when all these men returned to work at the same time, there was no talk of hunting or fishing. Then Renk found them working late into the night, well after Alaska Freight Lines' closing time. And they weren't working on trucks. "They were making aluminum ladders," Renk told us.

I immediately thought of the ladder we had found in the glacier.

After hearing the sounds of drills and saws whining late into the night,

Renk asked them what they were up to. At first, his questions were met with stony stares. But gradually, the men confided in him. They admitted they had located the Gold Wreck on Mount Sanford. They told him that after spending a week getting to a point high on the glacier, they had seen a sight that took their breath away. It was one of those moments when the fickle weather and the angry, heaving glacier grudgingly cooperated to reveal its secrets. Perched on an ice overhang about 40 feet above the men, part of the DC-4's fuselage stuck out. Dark blue and red patches of paint could be seen on some of the aluminum. It was part of the aft section, close to the tail, and it was tantalizingly close. But the men were used to handling monkey wrenches, not ice axes, so the overhang put the fuselage out of reach. The men returned to Anchorage.

Dutch Berck and the others became excited as they shared their deepest secret with Renk. They told him they were confident their aluminum ladders would enable them to reach the fuselage. Renk watched as they constructed several sections with slots that would fit together to make a ladder long enough to get them across crevasses and up to the overhang where the plane stuck out of the ice.

It was a race against time—they wanted to get back on the mountain before winter set in and buried the wreckage. They were lucky; the winter of 1956-1957 had an unusually small amount of snowfall. Now a warmer than usual summer increased their chances of getting back to the wreck before the snow started again. It was late July, 1957.

This was a group of men who were supremely resourceful and tough. Working for Alaska Freight Lines, they had conquered some of the most treacherous roadways in the world. They regularly drove over ice-and-snow-covered fields and frozen rivers to the DEW (Defense Early Warning) line. Their job was to make things work regardless of the conditions—and they were basically fearless. Other than their lack of ice-climbing experience, it was a group that was perfectly suited to find any treasure that might be aboard Flight 4422.

After constructing the ladders, Renk recalled that the men told the other guys in the shop they were going on a hunting trip, then they disappeared again. Renk wasn't sure whether the men used Henniger's Weasel, an all-terrain vehicle, to get to the mountain or whether the group had hired one of the local bush pilots to fly them in.

Dutch Berck told Renk that once back on Mount Sanford, armed with ladders, they made it up to a point just below the fuselage that stuck out of the overhang of ice. They hooked several sections of their ladders together and climbed up to the fuselage.

No one knows all of the details of what actually happened when they got to the glacier and returned to the wreckage. But, they did recover some treasure.

Dutch Berck's team would have climbed back down the ice, carrying their loot from 4422. Each man would have known he needed the others to survive the trek, at least for the moment. They must have been exhausted when they reached their high camp near the bottom of the ice falls.

No one knows how the men got back to Gulkana. From the base of the ice falls, it would have taken them at least a day to climb back down the glacier, then two or three more to make it to Gulkana in the Weasel. Hiking out would have taken them at least a week; flying, only a few hours at the most. All that's known for certain is that the men slipped back into Anchorage quietly.

Renk told us that about a week later, Berck and the other men returned to Anchorage. Berck told him and another AFL trucker, Dean Hart, "We recovered $250,000."

Whether it was gold, silver, gold certificates, or cash, no one knows for sure, because the men never revealed that information to Renk. Al told me, "All I remember is that they told me they got $250,000 from the wreck. I never knew if it was gold, cash, both, or something else."

According to Al Renk, over the next few weeks, each man turned in his resignation at Alaska Freight Lines. Renk said, "Within a few weeks they'd all left their well-paying jobs at AFL. They talked to Dean Hart and me several times after they got back. They told us again that they'd hit the jackpot on Mount Sanford and they'd decided to leave Alaska right away. They told their wives and girlfriends they'd send for them."

During a few weeks in Anchorage, the men constructed a wooden canopy over the back of Dutch Berck's dark-colored GMC pickup truck. Renk described the canopy. "They built the canopy over the bed of the half-ton pickup in such a way that no one could see inside. There were two rows of seats in the back, one on each side, that allowed them to all ride together— two up front, two or three in back, with room for storage under the seats."

Again, late at night, they talked with their good friends, Renk and Hart, entrusting them with their plans. Then they left town, and Berck stayed in touch with Hart, who had lent them some money. If most of their treasure was in gold, they would have needed cash.

In 1957, it was illegal for a U.S. citizen to own gold bullion—America was still on the gold standard and remained so until 1972 when President

Richard Nixon took the country off it. Taking the gold to another country was the only easy way to turn it into cash. Canada was too close and too risky. The men told Renk their destination was Lima, Peru.

They piled into the pickup and began the long drive south, through Alaska and Canada, then across the western United States. They crossed the border into Mexico, maybe posing as just another group of buddies on a long fishing trip. They drove on, through Guatemala, Honduras, Nicaragua, and Costa Rica, until they reached Panama, where the road stopped. Some of their friendships stopped as well.

They had thought they could drive all the way to Lima, but they were wrong. It may have been gold fever that caused a huge argument to break out among the men and they split up. John Henniger continued south. Al Renk believes Henniger made it to Lima. Berck stayed in Costa Rica for a few months, then sold the pickup and returned to Alaska in late fall, 1957. Renk didn't know what happened to the other two men. Such a tall tale is certainly one that is hard to swallow. So Marc and I did our best to confirm it.

It took us more than a year to find relatives of Dutch Berck. Finally, on an afternoon in June 2003, I visited Berck's second ex-wife, Jenny, in a Lake Worth, Florida, senior center. She recalled little about the 1940s and '50s. However, she graciously referred us to her daughter, Jeanette, and son, Jerry, who remembered their adventurous father. Jeanette lived near her mother, and Jerry was also in Florida, on vacation from Houston, Texas. They were enthralled with the stories we told them. Although these were tales they had never heard before, Jeanette and Jerry were able to fill many gaps in the stories and added a lot of credibility to what Al Renk had told us.

Jeanette remembered the men talking about driving the pickup to Central America, but she really didn't know why they had made the trip. She confirmed that her father had returned to Alaska in late 1957 and that he and his wife, Jenny, then sold their house and left Anchorage. Berck flew his wife, Jenny, Jeanette, and her three siblings to Seattle. They were supposed to fly on to Costa Rica, but for some reason the flight was canceled. They then took a train to Chicago, and flew from there to San Juan, Costa Rica, arriving in January 1958.

The children were comfortable attending the American school in Costa Rica, but their mother soon became unhappy with being unable to communicate; none of her family spoke Spanish. She also disliked the hot, damp climate. After just five months in Costa Rica, the couple and their children moved to Florida. Later that summer, Berck was sipping a beer in a bar when he met Dave Edgerton of the Burger King fast-food chain.

Edgerton talked him into buying Burger King Number 16, on Dixie Highway in West Palm Beach. Berck paid $16,000 for the franchise, and, according to Al Renk, "Berck became a millionaire as a result."

Jeanette wasn't certain about her father becoming a millionaire, but believes it's possible her father could have been involved with some type of treasure from 4422. "Dad was gone for many weeks at a time," she told us. "He was always a very adventurous man and this is the type of thing he would and could do. Yes, he could have had a second life unknown to his real family."

Her brother is not so certain. "Dad never mentioned anything about any of this to me," he said. "I got pretty close to him during his later years and it doesn't seem to make any sense."

Athough he did have motor homes, nice vehicles, and other grown-up toys, his father never flaunted any money he may have had. According to Jerry Berck, "Burger King number 16 was 100 percent financed, and we never lived high on the hog."

In 1964, Berck sold Burger King Number 16, moved to Houston, and bought Burger King Number 110 on Post Oak Road. Berck divorced Jenny and in 1975 married his third wife, Betty, originally from Costa Rica. Dutch Berck remained in Texas with his new family until his death in 1999, taking his secrets about Mount Sanford with him—well before we knew anything about his expeditions to Mount Sanford.

THE INCONSISTENCIES BETWEEN Jeanette's and Jerry's statements, and what Al Renk understood about Berck's financial status, raise questions we'll probably never be able to answer. But both of Berck's children agreed that, because of his injuries, their father could not have climbed up the glacier. Then again, he didn't have to. Other members of his team were capable of completing the climbs.

We tried to track down information about John Henniger. As a child, Jeanette Berck remembers the Hennigers in Anchorage, but lost all contact with them after moving to Costa Rica. Renk believed Henniger's wife and son moved to Lima shortly after John arrived there. Then in the 1980s, Henniger's son returned to Anchorage. Renk was at the Anchorage International Airport waiting to pick up a client when he recognized Henniger's son and spoke with him. He told Renk that his father had died and his mother didn't want to stay in South America by herself, so the son had brought her home to Seattle, and then came to Alaska for a visit. For many years, we searched for Henniger's son, but couldn't find any trace of him. Just as with Dutch Berck,

John Henniger probably took his secrets with him to the grave.

It's possible John Henniger spent many wonderful years living in relative wealth in Lima, Peru, or elsewhere in South America on the beach, sipping rum and Cokes.

As for the other two men, Jeanette Berck told us they were the Lucas brothers and she thought they also had eventually gone to Lima. One may have come back and worked at one of the Burger Kings for a while. We never located either of the Lucas brothers.

DURING THE 14 YEARS we spent uncovering the elusive truths about Flight 4422, Al Renk's story was perhaps the most amazing revelation. It was a secret he had kept for 40 years, and all of the men with firsthand knowledge of that treasure-hunting adventure had passed away. But there was one more living person who might have been able to confirm Renk's story: Dean Hart.

After searching for several months, we located Hart, who was in his 80s and living with his wife, Eleanor, in Yuma, Arizona. Hart was still healthy physically, but Alzheimer's disease had taken its toll on his memory. Like many people struck with that malady, he remembered some things clearly but others were a complete blank.

Hart confirmed several details of Renk's story. He remembered Dutch Berck and three other Alaska Freight Lines men planning "to go to Brazil or somewhere south in a pickup truck." He remembered the truck as having a topper with benches inside. He even remembered staying in touch with Berck by phone during the trip. In fact, Hart said Berck had asked him to go along on the trip to South America. But, Hart could not remember how the men acquired enough money to make the trip. He also had no memory of the famous crash of Flight 4422 or the attempts by so many to reach it. And even though he drove trucks for several decades, he could recall little about doing so.

Despite the fact that Dean Hart could only confirm a few details about Al Renk's story, we were inclined to believe what Hart told us. What he remembered was consistent with everything we had learned about Renk's story. The wreckage would have been in the upper ice falls in 1957 and 1958 and it could have been accessible. This is also consistent with many other reports that part of the tail section was in view high up on the glacier in the mid-1950s.

During an interview in February 2012, famous Alaskan bush pilot and airline owner Al Wright told us he'd flown over the crash site of 4422 many times in the 1950s. He remembered seeing two engines and the tail of the plane high up on the glacier at least during the first three years after the crash. He told me, "It was visible for many years after the crash."

The timing generally matches Layton and Lou Bennett's recollection that one other group either saw or brought out pieces of uniforms in the 1950s.

And finally, there was Renk's reputation. Mike Grimm, Sr.'s, father, Roy, of Maple Valley, Washington, worked with Renk at Alaska Freight Lines in the 1940s. During a 2007 interview, Roy Grimm told me that Renk was a stand-up guy and whatever he reported had to be true. During the interview, another ex-Alaskan trucker and friend of Roy Grimm, Gene Bailey of Shelton, Washington, told me he also knew Renk and vouched for his sterling reputation. That was good enough for me.

ANOTHER INTERESTING PIECE in the legend of Flight 4422 was the FBI's involvement. It came to light during my talks with native Alaskan dog musher Fred Ewan in July 2003 and again in the spring of 2005 at his home in the Alaskan village of Gakona. With his grandson on his knee and Mount Sanford looming in the background, Ewan told me about the wreck in 1948 and what he remembered about it.

Ewan told me that he and his dogsledding partner, Jack (Jake) Butler, were convinced there was gold or something else of great value on the plane. In 2003 Ewan told me, "We thought if we could make it to the site and recover the gold or whatever valuable treasure there was, we would get a big reward. We talked with several government officials about it but were never told exactly what we would find or specifically what to look for. But whatever it was, the government people wanted it badly...very badly! Everyone in town knew it, too."

Then, in 2005, Ewan reiterated his story and added, "The government officials told Jake and me, 'You'll know what it is when you find it.'"

Despite the prospect of a big reward, after careful consideration, Ewan and Butler decided that attempting to reach the crash site was just too dangerous.

For Marc and me, the term "government officials" was too general and needed narrowing. For years, we'd heard rumors that the FBI was involved in the crash investigation but we were unable to find any confirmation. Finally, in 2002, *London Times* international writer Barry Wigmore was able to obtain the FBI files. Among the files was a March 31, 1948, FBI radiogram that began, "Northwest Airlines, Inc., DC-4 crashed against mountain about 250 northwest of Anchorage March 12 killing its sixteen passengers and six crew members."

Although much of that information in the one-page report is incorrect, it proves that the Bureau had officially investigated the crash. In fact, the head man at the FBI took note of this particular investigation. Looking carefully at the document dated 3-31-48, one can see the initials JeH (John Edgar Hoover) inside the O of RADIOGRAM. Although his assistant, Mr. Tolson, is listed on the distribution list, Tolson did not initial it. This was an internal FBI document that proves the Bureau really did participate in the investigation. The point is, those rumors about government officials being in Glennallen were true and support the accounts of Fred Ewan, Sy Neely, and others. Indeed, officials from NWA, CAB, the U.S. military, and the FBI were all at Glennallen immediately after the crash.

This document, with many censored names, makes it clear the FBI investigated the crash for indications of sabotage. It states in part, "No indication whatsoever of sabotage."

The document also states, "Suggested possibility, but not for the records, that passengers may have been drinking and also crew members but no evidence developed to date that they were."

There is no mention of gold, cash, payroll, or other treasure. It's possible the FBI investigated the crash strictly because the DC-4 was still technically owned by the United States and leased to NWA. The radiogram ends with, "Since no indication of sabotage involved this office could conduct no investigation."

ON DECEMBER 14, 2006, I received an unsolicited phone call from retired NWA flight attendant Pat Olson. She had read an article about our discovery of Flight 4422 in the NWA Retired Pilots Association magazine and got my phone number from the magazine's editor.

In 1957, Olson had been a roommate of North Central Airlines flight attendant Connie Nelson when both women were in their early 20s. Olson relayed to me a story Nelson had told her about Flight 4422: "Nelson's father (or stepfather) called home sometime before Flight 4422's crash. He told Nelson's mother he would be home in a few days and that the plane had a lot of gold on it."

Although we tried, we could never confirm this story because we couldn't make a direct connection; No one named Nelson was on the plane and we haven't been able to locate Connie Nelson or any of her relatives. However, there certainly could have been an aircrew member named Nelson on 4422's legs between Tokyo and Shemya, or Shemya and Anchorage. Our research on her continues.

I contacted the CIA. Their response was along the lines of, "No information is releasable about any Canadian operations."

We never received a response from the agency's historian as to whether there were any operations that might have resulted in something of value having been placed on Flight 4422 in March 1948.

I NOW BELIEVE there is too much smoke rising from the pages of 4422's history to dismiss this story of treasure. The fact that the primary and backup files of 4422's military records were missing indicates someone had tried to make the records of the plane disappear. Placing a second DC-4 crash on Mount Sanford in the files of the Alaskan Rescue Coordination Center adds to the mystery. Intentionally placed false data often eliminates or confounds conclusions, supporting my theory of cover-up and deception. Then we have Connie Nelson's stepfather calling home to tell his wife about a lot of gold on the plane.

I found Al Renk to be a credible, firsthand source of information. Unfortunately, he passed away after an automobile accident in the fall of 2005. Luckily, we have the videotapes and taped phone conversations of our interviews with him.

The FBI was asked to investigate the crash of the chartered DC-4. That seems unusual with no cargo and no one on board other than the aircrew and the SS *Sunset's* crew of Merchant Mariners. I certainly believe Fred Ewan, who was convinced and willing to go to 4422's crash site in 1948. Overall, there is just too much evidence to ignore.

I believe that, in 1957, Dutch Berck's team of climbers retrieved whatever treasure was on board Flight 4422. But, exactly where that treasure originated remains a mystery—at least for now.

FLIGHT 4422'S CRASH site and debris field is a federally protected archaeological grave site carefully monitored by the National Park Service. In July 2003, I visited the Flight 4422's debris again and confirmed what we thought was happening to the glacier and the debris field. The debris field had changed significantly since 1999. It was rapidly disappearing underneath the growing surface layer of volcanic material. Glacial streams had continued cutting through the glacier's surface, thus collapsing the mantle of ice and rock. The natural churning action of the glacier surface was reburying the remains of the plane. Less debris from the plane was visible than had been in 1999 and nothing new had surfaced.

If the glacier's current movement continued, it would take about 1,100 years for all of the remnants of Flight 4422 to exit the glacier at its terminus either as identifiable pieces, or more likely, in microscopic bits after scraping between rock and ice. They would exit into the outflow stream, drift into the Sanford River, then join the Copper River near Gulkana. After dragging along the bottom for untold years, they would finally flow into the Pacific Ocean. Everything, it seems, in the end, drifts to the sea.

Throughout this project, Marc and I learned to look at ourselves carefully and to decide when we were pushing the limits too far. We also paid attention to the things we felt, but didn't necessarily understand. Maybe that is why we are still alive to tell this story. Our tenacity and refusal to give up took us right up to the edge—the edge where the goal was ultimately obtained.

Understanding others' passion proved to be just as important as our own. Family members of those lost and other researchers became infected with the same passion as Marc and me. They were all important and critical to our success. We learned not to discount anyone or any person's thoughts… everyone holds secrets and you never know who might hold the key.

HOWEVER, AMONG ALL THE things we learned, there was one lesson that overshadowed the rest: If you go looking for a Flight of Gold, walk softly, be careful and kind. Be prepared for anything. What you find might surprise you. The gold might not be what you can hold in your hand. It might be what you feel and share…that gold you find deep in your heart.

And…The mountains will stand tall and still in their insolent silence. Caring little about the actions and meanderings of humans, the monoliths created by Mother Nature's grand scheme reign superior, always have, and always will. The glacier will always have its secrets.

The explorers positioned 30 United States flags in the center of the Flight 4422 debris as a memorial to those lost, then framed the flags and distributed them to the families of those lost. *Photograph by author.*

Marc Millican views the wrecked engine again in 1999. The stream that it formerly had rested next to no longer exists at that spot, evidence of the rapidly changing face of the glacier. *Photograph by author.*

Werner ladder, old climbing rope, and ice screw from decades ago. There are scratches on the rungs consistent with the use of crampons on climbers' boots while walking across the ladder. Verbal testimony suggests many such ladders were used on the glacier. *Photograph by author.*

Author investigates quick disconnect panel used for hydraulic and other fluids on the DC-4. *Photograph by Marc Millican.*

The arm and hand as it looked minutes after its discovery just east of Propeller Point. Flesh and nails were still intact, which indicated that it had only recently just melted out of the glacier. *Photograph by author.*

Alaska State Trooper helicopter pilot Bob Larson flew the arm and hand to Anchorage days after its discovery. Larson would have a fatal accident a few years later. *Courtesy Alaska State Troopers.*

This ring stamped "Iran 1946" was located by Sergeant Rodney Dial not far from the arm and hand during the recovery operation and placed in safekeeping with the Alaska State Troopers. *Photograph by author.*

Genealogist Christine Lyon assisted in locating family members of the victims. She is pictured in Xenia, Ohio, returning the ring found near the arm and hand to Ron Oravetz, a family member of Arthur Eilertsen. *Photograph by author.*

Marc Millican (L), Sue Blei, and the author study the fingerprints at the Alaska State Troopers' main office in Anchorage. *Photograph by author.*

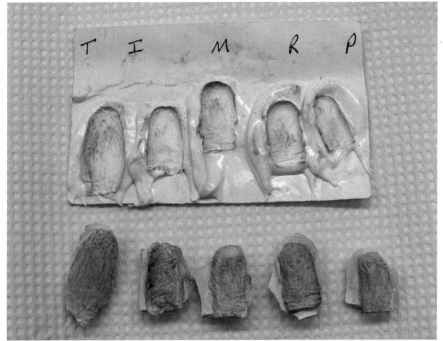

Ted Robinson used ID Enhancer to hydrate and raise fingerprint details on the much degraded hand so that fingerprints were visible. Then casts were made of the fingertips from which fingerprints were made. *Photograph by Ted Robinson*.

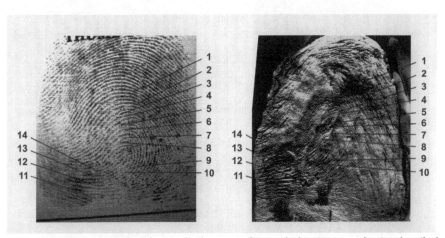

Mike Grimm, Jr., used enhanced photography and dusting to obtain detailed fingerprints from the fingerprints of the hand found on the glacier. *Courtesy Mike Grimm, Jr.*

Using the enhanced fingerprint images, Mike Grimm, Sr. (center), flanked by Ted Robinson (L) and Mike Grimm Jr. (R), makes the identification of Francis Joseph Van Zandt, the oldest known postmortem identification by fingerprints. *Photograph by author.*

The ID Enhancer solution kit manufactured by KDL Solutions, and distributed by Evident, is now sold regularly to help in identifying bodies. *Photograph by author.*

Dr. Odile Loreille, who conducted DNA studies on the arm and hand, at her work station at Armed Forces DNA Identification Laboratory. *Photograph by author.*

Family tombstone in Mt. Pleasant cemetery in Askeaton, Ireland. The details of the inscription provided the final clues to verify the Drumm/Conway family genealogy that connected them to victim Frank Van Zandt, whose arm and hand were discovered on the glacier. Pictured L to R are Andy Yeiser, Colleen Fitzpatrick, Chriss Lyon, and Maurice Conway. *Photograph by author.*

One of the gravestones of the many unknown soldiers buried at the Punchbowl Cemetery near Honolulu, Hawaii. It is hoped that, in time, the technologies developed to identify the human arm and hand found on the 4422 glacier may one day help to identify these soldiers. *Photograph by author.*

The 12 items recovered from among Flight 4422 wreckage are now kept in the National Park Service archives in Alaska. *Photograph by author.*

Author with famous bush pilot and writer Jorge Jorgensen, who flew hunters and fisherman in and around the areas near Mount Sanford in the 1950s. *Photograph by Marc Millican.*

Marc Millican with famous bush pilot and businessman Al Wright, who flew pilots in and around Mount Sanford in the 1950s. Wright saw a coroner's report in 1948 that noted $20,000 in gold certificates were on the plane. *Photograph by author.*

Gene Bailey   Ben Peters   Al Renk   Ernest Thayer   Bob Meier   Merle Rucker   Roy Grimm   Bob Nowell

BMR Trucking
Owned by Bob Nowell, Myrna Nowell, and Roy Grimm

BMR Trucking employees in 1953. Al Renk shared what he knew about Dutch Berck's claims regarding recovering $250,000 worth of something from the Flight 4422 glacier in 1957. Coincidentally, project fingerprint expert Mike Grimm Sr., is the son of Roy Grimm, pictured, one of the truckers. *Courtesy Mike Grimm Sr.*

Dutch Berck (circa 1952), one of the BMR truckers, may have recovered valuables from among the Flight 4422 wreckage in 1957. *Courtesy Jeanette Berck.*

360

EPILOGUE

February 2008 found me again driving five hours to Glennallen over ice-covered highways under an overcast sky. I pulled into the Alaska State Troopers' parking lot to take custody of the Iran 1946 ring. It had been stored in the evidence locker at the Glennallen jail for nearly nine years and now it was time for its release.

I presented an affidavit of history signed by Marc and me, along with a notarized statement from Ronald Oravetz stating identification and ownership. The evidence locker custodian, Jane Flygstad, handed the ring to me and I carefully placed it in a wooden display box donated by George Walton's Gold and Diamond Company in Anchorage. The ring was the only personal relic ever recovered from Flight 4422.

Five months later, at a ceremony in Xenia, Ohio, Researcher/Genealogist Christine Lyon and I returned the ring to Ron Oravetz. After more than 60 years, the ring had finally made it back to Arthur Eilertsen's family. There were tears of happiness, sadness, and closure as I gave the ring to Oravetz, Eilertsen's nephew. The local television station documented the event as Oravetz placed it on his little finger and told us how wonderful it was to have something from his long-lost uncle, who was also his recently deceased father's best friend and brother-in-law. One more chapter of the saga of Flight 4422 closed.

The other major recovery from Flight 4422—the arm and hand of Francis Joseph Van Zandt—remained at the Armed Forces DNA Identification Lab in Rockville, Maryland, thanks to an act of generosity by John Van Zandt. He authorized his uncle's arm and hand to be used for further scientific research.

Later that summer, I again visited the Punchbowl in Hawaii. I'd been there many times during the saga of 4422 and earlier—back in 1985, well before I knew anything about NWA Flight 4422 or the SS *Sunset*. This time, I went there to fully understand the strange connection of the Punchbowl with Flight 4422.

Leaves rustled in the warm wind. There it was again—the same haunting wind I'd heard in the American cemetery of Verdun, France; Normandy; and Arlington. In the Punchbowl, the hollow, timeless sound was the same; only the place was different, yet with the same rows and rows of soldiers lying in silent formation. The inhabitants of section U waited patiently for someone to discover who they are.

In February 2009, I again arranged a commercial flight to Dublin for our forensic genealogical team. We spent half a day with the news team of the national television of Ireland—RTE—taping a special program about Flight 4422 and how Ireland's own Maurice Conway helped solve the mystery. The next month West Limerick Radio-102 FM in Ireland aired a brief story about Flight 4422.

ON AUGUST 2, 2011, I was once more in the back of the Super Cub as Marc flew us back to Cub Valley. In 2003 I had vowed never to hike to the site of 4422 again. But we had recently agreed to take 64-year-old Randall Haslett, the son of 4422 purser Robert Haslett, to the site. An ex-Canadian Militia officer, he had the background, training, and physical conditioning to make the climb safely. Although a few other relatives of those lost on Flight 4422 had flown over the site, he would be the only living relative to actually visit the debris field. We had been discussing such a visit since 1999, after he located us following the news of our discovery. Now we were finally doing it.

The plan was for Marc to fly me to the site, where we would unload my equipment, and then fly back to Gulkana to pick up Haslett. Our research complete, my only goal was to get him to the debris field and back to Anchorage safely.

As we flew over the glacier Marc and I saw that the bottom, or tongue, appeared to have receded a hundred feet or so since 2003. We also noticed the glacier's exit river now flowed farther to the south as it flowed down the exit valley. From our viewpoint 2,500 feet above, the exit route looked tight, but the river appeared to have enough shoreline to be passable during our hike out.

We noticed other changes, too. The ice bridge at Green Point was not only gone, but had been replaced by sheer cliffs of ice. The undulations throughout the entire surface were generally more pronounced. We saw the 16-foot ladder, but it seemed to be farther south than before.

After one pass over the debris field, Marc flew to Cub Valley. Peering out of the windows, I noticed that the landing zone seemed unchanged since 2003. Repeating the approach we had followed in 1996, 1997, 1998, and 2003,

Marc brought the Cub in for a good backcountry landing. We unpacked my equipment, and Marc took off for Gulkana to pick up Haslett. An hour and a half later, they were back. The weather was closing in lower down in the valley at the Sanford River, so we unloaded the Cub in record time and Marc immediately departed to the west.

We needed to minimize the weight in the plane but in addition to our climbing equipment we now had a satellite telephone—an expensive, heavy communication device that increased safety and expedition efficiency. We also carried a special oversized waterproof tent fly, I called the Super Fly. My pack weighed 52 pounds, Haslett's just a little less.

In light rain, with the temperature at 46 degrees F., we departed Cub Valley at 10 a.m. Although he was an ex-military officer, I could detect a little trepidation on Haslett's part, wondering what it would be like in the Amphitheater of the Souls, where his father had died.

After following Green Ridge, we proceeded down into the glacier three-eighths of a mile short of Green Point. We had to do this due to the glacier degradation Marc and I had seen from the air. Getting on the center of the glacier was no easy task. What had taken 30 minutes in years past now took two-and-a-half hours. We placed 17 wands marking the new route as we negotiated around deep, blue glacial lakes; steep, slippery ice hills covered with rocks; crevassed areas; and streams. Comparing known points to the GPS, nothing was where it was in 1999.

We finally found a small piece of metal that looked like a piece of an airplane, then spotted a two-foot-square piece of cloth that could have been a seat cover. Fifteen minutes later, satisfied we were in the area of the debris field, we set up camp. We were one hundred feet west of a dark red, car-size boulder with a smaller rock on top. Haslett named this Madonna.

A mile up the glacier, on the left side of the ice falls, he saw a rock spire he thought looked like an owl. His mother loved owls. And then on the right side of the lower ice fall, he saw another spire he said looked like a bishop.

I suppose I could have been more accommodating, but I concentrated totally on safety. The three of us had earlier agreed we didn't want to have even the slightest of accidents. Randall Haslett was in his 60s, I was 56, and Marc was far away. Extreme caution was the watchword. Once we'd erected the tent complete with my Super Fly, we used the satellite phone to call Marc. We were relieved to learn he'd made it safely to Gulkana and was already in Anchorage where the weather forecast indicated steady rain, so he had driven my pickup back to Anchorage, leaving the Cub at the Gulkana Airport. That turned out to be a wise decision.

During an hour-long break inside the tent, with a light rain pitter-pattering on the roof, we ate freeze-dried food, rested, and talked about the crash. We discussed exactly where the plane had flown, how it impacted the mountain, the explosion, the flames, and how it fell 2,500 feet into the glacier. Then we talked about the aircraft parts Marc and I had located in previous years, their distribution, and what things we learned from them. Of course we also discussed the arm and hand and how we had identified it.

When the rain stopped, we left camp and headed southeast toward an area where we thought we might find the ladder and the center of the debris field. In just five minutes, we started seeing many pieces of aluminum—parts of the aircraft's skin ripped from the fuselage. But there was much less aircraft debris than Marc and I had seen on our expeditions. A few pieces of wood we hadn't seen before littered the rocky surface. We couldn't find the ladder, so we headed to what I thought was Propeller Point.

It looked completely different. Instead of a fairly flat area with gentle depressions, surface streams, and undercut ice cliffs, there were steep 50-foot walls of ice and a roaring river. As I'd suspected back in 2003, the glacier was melting rapidly, actually caving in on itself. We couldn't find any signs of the engine in the roaring stream. Above us, just north of the summit of what was left of Propeller Point, we thought we saw part of one of the propellers mixed among rocks. But there was no way we could get up there without technical ice climbing directly above a roaring glacier river—far too dangerous for us. By 9 p.m., we'd had enough, so we hiked back to camp. Of course the inevitable rain started, again.

We settled into the tent, and for an hour or so Haslett explained how lucky he had been to have a wonderful stepfather, but how often the faded vision of his real father haunted him, and how fortunate he had been to meet a nice young lady who became his wife. That night it rained hard and even turned to sleet, but we stayed nice and dry.

At 8 a.m. the next morning the veil of white clouds hiding Mount Sanford slowly dissipated and the rain stopped, allowing the mountain to show itself. It was a beautiful morning, perfect for this trip. The high cliffs were coated with fresh snow. Haslett used the satellite phone to speak with his wife in faraway Fredericton, Canada. It was during this conversation that this former military man shed some tears as the reality of where he was finally took hold.

We left camp an hour later. Haslett carried a small pack and I carried a small satchel of camera equipment. Over the next four hours, the son of Flight 4422's purser walked amid the wreckage of 4422—the remains of his father buried somewhere in the glacier. Then there came a special moment:

Lying on the glacier, Randall Haslett found a 12x6-inch rectangular, stainless steel top of a coffee pot commonly carried in airliners. This one was stamped AA for American Airlines. It was and still is common for airlines to lend, trade, or borrow similar items.

It could not have been more perfect; as the purser, Robert Haslett would have been in charge of the coffee and he would have touched this artifact on each flight. High up on a glacier in Alaska's wilderness, the personal connection between the son and his father was complete. Just as Haslett touched the top, a booming avalanche shot down from the highest cornices of Mount Sanford's west buttress. Huge plumes of snow billowed from the mountain's face as it flowed downward for several minutes and came to a stop well above us, near the lower ice falls to the left of Haslett's owl. But he didn't notice. He was in his own world with his father. He said it was "surreal, peaceful and calm."

Meanwhile, with Haslett involved in such a personal situation, I absolutely could not let my guard down. We could not make any mistakes.

THERE WERE NOT as many aircraft pieces as before, but there were a few I hadn't seen previously. A one-foot-long section of a propeller's tip possibly was part of a third engine. Another small piece apparently came from the leading edge of the tail—either the horizontal stabilizer or the vertical stabilizer. Its curved leading edge would have partially controlled the plane's vertical path. We saw what appeared to be an 8 by10-foot tarp partially covered with rocks. Four hundred feet to the east of the tarp lay a five-foot aluminum pole with a steel insert that could have been a tent pole. It may have been survival equipment or, perhaps, a maintenance tent from the plane. We had no way of knowing, since there was no cargo manifest for NWA 4422. It might have been a large tent pole from previous explorers.

We finally located the ladder. Taking careful GPS measurements, we determined the glacier had moved southwesterly 2,085 feet since 1999, or 178 feet per year. We verified this with some other known embedded airplane parts. Between 1948 and 1999, the glacier moved at an average speed of 254 feet per year. This could mean that as this glacier melts it loses mass, therefore slowing its movement. Although the ice melts, the embedded volcanic material does not. One could now hypothesize that if the current warming trend continues, this glacier will stop moving completely once all the ice and snow has melted, thus leaving only a glacial remnant.

Based on the trend we've observed since 1997, all of the wreckage of 4422 will most likely disappear into the volcanic rocks and subsurface streams within a decade or so. With the onset of the next ice age, the newly formed glacier will act like a giant bulldozer and push the remaining rocks and grit to the side, forming yet another moraine ridge running parallel to the glacier's edges. If so, pieces of Flight 4422 will remain in this volcanic rock moraine for a long, long time.

Just south of the ladder, we stopped and shook hands to commemorate our success in reaching the debris field. Just then, another avalanche roared down the mountain. A few minutes later, just as we were setting up a final video of the sun-blanketed mountain, one more avalanche cracked off from up on the west side of the mountain. It came from somewhere above 4422's impact point, slid down the same vertical valley though which 4422's debris fell in 1948, then flowed into the glacial cirque. Billowing puffs of snow dust covered the upper ice fall, just above the bishop. We took this to be a strong message that it was time to leave. So we did.

I was never so glad to get out of the debris field. This time was different and it had been a difficult journey for Haslett and me, both mentally and physically. I was older, and my physical conditioning was not as good as it had been during previous expeditions. And this time my only goal was to make sure Haslett remained safe even as he dealt with the personal tragedy that had affected his entire life.

He did great. It had been a safe, beautiful morning for exploring the debris field. After returning to our camp, he sat on a rock and wrote a letter to his father. The son, 15 months old in 1948, had grown to 64 years of age, while his father had died at this site at the age of 27. Randall Haslett had closure. It seemed as if the trip was in the bag, but we still needed to get down safely. While packing, I wondered what Mother Nature might throw at us.

Just before we took the spanning rods out of my dome tent, a huge gust of wind picked it up and lifted it 20 feet into the air, then it tumbled it like a giant beach ball another 200 yards to the east. Haslett chased it down, collapsed it, and brought it back.

After packing everything, we spent a few moments in silence, remembering those lost in the crash of 4422. At 3 p.m., we started back down the glacier to Cub Valley. Of course, as soon as we started hiking, it began to rain.

It took us three grueling hours to get off the glacier, collecting the wands as we passed them. The rain made the climb down more difficult than the climb up. The rocks slid easily on the underlying ice and we slid with them, several feet at a time. A 40- or 50-foot slide could take us into a crevasse or freezing pool. Each step was taken with care. We managed to make it to the lush grass and game trails of Green Ridge by 6 p.m. We continued to Cub Valley and set up camp at 8:45 p.m.

Exhausted, we called Marc and told him we thought we could be at the pickup zone down at 3,300 feet at 1 p.m. the next day. The fallback time was 3 p.m. Still in Anchorage, Marc said he would drive back to Gulkana the next morning and arrive by noon. It was good that Marc left the plane in Gulkana because Anchorage was socked in with low clouds and intermittently heavy rain.

We erected our tent at the west end of Cub Valley, right next to the 1950s' campsite where someone had left the five-gallon jerry can, pots, and pans. Again, we ate freeze-dried food. A 25-mile-per-hour wind blew all night from the east, along with mild rain. Intending on leaving the campsite by 7 a.m. the next morning, we waited until 9 a.m. when the rain finally subsided just long enough for us to pack up. I called Marc and left a message stating we were behind schedule at least two hours.

Finally, we hiked out of Cub Valley at 10 a.m. just as the rain started again. The temperature dropped to 42 degrees and the rain turned into sleet. This made our hiking even slower due to slippery grass and muddy trails. We were determined to avoid twisting an ankle or worse at the end of the expedition. Again, complete concentration on each step was critical. And then there it was—something I feared almost as much as avalanches.

"Randall," I said, "look at this."

"That looks like bear scat to me, all right," he said.

"And it's fresh. All those white hairs indicate it ate a sheep not more than a day ago."

"How big a problem is this?" he asked.

"It could be huge—depending on the size of the bear. Let's keep a close eye out, in front and behind us. Let's make a lot of noise every so often. Where's the gun?"

Haslett was carrying Marc's Smith and Wesson .44 Magnum.

"I have it right here. It's loaded and ready."

"Okay, let's go."

We found another pile of fresh bear scat 200 yards farther down the valley, right on our path, but luckily never saw any bears. Four hours later found us negotiating our way around the bottom end of the glacier. Because I had not been there since 2003, I was very concerned about this last part because the ice and rock could change quickly. But with no backtracking, we were able to locate a comfortable pass around the tongue and off the glacier, a few hundred feet south of where most of the water exited, still roaring like a tiger. Things were going well and we thought we might be able to make it to the pickup zone by 3 p.m. All we needed to do was to hike down the boulder-strewn side of the river for a mile or so, then travel south to the landing zone. That's when Mount Sanford threw us a curve ball, or in this case, a curve in the river.

We began to follow the exit stream just as I'd done before in '95 and '99. About halfway to the Sanford River, at the end of a small ridge, was the point where we would have to go left (south) and travel a mile and a half across the flats to the landing zone. After crossing one rushing tributary up to our knees in 33-degree water, we confirmed that the main channel had indeed moved south just as we had seen from the air two days earlier. But what we hadn't seen from the air was that the channel also had cut deeply into the 250-foot-high hill to the south.

With a depth of at least five feet, rushing water slammed against the cliffs, leaving nothing but undercut cliffs with no strip of rocks or sand at the river's edge. All we needed was 10 inches or so to hike on for a distance of 150 feet, but there was absolutely nothing we could walk on or wade through and we couldn't cross the main channel to our north—that one was 10 feet wide, waist deep and fast moving.

To me, it seemed that the glacial outflow volume of water had greatly increased since 2003. Even when physically at our strongest, it would have been extremely difficult and too dangerous to cross the river. We were stuck in the "V" between the tributary and the main channel.

One month earlier, I had flown an airline trip with First Officer Don Swanson. He had been a fishing guide and bush pilot in Alaska for many years, and I'd told him about my upcoming expedition to the site of 4422. He immediately recognized the story about the legendary crash.

He told me about several dangerous situations he'd encountered in Alaska's bush and then said something that stuck with me: "When faced with dangerous or critical situations in Alaska's bush, even the smallest error can result in tragedy. I absolutely had to make the right decisions the first time—especially when exhausted. I would always think about the situation and all the possibilities. Then I would think it over again. Then I would stop, sit back, and think it over one more time before taking any action. This saved my bacon more than once."

In my cold and tired state, Swanson's words swirled in the back of my mind. Sure, it would have been easiest to try crossing the main channel. But, that was also potentially deadly. At least for the moment, we were trapped, so I called Marc on the satellite phone, explained the situation, and told him we would not make our backup pickup time and would call him again when we figured it out. He understood exactly where we were and what I'd said. As a new backup plan, he would fly to the landing zone the next morning if he didn't hear from us.

Haslett and I sat on a couple of huge boulders and discussed the situation. We were exhausted at the end of a long expedition and something simple was wreaking havoc with our plans. We had two options: go back up the river's tributary a few hundred yards, cross it, and climb the hill to the south, or go all the way back to the glacier, cross the main channel where it was safe, hike down, then set up a Tyrolean Traverse (rope system) across the river about a half mile to our west.

We decided on the first choice as we sat there and looked up the hill again. Were there any other options? No. We stopped and thought about it one more time, and then agreed this was the best and safest plan. Then we discussed it one more time and decided going back and climbing the hill was the best choice. We knew it was not going to be easy—this wasn't just any hill.

At about 3 p.m. we moved out. After recrossing the knee-deep tributary, we started up the 45-degree slope, which was covered with 10- to-15-foot-tall alders. It was like hiking through a thick jungle and the tops of the alders continually grabbed our packs. With no way to go around, we pushed our way through them. Small limbs broke off as we forced our way through, while climbing. We were already soaked from crossing the cold water, and the rain made it so slippery we had to grab the alders' branches to keep from falling down into the stream as we made our way higher. There were no game trails—this was a route not normally traveled by animals, let alone people. Occasionally a branch would snap off in our hands, giving us a scare. This challenging and unexpected climb came at the worst time—the end of our trip.

Near the top, we were so tired we had to take five breaths for each step. Finally, after nearly an hour of climbing, we reached the uppermost part of the hill. We wasted no time and crashed down the other side—straight through more stands of alders and low branches of spruce trees. It took us just 20 minutes to descend the southwest side. At the bottom, we called Marc on the satellite phone and told him we should be at the landing zone within 30 minutes and that we would lay out an orange poncho at the touchdown point, just past the ditch I knew ran across the landing zone.

Although the rain had mostly stopped, we were cold and wet from the double tributary crossing. We hiked across flats in an attempt to make it to the pickup zone by 5 p.m. We gutted it out and continued zombie-like toward the landing zone arriving with just enough time to lay out the poncho, to give Marc a good, safe touchdown target. We cut the cords attaching the tent to my pack and were starting to erect it when we saw Marc approaching from the north. I was so cold, my hands were numb and I couldn't open the zipper on my pack to retrieve the portable aviation radio.

Marc made two passes over the runway before I finally used my hair comb to grab the zipper's end and get the radio out. I checked in and he let me know he was pissed that we were not already on the radio. All I could say is we were doing our best. After one radio call saying we were clear of the strip and that the winds were from the south at 10 knots, Marc landed—and already knew the weather was forecast to get worse, therefore, wanted to fly both of us out that evening.

Haslett and I quickly finished erecting the tent. By the time Marc had turned the plane around and taxied to our position at the north end of the usable takeoff zone, we had the tent up. It only took us five minutes to load Haslett's equipment in the plane. He strapped in, Marc pushed up the throttle and they roared off to Gulkana.

Now shivering, I slid into the tent, took off all my wet clothes, dried out, and put on my last set of dry clothes. Despite the light rain, a few afternoon rays of sun managed to shine into the tent. After firing up the stove, I drank some hot water which helped me warm up. That, and the sun, felt wonderful and I stopped shivering after 10 minutes.

At my home away from home, in the remote wilderness of the national park, I again felt solace—one with nature in the place we'd started the adventure 17 years earlier. The entire project had been a journey into the unknown and we'd been successful. But now, it felt different. I no longer felt the spirits of 4422's men calling to me. On the west side of the valley, the slopes of Mount Drum ascended; disappearing into clouds. Avalanches occasionally slid down its sides—the mountain hadn't changed a bit—but I had changed, and now it was time for me to go.

SURE ENOUGH, an hour later, Marc was back. We packed the tent and my other gear, then took off for Gulkana. During takeoff, I noticed that the airplane parts from the long-ago crash were no longer strewn alongside the landing zone. Apparently someone had taken them out.

I was too exhausted for any introspection as we flew by the glacier. I took a few photos of the river and the little hill we had just climbed. Never had something so simple been so difficult. As the mountain disappeared from view, I had only one thought; *Mount Sanford had certainly given us one last swift kick in the ass.*

I felt better as we approached the runway at Gulkana. After landing, then taxiing to the tie-down spot, Marc shut the engine down. Randall Haslett surprised us by meeting us. Right there on the tarmac, he popped open a bottle of champagne. We toasted his father and all the men lost on Flight 4422. The champagne tasted good, but the best thing was that the toast was being made by Randall Haslett, the son of one of the aircrew members—the only 4422 relative to have ever been on the site. That was very special for Marc and me. The entire project had come full circle.

Back at the New Caribou Hotel (its new name), the hot shower felt wonderful—it was the best shower I'd taken since one in Pheriche, Nepal, in 1986, after hiking up 18,000 foot Kala Patar, just west of Mount Everest. The next morning dawned beautifully clear in the Copper River basin. But, to the east, Mount Sanford was again covered with thick clouds and rain. Marc and I flew to Anchorage while Haslett drove my truck and spent a quiet day enjoying the sights of Alaska from the highway that roughly followed the route NWA 4422 had taken in 1948. He definitely was now in touch with the ill-fated flight and his father.

WE HAVE EXHAUSTED all of our research capability regarding 4422. There is no question the glacier is melting and the airplane debris is disappearing. There is nothing else Marc and I can do for the missing airliner, its passengers, aircrew, and relatives. The family members have closure and many of the mysteries have been solved. Now, it's time to put the saga of NWA Flight 4422, Alaska's Flight of Gold, behind us and consider the project complete.

We pushed fate as far as we dared. This was the last trip to the mountain for me. Marc has never revisited the site of Flight 4422 and says he never will. But maybe someday more can be learned from the Flight of Gold by future intrepid adventurers—those who follow their dreams and never give up. I truly wish them the best of luck.

In the meantime, if you happen to find yourself standing outside in Alaska on a cold winter night, open your mind and heart to the heavens. If it is one of those nights with shimmering colored skies, be silent...don't whistle in amazement...look into the sky. Against the backdrop of an infinite number of galaxies, full of brilliant stars, watch for a plane flying through the celestial curtains of northern lights—a DC-4 carrying 30 men on one last journey—a journey into the eternal sunset.

While surrounded by Flight 4422 wreckage, Randall Haslett writes a letter to his father, who died in the crash and whose remains likely lie buried in ice somewhere in the glacier behind him. *Photograph by author.*

Randall Haslett (L) and author in debris field of Flight 4422 on Mount Sanford. *Photograph by Randall Haslett.*

APPENDIX

MASTER FLIGHT 4422 KNOWN EXPEDITION LIST

Many people ventured to the 4422 glacier to hunt for the rumored gold or try to solve the mystery of the crash. This list only includes verified expeditions, not rumored expeditions. Expedition length is estimated and does not include access/egress times which would have ranged from 1 day (by plane) to many weeks (via foot or horseback).

NO.	DATE	NAME	Length	Source
1)	3-12-48	Layton Bennett/JerryLuebke	1 hour	L. Bennett
2)	3-12-48	Official air search parties	3 days	CAB report
3)	1948	Fred Ewan/Jake Butler	0 days	Fred Ewan

They started an expedition but canceled it once they saw how dangerous it was.

4)	1948	Woods, University of AK.	1 day	G. Hayden

Landed on Mount Sanford in an attempt to find Flight 4422.

5)	8-48	Rocky Goodman/H.Speerstra	Overflight	Newspapers
6)	Fall '48	George Hayden + 2 men	5 days	G. Hayden

They hoped to collect a piece of evidence to prove Flight 4422 crashed on behalf of a victim's brother for an insurance claim, but only got about half way then turned back due to heavy snow.

7)	Fall '49	Al Wright flew Burt Hallan	1 day	Al Wright
8)	Spring '49	Jorge Jorgenson/"Burt"	Unknown	Jorge Jorgenson

Jorgenson flew a man named "Burt" then dropped him off near the Sanford Glacier

9)	Summer '49	four climbers from Anchorage	4 days	Jorge Jorgenson

4 climbers from Anchorage with 1,000 feet of rope. Climbed the NE side.

10)	1950	Pilot Cleo McMahan	Unknown	*Copper River Journal*
11)	1950	Pilot Cleo McMahan	Unknown	*Copper River Journal*
12)	1950	Pilot Cleo McMahan	Unknown	*Copper River Journal*
13)	1950-54	Trapper "Burt" Holland	Varies	Luebke/Bennetts

Holland stayed up in the glacial valley each summer. He had ladders and a Cub. He told no one anything about what he did out there.

14)	1954	Herb Haley/Jack Wilson	Overflight	*Copper River Journal*
15)	1954	Ken O'hara	1 summer	Luebke/Bennett

O'hara owned Santa Claus Lodge and bus company (Anchorage-Fairbanks) and sponsored dogsledders Jake Butler and Fred Ewan. O'hara walked to site via the old trapper's trails with Jake Butler.

16)	1954	James Williams/Bill Holmes.	1 day	James Williams

They landed on Mount Wrangell with L-19 plane.

17)	1955	Dave Bennett, Italian climber	2 weeks	Layton Bennett
18)	1955	Army Corp Expedition	1 week	Lou Bennett
19)	3-10-57	Lewis/Kunkel/Levitt	1 week	Newspapers

Pilot Walter Lyons flew the team from Gulkana to Mount Sanford in an Aeronca Chief. He broke a ski. A second pilot, Claude E. Rogers, flew them out.

20)	1957	Dutch Burke + 3 men	1 week	Al Renk
21)	1957	Dutch Burke + 3 men	1 week	Al Renk
22)	1957	2 Soldiers from Ft. Richardson	Unknown	Newspapers
23)	1959	Military helicopter experiments	Unknown	Newspapers
24)	1950s.	Gulkana Service Station Mgr.	Several days	Lynn Ellis

Was witnessed on several occasions carrying aluminum ladder under his plane as he flew toward Mount Sanford with skis on his plane, unusual in summer. He measured the fuel for each flight by the quart, to be as light as possible. Then, after about 1957, he suddenly left the country.

25)	1960	Jack Wilson flew someone in	1 week	*Copper River Journal*
26)	6-60	Lucas/ Weber + 5 men	8 days	Whaley/News

On 7-27-60 journalist Tom Snapp reported this as 13th expedition, which used skiplane, over 1000 feet of rope, and a couple hundred feet of aluminum wire ladders.

27)	1989	Lowenthal/Kristi/Pluntke	3 days	Lowenthal/Plunt
28)	1989	Becker/Tejas/Ford	3 days	Ed Becker

One of the men got hit on the head by a falling rock.

29)	1990+/-	Paul Claus/Vern Tejas	1 day	Paul Claus

Landed at 13,000 at top and searched downward.

30)	1994	Ed Becker	3 days	Al Sebaka, Pilot
31)	1994	Millican/McGregor/Biasi	4 days	Author
33)	1995	Author's solo expedition	3 days	Author
34)	1996	Millican/McGregor	3 days	Author
35)	1997	McGregor/Millican	3 days	Author
36)	1998+/-	Canadian gold seekers	Unknown	NPS
37)	1998	Millican/McGregor	3 days	Author
38)	1999	McGregor/Millican	3 days	Author
39)	1999	NPS/NTSB/Troopers/Author	1 day aborted	Author
40)	1999	NPS/NTSB/Troopers	1 day	NTSB

Pilot Bob Larson and Lt. Rodney Dial used helicopter and recovered human arm/hand

41)	Fall 2000	NBC Dateline	1 day overflight	Author
42)	7-2003	McGregor/Wigmore/Millican	3 days	Author
43)	2002-12	Several charter flights over site carrying 4422's victims' relatives.		
45)	8-2011	McGregor/Haslett/Millican	3 days	Author

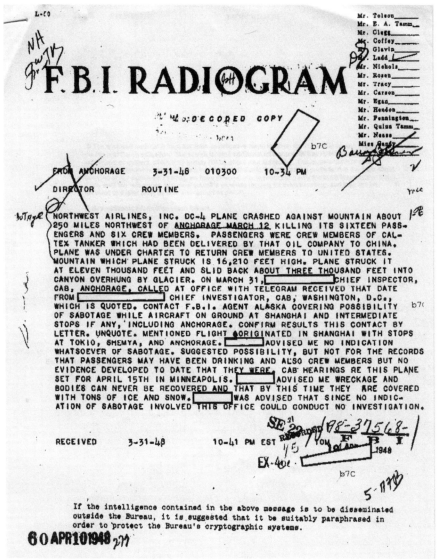

An FBI radiogram from 1948. Note the initial JeH, in the "O" of radiogram, indicating that J. Edgar Hoover, director of the FBI, reviewed the document. *FBI records.*

(Right) Official 45-513 record card for DC-4 No. N95422. This airplane was always owned by the United States government, which may explain the FBI's involvement. The "AIRLINES" entry indicates that it was leased to Northwest Airlines. The last three lines show a transaction cancellation on March 23, 1948, and RECL (reclamation) on September 14, 1948. The plane was written off as a total loss following the crash. *FAA records.*

KEVIN A. McGREGOR

377

BIBLIOGRAPHY

BOOKS

Boylan, Janet. *The Day Trees Bent to the Ground*. Anchorage: Publication Consultants, 2004.

Breihan, John R., Stan Piet, and Roger S. Mason. *Martin Aircraft 1909-1960*. Santa Ana, CA: Narkiewizc/Thompson. Greens, Inc. Printers and Lithographers, 1995.

Cohen, Stan. *The Forgotten War* . Vol. II. Missoula, MT: Arrow Graphics, 1988.

Davis, Neil. *The Aurora Watcher's Handbook*. Fairbanks: University of Alaska Press, 1992.

Dewalt, G. Weston, and Anatoli Bourkeev. *The Climb*. New York: St. Martin's Press, 1999.

Encyclopedia of Aviation. New York: Charles Scribner and Sons, 1977.

Ferguson, Sue A. *Glaciers of North America*. Golden, CO: Fulcrum Publishing, 1992.

Francillon, Rene J. *McDonnell Douglas Aircraft since 1920*. Vol. 1. London: Putnam, 1979; Oxford, England: The Alden Press, 1995.

Gann, Ernest K. *Fate is the Hunter*. New York: Touchstone, 1961.

Hoffman, Carl. *Hunting Warbirds*. New York: Random House, 2002.

Jackson, Lone E. *Mudhole Smith*. 4th printing. Anchorage: Color Art Printing, 1995.

Kessler, Ronald. *The Secrets of the FBI*. New York: Crown Publishing Group, division of Random House, 2011.

Kingsley, Norman. *Icecraft*. Glendale, CA: La Siesta Press, 1975.

Krakauer, Jon. *Into Thin Air*. New York: Villard Books, 1997.

Lane, Tony. *The Merchant Seamen's War*. Liverpool: Bluecoat Press, 1990. Originally printed by Manchester University Press.

McCarron, Ken, and Adrian Jarvis. *Give a Dock a Good Name*. Birkenhead, Wirral, Merseyside, England: Birkenhead Press Ltd., 1992.

Middlemiss, Norman. *World Tankers.* Newcastle, UK: Shield Publications, 1996.

Miller, Carolyn. *History of Alaska Land People and Events.* Anchorage: Arctic Circle Enterprises, 2002.

Mills, Stephen E. *More Than Meets the Sky.* Menasha, WI: George Banta, 1972.

Mountaineering: The Freedom of the Hills. 3rd ed. Seattle: Craftsman-Met Press, 1974.

Pollen, Sally McMahan. *Papa was a Bush Pilot.* Anchorage: Sally McMahan Pollen, 2000.

Rayner, Jay. *Stardust Falling.* Toronto: Penguin Group, 2002.

Read, Piers Paul. *Alive. The Story of the Andes Survivors.* Philadelphia and New York: J. B. Lippincott, 1974.

Robbins, Royal. *Basic Rockcraft.* Glendale, CA: La Siesta Press, 1971.

Ruble, Kenneth D. *Flight to the Top.* Viking Press, 1986.

Sawyer, Leonard Arthur, and William Harry Mitchell. *Victory Ships and Tankers.* Cambridge, MD: Cornell Maritime Press, 1974.

Selters, Andy. *Glacier Travel and Crevasse Rescue.* Seattle: The Mountaineers, 1990.

Sharp, Robert P. *Glaciers.* Eugene: University of Oregon Books, 1960.

Washburn, Bradford. *Exploring the Unknown.* Kenmore, WA: Epicenter Press, 2001.

White, Graham. *Allied Aircraft Piston Engines of World War II.* Warrendale, PA: Society of Automotive Engineers Inc., 1995.

Whitlock, Flint, and Terry L. Barnhart. *Capt. Jepp and the Little Black Book.* Superior, WI: Savage Press, 2007.

Whitworth, Rodney. *Merseyside at War.* Liverpool: Whitworth/Scouse Press, 1988.

Wilkinson, Paul H. *Aircraft Engines of the World.* New York: Paul H. Wilkinson, 1946.

Zim, Herbert S. *Air Navigation.* New York: Harcourt, Brace, 1943.

NEWSPAPER ARTICLES

ABC News.com, July 28-29, 1999. Multiple online articles regarding discovery of NWA 4422.

Anchorage Daily News,
--- March 12, 1948
--- March 11, 1957, "Fairbanks trio to seek gold on wrecked...."
--- March 18, 1957, "Three-man party fails to reach crashed plan."
--- July 27, 1960, "Seven climbers seek lost gold aboard old...."
--- August 9, 1989, "DC-4 wreck still glowing in..." by Peter Porco.

--- July 29, 1999, "Pilots find wreckage of '48..." by Peter Porco.
--- July 29, 1999, "Troopers work to close book..." by Peter Porco.
--- November 26, 1999, "A Personal Journey," by Helen O'Neill.
--- April 6, 1948, "O'Hara files bankruptcy, plans reorganization."
--- April 14, 1948, "CAB orders hearing of Mount Sanford crash."
--- April 18, 1948, "Chiang's change of heart."
--- April 20, 1948, "At the Hotels: At the Westward."
--- May 7, 1948. "CAA praises Gulkana pair."
--- May 12, 1948, "$2,000,000 gold shipment stolen."
--- June 1, 1948, "At the Hotels: At the Westward."
--- June 12, 1948, "Alaska U-Drive" advertisement.
--- August 2, 1948, "Chinese Communists claim Nationalist...."
--- August 2, 1948, "Chinese sells wife...$55,000,000 ($6.60 US)."
--- August 7, 1948, "Philippines gold sells at $51.25"
--- August 9, 1948, "Chinese money soars. Now 10,500,000 to $1."
--- August 19, 1948, "Chinese adopt new currency."
--- August 27, 1948., "U.S. Chinese aid 'drop in bucket'...."
--- March 11, 1957, --- July 28, 1960, "Gold seekers are miffed at expedition publicity."
--- June 24, 1963, "Lure of legendary gold."
--- June 24, 1963, "Mystery of plane with $4 million" by Tom Snapp.
--- June 2, 1972, "Tell it to Bud. Airplane void of any gold."
--- April 15, 1973, "Gold fever strikes again."
--- October 4, 1974, "Old gold rumor rises again."
--- September 7, 1977, "This tale of gold is a durable one."
Anchorage Public Library. "Lost $18M Fortune is yours for taking."
Associated Press national articles,
--- November 21, 1999. "Dead guard a dictator's treasure?" by Helen O'Neill.
--- November 28, 1999, "Dead men tell tales in the ice" by Helen O'Neill.
Canoe News online, November 15, 1999. Multiple articles.
Cincinnati (OH) *Times*, March 12, 1948.
CNN Interactive online news, July 30, 1999. Multiple articles on discovery of NWA 4422.
Copper River (AK) *Country Journal*, February 18, 1998 "Forget the gold...Are there diamonds?"
Denver Post, March 15, 1948.
Fairbanks (AK) *Daily Miner*, July 27, 1960. "Lost mountain climbers are found."
Fall River (MA) *Herald News*, March 15, 1948.
Jessen's Weekly (Fairbanks, AK), June 24, 1963.
Keyport (NJ) *Weekly*, March 18, 1948. "Keyporter dies in air accident."

London Times Two, April 27, 2000. "The Mystery of Flight 4422" by Barry Wigmore.

Minneapolis Star, April 13, 1948. "NWA plane missing over Alaska with 30 aboard."

--- April 16, 1948, "Pilots tell of fog in crash."

New Zealand Herald, April 8, 1963.

Northwest Airlines *On Course*, 1989 and 1994.

Paterson (NJ) *Morning Call*, March 15, 1948.

Seattle Post-Intelligencer, March 15, 1948.

Spokesman-Review (Spokane, WA), May 9, 1999.

Standard-Speaker (Hazleton, PA), August 7, 1999. "Mystery solved: The crash of Flight 4422."

United Press International, March 11, 1957. "Fairbanks trio to seek gold on wrecked plane."

Washington Post, March 15, 1948.

--- July 30, 1999, "1948 plane crash wreckage found in wilderness of..." by Will Woodward.

Yahoo News online, July 29, 1999. Multiple articles regarding discovery of NWA 4422.

Zanesville (OH) *News*, March 13, 1948. "30 reported on overdue plane."

--- March 14, 1948. "Zanesville flier on lost airliner."

--- March 16, 1948. "Snow avalanche covers plane wreckage."

Zanesville Signal, March 13, 1948. "Airliner with 30 aboard missing in Alaska."

Zanesville Sunday Times-Signal, March 14, 1948. "Airliner wrecked; local man co-pilot."

PAMPHLETS, REPORTS, LETTERS, AND OTHER DOCUMENTS

Blei, Sue R. Letter, January 12, 2001, referencing fingerprint comparisons.

Cameron, William P. Letter, February 11, 1982, regarding Flight 4422 crash on March 12, 1948.

Canadian Government. North West Air Command Admin. Unit Log, Whitehorse, YT, March 12/13,1948.

Gahn, Dr. Laura. Identigene Letter, April 26, 2002. Case #36307; Items # F86026: Hand and Forearm.

Grimm, Michael R. Friction Ridge & Impression Evidence Examinations. Certificate of Analysis, July 2007.

Hopkins, Bernard. Personal files from the SS *Grand River*, 1948.

McMahan, Cleo. Letter to Randall Haslett, October 13, 1980. Courtesy, Randall Haslett.

Merchant Mariners' lawsuit files based on and similar to *McCall v. OTC & NWA*. New York and other states.

Merchant Mariners' probate files. New York, New Jersey, and other states. 1948.

Overseas Tankship Corporation. Pay record, 1948. Courtesy, Bernard Hopkins.

--- Multiple telegrams to families of victims, March 1948.

Pratt and Whitney. R-2000 Engine serial numbers list.

Propst, Dr. Michael. Letters referencing SME Case 00-82, Agency Case #99-50657, July 24, 1999.

Swithinbank, Charles. *The Origin of Dirt Cones on Glaciers.* Oxford University Exploration Club, 1949.

Texaco Fleet *News*

U.S. Coast Guard Maritime Center. Personnel files of all 24 Merchant Mariners on board Flight 4422.

U.S. Government. *Civil Aeronautics Accident Investigation NC-95422 March 12, 1948. Mt. Sanford, AK*

--- C-54 manual circa 1940. Distributed by Western International Aviation, Tucson, AZ.

--- FAA aircraft records. All 14 NWA DC-4s registered in 1951 and those of NC-95422.

--- FAA weather data, Gulkana AK, 1950-1999.

--- *FBI Radiogram.* Re: NWA Flight 4422, March 31, 1948. FOIA document.

--- NTSB accident report FTW85FA259, Rock Springs, TX. June 19, 1985.

--- Personnel records of Arthur Eilertsen and Wilfred Beswick.

U.S. Government Information, Wrangell-Saint Elias National Park.

--- *10th Rescue Squadron history,* 1948.

--- USGS. *A Geological Guide to Wrangell-Saint Elias National Park and Preserve, Alaska.* Central Region, Denver, 1999.

Worsley, Wayne W. *Poems.* Navigators of Northwest Airlines, irca 1948. Courtesy, Gail Worsley.

INTERVIEWS

Argassi, Robert. Pratt and Whitney attorney

Avenson, Warren. NWA captain

Bailey, Gene. AFL trucker, 1950s

Bailey, Mrs. Gene

Bennett, Layton. Bush pilot, airline owner, radio operator; 1948 witness

Bennett, Lou. Radio operator; 1948 witness

Berck, Jeanette, daughter

Berck, Jenny, wife of Dutch Berck

Berck, Jerry, son

Biasi, Gerry. American Airlines pilot, expeditioner, mountaineer

Bleakley, Geoff. Historian, Wrangell-Saint Elias National Park

Borden, Jim. NWA captain
Bowyer, Mike. Son of Captain Charlie Ryan
Cameron, Helen. 1948 witness
Chamberlain, Kirk. Propeller expert, Hamilton Standard Propellers
Chellin, John. NWA station manager, Edmonton, Canada, 1948
Collins, Bruce. Aviation director, National Park Service, Anchorage, 1997
Crewdson, Ken. Radio operator, Northway, Alaska, 1940s
Delue, Carl. United Airlines captain, 1940s and later
Dial, Rodney. Sergeant, Alaska State Troopers
Diehl, Bill. Bush pilot, 1950s to 2012
Domer, Fred. Pratt and Whitney historian/archivist
Doyle, Vince. NWA captain
Edwins, David. NWA station manager, Shanghai, China, 1948
Eklund, Chet. NWA captain, 1948
Ellis, Lynn. Bush pilot. Owner, Ellis Air Taxi, Gulkana, Alaska
Erickson, Scott. National Transportation Safety Board investigator
Ewan, Fred. Dog musher, 1948 witness
Fallico, Franc. Alaska Medical Examiner
Freeman, Gerry. Explorer/author
Freesburg, Jim. NWA captain
Gap, Milton. NWA ground radio operator, 1947-1948
Goral, Alan C., DDS. Dentist in Littleton, Colorado
Grimm, Roy. Trucker in Alaska, 1950s
Grimm, Mrs. Roy
Halliday, Hugh. Canadian military historian, Victoria, BC, Canada
Hart, Dean. Trucker, Alaska Freight Lines, 1950s
Hart, Mrs. Dean
Hayden, George. First expedition attempt to find Flight 4422
Hess, Peter, Esq. Attorney
Holm, George. NWA mechanic, Minneapolis, 1948
Hopkins, Bernard N. Radio operator, OTC, Waiuku, New Zealand
Jarvis, Jonathan. Superintendent, Wrangell-Saint Elias National Park
Jorgenson, Jorge. Bush pilot, 1950s to present
Karcz, Steve. Bush pilot, Alaska
Kessler, Stanton. Alaska Medical Examiner
Kimm, Joseph. NWA System Chief Pilot, 1950
Klaus, Paul. Bush pilot and lodge owner
Koerner, Jerome. NWA radio operator, 1950s
Kottre, Tom. Alaskan pilot: Linden Airways, Desert Air, Air Ambulance.
Kramer, Vincent. First lieutenant, USAF, Laughlin AFB, TX
Larson, Bob. Helicopter pilot, Alaska State Troopers

Lofholm, Bill. Morrison-Knudsen paymaster, 1948
Lowenthal, Bob. NWA captain, 1989 expedition
Lowenthal, Kristi. 1989 expedition
Luebke, Jerry. Bush pilot, 1948 witness
McAbee, Frank. Pratt and Whitney European manager
McMahan, Cleo. Bush pilot 1948 witness
Meany, Don. Pilot and safety officer, North Slope Borough Search and Rescue
Neely, Sy. Hunter/trapper, 1948 witness
Neely, Carole. 1948 witness
Olson, Pat. NWA flight attendant, 1950s
Oneill, Helen. Associated Press reporter
Pluntke, Hartmut. NWA ramp agent 1980s, Anchorage. 1989 expedition
Polgar, Tony. NWA captain
Pollen, Sally. Daughter of bush pilot Cleo McMahan. Author, *Papa was a Bush Pilot*
Pryce, Michael. H. Ship captain, harbormaster
Propst, Michael. Alaska Medical Examiner
Renk, Al. Trucker, Alaska Freight Lines, 1950s
Renovitch, Mark. President D. Roosevelt Library, Hyde Park, New York
Rutan, Dick. Lieutenant Colonel, test pilot
Savory, Ralph. Captain, Pan American Airlines, 1948
Schumm, Kathryn. Daughter of Dave Edwins
Sebaka, Al. Helicopter pilot, Gulkana, Alaska
Seybert, Danny. CEO, PenAir
Sharp, Hunter. Chief ranger, Wrangell-Saint Elias National Park
Sowell, Randy. President, Harry S. Truman Library, Independence, MO
Stekel, Peter. Explorer and author, *Final Flight*
Swanson, Don. Bush pilot, Alaska back-country fishing guide. Pilot, Delta Air Lines
Vernon, Jerry. Canadian military historian, Burnaby, BC
White, Graham. Pratt and Whitney engine expert. Author, *Allied Aircraft Piston Engines of World War II*
Williams, James. Lieutenant colonel, base commander, Nome AFB, AK, 1948
Wilson, Jack. Bush pilot, 1950s
Wilson, Mrs. Jack
Worthington, Anne. Archivist, Wrangell-Saint Elias National Park
Wright, Al. Bush pilot mid-1900s to present. Airline owner
Young, Vic. Marine photographer, New Zealand

INTERVIEWS—FAMILY MEMBERS
Adler, Elizabeth

Andrascik, Audrey
Ault, Pearl
Bayley, Monica
Beglan, Matthew "Brick"
Bellehuemer, Mary Jane
Bellisimo, Gale
Boyce, Allison
Britt, Sophie
Brush, James and Ruth
Byerly, Holly
Calheiros, Judy
Chandler, Cindi
Cheslock, Florence
Comshick, Stanley
Conway, John
Conway, Kelly
Conway, Maurice
Conway, Shirley
Davidson, Audrey
Davidson, Carole
Davidson, Denise
Davidson, Leroy
Davidson, Robert
Davis, Jan
Delaney, Bernard
Denman, Dorothy
Depons, Lorraine and Lucy
Driver, Ann Worsley
Dryzga, Diane
Foote, Dave
Foote, Dorothy
Foote, Edward
Foote, John
Galpin, Susan
Gray, Myrtle
Hacker, Denise
Hamel, Dorothy
Harjehausen, Kathy
Haslett, Randall
Horrlocks, Katie
Hutt, Joyce

Jamele, Gwendolyn
Jamele, John
Jamele, Rich
Klein, Marcia
Koistenen, Kim
Kuxhause, Ann
Kwarta, Ann
Lewis, Lois
Maegli, Ruth
Malick, Carla and Dave
Manning, Francis
Manning, James
Matlosz, Nellie
McCall, Andre
McKay, Danny and Mary
Meehan, Janet
Mistal, Richard
Mustra, Edwin
Mustra, Ely
Mustra, James
Mustra-Leorna, Marlene
Oravetz, Frank
Oravetz, Gary
Oravetz, Linda
Oravetz, Ron
Ottaway, Eleanor
Paine, Melva Murray
Perugini, Genevieve
Petry-Purvin, Melva
Petry, Jim
Petry, Paul
Petry, Richard
Pile, Margaret
Price, Joan
Rector, Lester
Rector, Polly Logan
Reichart, Nancy
Rice, Rick
Rice, Sister Aileen
Scott, Pat
Sherff, Florence

Shusta, Anne
Sigmund, Carl
Sigmund, Dan
Sigmund, Joseph
Skilbred, George
Snell, Dorothy
Studemann, Marianne
Tisdale, Joanne
Tomek, Mavis Worsley
Van Cleef, James
Van Zandt, Brett
Van Zandt, John
Viega, Vincent A.
Wentworth, Gladys
Wilkowski, Karol
Worsley, Gail
Worsley, Greg
Zvolanek, Isabelle

NOTES/ACKNOWLEDGMENTS

I was 34 years old when I first heard about the lost DC-4. At that age, my friends and I felt we could accomplish anything and probably thought that we were immortal. So, the dream of locating Flight 4422 was not far-fetched to Marc Millican, Gerry Biasi, and me. We believed that we could accomplish something that others wouldn't consider and even thought was impossible. Locating the wreck of Flight 4422 and identifying the frozen arm and hand that had kept it company for 50 years fulfilled that dream. That venture filled us with an overwhelming sense of pride and purpose in having accomplished something meaningful.

Aviation and aerospace have always been a big part of my life. When I was young, I would lie on the grass of our front yard in Denver, Colorado, looking into the sky. I watched jets flying overhead— shimmering diamonds beyond my reach. But flying might have been in my blood. My father was a member of the Junior Board of Directors for Eddie Rickenbacker at Eastern Airlines. Later, Dad was an employment manager for the Glenn L. Martin (Aviation) Company.

Growing up at the foot of the Rocky Mountains, bicycling, hiking, skiing, and mountain climbing allowed me to enjoy and understand the magnificent, yet dangerous natural environment. Before turning 25, I had climbed 34 peaks over 14,000 feet in Colorado, and four more in California. In 1975, I twice climbed Mount Rainier. Mountaineering and aviation had become my cornerstones.

Although I wanted to learn to fly, it was just too expensive. In 1977, it cost $6.50 per hour to rent a Cessna 150, not counting aviation fuel at the outrageous price of 55 cents per gallon. An instructor cost $5 per hour. Instead, I studied law enforcement and worked as a cadet and dispatcher at the Littleton Police Department. Thus, I have a healthy respect and understanding for people involved in law enforcement.

I finally got my chance to fly when a promotion provided enough money for lessons. Every spare dollar went into flying lessons. I soon qualified as a private pilot, then as a commercial pilot, then as an instructor. In 1980, I joined the Air Force, influenced by my grandfather, Paul Bishop, who survived the trenches of World War I.

After instructing in T-37s, I rose to the rank of captain, served as an assistant safety officer, and participated in several accident inquiries. In 1985, I transferred to Travis Air Force Base and was promoted to aircraft commander, flying C-141 Starlifters all over the world. I left active duty military service in 1988 and was hired as a flight engineer for Delta Air Lines, then rejoined the Air Force as a reservist the next year—just in time for Desert Storm. I retired as a major in 1997.

I could not have predicted how this unique combination of education and experience would provide me with the unusual set of skills necessary to help embark on the Flight 4422 project. Nor could I have predicted that by 2008, Marc Millican and I (who had known each other for 23 years and had flown together in the Air Force), would both be flying for the same airline when Northwest Airlines would merge with Delta. My friendships with Marc and Gerry, the search for Flight 4422, and our interaction with the families of the victims have been important parts of my intellectual and spiritual journey. This has been an amazing adventure I wish to share—about the people, the plane, the ship, and the mysteries of Northwest Airlines Flight 4422, Alaska's legendary Flight of Gold.

HUNDREDS OF PEOPLE helped Marc Millican and me carry the Flight 4422 project and book to completion. Special thanks go to Dorothy Antrim, Robert Antrim, and Jon Shallop, who gave unwavering support from the very beginning, and the late Peter Hess who provided legal counsel and support critical to the project's success. The generous guidance and insight from journalist Barry Wigmore and authors and explorers Steve Lloyd and Valerie van Heest, who has written *Fatal Crossing* about another lost Northwest Airlines DC-4, were essential in making the Flight 4422 story come alive through the eyes of those lost in the crash, their friends, and families. Barry helped us interpret what we saw and felt, Steve helped us shape the story, and Valerie introduced us to her publisher, In-Depth Editions, who put *Flight of Gold* into print.

We thank the flight victims' relatives and friends for providing personal details of the men's lives and for treating us like members of their families. We also thank the scores of Northwest Airlines' pilots and other employees who helped us understand the airline industry of the 1940s and details of Flight 4422. Bernie Hopkins' knowledge of ships and the sailors' pay helped tremendously.

Bill Chubb and his staff at the Maritime Personnel Center in Arlington, Virginia, assisted us greatly in obtaining the personnel files, including fingerprints, of the sailors on board Flight 4422. We also appreciate the generous support, guidance, and expertise of many members of the Explorers Club. And we are especially indebted to Alaska State Trooper Rodney Dial, Trooper Helicopter Pilot Bob Larson, and NTSB Investigator Scott Erickson ,who helped investigate Flight 4422 at its remote crash site on Mount Sanford. We thank John Jarvis and the staff of the National Park Service who protect and preserve some of our nation's greatest assets, the huge, irreplaceable expanses of our national parks and preserves.

The final pieces of Flight 4422's puzzle were put into place by a world-class DNA and fingerprint forensics team spearheaded by Odile Loreille with co-worker Jodi Irwin, at the Armed Forces DNA Identification Lab in Rockville, Maryland. The entire expanded forensics team included Ryan Parr with assistant Kerry Robinson, Dongya Yang and assistant Camilla Speller, Genealogist Colleen Fitzpatrick, Professor Ted Robinson, Michael Grimm, Sr., Michael Grimm, Jr., Christine Lyon, and Andy Yeiser. The exceptional family research work of Maurice Conway in Askeaton, Ireland, and his gracious donation of DNA, helped tremendously in achieving the identification.

In Alaska, State Medical Examiners Michael Propst, Franc Fallico, Stanton Kessler, and fingerprint specialist Sue Blei all played important parts in coordinating the identification attempts of the arm and hand.

The unsung heroes of this project are the archivists, librarians, clerks, and others who protect and provide access to records and reference material. Their guidance and help with this project was paramount and we thank them for their efforts.

We deeply appreciate the editing assistance of Carleen Gonder, Peter Stekel, and Valerie van Heest, and the tireless and exceptional editing of Robert Yearick, whose ability to focus on the most important and poignant details led to a seamless story and, after a 12-year journey, pushed *Flight of Gold* across the finish line. Finally, Ann Weller's proofreading gave this book its final polish.

If you enjoyed **Flight of Gold**, *consider reading* **Fatal Crossing** *by V. O. van Heest about the loss and search for a similar Northwest Airlines DC-4 in the waters of Lake Michigan.*

PRAISE FOR FLIGHT OF GOLD

"While the chapters detailing the state of the art forensic science techniques and analysis were excellent, what grabbed and held my attention was the detailed and meticulous care given by Kevin and Marc to their research, recognition and recovery of critical evidence. Whether it's recovery of historical artifacts or items at a crash or crime site, how that evidence is handled can make or break a case; Kevin and Marc were superb investigators. On top of all that: It's a darned good read."
> *- Carleen Gonder, MIS, Founder and Executive Director of Wildlife Field Forensics*

"Break out the chips and beer... draw close to the fire... you're in for one hell of a story!"
> *- Bob Barrett, retired Merchant Mariner*

"Absolutely fascinating!"
> *- Leonard Nelson, Pan American Airways pilot*

"Kevin McGregor takes you along on a fantastic adventure back in time and high into Alaska's wilderness to unravel the legend of Northwest Flight 4422 and solve the many mysteries associated with its loss. Filled with hair-raising flights and treacherous climbs, this book keeps you on the edge of your seat and delivers surprises all along the way."
> *– V. O. van Heest, author of* Fatal Crossing:
> The Mysterious Disappearance of NWA Flight 2501 and
> the Quest for Answers

in-depth
editions